Reprints of Economic Classics

ESSAYS IN POLITICAL ECONOMY

Also Published In

Reprints of Economic Classics

By THOMAS EDWARD CLIFFE LESLIE

Land Systems and Industrial Economy of Ireland, England and Continental Countries [1870]

ESSAYS

IN

POLITICAL ECONOMY

BY

THOMAS EDWARD CLIFFE LESLIE

SECOND EDITION

[1888]

REPRINTS OF ECONOMIC CLASSICS

Augustus M. Kelley · Publishers

NEW YORK 1969

First Edition 1879

Revised Edition 1888

(Dublin: Hodges, Figgis & Co., *Grafton Street*;
London: Longmans, Green & Co., *Paternoster - Row*)

Reprinted 1969 by

AUGUSTUS M. KELLEY · PUBLISHERS

New York New York 10010

Library of Congress Catalogue Card Number

69 - 20305

PRINTED IN THE UNITED STATES OF AMERICA
by SENTRY PRESS, NEW YORK, N. Y. 10019

ESSAYS

IN

POLITICAL ECONOMY.

BY

THOMAS EDWARD CLIFFE LESLIE, LL.D.

SECOND EDITION.

DUBLIN: HODGES, FIGGIS, & CO., GRAFTON-ST.
LONDON: LONGMANS, GREEN, & CO., PATERNOSTER-ROW.
1888.

PREFATORY NOTE.

The present Volume is a new edition, modified in certain respects, of the 'Essays in Moral and Political Philosophy,' originally published in 1879, and now for some time out of print.

The alterations in the present Edition consist of—(1), omissions; (2), additions; and (3), changes in arrangement.

To render the Work more suitable for Students of Economics, those Essays which dealt mainly with the non-economic aspects of social life have been omitted. It is not thereby intended to depreciate their merits, which are, in our judgment, of a high order; but their preservation having been secured by the publication of the former Edition, it has been thought desirable in the present, which is specially designed for University use, to aim at greater unity of subject.

Seven Essays, published after the appearance of the former edition, have here been added. In the opinion of the Editors, they bear all the distinctive marks of Mr. Leslie's best work, and deserve to appear in a permanent form.

A different arrangement has been adopted for the purpose of bringing together Essays of a similar character. The guiding conception has been to group —(1) the Critical Essays; (2) those which are expository of the Author's general view of Economics; and (3), those dealing with the interpretation of actual phenomena, or with economic policy. In the first group are comprised Essays I.–XIII.; in the second, Essays XIV.–XVII.; and in the last, Essays XVIII.–XXVI.

The Student who desires to trace the development of Mr. LESLIE'S views can obtain the dates of publication of each Essay from the footnotes appended to the titles.

JOHN K. INGRAM.
C. F. BASTABLE.

July, 1888.

CONTENTS.

BIOGRAPHICAL NOTICE OF THE AUTHOR.*

THOMAS EDWARD CLIFFE LESLIE, one of the ablest and most original English economists of the present century, was born in the county of Wexford, in (as is believed) the year 1827. He was the second son of the Rev. Edward Leslie, Prebendary of Dromore, and Rector of Annahilt, in the county of Down. His family was of Scotch descent, but had been connected with Ireland since the reign of Charles I. Amongst his ancestors were that accomplished and energetic prelate, John Leslie, bishop first of Raphoe and afterwards of Clogher, who, when holding the former See, offered so stubborn a resistance to the Cromwellian forces, and the bishop's son, Charles, the well-known non-juror. Cliffe Leslie received his elementary education from his father, who resided in England, though holding Church preferment, as well as possessing some landed property, in Ireland. By him he was taught Latin, Greek, and Hebrew at an unusually early age. He was afterwards for a short time under the care of a clergyman at Clapham, and was then sent to King William's College, in the Isle of Man, where he remained until, in 1842, being then only fifteen years of age, he entered Trinity College, Dublin.† He was a distinguished student there, obtaining, besides other honours, a Classical Scholarship in 1845, and a Senior Moderatorship (Gold Medal) in Mental and Moral Philosophy at his Degree Examination in 1846. He became a law student at Lincoln's Inn, was for two years a pupil at a conveyancer's chambers in London, and was called to the English Bar. But his attention was soon turned from the pursuit of legal

---

* Reprinted, by permission, from the *Encyclopædia Britannica*, 9th ed.

† It is noteworthy that John Elliot Cairnes, William Edward Hearn (author of *Plutology*, 1864), and Richard Hussey Walsh (author of an *Elementary Treatise on Metallic Currency*, 1853), were in the same Junior Freshman Class of 1842–3.

practice, for which he never seems to have had much inclination, by his appointment, in 1853, to the Professorship of Jurisprudence and Political Economy in Queen's College, Belfast.* The duties of this Chair requiring only short visits to Ireland in certain Terms of each year, he continued to reside and prosecute his studies in London, and became a frequent writer on economic and social questions in the principal Reviews and other periodicals.† In 1870 he collected a number of his Essays, adding several new ones, into a volume, entitled, 'Land Systems and Industrial Economy of Ireland, England, and Continental Countries.' J. S. Mill gave a full account of the contents of this work in a Paper in the 'Fortnightly Review,' in which he pronounced Leslie to be 'one of the best living writers on applied political economy.' Mill had sought his acquaintance on reading his first article in 'Macmillan's Magazine.' He admired his talents, and took pleasure in his society, and treated him with a respect and kindness which Leslie always gratefully acknowledged.

In the frequent visits which Leslie made to the Continent, especially to Belgium and some of the less known districts of France and Germany, he occupied himself much in economic and social observation, studying the effects of the institutions and system of life, which prevailed in each region, on the material and moral condition of its inhabitants. In this way he gained an extensive and accurate acquaintance with Continental rural economy, of which he made excellent use in studying parallel phenomena at home. The accounts he gave of the results of his observations were among his happiest efforts. 'No one,' said Mill, 'was able to write narratives of foreign

---

* In the Preface to the former edition of this work Mr. Leslie has clearly explained the way in which his economic doctrine was formed:—"Whereas Mr. Mill, in his youth, attended the lectures of Mr. Austin, the author had the good fortune to attend those of Sir Henry Maine at the Middle Temple, and to learn first from them the historical method of investigation, followed with such brilliant success in *Ancient Law*, *Village Communities in the East and West*, and the *Lectures on the Early History of Institutions*. Holding a Professorship of both Jurisprudence and Political Economy, he was led to apply that method to the examination of economic questions, and to look at the present economic structure and state of society from Sir Henry Maine's point of view, as the result of a long evolution. Further investigation has convinced him that the English economist of the future must study in the schools of both Mr. Stubbs and Sir Henry Maine, as well as in that of Mr. Mill."

† In 1869 he was appointed Examiner in Political Economy to the University of London, which post he held for five years.

visits at once so instructive and so interesting.' In these excursions he made the acquaintance of several distinguished persons, amongst others of M. Léonce de Lavergne and M. Emile de Laveleye. To the memory of the former of these he afterwards paid a graceful tribute in a biographical sketch (Essay XII. in the present volume), and to the close of his life there existed between himself and M. de Laveleye relations of mutual esteem and cordial intimacy.

Two essays of Leslie's appeared in volumes published under the auspices of the Cobden Club, one on the 'Land System of France,' containing an earnest defence of *la petite culture*, and still more of *la petite propriété;* the other on 'Financial Reform' (1871), in which he exhibited in detail the impediments to production and commerce arising from indirect taxation. Many other articles were contributed by him to Reviews, including several discussions of the history of prices and the movements of wages in Europe, and a sketch of life in Auvergne in his best manner; the most important of them, however, related to the philosophical method of political economy, notably a memorable one which appeared in the Dublin University periodical 'Hermathena.' In 1879 the Provost and Senior Fellows of Trinity College published for him a volume in which a number of these articles were collected, under the title of 'Essays in Political and Moral Philosophy.' These and some later essays, which ought one day to be united with them,* together with the earlier volume on 'Land Systems,' form the essential contribution of Leslie to our economic literature. He had long contemplated, and had in part written, a work on English economic and legal history, which would have been his *magnum opus*—a more substantial fruit of his genius and his labours than anything he has left us. But the manuscript of this treatise, after much pains had already been spent on it, was unaccountably lost at Nancy in 1872; and though he hoped to be able speedily to reproduce the missing portion and finish the work, it is feared that but a small part of it, if any, has been left in a state fit for publication.† What the nature of it would have been may be gathered from an Essay on the 'History and Future of Interest and Profit' (Essay XVIII. in the present volume), which is believed to have been in substance an extract from it.

---

* The later Essays, here spoken of, are included in the present volume.

† The fear expressed above has since been confirmed; no part of the work was left in such a state as would admit of its publication.

That he was able to do so much may well be a subject of wonder, when it is known that his labours had long been impeded by a painful and depressing malady, from which he suffered severely at intervals, whilst he never felt secure from its recurring attacks. To this disease he in the end succumbed at Belfast, whither he had gone to discharge his professorial duties, on the 27th of January, 1882, in the fifty-fifth year of his age.

J. K. I.

ESSAYS IN POLITICAL ECONOMY.

I.

THE LOVE OF MONEY.*

THE Love of Money has always been in more or less disrepute with moralists. They have almost universally assigned to it nearly the lowest place in the scale of human affections. We say of human affections, for it is one which distinguishes man from all other animals, however intelligent. 'You call me dog,' said Shylock to the Christian merchant; 'hath a dog money?' Phrenologists have indeed laid down that all the propensities—combativeness, destructiveness, philoprogenitiveness, alimentiveness, love of life, &c.—are 'common to man with the lower animals;' but we are suprised that they have not discovered a peculiar protuberance on the outside of the human head corresponding with a peculiar propensity for money inside it. It is the more to be regretted that they have not ascertained the locality of this organ, since a claim has been set up on behalf of the lower animals to a close relationship to the human family. If a bump of philargyriveness or philonomismativeness could be shown on the human head, a conspicuous absence of this manifestation on the cranium of the former would enable us to disprove the connection, to the satisfaction at least of believers in phrenology. It would not, however, enable us, without further inquiry, to determine whether the love of money, which distinguishes us from the brutes,

* This Essay was published in November, 1862, in a periodical which has ceased to exist.

places us above or below them in moral character. To satisfy ourselves on this point, we must begin by inquiring what this thing 'Money,' of which men, and men only, are so fond, consists of. Sir Robert Peel's celebrated question—'What is the meaning of that word, a Pound, with which we are all familiar?'—was answered by himself in terms to the effect that a pound of money is a fixed quantity of gold or silver. But this answer, though highly appropriate to a discussion on the currency, is irrelevant to our present inquiry, whether money is a good or an evil; and whether the love of it is a good or a bad quality in mankind. Sir Robert Peel very justly ridiculed the definition given by one writer on the currency of a pound, as 'a sense of value in reference to currency as compared with commodities.' Yet in practical life this is really something like what men generally mean and want by money. They mean so much goods; so much of the commodities for sale in the market of the world. A pound to a 'navvy,' for instance, is so much beer and tobacco; to his mother it is so much tea and sugar. But these two cases are sufficient to show the extreme difficulty of pronouncing any moral judgment whatever upon the love of money, considered as a general human propensity; for the love of tea and sugar is universally admitted to be in itself an innocent affection, while the love of beer and tobacco is often condemned as combining two most pernicious desires. The love of money is really only a phrase for the love of a vast number of different things, which may be good, bad, or indifferent, regarded from a moral, religious, æsthetical, political, or medical point of view, but which are alike in one respect—namely, that they are all to be had for money, and are not to be had without it. As Solomon said, 'A feast is made for laughter, and wine maketh merry; but money answereth all things.' The love of money is that universal desire for wealth from which political economists have deduced a theory of commercial values, along with several important truths respecting the conditions of industrial energy and prosperity. Everybody wishes for some kind of wealth, and money is convertible into every other kind; and therefore everybody loves money for some purpose or other, from which we get the laws of competition, prices, wages, profits, and rent. Yet this general principle of pecuniary interest or love of riches by no means explains all the phenomena of the economic world. For it is, as we have said already, only a single expression for a great variety of wants, wishes, and tastes, which are not always the same from age to age, or from country to country, nor felt alike by every individual in any one age or country, and which, moreover, lead to very different consequences as regards the nature, amount, and distribution of wealth, and as regards the material as well as the moral welfare of human society.

That disease of language which metaphysicians call the realism of the schools still infests many of the terms and phrases which philosophy must employ. A host of different things are alike in some one respect, and a common name is given to them in reference to the single quality or circumstance which they have in common. It is simply a name for their common feature, but it puts their numerous differences out of sight and out of mind, and they come to be thought of in a lump as one sort of thing. Those moralists, accordingly, who feel themselves the better for heartily denouncing the general principle of the love of money or pursuit of wealth with which political economy sets out, confound, in their horror of a mere abstraction, the love of health, cleanliness, decency, and knowledge, with sensuality, avarice, and vanity. And perhaps political economists have not escaped a bias from their own phraseology, and are apt to imagine in their scientific discussions a much fuller explanation of the complete phenomena of wealth, and a much closer approximation to the complete philosophy of the subject, than lies within their province as commonly circumscribed by themselves at present.

It is obvious that the love of money includes a demand for various things, the production of which variously affects both the material interests of the consumers and the quality and distribution of the revenue of the whole community. It includes a love of pictures, toys, jewellery, plate, furniture, clothing, opium, soap, bibles, brandy, and, in short, everything in the International Exhibition, and many things not exhibited there. It includes a love of eating and drinking, both in moderation and in excess; of literature and science; of architecture; of the fine arts; of indolence and ease, and of business and sport; of foreign travel, and of a country house; of music; of charity, sensuality, cruelty, and power; of horses and dogs. It expresses sometimes a desire for the comforts of an old bachelor, and sometimes an inclination for matrimony; and when it takes the latter direction, it means with one young lady love in a cottage, and with another a palace without love; in one man it is fortune-hunting—in another, a disinterested attachment to Miss Aurora Penniless. The disciples of Malthus know how to discriminate between the economic consequences of these diverse matrimonial tendencies, and the important differences of their influence on the price of beef. Napoleon III. seems to behold in money the sinews of war; his friend Mr. Cobden connects it with commerce and peace. The poor man's love of money is a different feeling from the rich man's, and, accordingly, the writer of this essay never throbs with the emotions which must animate the breasts of Baron Rothschild and Lord Overstone. The American Southerner worships in the almighty dollar the giver of African slaves; the negro slave of Brazil adores it chiefly as the purchaser of liberty. The wealth which is coveted by men in the East is not that which is most prized by the men of the West. An Indian Rajah's chief wealth is a plurality of wives, personal attendants and elephants, and a load of gold trappings on both his elephant's body and his own—all which, not exclusive of the wives, would be more than an English duke or prince could bear. An old writer gives an account of a religious ceremony which he witnessed in Turkey, at which Prince Mustapha—a boy of eleven years old—'was so overloaded with jewels, both himself and his horse, that one might say he carried the value of an empire about him.' That is to say, the wealth which, in the hands of English capitalists, would have made a whole territory prosperous, and been distributed in wages through many hundred families, was concentrated upon making one small Turkish child vain and uncomfortable. And the oriental lust for jewels not only has effects upon the economic condition of the world which merit the attention of the political economist, but it has also, in a great measure, sprung from the absence, for many ages, of the conditions essential to general prosperity, and the accumulation of wealth in really useful forms. Wherever insecurity has long prevailed, a spirit of hoarding must exist, with a desire for that sort of wealth which contains much value in a durable and portable form, and which is easily hidden, easily removed, and none the worse for being buried for months or years in the ground. It is probable, therefore, that the love of gold chains and jewels for which the European Jew is remarkable has a European as well as an Asiatic origin, being inherited from his persecuted, plundered, and usurious ancestors in the middle ages, who found it necessary to pack their wealth into the smallest possible compass.

The existence of security, banks, and paper currency, have long exterminated from England that curious animal the genuine miser, with his treasure in a strong box, doing no good to anyone. Dr. Johnson, talking of misers to Boswell, said, 'A man who keeps his money has, in reality, more use of it than he can have by spending it. Why, sir, Lowther, by keeping his money, had the command of the county, which his family has lost by spending it.' But an English millionaire does not keep his money to himself, as the ancient miser, whether he spends it or not. If he saves it, instead of locking it up or carrying it about on his body, he puts it in a bank, and the banker's customers make use of the wealth he does not himself consume.

But when we say that the form of the love of money which displays itself in a love of dress, ornaments, and jewels, is almost confined to the men of Eastern countries, we must be understood as speaking of men in the narrowest sense, and as making no allusion in that comparison to the ladies of the two hemispheres. Women have everywhere their own peculiar notions of the value of money; and a world of either men alone or of women alone would contain a very different assortment of articles of wealth from that in the great mundane shop for both sexes which exists. With most species of animals, the male is more gorgeously dressed than the female; but so it seems to be with the human species generally, only in its less civilized forms. For we may perceive, with the growth of European civilization, a marked decline in the taste of men for the display of wealth on the body. A mediæval baron was much more expensively got up than his wife or daughter. Even in the last century the toilette of a gentleman was nearly as elaborate and splendid as that of a lady. Now, a gentleman thinks he makes a smart appearance with a flower in his button-hole, at an assembly at which the ladies are blazing with diamonds. It might be an instructive inquiry how far this difference in the desire for wealth is traceable to a radical difference in the natural mental constitutions of the sexes, and how far to restraints which confine the ambition of women in general to paltry objects, leading them to waste their time in hunting husbands, while men hunt seats in parliament, and foxes. Addison remarks, in the 'Spectator,' that 'One may observe that women in all ages have taken more pains than men to adorn the outside of their heads.' Perhaps one reason for this is, that men have in all ages prevented them from taking so much pains to adorn the inside. While we are on the subject of dress as one of the equivalents of money, and one of the objects of its pursuit, we may make a remark upon that singular revolution of the human mind through which it has come to be thought, by all men of a certain rank, in the Western world, becoming to attire themselves every evening in black from head to foot, as if for a funeral; and by most men, of all ranks, in that civilized region, becoming to clothe themselves in the dingiest hues all day long. The male apparel which is the last product of civilization appears to display a remarkable mixture of good sense and bad taste. The mistake made by the ladies of our time seems to be that of aiming at show and accomplishing waste; while the mistake of the gentlemen is that of aiming at plainness and accomplishing gloom.

Many other illustrations might be given of the curious turns taken by the fancy for clothing, as one of the uses of money. In the north of Ireland, for example, it is common to see a girl on the road with a smart bonnet, an extensive petticoat, and a gay parasol carried in the usual manner, but with a pair of shoes not upon her feet, but in her hands. Five-and-twenty years ago such a girl would have no more minded the effect of the sun on the skin of her face, than she now minds the effect of the earth on the skin of her foot; and five-and-twenty years hence it may be safely predicted that such a girl will not only think it advisable to wear her shoes on her feet, but will discover that they really hurt less there, when one is used to them, than the stones upon the road. At the same time, we must admit that the shoemakers of mankind—and of womankind, too, we presume—have left nothing undone to perpetuate a prejudice against their own particular production, and to weaken the force of the love of money for the sake of obtaining it. There is, again, in the inventory of modern wealth, and among the civilized uses of money, another article of dress of so obvious and simple a character that many persons may naturally suppose that it descends from the most remote antiquity. Yet, some centuries ago, all the wardrobes in England did not comprise a single night-dress for lady or gentleman, king or queen. Take again, another institution of the modern dressing-room—the bath. There is a history of civilization in the Tale of a Tub. There is a letter to the old 'Spectator,' on the effects of the love of money, in which the writer says that it is to that we owe the politician, the merchant, and the lawyer; 'Nay,' he adds, 'I believe to that also we are indebted for our 'Spectator.'' We are not prepared to explain the various motives which inspire the pens of authors. Did Shakspeare write for money? Did Pope? Did Dr. Johnson? Did Lord Macaulay? Does Sir Edward Bulwer Lytton? We are concerned at present with the motives of consumers rather than producers; and one thing at least is clear, that it is highly to the credit of the former to elicit such productions from the latter, and that the love of money in the modern world is to a great extent the love of good, elevating, and instructive objects—a love which meets with its return. New desires for health, decency, knowledge, refinement, and intellectual pleasures, have, in fact, revolutionised production. The antithesis to modern wealth is not so much poverty as a different kind of wealth. The change is more remarkable in the quality than in the quantity. No inconsiderable part of human wealth, it is true, still consists of the means of unhappiness rather than of happiness, and of the gratification of vice rather than of virtue. On the whole, however, there is a transformation in the moral character of wealth, and of the desires involved in the general love of money. For the most part, instead of representing wickedness, brutal delight, and idle pomp, or conquest, tyranny, and plunder, the wealth of Europe represents peace, culture, liberty, and the comfort of the many rather than the magnificence of the few. Where man's treasure is, there his heart is also; and the treasures of modern civilization seem to us to show as remarkable an improvement in the moral as in the intellectual and physical condition of society. 'Riches,' said Milton, 'grow in hell;' for even in his time much of the wealth that grew on earth bore many marks of being the property of bad and unhappy beings. But we may venture now to ask those well-meaning persons who, without regard to time and place, and without discrimination between good and evil, repeat ancient warnings against the love of money and the pursuit of wealth, whether they mean to praise dirt under the name of poverty, and whether they think idleness better than industry, ignorance better than science and art, and barbarism better than civilized progress? To political economists, on the other hand, we venture to suggest the cultivation of a department of the philosophy of riches which has never been scientifically investigated. The laws which regulate the value of the supply forthcoming from producers have been almost exhaustively developed in political economy; but the deeper laws which regulate the demand of the consumers, and which give the love of money all its force and all its meaning, have never yet received the regular attention of any school of philosophers.

II.

THE WEALTH OF NATIONS AND THE SLAVE POWER.*

It has long been a prevalent notion, that political economy is a series of deductions from the principle of selfishness or private interest alone. The common desire of men to grow rich by the shortest and easiest methods—to obtain every gratification with the smallest sacrifice on their own part—has been supposed to be all that the political economist desires to have granted in theory, or to see regulating in practice the transactions of the world, to ensure its material prosperity. A late eminent writer has described as follows the doctrine of Adam Smith, in the 'Wealth of Nations': 'He everywhere assumes that the great moving power of all men, all interests, and all classes in all ages and in all countries, is selfishness. He represents men as pursuing wealth for sordid objects, and for the narrowest personal pleasures. The fundamental assumption of his work is that each man follows his own interest, or what he deems to be his interest. And one of the peculiar features of his book is to show that, considering society as a whole, it nearly always happens that men, in promoting their own, will unintentionally promote the interest of others.'†

But, in truth, the acquisitive and selfish propensities of mankind, their anxiety to get as much as possible of everything they like, and to give as little as possible in return, are in their very nature principles of aggression and injury instead of mutual benefit: the mode of acquisition to which they im-

---

* *Macmillan's Magazine*, February, 1863.

† Buckle's *History of Civilization*, vol. ii.

mediately prompt is that of plunder or theft, and the competition which they tend to induce is that of conflict and war. Their first suggestion is not, 'I will labour for you,' but 'you shall labour for me;' not, 'Give me this, and I will give you what will suit you better in exchange,' but, 'Give it to me, or else I will take it by force.' The conqueror rather than the capitalist, the pirate rather than the merchant, the brigand rather than the labourer, the wolf rather than the watch-dog, obey the impulses of nature. The history of the pursuit of gain is far from being the simple history of industry, with growing national prosperity; it is the history also of depredation, tyranny, and rapine. One passage in it is thus given, in the early annals of our own country: 'Every rich man built his castle, and they filled the land with castles. They greatly oppressed the wretched people by making them work at their castles, and, when they were finished, they filled them with evil men. Then they took those whom they suspected to have any goods, seizing both men and women by night and day; and they put them in prisons for their gold and silver, and tortured them with pains unspeakable. . . . The earth bare no corn; you might as well have tilled the sea; for the land was all ruined by such deeds.'

But if misery and desolation are the natural fruits of the natural instincts of mankind, how has the prosperity of Europe steadily advanced in spite of the enemy to it which nature seems to have planted in every man's breast? How has the predatory spirit been transformed into the industrial and commercial spirit? Under what conditions are individual efforts exerted, for the most part, for the general good? These are the chief problems solved in Adam Smith's 'Inquiry into the Nature and Causes of the Wealth of Nations.' He has been careful to point out that 'the interests of individuals and particular orders of men, far from being always coincident with, are frequently opposed to, the interests of the public;' and he observes that 'all for themselves and nothing for other people seems to have been, in every age, the vile maxim of the masters of mankind.' The effort of every man to improve his own condition is, it is true, in Adam Smith's philosophy, a principle of preservation in the body politic; but his aim was to demonstrate that this natural effort is operative for the good of society at large only in proportion to the just liberty secured to every member of it to employ his natural powers as he thinks proper, whether for his own advantage or for that of others. Every infraction of, and every interference with, individual liberty he denounced as being as economically impolitic as morally unjust. His systematic purpose was to expose the losses which a nation suffers, not only from permission of the grosser forms of violence and oppression, but from every sort of restriction whatever upon voluntary labour and enterprise. Of laws regulating agriculture and manufactures for the supposed advantage of the public, he said, 'both were evident violations of natural liberty, and therefore unjust, and they were both too as impolitic as they were unjust. That security, he added, which the laws in Great Britain give to every man, that he shall enjoy the fruits of his own labour, is alone sufficient to make any country flourish. The history of Europe, in so far as it is the history of the progress of opulence, is not, in his pages, the history of selfishness, but of improving justice; of emancipated industry, and of protection for the poor and weak. It is, accordingly, the history of strengthening restraints upon the selfish disposition of mankind to sacrifice the happiness and good of others to their advantage or immediate pleasure. The fundamental principles on which the increase of the wealth of nations rests are thus summed up, at the end of Adam Smith's Fourth Book: 'All systems, either of preference or restraint, being thus completely taken away, the obvious and simple system of natural liberty establishes itself of its own accord. Every man, so long as he does not violate the laws of justice, is left perfectly free to pursue his own interest his own way, and to bring both his industry and his capital into competition with those of any man or order of men.'

The treatise on the 'Wealth of Nations' is, therefore, not to be regarded, as it was by Mr. Buckle, as a demonstration of the public benefit of private selfishness. Adam Smith denies neither the existence nor the value of higher motives to exertion. The springs of industry are various. Domestic affection, public spirit, the sense of duty, inherent energy and intellectual tastes, make busy workmen, as well as personal interest. And personal interest is itself a phrase for many different motives and pursuits, deserving the name of selfishness or not according to their nature and degree ; just as wealth under a single term includes many things of very different moral quality, according to their character and use. The aims of men in life may be high or low ; they may seek for riches of very different kinds and for very different purposes. In a recent essay in the 'Revue des Deux Mondes,' the eminent economist, M. de Lavergne, maintains that political economy and religion are, though essentially distinct, related to each other as the soul and body are. Wealth, he says, means food, clothes, and houses ; and religion, though it treats of higher things, does not teach that men should be left to perish of hunger and cold. Political economy has for its special end the satisfaction of the bodily wants, and religion that of the spiritual wants, of man. M. de Lavergne seems to have been led astray by the economic use of general terms, such as material wealth, material interests, and material progress. For wealth is not really or properly limited in political economy to such things as satisfy the bodily or material wants of humanity. It comprehends many things, the use of which is to minister to man's intellectual and moral life, but which have, notwithstanding, a price or value. Books, for example, as well as bread and meat, are wealth. Spiritual and other instructors are paid for as well as butchers and doctors. Wealth means, in fact, many different things, more or less material or immaterial, in different ages and countries. The highest kinds of wealth will be found where there is most general freedom for the development of the highest powers of humanity, and where no class have a licence for the gratification of their selfish passions at the expense of any other class. But what Adam Smith contended for was, that no class of men, be their motives good or bad, should be suffered, under any pretext, to encroach upon the industrial liberty of other men. The true moving power of the economic world, according to his system, is not individual selfishness, but individual energy and self-control. His fundamental principle is perfect liberty. The 'Wealth of Nations' is, in short, an exhaustive argument for free labour and free trade, and a demonstration of the economical policy of justice and equal laws. Arguing against the law of apprenticeship, the philosopher said: 'The property which every man has in his own labour, as it is the original foundation of all other property, so it is the most sacred and inviolable. The patrimony of a poor man lies in the strength and dexterity of his hands; and to hinder him from employing his strength and dexterity in what manner he thinks proper for his own advantage is a plain violation of that most sacred property. It is a manifest encroachment upon the just liberty both of the workman and of those who might be disposed to employ him. As it hinders the one from working at what he thinks proper, so it hinders the others from employing whom they think proper.'

The system, therefore, which is most subversive of the doctrines of political economy, as taught by Adam Smith, is that most selfish of all possible systems—slavery. The political economist must condemn it as loudly as the moralist. It attacks the life of industry, and prevents the existence of exchange. It robs the labourer of his patrimony; it robs those who would hire him in the market of their lawful profits; and it is a fraudulent abstraction from the general wealth of nations, the quantity and quality of which depend upon the degree of industrial liberty secured to every individual throughout the world for the exercise of his highest powers. Of the property of the slaveholder in the industry of his slaves, the paradox, *la propriété c'est le vol*, is a literal truth according to political economy as well as common morality, and as regards not only the slaves, but the whole commercial world. Yet slavery is a system within the legitimate range of economic inquiry, which is by no means limited, as has sometimes been contended, to the phenomena of an imaginary world of free exchanges, but extends to all the economic phenomena of the real world, in which wealth is produced and distributed according to very different systems. Injustice and oppression have their natural train of economic consequences as well as liberty and equal laws, and the economist is concerned with both, as the physician studies the laws of disease as well as health. 'Writers on political economy,' says the chief among them in our time, 'propose to investigate the nature of wealth, and the laws of its production and distribution, including, directly or remotely, the operation of all the causes by which the condition of human beings is made prosperous or the reverse.' There is not a country in Europe at this day, not excepting our own, the economic phenomena of which the principle of exchange would be sufficient to interpret. But, even if pure commercial competition now regulated, throughout the whole of Europe, the production and distribution of every article of wealth, the whole domain of history, and the breadths of Asia, Africa, and America, would remain for the economist to explore, and to account on other principles for the direction and results of human industry, the use of natural resources, and the division of the produce. The economy of the Slave States of America, for example, afforded an opportunity for this inquiry, of which Mr. Cairnes availed himself in his admirable essay on the Slave Power. In an earlier essay, he described political economy as belonging to 'the class of studies which includes historical, political, and social investigations,' and defined it as 'the science which traces the phenomena of the production and distribution of wealth up to their causes in the principles of human nature, and the laws and events of the external world.'* In the later essay, instead of deducing unreal consequences from the hypothesis of industrial liberty, he has traced the origin and consequences of the opposite order of things. Instead of the theory of wages, profit, and rent, applicable to a free society, he lays bare the structure of a society which excludes wages, for the labourer is fed and flogged like a beast of burden; in which there is no profit, according to the economist's defi-

* *Logical Method of Political Economy.* By J. E. Cairnes, Professor of Political Economy in the University of Dublin.

nition, for labour is not hired, but stolen; in which there is little or no rent, for only the best soils can be cultivated, and they are constantly becoming worthless instead of growing in value; in which fear is substituted for the hope of bettering his condition, and torment for reward, as the stimulus to the labourer's exertion; and in which wealth exists only in its rudest forms, because the natural division of employments has no place, and only the rudest instruments of production can be used. Adam Smith had previously examined the milder conditions of feudal servitude, demonstrating that the backwardness of mediæval Europe was attributable to these and similar discouragements to industry, and showing how it was forced into unnatural channels by such obstructions. For, through every part of his philosophy, 'Dr. Smith sought,' as Dugald Stewart relates, 'to trace, from the principles of human nature and the circumstances of society, the origin of the positive institutions and conditions of mankind.' The 'Wealth of Nations' contains the substance of the last division of a complete course of lectures upon moral science, in which Adam Smith expounded, in succession, Natural Theology, Ethics, Jurisprudence, and Political Economy. His lectures on Jurisprudence have not survived; but his pupil, Dr. Miller, states that 'he followed in them the plan suggested by Montesquieu, endeavouring to trace the gradual progress of jurisprudence from the rudest to the most refined ages, and to point out the effect of those arts which contribute to subsistence and to the accumulation of property, in producing corresponding improvements or alterations in law and government.' From this it is clear that his conception of the true scope and method of jurisprudence agreed with his conception of the true scope and method of economic inquiry. And in the 'Wealth of Nations,' accordingly, he traced the operation both of the causes which rescued Europe from barbarism and occasioned its progress in opulence, and of those which impeded the action of the natural principles of preservation and improvement. In short, his treatise included an inquiry into the causes of the poverty as well as of the wealth of nations, and an investigation of the actual constitution and career of industrial society. He showed how rural industry and progress were thwarted in the middle ages by such impediments that, but for the happier circumstances of its towns, Europe could never have emerged from the calamities which befel it after the dissolution of the Roman Empire. The servile and insecure position of the cultivators of the soil prevented industry from achieving its first triumphs in the country according to the course of nature, which makes agriculture the primary, because the most necessary, business of mankind. 'Order and good government, on the other hand, and along with them the liberty and security of individuals, were established in cities at a time when the occupiers of land in the country were exposed to every sort of violence. But men in this defenceless condition naturally content themselves with a bare subsistence, because to acquire more might only tempt the injustice of their oppressors. On the contrary, when they are secure of enjoying the fruits of their industry, they naturally exert it to better their condition, and to acquire, not only the necessaries, but the comforts and elegancies of life. That industry, therefore, which aims at something more than necessary subsistence, was established in cities long before it was commonly practised by the occupiers of land in the country.' In this manner, Adam Smith has traced the causes of the actual and, as he calls it, the 'unnatural' course of industry in the slow and chequered progress of modern Europe. He investigated the phenomena of what was, happily for us, on the whole, a progressive society. Mr. Cairnes, on the contrary, has investigated those of a retrograde one.

In the Slave States of America Mr. Buckle might have seen the economical results of a society based upon selfishness instead of justice. The negro shows elsewhere* his capacity to take

* The following statement, affording evidence as to the character, capacity, and enterprise of the negroes, is contained in a letter to the writer of this Paper from one of the principal English residents in Victoria, the Capital of Vancouver's Island. It formed part of a general description of the Colony, furnished without any reference to the question of slavery :—' Before the gold excitement, but during the same year (1858), the Legislature of California passed a law forbidding the immigration of negroes. This caused the latter to appoint a deputation, which visited the British possession of Vancouver's Island ; and so favourable was their

his part in the free division of labour, and the consequent multiplication of the productions of the different arts, which occasions, in the words of Adam Smith, in a well-governed society that universal opulence which extends itself to the lowest ranks of the people. In the squalid and comfortless homes even of the higher ranks of the people in the American Slave States we see the consequence of oppressed and degraded industry. 'It may be,' says Adam Smith again, 'that the accommodation of a European prince does not always so much exceed that of an industrious and frugal peasant, as the accommodation of the latter exceeds that of an African king, the absolute master of the lives and liberties of ten thousand naked savages.' The American slave-owner is, as it were, a petty African king, and in real penury, as well as in power, resembles such a ruler. It is said, indeed, that we owed to slavery the produce which supplied the principal manufacture of Great Britain. But the whole of this production was in truth to be credited to free industry, while all the waste and ruin which accompanied it must be ascribed to slavery. The possibility of the profitable growth of so much cotton was caused by the commerce and invention of liberty, while the barbarism of the poor whites, the brutifying of the negro population, and the exhaustion of the American soil, are the net results of slavery. In truth, to Watt, Hargreaves, Crompton, and Whitney—free citizens of England and the Northern States—the southern planters owed the whole value of their cotton. What slavery may really claim as its own work is that, by exhausting the soil it occupies by a barbarous agriculture, which sets the laws of chemistry as well as of political economy at defiance, it hastens its own extinction from the day that its area is once definitely and narrowly

report, that it not only caused many coloured people to leave California, but also aroused general attention, particularly that of British subjects; for by all who had occasionally heard of the island before it was considered a sort of petty Siberia. While people were reading accounts of the climate, soil, and low price of town lots in Victoria, there came rumours of rich gold sands on the banks of the Frazer River in British Columbia. Two or three small coasting vessels had previously sailed with coloured passengers; but the demand for passages by white people became so great, that large steamships departed every few circumscribed. This its own advocates admit, but with a singular inference: 'Slavery has, by giving to the laws of nature free scope, moved over a thousand miles of territory, leaving not a slave behind. Why should good men attempt to check it in its progress? If the laws of nature pass slavery farther and farther south, why not let it go, even though, in process of time it should, by the operation of natural laws, pass away altogether from the territory where it now exists?' Why, we may ask, should devastation be suffered to spread? Should fires in a city be suffered to burn themselves out by advancing from street to street until not a house remains to feed the conflagration? The slaveholder, as he moves southward or westward, not only carries moral and material destruction with him, but leaves it behind for those who come after him. The rich slavebreeder follows him with his abominable trade, and the poor white sinks back into barbarism in the wilderness the slaveholder has made. The order of European progress has been reversed. In Europe, justice, liberty, industry, and opulence grew together, as Adam Smith described. In the Slave States of America, as Mr. Cairnes has shown, the Slave Power constitutes 'the most formidable antagonist to civilized progress which has appeared for many centuries, representing a system of society at once

days with from 300 to 1000. Among them were some coloured people, and they have increased in number until, I think, we may safely estimate them at 500. The occupations of these coloured people in Victoria are, to the best of my recollection, porters, sawyers, draymen, day-labourers, barbers, and bathkeepers; eating-house keepers; one hosier, as black as a coal, with the best stock in the town; and two or three grocers. Some of them went to the mines, and were moderately successful. Their favourite investment is in a plot of ground, on which they build a neat little cottage and cultivate vegetables, raise poultry, &c. Nearly all had been prosperous, and a few had so judiciously invested that they were in receipt of from £10 to £40 a month from rents. They are industrious, economical, and intend to make the colony their permanent home; the outskirts of the town are well sprinkled with their humble but neat dwellings, and their land is yearly increasing in value. By this showing they are a quiet, industrious, and law-abiding people; but there is a drawback, taking them altogether as citizens, which arises from their earnest desire to be on a perfect social equality with the whites at church, the theatre, concerts, and other public places of assembly. When you consider the strong disinclination for their company, not only of our large American population, but also of Englishmen, who very quickly imbibe the American prejudice, you can readily conceive that a number of disagreeable scenes occur.'

retrograde and aggressive—a system which, containing within it no germ from which improvement can spring, gravitates inevitably towards barbarism, while it is impelled by exigencies inherent in its position and circumstances to a constant extension of its territorial domain.'

> *ἄνω ποταμῶν ἱερῶν χωροῦσι παγαὶ*
> *καὶ δίκα καὶ πάντα πάλιν στρέφεται.*

For the perpetuation and extension of the system to which is owing this retrogressive movement of the English race, in a region endowed with every natural help to progress, the slaveholders are in arms. They have not been slow to point, indeed, at General Butler's misrule in a southern city, and to ask if the cause of their adversaries is the cause of liberty? But such men as General Butler are living arguments against a Slave Power. General Butler was absolute master at New Orleans; and, even in the words of an ardent apologist for slavery, 'that cruelties may be inflicted by the master upon the slave, that instances of inhumanity have occurred and will occur, are necessary incidents of the relation which subsists between master and slave, power and weakness.'* There was never a more striking example of the ease with which men are cheated by words than the generous sympathy given in England to the cause of the slaveholders, as the cause of independence, and therefore of liberty! It is the cause of independence, such as absolute power enjoys, of every restraint of justice upon pride and selfish passions. The power of England is in a great measure a moral power, founded on the respect of the civilized world for the courageous opposition of her people for centuries to such independence both at home and abroad. And, if the public opinion of England and the leaning of her policy be found ultimately upon the side of the maintenance and extension of the Slave Power in America, she will sustain in the end as great a loss of actual power, as well as of moral dignity, as if she entered into a league with the despots of Europe, and closed her

---

* *The South Vindicated*, p. 82.

cities of refuge against their victims. The Slave Power fights against all the principles of civil and religious liberty on which England rests her glory, and all the principles of political economy to which she ascribes her wealth. In policy, as well as in justice, England must refuse her countenance to that Power, as the enemy of the liberty as well as of the wealth of nations.

III.

THE POLITICAL ECONOMY OF ADAM SMITH.*

'Political Economy belongs to no nation; it is of no country: it is the science of the rules for the production, the accumulation, the distribution, and the consumption of wealth. It will assert itself whether you wish it or not. It is founded on the attributes of the human mind, and no power can change it.'† In these words—accompanying an admission that the Irish Land Bill, which he nevertheless defended on other grounds, 'offended against the principles of political economy'—Mr. Lowe gave expression last session to the conception of one school of the followers of Adam Smith, that Political Economy is, not what Adam Smith called his own treatise, 'An Inquiry into the Nature and Causes of the Wealth of Nations,' but a final answer to the inquiry—a body of necessary and universal truth, founded on invariable laws of nature, and deduced from the constitution of the human mind.

I venture to maintain, to the contrary, that political economy is not a body of natural laws in the true sense, or of universal and immutable truths, but an assemblage of speculations and doctrines which are the result of a particular history, coloured even by the history and character of its chief writers; that, so far from being of no country, and unchangeable from age to age, it has varied much in different ages and countries, and even with different expositors in the same age and country; that, in fact, its expositors, since the time of Adam Smith, are substan-

---

* *Fortnightly Review*, November 1st, 1870.

† *Speech on the Irish Land Bill*, April 4th, 1870.

tially divisible into two schools, following opposite methods; and that the method of one of them, of which the fundamental conception is, that their political economy is an ascertained body of laws of nature, is an offshoot of the ancient fiction of a Code of Nature and a natural order of things, in a form given to that fiction in modern times, by theology on one hand, and a revolt against the tyranny of the folly and inequality of such human codes as the world had known on the other.

No branch of philosophical doctrine, indeed, can be fairly investigated or apprehended apart from its history. All our systems of politics, morals, and metaphysics would be different if we knew exactly how they grew up, and what transformations they have undergone; if we knew, in short, the true history of human ideas. And the history of political economy, at any rate, is not lost. It would not be difficult to trace the connection between every extant treatise prior to the 'Wealth of Nations,' and conditions of thought at the epoch at which it appeared. But there is the less occasion, for the purpose of these pages, or of ascertaining the origin and foundation of the economic doctrines of our own day, to go behind the epoch of Adam Smith, that he has himself traced the systems of political economy antecedent to his own to a particular course of history, to 'the different progress of opulence in different ages and nations,' and 'the private interests and prejudices of particular orders of men.' What he did not see was, that his own system, in its turn, was the product of a particular history; that what he regarded as the System of Nature was a descendant of the System of Nature as conceived by the ancients, in a form fashioned by the ideas and circumstances of his own time, and coloured by his own disposition and course of life. Still less could he see how, after his time, 'the progress of opulence' would govern the interpretation of his doctrines, or how the system he promulgated as the system of liberty, justice, and divine benevolence, would be moulded into a system of selfishness by 'the private interests and prejudices of particular orders of men.'

'The Wealth of Nations,' says Mr. Buckle, 'is entirely

deductive. Smith generalizes the laws of wealth, not from the phenomena of wealth, but from the phenomena of selfishness. He makes men naturally selfish; he represents them as pursuing wealth for sordid objects, and for the narrowest personal pleasures.'* This description is not misapplied to a political economy of later days, which has guided Mr. Buckle's interpretation of the system of Adam Smith; but with respect to that system itself, it involves two fundamental misconceptions. Selfishness was not the fundamental principle of Adam Smith's theory; and his method, though combining throughout a vein of unsound *a priori* speculation, was in a large measure inductive. The investigation which establishes this will be found also to exhibit the connection between his economic system and the chief problems pressing for solution in his time; the methods which the philosophy of the age provided for their solution; and the history and phenomena of the economic world in which he lived, and from which his ideas, his inductions, and his verifications were drawn.

One consideration to be carried in mind in the interpretation of the 'Wealth of Nations' is that its author's system of philosophy ought to be studied as a whole; his economic system was part of a complete system of social, or, as he called it, moral philosophy. Mr. Buckle, who on other points has much misconceived the 'Wealth of Nations,' properly says of it, and the 'Theory of Moral Sentiments,' that the two must be taken together and considered as one, both forming part of the scheme embraced in his course of moral philosophy at Glasgow—a course which, it is important to observe, began with Natural Theology, and included, along with Ethics and Political Economy, the Philosophy of Law. Again, as his social philosophy should be considered as a whole, so the whole should be considered in connection with the philosophical systems or methods of investigation of his time. Two essentially opposite systems of reasoning respecting the fundamental laws of human society were before the world at that epoch, which may be respectively

* *History of Civilization in England*, i. 228; ii. 449.

designated as the theory of a Code of Nature, and the inductive system of Montesquieu—the former speculating *a priori* about 'Nature,' and seeking to develop from a particular hypothesis the 'Natural' order of things; the latter investigating in history and the phenomena of the actual world the different states of society and their antecedents or causes—or, in short, the real, as contrasted with an ideal, order of things. The peculiarity of Adam Smith's philosophy is, that it combines these two opposite methods, and hence it is that we have two systems of political economy claiming descent from him—one, of which Mr. Ricardo was the founder, reasoning entirely from hypothetical laws or principles of nature, and discarding induction not only for the ascertainment of its premises, but even for the verification of its deductive conclusions; the other—of which Malthus in the generation after Adam Smith, and Mr. Mill in our own, may be taken as the representatives—combining, like Adam Smith himself, the *a priori* and the inductive methods, reasoning sometimes, it is true, from pure hypotheses, but also from experience, and shrinking from no corrections which the test of experience may require in deductions. Of the two schools, distinguished by their methods, the first finds in assumptions respecting the nature of man, and the course of conduct it prompts, a complete 'natural' organization of the economic world, and aims at the discovery of 'natural prices,' 'natural wages,' and 'natural profits.'

An examination of Adam Smith's philosophy enables us to trace to its foundation the theory upon which the school in question has built its whole superstructure. We shall see that the original foundation is in fact no other than that theory of Nature which, descending through Roman jural philosophy from the speculations of Greece, taught that there is a simple Code of Nature which human institutions have disturbed, though its principles are distinctly visible through them, and a beneficial and harmonious natural order of things which appears wherever Nature is left to itself. In the last century this theory assumed a variety of forms and disguises, all of them, however, involving one fundamental fallacy of reasoning *a priori* from assumptions obtained, not by the interrogation but by the anticipation of Nature; what is assumed as Nature being at bottom a mere conjecture respecting its constitution and arrangements. The political philosophy flowing from this ideal source presents to us sometimes an assumed state of nature or of society in its natural simplicity; sometimes an assumed natural tendency or order of events, and sometimes a law or principle of human nature; and these different aspects greatly thicken the confusion perpetually arising between the real and the ideal, between that which by the assumption ought to be and that which actually is. The philosophy of Adam Smith, though combining an inductive investigation of the real order of things, is pervaded throughout by this theory of Nature, in a form given to it by theology, by political history, and by the cast of his own mind. 'The great and leading object of his speculations,' says Dugald Stewart, by no means intending a criticism, for Mr. Maine had not then explored the fallacies lurking in the terms Nature and Natural Law, 'is to illustrate the provisions made by Nature in the principles of the human mind, and in the circumstances of man's external situation, for a gradual and progressive augmentation in the means of national wealth, and to demonstrate that the most effectual means of advancing a people to greatness is to maintain that order of things which Nature has pointed out.' At the end of Book IV. of the 'Wealth of Nations' we find the Code of Nature and its institutions definitely marked out: 'All systems either of preference or restraint being completely taken away, the obvious and simple system of natural liberty establishes itself of its own accord. According to the system of natural liberty, the State has only three duties to attend to:' namely, to protect the nation from foreign aggressions, to administer justice, and to maintain certain great institutions beyond the reach of individual enterprise—a supposed natural limitation of the province of law and government which has been the cause of infinite error in both theoretical political economy and practical legislation.

The same fundamental conception pervades both Smith's

system of ethics and his philosophy of law. Investigating the character of virtue, he treats first of 'the order in which Nature recommends objects to the care of individuals' for their own personal happiness; next, of 'the order which Nature has traced out for the direction of our powers of beneficence: first, towards other individuals; and, secondly, towards societies.' So, in the description given by himself of his proposed history of jurisprudence, he states that 'every system of positive law may be regarded as a more or less imperfect attempt towards a system of natural jurisprudence;' and that the main end of jural inquiry is to ascertain 'what were the natural rules of justice, independent of all positive institutions'—a description, perfectly coinciding with Mr. Maine's, of the place which the law of Nature filled in the conception of the Roman jurist. 'After Nature had become a household word, the belief gradually prevailed among the Roman lawyers that the old Jus Gentium was in fact the lost Code of Nature. The Roman conceived that, by careful observation of existing institutions, parts of them could be singled out which either exhibited already, or could by judicious purification be made to exhibit, the vestiges of the reign of Nature.'*

But abstraction would never have played so great a part in Adam Smith's philosophy, would never have resulted in such sweeping generalizations respecting the beneficent and equitable economy resulting from the play of the natural inclinations and individual interests of men, had not the classical conception of Nature's harmonious code become blended with the theological conception of 'that great, benevolent, and all-wise Being, who directs all the movements of Nature, and who is determined to maintain in it at all times the greatest possible quantity of happiness.' Ideas thus derived from early philosophy became converted into the plans of Providence. Mr. Buckle displays less than his customary erudition when he states that theology had been finally separated from morals in the seventeenth century—from politics before the middle of the eighteenth.

* *Ancient Law*, pp. 56, 88.

Natural theology makes the first part of Adam Smith's course of moral philosophy, and its principles pervade every other part. The law of Nature becomes with him an article of religious belief; the principles of human nature, in accordance with the nature of their Divine Author, necessarily tend to the most beneficial employments of man's faculties and resources. And as the classical conception of Nature supposed simplicity, harmony, order, and equality in the moral as in the physical world, in Adam Smith's philosophy it becomes associated with divine equity and equal benevolence towards all mankind, and by consequence with a substantially equal distribution of wealth, as the means of material happiness. Nothing, therefore, is needed from human legislation—and this conclusion was powerfully fortified, as we shall afterwards see, by the political ideas of the age—beyond the maintenance of equal justice and security for every man to pursue his own interest in his own way. In the 'Wealth of Nations,' after laying it down that every individual endeavours as much as he can both to employ his capital in the support of domestic industry, and so to direct that industry that its produce may be of the greatest value, and therefore necessarily labours to render the annual revenue of his own nation as great as he can, Adam Smith adds: 'He generally, indeed, neither intends to promote the public interest, nor knows how much he is promoting it. By preferring the support of domestic to that of foreign industry, he intends only his own security; and by directing that industry that its freedom may be of the greatest value, he intends only his own gain, and he is in this, as in many other cases, led by an invisible hand to promote an end which was no part of his intention.'

So in the 'Theory of Moral Sentiments:'* 'The produce of the soil maintains at all times nearly that number of inhabitants which it is capable of maintaining. The rich only select from the heap what is most precious and agreeable. They consume little more than the poor, and, in spite of their natural selfish-

* *Theory of Moral Sentiments.* Part IV., chap. i.

ness and rapacity, though they mean only their own conveniency, though the sole end which they propose from the labours of all the thousands whom they employ be the gratification of their own vain and insatiable desires, they divide with the poor the produce of all their improvements. They are led by an invisible hand to make nearly the same distribution of the necessaries of life which would have been made had the earth been divided into equal portions among all its inhabitants; and thus without intending it, without knowing it, advance the interest of the society, and afford means to the multiplication of the species. When Providence divided the earth among a few lordly masters, it neither forgot nor abandoned those who seemed to have been left out in the partition.'

The mischief done in political economy by this assumption respecting the beneficent constitution of Nature, and therefore of all human inclinations and desires, has been incalculable. It became an axiom of science with many economists, and with all English statesmen, that by a natural law the interests of individuals harmonize with the interests of the public; and one pernicious consequence is, that the important department of the consumption of wealth has—though Mr. Lowe properly includes it in his definition of political economy—been in reality either altogether set aside, as lying beyond the pale of economic investigation, or passed over with a general assumption, after the manner of Mandeville, that private vices are public benefits. The real interests which determine the production, and subsequently, in the course of consumption, in a great degree the distribution, of wealth, are the interests of consumers; although the truth is veiled by the division of labour, the process of exchange, and the intervention of money, which makes wealth in the abstract, or pecuniary interest, seem the motive of producers. If every man produced for himself what he desires to consume or use, it would be patent how diverse are the interests summed up in one vague general term, self-interest—interests which vary in different individuals, different classes, different nations, and different states of civilization. And economic investigation would long since have penetrated beneath the surface of pecuniary interest to the widely different character of the real aims determining the nature and uses of wealth, but for that assumption of an identity between public and private interest which Adam Smith's authority converted into an axiom. Under its influence we find him assuming that the great landowners of the sixteenth century, in enclosing their manors and dismissing tenants, retainers, and labourers, to purchase luxuries for themselves, employed no less national labour than before; although the land fed sheep instead of men, and the wool of the sheep, in place of clothing labourers at home, went from the country to foreigners in exchange for wines, silks, velvets, and trinkets, for the personal consumption of the lord of the manor. When William the Conqueror afforested at once some three-score parishes, he did only what landowners have done from the fifteenth century to the present time. To take the children's food and give it unto dogs is, by this reasoning, to give it back to the children!

The Nature hypothesis had, however, with Adam Smith another powerful ally besides theology in the idea of liberty. The idea of civil and religious liberty, of resistance to arbitrary government and unequal laws, of confidence in individual reason and private judgment as opposed to the dictates of external authority, had begun even in the seventeenth century to spread from the world of religion and politics to the daily business of life. At the beginning of the second half of the eighteenth century the predominant form which this idea took was the liberation of individual effort in the world of industry and trade from oppressive restrictions and arbitrary and unequal imposts; and it found in the Code of Nature a quasi-philosophical basis on which to build a complete economic 'system of natural liberty.' The French Revolution, of which the seeds were then being sown by the Economistes (or Physiocrates, as they were afterwards called, from the name they gave to their system, a name denoting the government of society by nature or natural laws), was, in its origin, an economic revolution, a 'rebellion of the belly,' stirred up *ab initio* by the Économistes, who saw in the fetters and insecurity of industry the cause of the poverty of France, and in the superior freedom and security of its cultivators and tradespeople the secret of the superior prosperity of Great Britain. Living in such a world of human misgovernment and suffering toil, beholding, as the Physiocrates did, all the natural sources of wealth locked up by human laws, it is not surprising that the doctrine of a Code of Nature, of natural rights of liberty and property, of a natural organization of society for the increase of human prosperity and a just distribution of the fruits of the earth and of industry, came upon them like a new revelation, and carried the authority of one. Thus, like Adam Smith, on whom their doctrines had no small influence, the Physiocrates invested the ideal Code of Nature, which had come to them through the lawyers of their country from the jurisprudence of Rome, with a divine origin, and found in it a complete circumscription and definition of the province of human sovereignty. The three same fundamental conceptions derived from the three same sources—from Græco-Roman speculation, from Christian theology, and from the revolt of the age against arbitrary interference with private industry and unequal imposts on the fruits of labour, formed the groundwork of the political economy of Adam Smith and the Physiocrates: the sole difference in this respect is, that the latter gave the name political economy to the whole of social philosophy, while Adam Smith limits the particular name to a department of social philosophy relating to wealth, and that they enunciated these doctrines as laws of Nature and God with more passionate emphasis. Adam Smith had not derived any of the three fundamental ideas of his political economy from the Physiocrates—for those ideas came to both from the history and philosophy of the past, and from the circumstances of the age—but he was strongly confirmed in them by his visits to France, his personal intercourse with them, and his study of their writings; he caught from them, moreover, not only particular propositions and expressions, but something of the form which his doctrine of natural distribution has taken, and also the precise limitation which he gives to the functions of the State.

Smith was himself so sensible of his debt to the Physiocrates, that he not only speaks of Quesnay's system as 'the nearest approximation to the truth that had been published upon the subject of political economy,' but was prevented only by Quesnay's death from dedicating to him his own great treatise. He was, however, under a much more solid obligation to a much greater Frenchman, the illustrious Montesquieu. Mr. Buckle, who in his excellent chapters on the 'Intellectual History of France' justly traces to England the origination of the spirit of liberty which in the eighteenth century took possession of French philosophy, nevertheless does injustice at once to France and to Great Britain in overlooking the influence of Montesquieu over Scotch philosophy in Adam Smith's age. And the same oversight, coupled with a view of political economy which Mr. Buckle himself adopted from Ricardo and his school, leads him to describe Adam Smith's method as entirely deductive. The philosophy of Great Britain, Mr. Buckle affirms, owes nothing to France; and he represents the intellect of Scotland as having, under clerical guidance, become wholly deductive, referring as a crucial example to Adam Smith, Scotland's most eminent political philosopher. The clerical system of deductive reasoning certainly runs through and warps the whole philosophy of Adam Smith. Nevertheless, his philosophical love of truth, and of interrogating nature itself in its real phenomena, and the inductive method of doing so which Scotch philosophy in his age had adopted from Montesquieu, preserved him from many errors into which the method of deduction from assumptions respecting Nature and its laws has led one school of his followers, which at the present day is not backward in claiming the clerical prerogative of orthodoxy. It has already been observed that two opposite systems of reasoning were before the world in Adam Smith's age, and that he combined them both—the system of reasoning from a theoretical law of Nature, and the historical inductive method of Montesquieu, which traces the real order of things, and seeks in the circumstances and history of society the explanation of its different states in different ages and countries. The latter method had a powerful attraction for a new school of political and jural philosophy in Scotland to which Adam Smith belonged. Lord Kaimes, his literary patron, and Millar, his own pupil, alike followed Montesquieu's method. Dalrymple, also a disciple of Lord Kaimes, states in the dedication of his 'History of Feudal Property'—a work which seems to have afforded Adam Smith not a few important suggestions—that much of his manuscript had actually been 'revised by the greatest genius of the age, President Montesquieu.' And Millar expressly states that in his lectures on the Philosophy of Law, his great master 'followed the plan which seems to have been suggested by Montesquieu; endeavouring to trace the gradual progress of jurisprudence from the earliest to the most refined ages, and to point out the effect of those arts which contribute to subsistence and to the accumulation of property in producing corresponding improvements in law and government.' But, as Mr. Buckle himself says, Adam Smith's political economy and the rest of his philosophy were 'part of a single scheme.' And a comparison of Books III., IV., and V. (chapter i.) of the 'Wealth of Nations' with Adam Smith's own description, on the one hand, of the work he had previously contemplated on the History of Law, and Millar's account of his lectures, on the other, shows how closely connected were his economic and his jural researches. So closely indeed were they so, that internal evidence confirms the statement of Dugald Stewart, that he actually published in the 'Wealth of Nations' a valuable part of the work he had long before announced on the jural history of mankind; and we have in this fact a probable explanation of the story that he destroyed a few days before his death the manuscript of his lectures on jurisprudence. He preserved in the 'Wealth of Nations' what he probably thought their most valuable results.*

* An eminent Scotch philosopher of the present day, Mr. Alexander Bain, has expressed to me a doubt that Adam Smith destroyed anything which he considered valuable; adding, that he was little disposed to consider anything to which he had given research and thought of small value. The preservation of the chief results of his jural studies in the *Wealth of Nations* reconciles Mr. Bain's opinion on this point with the destruction of the manuscripts, of which there seems to me conclusive evidence.

The problem which Adam Smith proposed to himself was by no means only the illusive one, What is *a priori* the order of Nature, or 'the natural progress of opulence?' He inquired further 'What had been the actual order of things, the actual progress of opulence, and its causes?' What had occasioned the slow progress of Europe from the time of the barbarian conquests down to modern times? What the more rapid advance of Great Britain than of France and other parts of the continent? To answer these inquiries he subjected the phenomena of history and the existing state of the world to a searching investigation, traced the actual economic progress of different countries, the influences of laws of succession, and of the political distribution of property, the action and reaction of legal and industrial changes, and the real movements of wages and profits so far as they could be ascertained. Nor was he content with the inductions of the closet from written evidence—though necessarily the most important field of inductive investigation in social philosophy—he compared all the phenomena which careful personal observation, both in his own country and in France, had brought under his view. In short, he added to the experience of mankind a large personal experience for inductive investigation. Even the Physiocrates, although their study of actual phenomena was much less comprehensive and minute, though they were far more given to accepting at once their own unverified ideas as laws of nature, yet by no means neglected experience entirely. They had studied the economic condition of their own country, and compared it with what they knew of Great Britain; and they believed their theories of the natural order of things founded on the evidence of the results of interference with industry and spoliation of its fruits on the one hand, and of individual liberty and security of property on the other. The extent to which observation guided their doctrines is remarkably illustrated by their division substantially into two schools, whose conclusions, though converging in the main, were reached by different paths of personal experience, and moulded by it. Quesnay, the son of a small farmer, reared in the country amid the sufferings of the peasantry and the stagnation of agriculture under despotic restriction and ruinous imposts, and knowing of what imprisoned riches the soil was possessed, taught that land was the sole original source of wealth, agriculture the sole really productive employment, to whose fruits other industries gave only changes of form or place. Gournay, on the other hand, a merchant himself, and of a line of merchants, made the freedom of trade his staple doctrine, and summed up in the maxim, *Laissez faire et passer*, the duties of government.* The distinction exemplifies, moreover, that influence of personal history on the forms of political economy to which reference has been made.

There ran thus through the political economy of both Adam Smith and the Physiocrates, though much more extensively and systematically in the former, a combination of the experience philosophy, of inductive investigation, with *a priori* speculation derived from the Nature hypothesis. Hence, while on one hand the inductive method preserved the great Scotchman from grave errors into which not a few of his English followers in the mother-country of inductive philosophy have been led by the *a priori* method, on the other hand the bias given by preconceived ideas was so strong in the case of Smith himself, as to cause him to see in all his inductions proofs of a complete code of nature—of a beneficent order of nature flowing from individual liberty and the natural desires and dispositions of men. Like the Physiocrates, he blended the so-called 'evidence,' or self-evidence, of the law of nature in itself, with the evidence of phenomena carefully collated and sifted. The truth is, that Smith wrote before the physical sciences had developed canons of induction, and he thought an induction complete when he had obtained an immense number of instances, and a theory proved when it seemed to fit every observed case. Throughout history, and over Europe, he saw nothing but disorder and misery from such human legislation as the world had known, wherever it went beyond protecting personal liberty and property; he saw on all sides a mass of poverty traceable to State interference; the only

---

* *Les Économistes Français du XVIIIme Siècle*, by M. Léonce de Lavergne, pp. 173-5.

sources of whatever wealth and prosperity existed were the natural motives to industry, and the natural powers of production of individual men, and he leaped to the conclusion that nothing was requisite but to leave Nature to itself, that complete harmony existed between individual and public interests, and that the natural conduct of mankind secured not only the greatest abundance, but an equal distribution of wealth. He thought he found in phenomena positive proof of the Law of Nature, and of the character of its enactments. We find here the explanation of the seeming contradiction which Adam Smith's combination of the theory of natural Law with the inductive historical method gives to Mr. Maine's proposition 'that the book of Montesquieu, with all its defects, still proceeded on that Historical Method, before which the Law of Nature has never maintained its footing for an instant.' It is incontrovertible that historical investigation convicts the Nature hypothesis of reproducing a mere fiction of ancient philosophy; nevertheless Adam Smith, partly under the bias given by the theory itself, partly because the method of interrogating Nature itself was new, and the canons of induction unsettled, conceived that the method of Montesquieu proved the truth of the theory of Nature; in short, that nature, when interrogated, confirmed his anticipations of Nature.

One cause of the misconception that Adam Smith's economic method was one of mere *a priori* deduction is the arrangement he has adopted in the order of the five books of the 'Wealth of Nations.' In the order of logic the third and fourth books come before the first and second. They contain the induction on which is based the conclusion that the State has only to protect individual liberty, and the natural effort of every individual to better his own condition—or, in one word (with which his first book begins), labour—will supply in the most ample manner all the necessaries and conveniences of life, will divide its functions spontaneously in the best manner, and will distribute its produce in a natural order, and with the utmost equality. It has already been suggested that no such complete organization for the distribution of wealth is made by individual action, or what Adam Smith called Nature. Mr. Mill has shown the fallacy of defining political economy as the science of exchanges ; a definition which, besides omitting some of the most important conditions determining the production of wealth, overlooks the truth that human institutions, laws of property and succession, are necessarily chief agencies in determining its distribution. And it affords an instructive exemplification of the two methods which Adam Smith combined, *a priori* deduction from supposed principles of Nature, and inductive investigation of facts, that when the order of Nature is present to his mind, he finds a complete natural organization for the distribution of wealth, and no function for the State in the matter; but when he traces the actual progress of opulence, his readers are confronted at once with laws of succession, to which he traces the slow and irregular course of European progress after the barbarian conquests; laws founded on those conquests, and designed to perpetuate the unequal distribution of wealth they effected; laws which are potent agencies in the distribution of wealth in England to this day, and in the determination of its whole social and industrial economy.

But even while tracing in his first book the 'natural' distribution of wealth by exchange, or as he expresses it, 'the order according to which the produce of labour is naturally distributed among the different ranks of the people,' Adam Smith has been preserved by the inductive method which he combined with *a priori* deduction from enormous fallacies into which the school of Ricardo has since been betrayed by their method of pure deduction. The ancient theory of natural law involved the idea of uniformity and equality; and this idea in Adam Smith's case was powerfully reinforced both by that of an ideal order deducible from the equity and equal benevolence towards mankind of the Author of Nature, and by the love of system, symmetry, and harmonious arrangement which plays a conspicuous part in the 'Theory of Moral Sentiments,' because it did so in the author's own mind. With all these conceptions the theory of a complete equality of the advantages and disadvantages of different human occupations, and an equality, in that sense, of wages and profits, had obviously a powerful attraction for

Smith. It affords surprising evidence of his true philosophical spirit of inquiry into facts that he should nevertheless have denied the actual equality of wages and profits, traced the great actual inequalities to their causes, and defined the conditions of equality and inequality, and the actual effect of industrial progress on these movements, in such a manner as to indicate the very progressive divergence which can be shown to have since taken place, and which a school of modern economists not only ignores, but sometimes angrily denies, as inconsistent with its *a priori* deductions. Adam Smith, for his own part, not only limited *ab initio* the tendency to equality to what was practically the same neighbourhood, but pointed out that the kingdom was in fact divided into a number of different neighbourhoods with very different rates. Secondly, he traced many of the actual inequalities to pernicious institutions, a class of causes of inequality which later economists have done much to perpetuate by affirming a substantial equality. Thirdly, in place of insisting that competition alone determines the rate of wages, and gives the labourer the utmost value of what he produces, Adam Smith maintained that combination on one hand, tacit or open, on the part of employers, was the normal condition of things; while, on the other, the necessitous position of the labourer exposed him to the exaction of very unequal terms. Fourthly, he expressly confined the tendency to equality in the case of both wages and profits, even where competition was in full and free activity, to a stationary and simple condition of the industrial world. Fifthly, he showed that in place of equalizing wages, industrial progress had already produced great inequalities in England, and was beginning to do so in Scotland.

After observing that the price of labour varied much more in England than in Scotland, he adds: 'In the last century the most usual day wages of common labour through the greater part of Scotland were sixpence in summer and fivepence in winter. Three shillings a-week, the same price very nearly, still continues to be paid in some parts of the Highlands. Through the greater part of the low country the most usual wages of common labour are now eightpence a-day; tenpence, and sometimes a shilling about Edinburgh, in the counties which border upon England, and in a few other places where there has lately been a considerable rise in the demand for labour, about Glasgow, Carron, Ayrshire, &c. In England the improvements of agriculture, manufactures, and commerce began much earlier than in Scotland. The demand for labour, and consequently its price, must necessarily have increased with those improvements.'

Manufactures and trade on a great scale were only beginning in Scotland; the steam-engine had not yet been brought to bear on the mine or the loom when the 'Wealth of Nations' was composed; and the great inequalities in the local demand for labour throughout the kingdom, which have followed in the wake of steam, were yet to appear. Adam Smith, in truth, lived in a very early industrial world; the only steam-engine he refers to is Newcomen's; the word 'manufacture' had not lost its true meaning and become as inappropriate as hideous. In the clothing manufacture, he expressly says, the division of labour was nearly the same as it had been for a century, and the machines employed were the same; adding that only three improvements in them of any importance had taken place since the reign of Edward IV. In place of the infinite diversities of complexity and difficulty in the different employments of capital which have followed the progress of mechanics and chemistry, all modes of employing capital were, he says, about equally easy. The foreign trade of the kingdom was so small that he computed the annual importation of corn at only 23,000 quarters, and concluded that the freest importation never could sensibly affect prices in the home market.

In short, he applied the doctrine of equality only to a simple and almost stationary condition of industry and neighbourhood trade, in which few changes in the mode of production or the channels of trade took place from one century to another, and in which the inhabitants of each neighbourhood might comparatively easily estimate the profits and prospects of each different employment; and even to such a world, only with many modifications and exceptions. To such a world, in positive terms, he limited the tendency to equality which has been made by his successors, not only an unconditional assumption, but the basis of finance. The truth is, that the doctrine of a tendency to equality is a mere theorem in political economy; and a theorem which imports the tendency only under special conditions well enunciated by Adam Smith—conditions the opposites of those which prevail in the present industrial world.

A state of the industrial world which was exceptional in Adam Smith's time is the normal state in our own; and it is certain, both from his positive doctrine and from his close attention to the realities of life, that had he lived even two generations later, his general theory of the organization of the economic world and the results of the competition for economic life would have been cast in a very different mould. Alike in the theory of Nature which pervades his entire philosophy of society, and in his general conceptions of the industrial world, we trace the influence of the early world in which he lived. One striking example of this is that one-half of society has been almost entirely overlooked in his philosophy. His language appears at first sight to point to unrestricted liberty as the unconditional principle of a true political economy, and the indispensable requisite of the full development of the economic resources of nature; but on closer inspection it will be found that where he speaks of 'the natural effort of every individual to better his own condition, when suffered to exert itself with freedom and security,' as the cause of national wealth and prosperity, he had only the half of the nation denoted by the masculine pronoun in his mind; he meant only what he elsewhere says, 'the natural effort of every man.' He seems to have been perfectly content—though it involves an inconsistency which is fatal to his whole theory—with the existing restraints on the energies of women; and the only effort on the part of a woman to better her own condition which he has in view is 'to become the mistress of a family.' In the only passage in the 'Wealth of Nations' in which women are referred to, we discover at once how far was he from having developed universal laws of industry and wealth, how far he was from escaping from the ideas of a primitive world. 'There are,' he said, 'no public institutions for the education of women, and there is accordingly nothing useless, absurd, or fantastical, in the common course of their education. They are taught what their parents or guardians judge it necessary or useful for them to learn, and they are taught nothing else. Every part of their education tends evidently to some useful purpose—either to improve the natural attractions of their person, or to form their minds to reserve, to modesty, to chastity, and to economy; to render them both likely to become the mistresses of a family, and to behave properly when they have become such. In every part of her life a woman feels some convenience or advantage from every part of her education.'

Although 'the obvious and simple system of natural liberty' is the foundation of Smith's whole system, though he regarded it as the law of the beneficent Author of Nature, it turns out that he applied it only to one-half of mankind. The reason is that the law and the exception alike came to him from the age in which he lived, and the ideas of a yet earlier state of society. The insurrection against the oppressive and unequal economic *régime* of the past was as yet only on the part of men; and the very theory of the Law of Nature which men invoked for their own emancipation, as it was the offspring of the speculation of the ancient world, so it bore the impress of its narrowness and injustice.

IV.

'SOME LEADING PRINCIPLES OF POLITICAL ECONOMY NEWLY EXPOUNDED,' BY PROFESSOR CAIRNES.*

ANY new work by Mr. Cairnes would be sure of a *succès d'estime*, but the present is one, the importance of which the economist most opposed to some of the principles it expounds with so much force, clearness, and skill, will not call in question. Its very importance, on the other hand, the high reputation of its author, and the consummate literary art it displays, impose on a reviewer the duty of sifting it closely. Mr. Cairnes himself sets an example of independent criticism. Thus he speaks of Mr. Mill's doctrine of cost of production as 'radically unsound, confounding things in their own nature distinct and even antithetical, setting in an essentially false light the incidents of production and exchange, and leading to practical errors of a serious kind, not merely with regard to value, but also with regard to some other important doctrines of the science.'

As we, for our own part, think not a few of Mr. Cairnes' own positions, including his doctrine of the relation of cost of production to value, untenable, we must claim for ourselves like independence of judgment and freedom of speech. Mr. Cairnes, we may observe, overestimates sometimes the amount of authority opposed to his own views, sometimes the amount on their side. In the case just referred to he too hastily assumes that the view he dissents from 'has the general concurrence of economists.' The English market for economic publications is extremely limited; the works on the subject are necessarily few; but it is notorious that various doctrines to be met with in the

---

* *The Academy*, June 27, 1874.

English text-books have often been questioned in lectures, articles, discussions, and private conversation; and that the general concurrence even of English economists—of whom alone English economists are apt to take account—ought not to be assumed from the agreement of those books. In the second place, the definition of cost of production which Mr. Cairnes puts forward had, in fact, been set forth in very similar terms in a treatise which has gone through many editions. Mr. Senior, criticising Malthus for terming profit a part of the cost of production, says, 'Want of the term abstinence has led Mr. Malthus into inaccuracy . . . an inaccuracy precisely similar to that committed by those who term wages a part of the cost of production.' Mr. Senior proceeds to define cost of production as 'the sum of the labour and abstinence necessary to production.' Mr. Senior's analysis is, indeed, defective in omitting the element of risk, but that defect is beside the question, and in respect to it we may observe that Mr. Cairnes too narrowly limits it, in the case of the labourer, to risk to mental and bodily faculties. The labourer often shares the pecuniary risks of the capitalist's enterprise; he runs the risk of being thrown out of work and wages at a critical time; and this is only one of a number of facts inconsistent with the assumption of an equality of wages, even within the limits which Mr. Cairnes sets to it.

The doctrine of cost of production involves the whole theory of wages and profit: and an immense superstructure which has been built on what Mr. Cairnes would call the orthodox theory, must stand or fall with that theory. The subject may be conveniently approached by an examination of the doctrine of 'the Wages Fund' and an 'average rate of wages,' for which Mr. Cairnes contends. An instance has just been noticed of an over-estimate, on his part, of the amount of difference between his own views and those of other economists: we here meet with one of an over-estimate of the amount of support from authority which Mr. Cairnes is entitled to claim for his own view. He terms his own side of the question with respect to the Wages Fund 'the orthodox side.' If orthodoxy in economics is to be determined by authority, some weight surely is to be attached to continental authority. And in Germany, as Dr. Gustav Cohn has lately pointed out, the doctrine of a Wages Fund was controverted more than fifty years ago, and has been repeatedly assailed since; nor does it now form, we believe we may affirm, an article of the creed of any scientific school of German economists. It is condemned by M. Emile de Laveleye, of Belgium, to whom Mr. Cairnes will not deny a place in the front rank of European economists. French economists have never been polled on the question, but it is at least certain that the notion that there is an aggregate national wages fund, the proportion of which to the entire number of labourers determines the general rate of wages, is incompatible with the exposition which M. Léonce de Lavergne—who, it is needless to say, combines the highest theoretical attainments with the most extensive knowledge of the actual economic phenomena of his own country—has given of the diversity of the rates of wages and the causes determining them, in different parts of France. In England the doctrine was, after mature consideration, abandoned by Mr. Mill; it has been vigorously assailed by Mr. Thornton; it is repudiated by Mr. Jevons; and among other economists in this country the present reviewer long ago combated it. On the whole, we believe that the chief weight of European authority is against the doctrine, and that it is a heresy, if that constitutes one. But the terms orthodoxy and heresy are singularly inappropriate in philosophical discussions. What philosophy seeks is reason and truth, not authority; and we will briefly state some of the grounds of reason and fact on which we take our stand in maintaining that an aggregate wages fund and an average rate of wages are mere fictions—fictions which have done much harm, both theoretically and practically, by hiding the real rates of wages, the real causes which govern them, and the real sources from which wages proceed. In every country in Europe, the rates of wages even in the same occupation vary from place to place; in other words, the same amount of labour and sacrifice of the same kind is differently remunerated in different localities. The Devonshire,

Somersetshire, or Dorsetshire labourer has been earning for the last fifty years less than half what the same man might have earned in Northumberland; the pay of Belgian farm labour is three times higher in the valley of the Meuse than in the Campine, and twice as high as in Flanders; it varies likewise prodigiously in Germany, even in adjoining districts. Whence these diversities? The reason, obviously, is that distinct and dissimilar conditions determine wages in different parts of each country. Mr. Cairnes urges: 'A rise of wages, let us suppose, occurs in the coal trade: does anyone suppose that this could continue without affecting wages, not merely in other mining industries in full competition with coal mining, but in industries the most remote from coal mining—industries alike higher and lower in the industrial scale? Most undoubtedly it could not.'

We answer, most undoubtedly it could, and actually did. Wages rose continuously for a century in mining and other industries in some counties in England, while in others the earnings of the agricultural labourer remained stationary throughout the whole period. In 1850, Mr. Caird found the rate of agricultural wages in one northern parish 16s. a week, in another parish in the south only 6s. a week. In the former parish, mines and manufactures competed with farming for labour; in the latter, the one employer was a farmer holding 5000 acres. Would it be reasonable to say there was an average rate in the two parishes of 11*s*. a-week, resulting from the ratio of the aggregate wages fund to the number of labourers in both? What share had the southern labourer in the funds from which his fellow in the north earned his 16*s*. a-week? In like manner the funds expended in wages in the Rhine Province no more govern the price of labour in Pomerania and Posen than in Cornwall or Kent. A farm labourer in Flanders earns 1 fr. 50 c. a-day; an inferior labourer in another part of Belgium may earn 3 fr. 50 c. and upwards. Why? Because the Fleming no more shares in the funds which afford such high wages around Charleroi and Liége than a provincial journalist does in the funds from which the writers of the 'Times' are remunerated. Moreover, to speak of the ratio of an aggregate wages fund to the number of labourers as determining wages in each country surely implies that the sum expendible in wages at any given time is a fixed quantity; and, accordingly, M. de Laveleye remarks that one of many facts which give a practical refutation to the doctrine is that wages have recently risen in some parts of Belgium at the expense of rent. The demand for labour in manufactures on the one hand, and the novel attitude of the Belgian farm labourer on the other, have compelled farmers in certain districts to raise wages to a point at which farming has become a losing business; rents, therefore, are falling. It was seriously urged against trade-unions and combinations of labourers in England a few years ago by some advocates of the doctrine of the wages fund, that wages could not be raised by combination in one trade or locality without a proportionate fall of wages elsewhere, there being only a certain aggregate fund to be distributed. Mr. Heath's statement, however, is incontrovertible, that the mere report of the formation of an agricultural labourers' union in Warwickshire raised wages immediately in several neighbouring counties, and it will hardly be contended that there was a corresponding fall in other counties.

It is evident that the result has been mistaken for the cause; that the aggregate amount of wages is nothing but the sum of the particular amounts in all particular cases taken together; and that it would be as rational to say that the income of each individual in the United Kingdom depends on the proportion of the total national income to the number of individuals, as to say that the wages of each labourer in every place and in every occupation depend on the ratio of the sum total of wages to the total number of labourers. The statistician may find some interest in calculating the average rate resulting from the ratio of the aggregate amount of wages, if it could be ascertained, to the number of labourers in the kingdom; but the economist deludes himself and misleads others by representing this as the problem of wages. If farm wages be 10*s.* a-week in Devonshire, and 20*s.* in Northumberland, to say that the average rate is 15*s.* a-week is to speak of a rate which has no existence in either, and to withdraw attention from the causes of the real rates in both. In every country, instead of an average or common rate of wages, there is a great number of different rates, and the real problem is, What are the causes which produce these different rates? Hence we are driven to conclude that Mr. Cairnes is not 'justified,' to use his own words, 'in generalizing the various facts of wages into a single conception, and in discussing "general" or "average wages."'

At this point we are brought to inquire whether there is any better reason for maintaining the existence of an average rate of profit. The doctrine of average profit is closely connected in Mr. Cairnes' exposition with that of average wages. While contending, erroneously as we have shown, for an equality of wages throughout all similar occupations in the same country, he admits that working classes of very different degrees of skill do not compete, and may be paid at different rates for equal sacrifice and exertion. But, he adds, 'though labourers in certain departments of industry are practically cut off from competition with labourers in other departments, the competition of capitalists is effective over the whole field. The communication between the different sections of industrial life, which is not kept open by the movements of labour, is effectually maintained by the action of capital constantly moving towards the more profitable employments. In this way our entire industrial organization becomes a connected system, any change occurring in any part of which will extend itself to others, and entail complementary changes.'

In Mr. Cairnes' view, if wages were below par in any trade or locality, although the labourers there might not be able to migrate, a movement of capital seeking cheap labour would at once set in. It might almost be a sufficient refutation of this doctrine, in relation both to wages and to profit, to point out that no migration of capital has equalized the wages of agricultural labourers in any country in Europe. What migration there has been—and it has been altogether inadequate to produce an approach to equality of wages—has been almost altogether a migration of labour. Moreover, if in a single occupation so simple as that of agricultural labour there has been no such effective competition as Mr. Cairnes assumes, there seems some antecedent reason for suspecting error in the assumption of such an effective competition among capitalists as to equalize the rates of profit in all the countless employments of capital. There is something like a circular movement in Mr. Cairnes' reasoning on this subject. He first argues—'Each competitor, aiming at the largest reward in return for his sacrifices, will be drawn towards the occupations which happen at the time to be the best remunerated; while he will equally be repelled from those in which the remuneration is below the average level. The supply of products proceeding from the better paid employments will thus be increased, and that from the less remunerative reduced, until supply, acting on price, corrects the inequality, and brings remuneration into proportion with the sacrifices undergone.'

But afterwards we read—'The one and sufficient test of the existence of an effective industrial competition is the correspondence of remuneration with the sacrifices undergone—a substantial equality, that is to say, making allowance for the different circumstances of different industries, of profits and wages. Such a test applied to domestic transactions shows the existence of a very large amount of effective industrial competition throughout the various industries carried on within the limits of a single country. The competition of different capitals within such limits may be said to be universally effective.'

Is not this very like arguing that the equality of profits is proved by the fact that there is an effective competition of capital, and that the equality of profits proves the fact of an effective competition? Nor is this the only seeming flaw in Mr. Cairnes' logic. In proof of the equalization of profits, he urges that capital deserts or avoids occupations which are known to be comparatively unremunerative; while if large profits are known to be realized in any investment, there is a flow of capital towards it. Hence it is inferred that capital finds its level like water. But surely the movement of capital from losing to highly profitable trades proves only a great inequality of profits. There is, in like manner, a considerable emigration of labourers from Europe to America: does that prove that wages are equalized over the two continents? Let Mr. Cairnes himself answer—'Great as has been the emigration from Europe to the United States, it may be doubted if any appreciable effect has been produced on the rates of wages in the latter country. Throughout the Union, wages remain in all occupations very considerably higher than in the corresponding occupations in this country.'

Elsewhere he estimates American wages at twice the English, and four times the German rate. The emigration of labour, thus, is neither sign nor cause of an equality of wages; it is, on the contrary, consequence and proof of their inequality; and the migration of capital from losing or unprofitable to promising businesses, in like manner, only lands those who refer to it in evidence of the equalization of profits in an *ignoratio elenchi.* Mr. Cairnes, it seems clear, has not taken into consideration the main objections to the doctrine he espouses. The only objections he notices are the difficulty of transferring buildings, plant, and material from one use to another, and of learning a new branch of business. The fact is, that there are, in the first place, no means whatever of knowing the profits and prospects of all the occupations and investments of capital. No capitalist knows so much as the names, or even the number of the trades in the London Directory, only a part of the trades of the kingdom; and their number and names are yearly increasing. If, again, there were any statistics showing the actual gains of the different trades, they would show that the profits of the individual members of each trade vary immensely.

The business of insurance used to be thought one in which there was a certain general rate of profit. But a few years ago the subject was investigated by Mr. Black, and also in the 'Economist,' and the result arrived at was the fact of 'extremes of success and disaster in the experience of companies still underwriting.' Mr. Cairnes' reasoning assumes that the profits of every business are well known; but as they vary greatly with different companies and different individuals, the assumption implies that individual profits are known. If they were, it would be seen that to speak of the average profits, even of a single business, is idle. Moreover, even if the past profits of every individual in every trade were known, it would be a serious error on the part of capitalists, though one which they often commit, to judge of the future from the past. The changes in production and the conditions of trades, in international competition, and in prices, the effects of speculation, fluctuations of credit, and commercial crises, of scarce and abundant seasons, wars and other political events, new discoveries and inventions, would upset all these calculations. Curiously enough, Mr. Cairnes himself has maintained that the new gold mines introduced a disturbing element which will probably affect profits for thirty or forty years. Ricardo admitted that at the very time he was building a pile of theory on the assumption of an equality of profits, the return of peace had made them in fact very unequal. Had he looked back for a quarter of a century, he would have found abundant proof that they had been very unequal throughout the long war; and had he been able to foresee the immediate future, he would have learned from the crisis of 1825, which Mr. Tooke so well described, how blindly mercantile men often reason, how far they are from possessing the knowledge, sagacity, and prescience his theory supposed. So far, indeed, are men in business from knowing the conditions on which future prices and profits depend, that they are often ignorant, after the event, of the causes of their own past profits and losses. Not a single farmer or corn merchant, no witness whatever before the parliamentary committees save himself, Mr. Tooke states, dreamt of referring the high prices of corn in the early part of this century to the succession of bad harvests. It is not even true that losing businesses are always abandoned. Hope springs eternal in the human breast, and it is an old saying that all the mines in Cornwall are worked at a loss—that is to say, the average result is a balance on the wrong side. Mr. Mill, indeed, has reduced the supposed equality to one not of actual profits, but of expectations of profit. There is not, however, even this: no capitalist ever attempts to survey the whole field, or to estimate the probable relative gains of every investment.

The doctrine of average profit, like that of average wages, thus falls to the ground, and with it falls the superstructure built on it, including Mr. Cairnes' doctrine of value. 'The indispensable condition,' he states, 'to the action of cost of production is the existence of an effective competition amongst those engaged in industrial pursuits'—that is to say, a competition which equalizes profits; and we have seen that no such competition is possible. If we are, in economic theory, to exhaust space and time of their contents, and to suppose a vacuum in which no obstacles to the movements of labour and capital in pursuit of gain exist within the limits of each country, so that wages and profits are equalized, why not apply the same supposition to international trade and international values? We might, in like manner, theorise about wages, profit, prices, and rent at the bottom of the ocean on the supposition of the absence of water. The truth is—and it is a truth which Mr. Cairnes has missed, though he has made an important step towards it—that the principle regulating domestic as well as international values is not cost of production, but 'the equation of demand,' or 'demand and supply;' though the formula is one which requires much interpretation, and by no means contains in its very terms the full explanation of values and prices which many people suppose.

But more than the superstructure of economic theory built on the doctrine of cost of production falls to the ground along with it. The method of deduction from assumption, conjecture, and premature generalization falls too. Mr. Cairnes speaks in his preface of certain 'assumptions respecting human character and the physical conditions of external nature,' as constituting 'the ultimate premisses of economic science;' and of the 'method of combined deduction and verification by comparison with facts,' as 'the only fruitful or, indeed, possible method of economic inquiry.' But is a theorist likely to be very searching in his verification of assumptions on which he has built his whole science and his own reputation? Have the economists of the deductive school ever verified their doctrines respecting the equality of profits and of wages? If they are at liberty to set aside as ' disturbing causes,' all the obstacles to the pursuit of gain resulting from other principles of human nature, and from external circumstances, and to theorise respecting wages, profits, and prices *in vacuo*, what right have they to assume the existence of the love of gain itself in such an imaginary world? The only facts in human nature, we may add, which abstract political economy takes account of are far indeed from being ultimate facts, or from being susceptible of treatment in economic reasoning as simple, universal, and invariable principles. Self-interest and the desire of wealth are both names for a multitude of different passions, ideas, and aims, varying in different ages and countries, and with different classes and different individuals; and each having its own peculiar effects on the nature, production, and distribution of wealth.

The ' principle of population,' again, so far from being an ultimate fact in human nature from which general conclusions can be drawn, is a highly artificial and widely varying principle, inseparably interwoven with religious and moral ideas and historical causes. Its force in Bengal is the result mainly of a particular superstition; and, owing to causes which have never been probed to the bottom, its force varies greatly, not only in neighbouring countries like England and France, but in different parts of the same country, Normandy and Britanny for example.

Our limits prevent our even alluding to many special questions of great interest raised by Mr. Cairnes, but we will take two or three examples from the chapter ' On some Derivative Laws of Value.' In the early stages of a nation's growth, tillage for the production of corn steadily gains ground on pasture; but Mr. Cairnes treats it as a 'law of industrial progress' that in the later stages this process is reversed, and pasture constantly encroaches on tillage. We think we find here an instance of the economic error resulting from inattention to both continental phenomena and continental literature. Save in exceptional situations, the increasing supply of meat in

Europe is obtained by stall-feeding and tillage, not by the extension of pasture. As Professor Nasse states, the aridity of the climate and the character of the soil preclude pasture throughout the greater part of Germany. M. de Laveleye maintains that, by means of stall-feeding, Flanders, in spite of the poverty of its soil, supports more cattle to the acre than England. It is noticeable that both these distinguished economists point to one condition unnoticed by Mr. Cairnes, which may in future, to some extent, counteract the causes hitherto operating so decisively in favour of tillage for the production of meat over most of the Continent—namely, the rise in the price of labour. How far mechanical art, on the other hand, may neutralize this condition it is useless here to inquire; but M. de Laveleye makes the important observation, that even where a country like England, with exceptional advantages for pasture, imports a great part of its corn, the importing and exporting countries become virtually one economic region in which tillage is constantly advancing. Hence an enormous extension of tillage in the United States, for the supply both of its own population and that of Europe, is as certain as any fact in the economic future can be. Connected with the foregoing question is one respecting the price of corn, which, according to Mr. Cairnes, 'at length, in the progress of society, reaches a point beyond which (unless so far as it is affected by changes in the value of money) it manifests no tendency to advance further.' This point, in Mr. Cairnes' judgment, was already reached in England three centuries ago, if not, as he has no doubt, some centuries earlier; the reason he assigns being that, after a certain point, an advance in the price of corn reacts on population and checks the demand. There are, however, several methods by which a nation may meet an advancing cost of corn—by a diminished consumption of animal food, for instance, or a diminished cost of manufactures. As a matter of fact, the labouring population of England has much diminished its use of animal food since the fifteenth century, while it clothes itself cheaper. The enormous prices of corn towards the close of the last, and during the early part of the present century, again, show how an advance in the price of bread may be met by privation. The whole population of the United States is now a meat-consuming one; but if Macaulay's prediction should be fulfilled, at no very distant future an increased cost of corn would be met by relinquishing meat; and a part of the nation might possibly even fall back on potatoes, or some other cheap vegetable; so that the future price of corn can only be matter of speculation. The price of timber, it may be observed, has followed a different course on the Continent from that which Mr. Cairnes lays down for it. Its value, he says, 'rises in general slowly, but never attains a very great elevation, reckoning from its height at starting.' Professor Rau, however, has given the following prices of a given measure of the same wood in Würtemberg, in florins and kreuzers:—1690-1730, 57 kr.; 1748-1780, 2 fl. 14 kr.; 1790-1830, 8 fl. 22 kr. And Dr. Engel's statistics show that the price of wood in another part of Germany nearly quadrupled itself between 1830 and 1865.

While we dissent altogether from most of the fundamental propositions of Mr. Cairnes' book, from the economic method it follows, and from not a few of its inferences and speculations, we see much to admire in it. It abounds in valuable criticisms, such as that of Mr. Brassey's proposition that dear labour is the great obstacle to British trade, and of the argument of American protectionists that the States with their high-priced labour cannot compete with the cheap labour of Europe.

V.

JOHN STUART MILL.*

The volume which completes the series of Mill's 'Dissertations and Discussions' illustrates a passage in his Autobiography, in which he describes his own as 'a mind which was always pressing forward, equally ready to learn either from his own thoughts or from those of others.' History affords scarcely another example of a philosopher so ready to review his positions, to abandon them if untenable, and to take lessons from his own disciples, as the discussion, for instance, of Mr. Thornton's book 'On Labour' shows Mr. Mill to have been. On the other hand, the volume adds links to a chain of evidence against another judgment pronounced by Mr. Mill on his own intellect, in a passage of his Autobiography which speaks of his natural powers as not above par but rather below it, and of his eminence being due, 'among other fortunate circumstances, to his early training.' His early training had undoubtedly a remarkable effect on his intellectual career—though in our judgment a very different one from that attributed to it by himself; and certainly, without reference to it, neither his system of philosophy nor his mental calibre can be properly estimated. It ought to be taken into particular account in connexion with some phases of his economics exhibited in the volume before us; but the question with respect to its influence has a much wider importance. It is a special instance of the great general question concerning not only the causes which produce great minds and direct their energies, but also those which govern the general course of

* *The Academy*, June 5, 1875.—This Article appeared as a review of Volume IV. of Mr. Mill's *Dissertationsand Discussions.*

philosophy and thought, since Mr. Mill's works had no small share in determining the ideas held in his time by a great part of the civilized world on some of the principal subjects of both theoretical speculation and practical opinion. For it will not be disputed that he was looked up to in several countries as the writer of chief authority on logic, political economy, and politics, and one of the first on psychology and morals. Latterly, however—not to speak of the passing influence of a political reaction on his popularity—it has been generally admitted that his methods in mental and social philosophy were inadequate; and his political economy is now censured, especially in Germany, for inconsistency and insufficient breadth of conception. 'His ground-plan,' says Dr. Roscher in his "History of German Political Economy," 'is a mere theory of the tendencies of undisturbed individual interest, yet he frequently admits the existence of practical exceptions to the theoretical rules thus arrived at, and the presence of other forces and motives.' Other writers, English, Germans, and Americans, have expressed astonishment that he could ever have adopted the doctrine of the wages-fund, which two of the dissertations in the present volume show that he finally discarded. The inquiry follows, Are the defects of his system to be traced to his own mind, or to his education?

One thing is plain in the matter. Education can nurture, develop, and direct the application of great mental powers; it can also misdirect, and even cramp and distort, but cannot create them. And no man without great and varied powers could have produced such works as Mr. Mill's 'System of Logic,' 'Principles of Political Economy,' 'Examination of Sir W. Hamilton's Philosophy,' and the four volumes of 'Dissertations and Discussions'; not to speak of minor works, such as his essays on 'Utilitarianism' and 'Liberty.' One of his Dissertations shows that even a poetical fibre—one rarely found in the logician or the economist—was not absent from his mental constitution and more than one of them refutes Dr. Roscher's criticism that 'his was not an historical mind,' if by that is meant that he lacked the genius for historical inquiry; though it must be confessed that the historical method is rarely applied in his philosophy. Add to this, that thirty-six of the best years of his life were spent in a public office, in which he displayed administrative powers of the first order, and discharged his official duties not only with efficiency, but such ease and despatch, that he found time to distinguish himself among the foremost writers in several departments of intellectual speculation ; and that he afterwards took a considerable place as a debater in Parliament. The man who did all these things also exhibited in private society remarkable conversational powers, quickness of apprehension and reply, a facility of allusion and anecdote, with a vein of gentle humour, and such felicity and force of expression, that even when his conversation was grave, the present writer was often reminded of Steele's description of Sir Andrew Freeport that 'the perspicuity of his discourse gave the same pleasure that wit would in another man.'

If, however, Mr. Mill's 'early training' does not account for his intellectual eminence, it assuredly went far to form his philosophy; but a great deal more than the peculiar mental discipline to which his father subjected him must be included in that early training. We must include the fundamental conceptions, and the method of inquiry, of the leading intellects of the age from which he received his education. It was an age in which Bentham was justly regarded as the first social philosopher —Ricardo, less justly, as the highest authority in political economy, in spite of the protest of Malthus against his abstractions and precipitate generalization; Mr. Mill's father, James Mill, as the most eminent political thinker and writer of the time, and one of its chief lights in psychology ; and John Austin as *facile princeps* in jurisprudence. No leaders of thought ever reposed more unbounded confidence in their own systems than did this famous band. They seemed to themselves to hold in their hands the keys to every problem in the science of man. In psychology the master-key was the association of ideas ; in morals it was utility ascertained by a balance of pleasures and pains ; in political philosophy it was utility combined with representative government ; in political economy it was pecuniary self-interest together with the principle of population; in jurisprudence it was a particular definition of law and classification of rights. All these methods the younger Mill applied with a power never surpassed, and in addition he in good part created a system of logic which may be corrected and improved, but will ever hold a place among the chief works of the human mind. It was the fault of his age and of his education if the doctrine of evolution found no place in his psychology or his social science; if the historical method was taken up in his 'Political Economy,' as it was in the preliminary remarks of his treatise, only to be laid aside; and if corrections from observation and fact of the inferences from *a priori* reasoning appear, both in that treatise and in the present volume of his 'Dissertations and Discussions,' only in the form of practical exceptions to abstract theory, or of 'applications' of economic science, when the fault really lay in the original conception of the science itself. It was not possible to weld the abstractions of Ricardo and the actual forces governing economic phenomena into a consistent and scientific system; or to furnish an adequate theory of the origin and growth of human ideas without investigation of the entire history of human society. But if any one individual is especially to be blamed for the shortcomings of his system, it is not John, but James Mill. No training ever was more carefully adapted at once to crush all originality and to inspire excessive confidence in the methods adopted, than that which the younger Mill received from his father. It should, too, be borne in mind that the *a priori* political economy had its chief charm for John Mill, not in the simplicity and symmetry which recommended it to narrower and shallower minds, but in the complete individual liberty which it supposes. How far he was from trusting to individual interest to secure the best economy in all cases is sufficiently shown in the remarks in the first dissertation in the present volume (on Endowments) with respect to free trade in general, and to the doctrine that education should be left to demand and supply, in particular.

The action of demand and supply in another economic

aspect, namely on value, is discussed with conspicuous ability in the second dissertation on Mr. Thornton's book. The theory of a wages-fund, the proportion of which to the number of labourers in the country determines the price of labour, is there rejected; and it should be observed that this doctrine was not originated by Mill, but appeared in its most uncompromising and fallacious forms in the works of his predecessors, MacCulloch and Senior. It is, in fact, a corollary to the doctrines of an average rate of profit and an average rate of wages. If profits could not be higher, nor wages lower, in one employment or place than in another, there would really be such a mobility of capital and such a connexion between the funds out of which wages are everywhere paid, that it would not be very inaccurate to speak of them as forming a general fund on which the price of labour depends; though even in that case the combination of labourers might produce a higher general rate of wages and a lower general rate of profit than competition had done. What neither Mr. Mill nor Mr. Thornton seems to us sufficiently to bring out, is that the main power of trades unions to raise wages in particular cases has arisen from the actual inequalities of both profits and wages. Where extraordinary gains have been made in a business, the labourers have been enabled by concerted action to extort a share which competition would not have assigned to them; and again, where wages have been abnormally low, they have been able in like manner to compel a rise. The dissertation on the land question, and the papers on land reform in this volume, show that Mr. Mill, like most people of all political parties when they were written, underrated the strength of the forces on the side of the existing land systems; and the same remark is applicable to some passages in a review of Sir H. Maine's 'Village Communities,' which deserves particular notice for the generous interest and admiration which it shows that Mr. Mill felt for works of genius and learning, even when allied to far more conservative tendencies than his own. The essay on Bishop Berkeley's works, besides its great intrinsic merits as a piece of psychological criticism, is remarkable likewise for the sympathy it evinces with genius allied to religious opinions widely opposed to Mr. Mill's.

The volume contains, besides other instructive essays, a review of Grote's Aristotle by one to whom few will deny the highest claim to be listened to as a critic on such a subject, and to whom many will assign a place beside Bacon among the most illustrious successors of the original founder of logic.

VI.

PROFESSOR CAIRNES.*

PROFESSOR CAIRNES has been laid to rest with extraordinary honour. No other author's death in our time, save Mr. Mill's, has called forth so strong and general an expression of feeling; and Mr. Mill had been a leader of a philosophical school for a generation, and for several years a distinguished and active member of Parliament, while Mr. Cairnes had resided in England only for a few years, during the greater number of which he was the victim of a cruel malady which secluded him from the world and deprived him latterly even of the use of his pen. It is but thirteen years since Professor Cairnes, then holding a chair of Political Economy in Ireland, and known only to a few of the more studious economists in England, suddenly attained a wide celebrity by the publication, at the most critical moment in the American civil War, of 'The Slave Power;' one of the most masterly essays in the literature of political controversy, and, even now that American slavery is extinct, one of the most instructive and interesting treatises which students either of politics or of economics can find in the English language. The progress of economic science, and the changes in the views of economists, of which there are indications all over Europe, may disturb some of the conclusions of Mr. Cairnes' other works, but 'The Slave Power' will ever defy criticism; and no serious answer was attempted to be made to it, even when the war was at its height, and when the Southern States had the sympathy and support of some of the most powerful organs of the English press.

---

* *The Academy*, July 17, 1875.—This Article appeared as an obituary notice immediately after the death of Mr. Cairnes.

The practical object for which 'The Slave Power' was published has been triumphantly accomplished, but it had also a philosophical purpose which gives it a permanent value as an economic classic, for its subject was originally selected by Mr. Cairnes for a course of lectures 'to show that the course of history is largely determined by economic causes.' The skill and ability with which this purpose was carried into effect will, we believe, make future economists regret more and more as their science advances that Mr. Cairnes did not in his subsequent works develop another side of the relation between history and political economy, namely, the connexion between the whole social history of a country and its economic condition as one of the phases of the entire movement, and not as the result of a single principle or desire.

Before the publication of 'The Slave Power,' two essays in 'Fraser's Magazine,' 'towards the solution of the Gold Question,' had attracted the attention of economists in this country, especially Mr. Mill, to Mr. Cairnes' remarkable talent for deductive reasoning and exposition in economics. We think for our own part, and we have reason to believe that such was subsequently Mr. Mill's view, that in his practical conclusion Mr. Cairnes took insufficient account of the influence on prices of the acquisition by France, Germany, and other continental countries, of the power of production and communication by steam, contemporaneously with the diffusion of the new gold; but those who dissent from the proposition that prices have risen more in England since the discovery of the new gold mines than in any continental country, will nevertheless find nothing to dispute in the principles which Mr. Cairnes applied with consummate skill to the solution of the problem. The causes which have raised prices on the continent so greatly above their former low level are causes of the same order with those whose operation Mr. Cairnes discussed in relation to England.

Although an invalid, impeded in every physical movement by the malady from which he suffered, Mr. Cairnes took an active, though sometimes an unseen, part in the discussion of all the chief political controversies in this country during the last ten years, especially the Irish land question and Irish University education; and to him more than to any other single person it is due that University education in Ireland is not now under the control of an Ultramontane hierarchy, and that some of the chief subjects of historical and philosophical study have not been banished from the University of Dublin and the Queen's Colleges.

Last year, although then no longer able to write with his own hand, Mr. Cairnes published his 'Leading Principles of Political Economy newly Expounded,' a work which ought to be regarded, even by those who dissent most from some of its principles, as an important contribution to economic science. To state with the greatest possible clearness and force the reasons for espousing one side of a scientific controversy, is to render one of the best services to those who seek to know all that can be said on both sides. And if any position which Mr. Cairnes takes up is unsuccessfully maintained, the student may feel assured that if literary and dialectical skill could have defended it, it would be impregnable. The second edition of Mr. Cairnes' 'Logical Method of Political Economy,' which has recently been published, and which we hope on a future occasion to review, ought in like manner to be welcomed by those economists who incline to the inductive or historical method, not only for the intellectual interest which the reasoning of a powerful mind must always excite, but also as a masterly exposition of the deductive method, and a complete presentation of all that can be said for it or got out of it.

We have no words to express our admiration of the heroic fortitude and public spirit without which no amount of intellectual power would have enabled Mr. Cairnes, under sufferings of the most prostrating kind, to maintain so high a place in the philosophical and political history of his time as that which is assigned to him by universal consent. His moral as well as his intellectual qualities won for him the reputation which has now become historical.

VII.

MR. BAGEHOT.*

MR. WALTER BAGEHOT, the eminent editor, author, and political economist, died on Saturday last, at the same early age as the late Professor Cairnes, having reached only his fifty-second year. He was educated at University College, and graduated with distinction in the University of London, in which he was lately examiner in Political Economy. He was known to the public chiefly as editor of the 'Economist,' and by his books and essays; but he was also a partner in a bank, and was thus one of four remarkable men of letters in this century who have also been English bankers—Samuel Rogers, the poet; Grote, the historian; and Sir John Lubbock making the other three. As editor of the 'Economist,' Mr. Bagehot was the successor of its founder, the late Right Honourable James Wilson, whose son-in-law he was. He conducted that journal with consummate ability, and raised it to the first rank, both as a financial and as a political authority. He might, doubtless, have augmented his fortune by lending adroit support from time to time to particular financial and commercial speculations, but no line of the Economist ever showed the smallest favour of that kind, and it did honour to the English press under his management, alike by its absolute integrity and impartiality, and by its intellectual calibre.

As a political economist Mr. Bagehot belonged to the older deductive school, but his recent essays in the 'Fortnightly Review' mark an epoch in the history of English political economy, by abandoning the ground hitherto claimed by the leaders of that school for their method and doctrines. It is not many years

---

* *The Academy*, March, 31, 1877.—This Article appeared as an obituary notice.

since Mr. Lowe affirmed that 'political economy belongs to no nation, is of no country, and no power can change it.' Mr. Bagehot, on the contrary, emphatically limited the application of the postulates of the *a priori* and deductive method to England at its present commercial stage. And within this limit he further circumscribed and qualified what he termed 'the fundamental principle of English political economy,' by assuming only 'that there is a tendency, a tendency limited and contracted, but still a tendency, to an equality of profits through commerce.' Thus circumscribed, the principle can no longer serve as a foundation for the superstructure erected upon it, which is built on the assumption that the tendency is so effectual, and so arithmetically true and exact in its operation, that every shilling of cost to which every producer is put by any special tax or burden is nicely recovered, with neither more nor less than ordinary profit in the market. Besides the essays referred to, and the numerous articles which he wrote in the 'Economist,' Mr. Bagehot contributed to economic literature an excellent work on banking and the money-market, under the title of 'Lombard Street.' He was the author, also, of a work entitled 'Physics and Politics,' which embodies a series of ingenious, though rather fragmentary, essays on the natural history of political society.

The work which displays in the highest degree both the original powers and some of the peculiar characteristics of Mr. Bagehot's mind is his 'English Constitution,' which is unquestionably entitled to a place among English political classics. It is not without a tinge of cynicism, but it undoubtedly brings to light principles overlooked in all previous works on the Constitution, and which must be admitted by the disciples of Mr. Mill as qualifying to some extent the doctrines of that great writer's 'Representative Government.' One of the curious practical contradictions which, as Mr. Bagehot has pointed out, the political history of England gives to political theory is, that the £10 householders, who, under the Reform Act of 1832, formed the bulk of the constituency, were, above all classes, the one most hardly treated in the imposition of taxes; so little did representation secure especial care for their interests.

Although of the Liberal party, Mr. Bagehot was, by disposition and cast of thought, what, for want of a more appropriate word, we must call an aristocrat in political opinion and feeling—a Whig, not a Radical. In his 'English Constitution' he speaks of the order of nobility as useful, not only for what it creates, but for what it prevents, and in particular as preventing the absolute rule of gold, 'the natural idol of the Anglo-Saxon,' who is 'always trying to make money,' and who 'bows down before a great heap, and sneers as he passes a little heap.' If Mr. Bagehot did not himself bow down before the great heap, he was a little disposed to sneer at the little heap. Thus in 'Lombard Street,' speaking of the democratic structure of English commerce as preventing a long duration of families of great merchant princes, he says 'they are pushed out, so to say, by the dirty crowd of little men.' And in the discussions which arose out of the agitation for a reform of the Irish law of landlord and tenant, he could not conceal his scorn for little farms and little properties in land, such as form the main foundation of the prosperity of France.

Mr. Bagehot unsuccessfully sought at one time a seat in Parliament, but with all his political sagacity, knowledge, and talent, he was scarcely qualified to make a considerable figure in the House of Commons; for, although he might have made an administrator of a high order in a public office, he remarkably exemplified the essential difference between the qualifications of a writer and those of a speaker. The position that actually fell to him in life was the one he was best fitted for, and it was one really more honourable and more useful than that of many eminent members of Parliament.

VIII.

JEVONS' 'THEORY OF POLITICAL ECONOMY.'*

THE high reputation of the author, and the unsettled state of opinion with respect to both the limits and the method of political economy, make it the duty of every economist to master the doctrines of this work; and that can be done only by careful study of the book itself. A reviewer limited to a few dozen sentences can at best only assist a reader to form a judgment on some of its main topics. The principal questions it raises are, whether political economy should be confined within the limits that Mr. Jevons assigns to it, and whether the method which he applies to the solution of the problems within those limits is legitimate and adequate. On both questions our own opinion differs from that of Mr. Jevons; but, with respect to the first, the difference, though important, is one mainly of classification and naming. For Mr. Jevons fully concurs in the necessity of historical induction to ascertain the economic phenomena of society and their laws, but would set it apart as a branch of the general science of society under the name of 'economic sociology,' confining the term 'political economy'—or, as he prefers to call it, 'economics'—to a theory deduced from known facts, axioms, or assumptions, respecting the conduct dictated by personal interest, such as, 'that every person will choose the greater apparent good, that human wants are more or less quickly satisfied, and that prolonged labour becomes more and more painful.' The theory of population, accordingly, though pronounced by Mr. Jevons 'as scientific in form as consonant with facts,' forms, in his view, 'no part of the direct problem of economics,'

---

* *The Academy*, July 26, 1879.

and is not discussed in his present work. The majority of the most eminent economists of all schools—including Mr. Senior, who attempted to make political economy purely deductive, and whom Mr. Jevons estimates highly—are, it need hardly be said, against so narrow a limitation of the province of the science, and Mr. Jevons gives only the following reason for it:—'The problem of economics may be stated thus: given a certain population, with various needs and powers of production, in possession of certain lands and other sources of material; required the mode of employing their labour which will maximise the utility of the produce.' He adds, that 'it is an inversion of the problem to treat labour as a varying quantity, when we originally start with labour as the first element of production, and aim at its most economical employment.' The answer seems to be that land, like labour, is a primary element of production, and the area in cultivation and the productiveness of that area are both varying quantities. Were labour, moreover, not a varying quantity—as it is, because population is so—inferior soils and costlier methods of cultivation would not have been resorted to, and rent, to which Mr. Jevons gives a high place in economics, would not have arisen. But if, for these reasons, the laws of population come properly within the pale, political economy is clearly not limited to an assemblage of deductions or calculations from self-interest. Nor can any other natural laws, directly and deeply affecting the amount and distribution of wealth, be in consistency excluded. Admit the theory of population, and all that Mr. Jevons classes apart, under the name of economic sociology, has a logical title to a place within the domain of political economy.

Since Mr. Jevons, however, is an advocate, not an opponent, of the most extensive historical and inductive investigation, it is, as we have said, mainly a question of naming and classification, whether the term 'political economy' or 'economics' should be confined to a narrower field. But the question follows—Within that narrower field can we proceed, as Mr. Jevons contends, not only by simple deduction, but by mathematical process? 'There can be,' he says, 'but two classes of sciences—

those which are simply logical, and those which, besides being logical, are also mathematical. If there be any science which determines merely whether a thing be or not, whether an event will or will not happen, it must be a purely logical science; but if the thing may be greater or less, or the event may happen sooner or later, nearer or farther, quantitative notions enter, and the science must be mathematical in nature, by whatever name we call it.' Nevertheless, it can hardly be contended that Adam Smith's reasoning respecting the nature and causes of the wealth of nations is in its essence, and ought to be in actual form, mathematical; or that the process by which his main propositions are established is anything more than logical. We might add that they rest in good part on inductive, and not simply on deductive, logic; but the question before us is whether mathematical methods could properly be applied to their demonstration. That wealth consists, not of money only, but of all the necessaries and conveniences of life supplied by labour, land, and capital; that man's natural wants are the strongest incentives to industry; that the best assistance a government can give to the augmentation of national opulence is the maintenance of perfect liberty and security; that the division of labour is the great natural organization for the multiplication of the products of industry; that it is limited by the extent of the market; and that the number of persons employed in production depends in a great measure upon the amount of capital and the modes of its employment—these are the chief propositions worked out in the 'Wealth of Nations,' and it can hardly be said that mathematical symbols or methods could fitly be used in their proof. We need not controvert Mr. Jevons' proposition that 'pleasure, pain, labour, utility, value, wealth, money, capital, are all notions admitting of quantity; nay, the whole of our actions in industry and trade depend upon comparing quantities of advantage or disadvantage.' But the very reference which Mr. Jevons proceeds to make to morals militates against the assumption that 'political economy must be mathematical, simply because it deals with quantities,' and that 'wherever the things treated are capable of being greater or less, there the laws and relations must be mathematical.' The author instances Bentham's utilitarian theory, according to which we are to sum up the pleasures on one side and the pains on the other, in order to determine whether an action is good or bad. Comparing the good and evil, the pleasures and pains, consequent on two courses of conduct, we may form a rational judgment that the advantages of one of them preponderate, that its benefits are greater, its injurious results, if any, less; but it by no means follows that we can measure mathematically the greater or less, or that the application of the differential calculus would be appropriate or possible in the matter. We do not go the length of saying that there are no economic questions to which mathematical calculation could be fairly applied. The precious metals, for instance, move so easily between adjacent countries, that the variations of the foreign exchanges might perhaps be mathematically treated. But the immense inequalities in wages and profits, and the extraordinary fluctuations of prices under the uncertain influence of credit and speculation, are enough to baffle any attempt to apply the calculus to questions of value in general.

Were the application of mathematical processes and symbols to all economic reasoning, however, possible, it does not follow that it would be expedient. Bastiat's conception of the main problem of political economy was not very different from that of Mr. Jevons, who says, that 'to satisfy our wants to the utmost, with the least effort—to procure the greatest amount of what is desirable at the expense of the least that is undesirable—is the problem of economics.' Suppose that Bastiat could have put his 'Sophismes Economiques' into a mathematical form, with symbols for words, and equations for syllogisms and epigrams, would not political economy and the world have suffered a heavy loss by his doing so? The 'Times' might be printed in shorthand, and much ink and paper thereby saved, but would it conduce to the enlightenment of the public to make that economy? We regret that so much of Mr. Jevons' own reasoning is put into a mathematical form, because it is one unintelligible or unattractive to many students of considerable intellectual power and attainments. On the other hand, we not only concede that a mathematical shape might have been given to a great part of Ricardo's system, but we regret that it ever received any other, because his theory of value, wages, profits, and taxation is misleading and mischievous. Assume that the products of equal quantities of labour and abstinence are necessarily of equal value and price, and that exertions and sacrifices of different kinds are commensurable, and a number of mathematical equations and calculations can be based on those assumptions. But since the basis is false, the more the superstructure is hidden the better; and we should be glad to see it obscured, in every treatise in which it is put forward, by a liberal use of the calculus. Taking utility in the sense in which Mr. Jevons uses the word, we should acquiesce in his 'general law that the degree of utility varies with the quantity of commodity, and ultimately decreases as that quantity increases.' Yet, in one case only are the variations of utility and value, consequent on variations in the quantity of commodity, susceptible of mathematical measurement and calculation. The purchasing power or value of currency is inversely as its quantity, because there is an unlimited demand for it; but the variations in the value of other commodities bear no regular ratio to their quantity. Davenant's estimate, to which Mr. Jevons refers, that a defect of one-tenth in the harvest raises the price of corn three-tenths, and that a defect of one-half more than quadruples its price, is useful as an illustration, and made a rough, though only a rough, approximation to truth, so long as little corn came from abroad. Now the supply comes from the harvests of the world, and a defect of one-tenth in our own harvest might be followed by a fall instead of a rise in the price of grain. Could we even get accurate statistics of the harvests of the world, it would be found that its price is affected by so many other conditions that it bears no constant mathematical ratio to the amount of supply.

On the other hand, the stress which Mr. Jevons lays on the relation between value and quantity of supply seems to us to afford an answer to an objection which Mr. Cairnes has made to the proposition for which Mr. Jevons contends, that 'value depends on utility.' When Mr. Cairnes asks whether commodities are exchanged for each other simply in proportion as they are useful, we should reply in the affirmative, if by usefulness is meant, what Mr. Jevons and most other economists mean by it, the power of satisfying any human desire. If, in a siege or a famine, a loaf is refused in exchange for a large diamond, it is because the loaf is more desired or more useful; if, in ordinary times, a large diamond would not be given for a thousand loaves, the reason is that the diamond is preferred, or has greater utility in the economist's sense. It may, indeed, be urged that the comparative usefulness of diamonds and loaves, in the two cases, gives only the proximate cause of their relative value in exchange, and that the ulterior cause is comparative limitation of supply. A loaf contains as much nourishment in a time of plenty as in a famine; but in the former case no particular loaf is much wanted, or has any particular utility, while in a famine every loaf has a utility proportionate to the amount of food it contains. Mr. Jevons' proposition is in substantial accordance with the generally accepted doctrine that value depends mainly on limitation of supply. It depends, however, also, on other conditions, which defy all mathematical powers of calculation. Given the supply of a commodity, the urgency of the desire for it, and the amount of the funds in the hands of the persons desirous to purchase it, its price is still indeterminate. It will vary, according as buyers and sellers combine or compete, according to the activity of credit and speculation, and according to other conditions which are subject to no ascertainable laws.

A proposition laid down by Mr. Jevons, in which we fully concur, is, 'that economics must be founded on a full and accurate investigation of the conditions of utility, and to understand this element we must examine the wants and desires of man.' An urgent desideratum in political economy is certainly the substitution of a true theory of what Mr. Jevons terms 'the laws of human wants' for vague abstractions, such as the love of wealth and the aversion to labour. But wide historical investigation must precede the construction of the true theory. The authors to whom Mr. Jevons refers have made some instructive suggestions respecting the subordination and successions of human wants; but they seem not to have perceived that these wants vary under different surrounding conditions and in different states of society. The order which the evolution of human wants follows is one of the inquiries that await a rising historical and inductive school of economists, which happily has no opposition to encounter from Mr. Jevons. But with respect to the deductive method, Mr. Jevons does not quite fairly represent the view of that school when he says, 'I disagree altogether with my friend, Mr. Leslie; he is in favour of simple deletion; I am for thorough reform and reconstruction.' We are, it is true, for deletion of the deductive method of Ricardo: that is to say, of deduction from unverified assumptions respecting 'natural values, natural wages, and natural profits.' But we are not against deduction in the sense of inference from true generalizations and principles, though we regard the urgent work of the present as induction, and view long trains of deduction with suspicion.

We have been able to touch only a few of the problems discussed in Mr. Jevons' treatise. It is one which requires a considerable intellectual effort on the part of the reader, but the effort will bring its reward, even where it may not end in entire assent to the views of the eminent author.

IX.

MARSHALL'S 'ECONOMICS OF INDUSTRY.'*

An eminent scholar lately said to the writer that he preferred the old kind of review, which simply told what a book contained. The preference is intelligible on the part of a man who likes to know the gist of every new book, and to judge for himself of its soundness. The system would save readers both money and time. For threepence they might get the pith of a number of new works in a weekly review. Yet there are objections to this definition of the province of the reviewer. The editor of a famous journal, who knew his public well, used to tell a new writer, when sending him a book, that he wanted an original article on the subject, not a mere review. Competent critics, indeed, would not be content to write summaries—a business which could be done by mere drudges. Nor is it quite fair to an author to sell a little compendium of his work. Even a reader may sometimes object. The novel-reader, as well as the novelist, has no such enemy as the reviewer who tells the whole story in a few words. We shall, therefore, not attempt to summarise the contents of Mr. and Mrs. Marshall's work. Mr. Marshall has been known for several years, though less widely than if his pen had been more active, as one of the most accomplished and learned economists in England; and Mrs. Marshall bore a high reputation as lecturer at Newnham Hall, Cambridge. The theory of the economics of industry, set forth by two such authors, is not to be compressed into a few columns, to say nothing of the right and duty of criticism.

The book before us makes greater changes in economic

---

* *The Academy*, November 8, 1879.

method and doctrine, compared with previous text-books, than might be perceived at first sight; for they are made without sound of trumpet, and for the most part without controversy. Sometimes, indeed, they seem to us made without sufficient warning to call the student's attention. Still, the authors have, in their statement of general principles, adhered to the main lines of the economic system hitherto generally followed in England. Like a lecturer, the writer of a text-book ought to put the reader in possession of the system hitherto in vogue, and may find it necessary to begin with propositions which he afterwards subjects to such qualifications, exceptions, and limitations, that they turn out to be mere introductory observations and provisional assumptions; though, unfortunately, it is the custom, in political economy, to dignify preliminary generalities of this sort with the title of laws.

One characteristic merit of Mr. and Mrs. Marshall's work is that they do not make use of provisional doctrines or generalizations, of the class just referred to, as premisses from which trains of deduction can be made, but as starting-points for the investigation of actual phenomena, and the ascertainment of the presence and operation of their actual causes and conditions. Thus, the 'theory of normal value,'—a term, indeed, the appropriateness of which we shall have to question—which assumes the equalization of wages and of profits, and the conformity of prices with the expenses of production, is only used by the authors 'as the starting-point from which we must set out to explore all the various irregularities and unevennesses of market values.' A provisional assumption that competition tends to equalize the earnings of labour in the same trade in different localities may, for example, lead to the discovery of the causes of their actual inequalities. Suppose agricultural wages more than fifty per cent. lower in Dorsetshire than in Yorkshire, the inference from the assumption would be that there are obstacles to the migration of labourers, and the causes determining the actual market rates in the two counties might be thence ascertained. The discussion of local variations of value, of market fluctuations, and of the influence of trade unions on wages, in Mr. and Mrs. Marshall's book, is admirable, and, among other results, ought finally to dispose of the doctrine of the wages fund. 'The whole net annual income of the country,' say the authors, 'consists of all those commodities and conveniences of life which are produced during the year, after replacing the auxiliary capital that is consumed or worn out during the year. This net annual income is divided into —firstly, earnings of all kind of work, including business management; secondly, interest on capital; thirdly, rent obtained for the use of land or any other property that is artificially limited; fourthly, taxes paid to the State.' The first remark which this passage suggests is, that the authors appear to include, like Mr. Senior and most German economists, not only material commodities, but services and utilities which bear a price in the market, in the wealth of a nation; and accordingly the definition of wealth in their first chapter ought to be enlarged. Much thin sophistry has been expended by some English economists on an attempt to exclude services and the conveniences of life, when not, to use Adam Smith's phrase, fixed in some material and vendible commodity, from the category of wealth, although useful, limited in supply, exchangeable for commodities, and not to be had without purchase. The consequence is, that a fundamental change is overlooked which takes place in the real revenue and wealth of a nation as civilization advances—namely, that it consists more and more of material and durable articles, and less and less of perishable services, to perform which much trouble is undergone, but which leave nothing behind them. The mediæval baron sometimes maintained thousands of attendants and followers, whose services, not the commodities he gave for them, constituted a large part of his real wealth; for the commodities became the wealth of the retainers. On the fall of the baronial power, services of this kind gave place to commodities, some of which were of a durable kind, and made lasting additions to the national wealth.

But the point which especially calls for consideration in the passage cited relates to the remuneration of superintendence, or, as Adam Smith called it, of the labour of inspection. By

Mr. Mill this element is treated as forming, along with interest, a constituent of profit. Mr. and Mrs. Marshall, on the other hand, transfer it from the profit side of the account to that of wages, classing it, under the name of earnings of management, with the earnings or wages of skilled labour in general. There are some tendencies in modern industrial economy to make this eventually the proper classification, but it requires, at least, more explanation and qualification than it has received from the authors. They say, only, that 'We shall find it best to class earnings of management with the earnings of other kinds of work, because they are similar in nature to other earnings, and are, in the long run, governed by the same laws. For though, in the passing vicissitudes of trade it is somewhat difficult to draw a clear line between the interest on a business-man's capital and his earnings of management, yet we shall find that there is little in common between those fundamental laws which determine, in the long run, the normal rate of interest, and those which determine, in the long run, the normal earnings of management.' The authors do not seem to have had in view the objection to their classification suggested by Adam Smith's observation, that the earnings of two men of business, whose labour of inspection may be nearly the same, may differ widely, because varying, like interest, with the amount of capital they turn over, not with the amount of their labour. 'If,' he said, 'we suppose two manufacturers, the one employing a capital of £1000 and the other of £7300, in a place where the common profits of stock are ten per cent., the one will expect a profit of about £100 a-year, while the other will expect about £730. Yet their labour of inspection may be nearly or altogether the same.' To put the case in another way: a grocer, with a capital of £1000, sells at prices which leave him, let us say, after replacing his stock with insurance, a profit of £100 a-year for interest and trouble together. A neighbouring grocer, with ten times the capital, gets the same prices, and makes a net profit of £1000 a-year, with perhaps little more trouble. In such a case the earnings of management are surely not determined by the laws which regulate wages in general, and have much more in common with those which govern the rate of interest. Nevertheless, causes are at work, though the authors do not bring them out clearly, tending to regulate ultimately the earnings of management by the amount of skill and trouble it requires, instead of by the amount of capital. The scale on which modern business is carried on, and the growth of joint-stock companies, have given rise to a class of managers who are not partners, but paid by salaries for their work. And it is a tendency of competition to force the owners of the capital so employed to sell at prices which yield only what the management actually costs in this way. The system tends to drive small producers and dealers out of the market; for, a large salary to the manager of a big business may make no sensible addition to prices, while a proportionate remuneration to a small capitalist for his trouble would seriously raise the price of his goods. The growth, too, of the system of doing business on borrowed capital, due largely to modern banking facilities, has a similar tendency. The man working with borrowed capital may be content with an equivalent to a large salary, and his competitors, with capital of their own, must sell at the same prices. These tendencies are, however, to a great extent counteracted by other causes, which make profit include an element, over and above interest, that varies with the amount of capital, not with the labour of management, and which tend to assign this element chiefly to the owners of the capital as such, not to the managers as such. According to the authors, net profit contains no elements, save interest and the earnings of management, which they say are regulated by the same laws as the earnings of skilled labour. If so, the profits of trade ought to exceed interest only by the amount of a good manager's salary, and the ordinary fees of directors. Yet it is certain that the dividends received by the shareholders of a company may much exceed bare interest, in consequence partly of good management, while the managing staff receive only the ordinary remuneration. One reason for this is, that profit includes elements which cannot be disentangled and measured so as to determine the share due to the management. Luck, situation, connexion, prestige, and other elements enter, along with interest and superintendence, into profit; and it is impossible to say how much is due to each. The returns to all together usually vary in proportion to the amount of the capital embarked, not to the skill and trouble of management, and its owners legitimately claim the surplus. The authors' analysis of profit, accordingly, appears to us not quite complete, and we cannot think the subject is really made clearer by getting rid of the term profits altogether, as they seek to do, and speaking only of interest in reference to the gains of capital.

Another aspect of the problem of the rate of profit, as to which Mr. and Mrs. Marshall's exposition seems to us not entirely satisfactory, relates to the amount of the fund to be divided between capital and labour. 'The total net annual produce of a country's capital and industry,' they say, 'after rent and taxes have been deducted from it, consists of the interest on capital, and the earnings of different kinds of industry, and we have called it the earnings-and-interest fund.' The share, they add, which capital obtains, depends, first, upon the amount of the fund, secondly, on the manner in which it is divided between labour and capital. The amount of this 'net annual produce of the country,' or aggregate national 'earnings-and-interest fund,' depends, as they show, on the productive powers of land, labour, and capital, the state of science and art, and so forth; and their exposition of this subject is full, though concise. It is, too, undoubtedly important to the economist to have a clear view of the causes determining the amount of the annual revenue of the nation as a whole. Yet the problem respecting the rate of profit is a different one. The capitalists and labourers in a trade do not simply divide between them a share in a definite national fund, created by the general productiveness of the whole national capital and labour; they themselves, in a great measure, create the particular fund which they divide, and the amount which they will receive depends largely on the amount of their own produce, and the economy, as well as the skill and energy, which they exercise in its production. Much waste and loss practically arises from the tendency of both capitalists and workmen to regard the amount of profits and wages as a question, simply, of sharing a given fund, when the most important matter is to produce it.

The authors next inquire, 'how the earnings-and-interest fund is divided into the share which capital takes as interest, and that which industry takes as earnings.' They proceed, accordingly, to discuss the problem of the rate of interest, and it is certainly one which calls for investigation in a treatise on the economics of industry. Yet the owners of capital in business have much else to look to. For them the point is not merely what interest they could get on the best security, but what profit the particular businesses or investments they have under their eye are likely to afford: here they must take into account the influence of many conditions and elements which but remotely and slightly affect the general rate of interest. But, confining ourselves to the question of the rate of interest, the general proposition which Mr. and Mrs. Marshall lay down is, that 'it will be found to depend upon the urgency of the demand of industry for the aid of capital.' Industry is rather a vague term, and one of its misfortunes is, that it is commonly used by French economists in a narrow and special sense. The authors appear to mean by it, in the proposition before us, simply labour, since they say that, 'The demand of industry for the aid of capital will not be urgent if there is a large supply of capital in proportion to the population. Industry will not then be compelled to resign to capital enough of the produce to afford a high rate of interest.' But labour has many competitors at home and abroad for capital. Our National Debt, and the sums which foreign States have raised in Great Britain since the Crimean War, show how formidable is the competition of public borrowers, and to their demand must be added that of private borrowers for unproductive purposes, of the intensity of which the extent to which land in the United Kingdom is mortgaged affords an indication. Looking, however, only to the side of the question which the authors discuss, it seems to us important to bear in mind that the shares of labour and capital will depend, not merely on the demand of labour for capital, but also on the demand of capital for labour, which varies much with the mode of production. When, in the sixteenth century, pasture largely superseded tillage, labourers suffered heavily from a diminished demand on the part of capital. The authors clearly show that 'The progress of civilization increases the demand of industry for the aid of capital, independently of any increase in the population, for it causes a continual increase in the amount and expensiveness of the machinery and other things which men use as means to the attainment of their ends.' Several writers have inferred from this fact that the increase of fixed capital is detrimental to labourers. But this is not a necessary consequence, nor has it been the usual consequence hitherto. The construction of railways, it is true, resulted in the conversion of much circulating capital into rails, rolling stock, and plant. But the railways themselves, instead of diminishing, vastly augmented, the demand for labour. It was not men, but horses, they superseded in the business of carriage, and more men are now employed by railway companies in London alone than were employed formerly by all the coaches in England. The power-loom, again, superseded the hand-loom, but it did not diminish the demand for manual labour in spinning and weaving; on the contrary, largely augmenting it. And wherever railways and machinery have made their way on the Continent the demand for labour has gone up with a bound.

In connexion with the constituents of the rate of profit, it is observable that the authors ignore altogether Mr. Mill's analysis of gross profit into indemnity for risk or insurance, as well as interest and remuneration of superintendence. Their reason appears to be that they include insurance among the expenses of production, not in the net income which the owners of capital receive; but the point is one which ought to be made clear to the student. Moreover, the actual indemnity for risk that business investments afford by no means corresponds accurately with the actual amount of risk. In a country like America, and in a less degree in England, the love of speculation and enterprise is such that risk is commonly underrated. On the

Continent of Europe, on the other hand, it has hitherto been generally over-estimated through timidity, and the reluctance of people to trust money out of their sight. These different tendencies of national character would *pro tanto* cause the average net rate of profit in business to be higher on the Continent of Europe than in the United States or Great Britain, in proportion to the rate of interest.

Another remark which the subject suggests is, that the rate of interest on the best security, or the price of the funds, by no means affords a measure of the amount which ought to be set aside as insurance, and therefore as part of the cost of production. Some of the most lucrative businesses have the good fortune to be also the safest; others, whose returns are scanty, are at the same time shaky, and perhaps on their last legs. It is not true of trade that high profits are another name for bad security, nor does the converse hold good. The equality of profits is an illusion.

The authors distinguish emphatically between what they call normal values, or those which would result from the undisturbed action of competition, and market values, or those actually resulting from the existing constitution and usages of the industrial world. 'The theory of normal value' is, in their words, 'the starting-point from which we must set out to explore all the various irregularities and unevennesses of market values.' The normal value of a thing, in their view, is equal to its expenses of production; its market value, they show, may widely deviate from that standard. The deviations are actually greater than they show; but the main comment we have to make is, that competition itself is the main cause of these deviations, and of the irregularities and unevennesses of market values. Industrial liberty, and the eager pursuit of gain, produce an economic world, the vastness, variety, complexity, incessant change, speculation, and potent influence of chance in which are absolutely incompatible with the knowledge and nice calculation of relative profits, upon which the theory rests that the prices of commodities are regulated in the long run by their cost of production. Market values, in fact, with all their 'irregularities and unevennesses,' are the true normal values, if by that phrase be meant what the authors mean—the values resulting from the action of competition. That even in the long run—to use the somewhat lax and unscientific phrase which we are not a little surprised to find writers of their powers of accurate thought and expression repeatedly and emphatically employing—profits are not equalized, or prices adjusted to the expense of production, as their theory of normal value assumes, appears by their own statement. Even in little villages, they say, in which one might imagine at first that everyone knows all his neighbours' affairs, and what profit every trade yields, it is not so, and very little beyond the fact that one man seems to be prosperous, another the reverse, is really known. Some of the villages in which this is so have existed for several centuries—a tolerably long run. How much less can the relative gains of all the different occupations of the great industrial world be known to the owners of capital, and equalized by their competition? The more people investigate market values by such lights as the book before us affords, the less heed they will give to the values of Ricardo's theory, and the more they will be led to reverse his mode of procedure, and to make market values the starting-point from which to arrive at true normal values—that is to say, those resulting from the operation of unrestricted competition.

Mr. and Mrs. Marshall's book is full of information and novel and apposite illustration. It will, we hope, pass through several editions; and among the changes which we venture to suggest are, the total dismissal of the phrase 'in the long run' from their pages, and a less sparing application of the term 'laws' to provisional and hypothetical assumptions. There is a kind of brain that is prodigiously fertile in the production of 'economic laws,' giving the name to every crude and hasty generalization or guess that occurs to it; but authors of the scientific culture and ability which the work before us displays need no such parade of scientific terminology to command respectful attention.

X.

THE HISTORY OF GERMAN POLITICAL ECONOMY.*

Two different conceptions of Political Economy now divide economists throughout Europe; of which, looking to their origin, one may be called English, the other German, though neither meets with universal acceptance in either England or Germany. English writers in general have treated Political Economy as a body of universal truths or natural laws; or at least as a science whose fundamental principles are all fully ascertained and indisputable, and which has nearly reached perfection. The view, on the other hand, now almost unanimously received at the universities, and gaining ground among practical politicians, in Germany, is that it is a branch of philosophy which has received various forms in different times and places from antecedent and surrounding conditions of thought, and is still at a stage of very imperfect development. Each of these conceptions has its appropriate method; the first proceeding by deduction from certain postulates or assumptions, the second by investigation of the actual course of history, or the historical method. In England it is usual to speak of induction as the method opposed to *a priori* deduction, but the inductive and historical methods are identical. Both aim at discovering the laws of succession and co-existence which have produced the present economic structure and condition of society. A subsidiary branch of historical investigation traces the progress of thought and philosophical theory, but this branch has the closest relation to the main body of economic history, since one

* *Fortnightly Review*, July 1, 1875.

of the chief conditions determining the subjects and forms of thought at each period has been the actual state of society; and ideas and theories, again, have powerfully influenced the actual phenomena and movement of the economic world. Dr. Wilhelm Roscher's 'History of Political Economy in Germany' (*Geschichte der National-Oekonomik in Deutschland*) is by far the most considerable contribution that has yet been made to this subsidiary branch of inquiry. It would be impossible in a few pages to review a book which ranges over several centuries, and discusses the doctrines of several hundred authors, besides drawing from numerous unnamed works. What is sought here is to indicate some of the leading features in the history of this department of German thought, with some observations suggested by Roscher's book, or by its subject.

An English historian cited by Roscher speaks as if the history of political economy had begun and almost ended with Adam Smith. Roscher himself begins with the Middle Ages, and ends with the conflicting doctrines of different schools and parties in Germany at the present day. The structure and phenomena of mediæval society in Germany, as elsewhere, were far from suggesting an economic theory based on individual interest and exchange. Common property in land, common rights over land held in severalty; scanty wealth of any kind, and no inconsiderable part of it in mortmain, or otherwise intransferable; labour almost as immovable as the soil; production mainly for home consumption, not for the market; the division of labour in its infancy, and little circulation of money; the family, the commune, the corporation, the class, not individuals, the component units of society: such are some of the leading features of mediæval economy. In the intellectual world the division of labour was even less advanced than in material production; philosophy was in the hands of an ecclesiastical order, antagonistic to both the individual liberty and the engrossing pursuit of wealth which modern political economy assumes. Roscher points to the Canon Law as embodying the earliest economic theory, and it is deeply tinctured with both communism and asceticism; poverty is the state pleasing to God, superfluous wealth should be given to the Church and the poor, interest on money is unlawful, to buy in the cheapest and sell in the dearest market is a twofold wrong. Nor did the secular law harmonize better with modern economic assumptions. Every system of positive law, as Roscher observes, has a corresponding economic system as its background; and the economic system at the back of the secular law was based on status, not on contract—on duty and loyalty, not on individual interest. Thus whether we look to the actual economy of mediæval Germany, to its moral philosophy, or to its positive law, we find a condition of things incompatible with the economic doctrines of modern times.

A new era opened with the Reformation, and Roscher divides the history of modern political economy in Germany into three periods, the first of which he calls a theological and humanistic one (*das theologisch-humanistische Zeitalter*), on account of the influence of both the doctrines of the Reformers and the literature of classical antiquity. But the economic movement of society itself tended to awaken new ideas. The Reformation not only created considerable economic changes of a material kind, but was in fact the result of general social progress, one aspect of the economic side of which shows itself in the discovery of the new world, and the consequent revolution in prices. In Germany, too, though to a less extent than in England, something doubtless was visible of that change from status to contract, and from service for duty to service for personal gain, which struck the great English poet, who was himself among the productions of the new age.* We may take Erasmus and Luther as representatives of the economic influences of the new theology and classical literature in Germany. The saying of the mendicant friars with respect to theology is true

---

* 'O good old man! how well in thee appears
The constant service of the antique world,
When service sweat for duty, not for meed!
Thou art not for the fashion of these times,
When none will sweat but for promotion.'
As You Like It, act ii., sc. 3.

also, Roscher observes, in the region of economics, that Erasmus laid the egg which Luther hatched. 'Erasmus, going back to the best age of classical antiquity as well as to pure Christianity, proclaimed that labour was honourable.' Luther preached the same doctrine, and moreover anticipated Adam Smith's proposition, that labour is the measure of value. Luther's enthusiasm for the increase of population illustrates the connexion of the economic ideas of the age with both its theology and its material condition, since it sprang on the one hand from antagonism to monastic celibacy, and on the other hand from the rapid increase in the means of subsistence. The chief economic influences of classical antiquity are classed by Roscher under five heads. Its literature, being that of a high state of civilization, furthered the rise of Germany to a higher social stage. The States from which this literature emanated were cities, whose example fostered the development of town life and economy. They were also highly centralized States, with the liveliest national spirit; and their history and ideas could not but promote the development of the modern State and of national unity, as opposed to the mediæval division of each nation into innumerable petty groups and governments. They were also either monarchical or democratic States, the study of which tended to accelerate the decline of the feudal aristocracy. Lastly, types of life and thought so unlike those which the mediæval world had bequeathed could not but nurture a critical and inquiring spirit, which made itself felt in the economic, as in other directions of the German mind. The only indications, however, of an independent economic literature in this period seem to have been the writings of Camerarius and Agricola on currency. Germany seems to have produced nothing so remarkable as the famous tract by W. S., once attributed to Shakespeare, which the revolution in prices and the contemporary economic changes gave birth to in England.* The period closes with the Thirty Years' War,' in connexion with which Roscher adverts to the

---

* See an Essay by the present writer on the 'Distribution of the Precious Metals in the Sixteenth and Nineteenth Centuries,' reprinted in this volume.

influence on Germany, both for good and for evil, of its geographical position; including among its beneficial effects a disposition to learn from all sides, which is visible in the subsequent history of its economic ideas and literature.

The second period in the history of German political economy, which covers more than a century from the Thirty Years' War to the period of Frederick the Great, is called by Roscher *das polizeilichcameralistiche Zeitalter*, as being one of State regulation and fiscal science. The term 'cameralistic,' which makes a great figure in early German economics, originated (as Roscher mentions in another work) in the office or chamber (Cammer), which in each German State was charged with the supervision and administration of the Crown revenues. Hence the science called *cameralistische Wissenschaft*, which is perhaps best explained by reference to one of the two objects which Adam Smith, at the beginning of his account of the Mercantile system, says political economy, 'considered as a branch of the science of the statesman or legislator,' has in view. It proposes, he says, to provide a plentiful revenue both for the State and the people. Cameralistic science aimed at augmenting the revenue of the State or the sovereign, rather than the people. Roscher's second period might, more intelligibly to English readers, be distinguished as the Mercantile period, since one of its chief features was the Mercantile system, interwoven with the system of State regulation and finance. It is a modern error, which, as Roscher remarks, is not attributable to Adam Smith, to ascribe to the Mercantile school the notion that money is the only wealth. What that school really taught was that money, in Locke's words, was the most solid and substantial part of the moveable wealth of a country; that it had more extensive utility than any other kind of wealth, on account of its universal exchangeability abroad as well as at home; and that a considerable stock of the precious metals in the treasury of the State, or within its reach, was requisite as a provision for foreign wars. Money had really acquired great additional usefulness and importance by the change from the mediæval to the modern economy, with the substitution of payments in coin for payments in kind, and the great increase in the division of labour, and in trade, both internal and foreign. And as the Mercantile system was thus connected on the economic side with the actual movement of society, so on the political side it was connected with the growth of monarchical States, increased activity and interference on the part of the central governments, and the maintenance of monarchical armies, and increased need for money in State finance. A circumstance not adverted to by Roscher, which doubtless contributed to the growth of the Mercantile system, was the revolution in prices, and in international trade, consequent on the influx of American gold and silver, which really placed the countries with a small stock of money and a low range of prices at a disadvantage. They bought dear and sold cheap in the foreign market. The system was thus not so irrational in its objects as many modern writers have supposed; but its history is chiefly important, in the point of view with which we are concerned, as illustrative of the connexion between economic theories and surrounding phenomena and conditions of thought.

The first period in Roscher's division is, as already said, classed by him as theological and humanistic. In the second period German Political Economy in his view disengaged itself finally from both theology and jurisprudence, and became an independent science. It is, however, a fact of no small importance to a right understanding of economic history, and to a due appreciation of the authority of some of the economic doctrines of our own day, that economic philosophy was so far from emancipating itself in the seventeenth century completely and finally from theological and juridical theories, that the system not only of the French Physiocrates, but also of Adam Smith, whose 'Wealth of Nations' had a prodigious influence over Germany, was in great part built on an ancient juridical theory in a modern theological form, and penetrated by a theological spirit. Roscher's third period, which reaches down to the present day, begins with the introduction of the system of the Physiocrates into Germany, where, he says, it influenced only some individual minds, adding that in England it could gain almost no ground. But the influence of the 'Wealth of Nations,' both in Germany and elsewhere, was so great that 'the whole of political economy might be divided into two parts—before and since Adam Smith—the first part being a prelude, and the second a sequel (in the way either of continuation or opposition) to him.' The system of the Physiocrates had doubtless some peculiar features, traceable to its country and parentage, the study of which throws much light on the causes which have shaped economic ideas, and forms an instructive chapter in the general history of philosophy. Nevertheless its main foundation was essentially the same as that on which Adam Smith's political economy rested. Roscher himself, along with other eminent German economists, has drawn attention to the connexion between both systems and the idea of a Law of Nature, which eighteenth century philosophy had derived from Roman jurisprudence. What they seem to have overlooked is, that both with the Physiocrates and with Adam Smith the Law of Nature distinctly assumed a theological form. The simple, harmonious, and beneficent order of Nature which human laws should leave undisturbed and only protect, became of divine institution, and Nature in short became Providence. Dupont de Nemours, who invented the name Physiocratie, to signify the reign of natural law, says in the dedication of the system to the sovereigns of the world, 'Vous y reconnaîtrez la source de vos droits, la base et l'étendue de votre autorité, qui n'a et ne peut avoir de borne que celle imposée par Dieu même.' In Adam Smith's lectures on moral philosophy, political economy formed one part of a course of which natural theology was another part, and the real ground of his confidence in the beneficial economy resulting from the undisturbed play of individual interest is expressly stated in the 'Wealth of Nations,' as well as in his 'Theory of Moral Sentiments,' to be the guidance of Providence. 'Every individual necessarily labours to render the annual revenue of the society as great as he can. He generally, indeed, neither intends to promote the public interest, nor knows how much he is promoting it. He intends only his own gain, and he is in this, as in many other cases, led by an invisible hand to promote an end which was no part of his intention.'* The process of specialization, which has differentiated one branch of secular knowledge after another from theology, had not reached political economy in Adam Smith's age, nor with many of his successors. Scientifically regarded, the theory of Malthus was fatal to the assumption of a beneficent tendency of the natural desires of mankind, but it did not prevent Archbishop Whately from finding in political economy the strongest evidences of natural theology; and the harmony of a beneficent economy of Nature with the theism of modern times unquestionably contributed, though often by an unperceived connexion, to the success which the political economy of Adam Smith and the system of *laissez faire* met with in Germany as well as England.† The principal merit of Adam Smith's economic philosophy has been generally overlooked. He combines the historical method of Montesquieu with the theory of Natural Law; and although that theory, together with his theological system, gave a bias to his inductive study of the real order of social progress, he has a true title to be regarded as the founder of the historical method in political economy, in the sense at least of having been the first to apply it. In Germany, it is true, this method has been of indigenous and more recent growth, having been transferred from other branches of German historical science, especially in relation to law. And as Adam Smith's system has been generally associated only with that portion of it which is based on Natural Law, the historical school of German economists have for the most part assumed an attitude of antagonism to what they call Smithianismus.

The last chapter of Roscher's history describes the tenets and methods of the different schools and parties which the economic and political condition of Germany on the one hand, and the progress of science on the other, have evolved during the last thirty years. Dr. Roscher does not exclude even

---

* *Wealth of Nations*, book iv. chap. ii.

† American political economy to this day is theistical, and its principles drawn in great measure from assumptions respecting the method of Divine government.

socialism from a place in his history, his object being to portray all the principal phases of German thought on the subject of the production and distribution of wealth. Two conditions concurred to stimulate economic inquiry and discussion in Germany in recent years: the material progress of the country in population, production, trade, and means of communication, presenting new economic phenomena and raising new problems, especially in relation to the working classes; and the great contemporary progress of the sciences of observation, especially history. Political causes, too, have had a share in producing a diversity of economical creed. Roscher distinguishes five different groups, designated as free traders, socialists, reactionary conservative economists, officials, and the historical or 'realistic' school. Of these five groups, two, however (the 'reactionary' and the 'official' economists), may be left out of consideration here—the former as insignificant in number, and the latter as distinguishable only in reference to the subjects on which they write, and the special knowledge they bring to bear on them. We need concern ourselves only with the free-trade school—sometimes called, by way of reproach, the Manchester party—the socialists, or socialist-democrats (*Socialdemokraten*), and the realistic or historical school. The free traders, under the leadership of Prince Smith, Michaelis, and Julius Faucher, formed, some years ago, an association called the German Economic Congress (*Volkswirthschaftlicher Congress*), and all German economists are agreed that they rendered great service to Germany by their strenuous exertions for industrial and commercial liberty. Roscher, too, refuses to stigmatize them with the name 'Manchester party,' on account of their patriotism; but he objects to their economic theory, which was that of Bastiat and the old English *laissez faire* school, as too abstract, too optimist, and too regardless of history and reality. But many of the younger members are broader in their creed, and by no means opposed to the historical or realistic method of economic inquiry. The socialists or social democrats, of whom Karl Marx and the late Ferdinand Lassalle may be taken as the exponents, aim both at political revolution and at the abolition of private property in land and capital; and Roscher points out that they are even more unhistorical in their method, and more given to misleading abstractions—for example, the argument that capital is accumulated labour, and labour therefore should have all its produce—than the extremest of the elder free traders. Signor Pozzoni signally errs in classing, in a recent article in this Review, the realistic German school with the socialists. The realistic school, which has its chief strength in the universities, is no other than the historical school, which Signor Pozzoni classes apart; and the Association for Social Politics (*Verein für Social-politik*) which its members have formed, and which, by a play on words, led to the nickname of *Katheder-Socialisten*, now includes some of the Economic Congress, or free-trade party, along with Government officials, merchants, and manufacturers, as well as professors and working men. The true meaning of the term 'realistic' is sufficiently explained by Roscher's words:—'The direction of the political economy now prevailing at our universities is with reason called realistic. It aims at taking men as they really are, influenced by various and withal other than economic motives, and belonging to a particular nation, state, and period of history.' Man, in the eyes of the historical or realistic school, is not merely 'an exchanging animal,' as Archbishop Whately defined him, with a single unvarying interest, removed from all the real conditions of time and place—a personification of an abstraction; he is the actual human being such as history and surrounding circumstances have made him, with all his wants, passions, and infirmities. The economists of this school investigate the actual economy of society and its causes, and are not content to infer the distribution of wealth from the possible tendencies of undisturbed pecuniary interest. Such a practical investigation cannot be without practical fruit, but its chief aim is light. And it is needless to say what a boundless field of instruction the study of the economic progress and condition of society on this method opens up. Among the works which it has recently produced in Germany may be mentioned Roscher's 'Nationalökonomik des Ackerbaues,' Schmoller's 'Geschichte der deutschen Kleingewerbe,' Brentano's

'Arbeitergilden der Gegenwart,' and Nasse's well-known 'Essay on the Agricultural Community of the Middle Ages in England.' Nor has the historical method been unproductive in England. A great part of the 'Wealth of Nations' belongs to it; and to it we owe Malthus' 'Treatise on Population,' Tooke's 'History of Prices,' and Thorold Rogers' 'History of Agriculture and Prices.' Sir Henry Maine's works on 'Ancient Law,' 'Village Communities in the East and West,' and the 'Early History of Institutions,' not only afford models of the historical method, but actually belong to economic as well as to legal history, and exemplify the nature and extent of the region of investigation which those English economists who are not content with barren abstraction have before them.

Nothing can be more unfounded than the imputation of socialist or destructive tendencies which the nickname of *Katheder-Socialisten* has linked with the historical school of German economists. Historical philosophy has assuredly no revolutionary tendencies: it has been with more justice accused of tending to make its disciples distrustful of reforms which do not seem to be evolved by historical sequence and the spontaneous births of time. But, as a matter of fact, a great diversity of opinion is to be found among the economists of this school in Germany; some being conservative and others liberal in their politics; but no revolutionary or socialist schemes have emanated from its most advanced Liberal rank. Their principal practical aims would excite little terror in England. Some legislation after the model of the English Factory Laws, some system of arbitration for the adjustment of disputes about wages, and the legalization of trade-unions under certain conditions, are the main points in their practical programme; and they are supported by some of the warmest friends of the German throne and aristocracy.

It is impossible to praise too highly the extraordinary erudition, the immense industry, and the manysidedness of intellectual sympathy which distinguish Roscher's history of German political economy; but we venture to suggest to him a revision of the brief notice which it includes of the history of

English political economy in the last thirty years. Generous in the extreme in his estimate of the earlier economic literature of this country, he is less than just in his criticism of it in recent years—an injustice of which the present writer may speak without prejudice, being excepted along with Thornton and Thorold Rogers from Dr. Roscher's unfavourable judgment: one for which no other reasons are assigned than some defects in Mr. Mill's system, on the one hand, which are really attributable to Mr. Mill's predecessors, and the doctrines of a writer,* on the other hand, who represents no English School, and has no supporter among authors of economic works or professors of political economy in this country. In this single instance Dr. Roscher has deviated from the impartiality which is one of the great merits of his 'History.' Readers interested in the historical study of political economy will find an excellent companion to Dr. Roscher's 'History' in Dr. Karl Knies' highly philosophical treatise, 'Die Politische Oekonomie vom Standpunkte der geschichtlichen Methode.'

---

* Mr. H. D. Macleod.

XI.

ROSCHER'S 'PRINCIPLES OF POLITICAL ECONOMY.'*

MONTALEMBERT said he came to England from time to time to take a bath of liberty, and the economists of his day, in England as well as France, might have done well to take a bath now and then of both liberty and learning in Germany, although industrial life was less free there than even in France at that time. It is an indication of the narrow groove in which the study of political economy has moved in this country under the influence of the *a priori* method, that the first translation into English of one of Roscher's works should be that before us by Mr. Lalor, an American, who has thus done a service to literature and philosophy that might have been done more than twenty years ago by an Englishman.

A French translation of an earlier edition of this very work was made in 1857—a period at which it is doubtful if there was an economist in the United Kingdom, besides Mr. Mill, who knew so much as the names of the three most eminent German economists then living—Roscher, Knies, and Hildebrand. Germany is, indeed, so entirely overlooked to this day by English opponents of the historical method, that they speak of its advocates as followers, or at least admirers, of Auguste Comte. The German historical school is, in point of fact, strangely ignorant of the 'Positive Philosophy:' a curious instance of which is, that the only Comte referred to in Roscher's erudite pages before us is, not Auguste, but Charles, while so little

---

* *The Academy*, March 29, 1879.

known a French writer of the last century as Cantillon is often cited in them.

Sympathy with the working classes led in recent years to a strong reaction on the part of a number of German professors against the optimism of 'orthodox' political economy, and to the rise of the so-called or nicknamed *Katheder-Socialisten*, sometimes ignorantly or artfully confounded with socialists; but the historical method, which Roscher, Knies, and Hildebrand had long before begun to apply, and the tendencies of German philosophical inquiry, must in any case have produced a revolt against the abstractions and fictions of the *a priori* method. As Erasmus is said to have laid the egg that Luther hatched, so doctrines of economic reform, now strong on the wing in Germany, may owe their origin in good part to Roscher, though their incubation may not be seen in his works. At first sight one might say, indeed, that the difference between Ricardo's work on the 'Principles of Political Economy' and Roscher's lies rather in the amount of historical research in the latter than in fundamental diversity of doctrine. So far as doctrine is concerned, the difference is for the most part one more of tone than of principle, and often makes itself felt chiefly in the absence of dogmatic formula, and of the use of rigorous and infallible logic affected by Ricardo's school. Mr. Cairnes and Mr. Bagehot might have put Roscher's chapters on profits, cost of production, and price, for example, into the hands of their followers without fear of shaking their faith: indeed, the dissent from this part of the Ricardian system originated here, not in Germany. Again, like most English and French economists, Roscher treats Ricardo as the discoverer of the law of rent, observing that, although he may not have given it the best form, he is as unquestionably entitled to the honour of having discovered it as Malthus to that of having discovered the law of population. The truth is, that putting aside the claim of Dr. Anderson, we might as well speak of the Ricardian doctrine of population as of the Ricardian theory of rent, Ricardo having borrowed both alike from Malthus. His own words are:—'In all that I have said concerning the origin and progress of rent, I have repeated the principles which Mr. Malthus laid down in his "Enquiry into the Nature and Progress of Rent," a work abounding in original ideas.'

On the subject of population, as on that of rent, Roscher's doctrine coincides substantially with that of Malthus, Ricardo, and John Mill. Those who imagine that the rapid growth of the English population in the last three generations, while general wealth has advanced with equal rapidity, refutes the Malthusian doctrine of an inevitable check, preventive or positive, to its increase at the potential rate, would do well to consider the evidence in Roscher's book as to what the potential rate is: for instance, that a woman between fifty and sixty years old has been known to have two hundred and four descendants in her lifetime. Had the population of England increased at the potential rate, even since the beginning of the present century, it would now much exceed a hundred millions, and would be more than two hundred millions at its close. At that pace, after a few more generations, there would not be standing-room not to say breathing-room, for the nation. The most rigorous Malthusian may, however, be content with Roscher's language respecting the relation between population and wages. The working class can, indeed, he says, exercise little control over the immediate supply of labour, on account of their immediate need of subsistence; but the future supply depends on their own will; and it is here that a permanent working-men's union, controlling the whole class, might exert powerful influence. A higher economic condition of the class is maintainable only on condition that they create families no larger than can be supported consistently with the maintenance of a higher standard of wants. It might, perhaps, be suggested that a higher standard of economy is in England more needed than a higher standard of wants, and that a working-man might better be required by public opinion or by the opinion of his class to save a certain amount before marriage than merely to be earning some specified rate of wages. The reason for the necessity of external influence or moral control in the matter, one may add, is that it is not his own wife and children, but other people's, that raise the price of food and lower the price of labour against the working-man. His own wife is generally worth more than her keep as a housekeeper and cook, and his children soon bring in more than they take out of the family till. Nevertheless, Roscher properly rejects the doctrine of a 'wages-fund,' determining, by its proportion to the number of labourers, the 'average' rate of wages. His arguments on the subject are, however, hardly the strongest that may be advanced, and, like several English writers, he ascribes the first refutation of the doctrine in this country to Mr. Longe, whose essay in its original shape contained no real disproof of the doctrine, while it was not itself free from fallacy. The true refutation is, that there is no such mobility of capital and labour as would make all the sums expendible in wages practically one fund, and the actual rates of wages are determined by different conditions in different cases—for example, by competition, by combination, by monopoly, and sometimes by the liberality of employers—so that the aggregate amount of wages is simply the sum of all the particular amounts, and the effect, not the cause, of the actual rates. Mr. Longe's essay, like Single-speech Hamilton's discourse, produced an effect beyond its desert. Had Hamilton made a great number of good speeches they might have all been forgotten, for people seldom remember much about anyone; but a single oration was a surprise, and left an impression. Much of Mr. Longe's criticism of Mr. Mill was erroneous. There is, no doubt, an element of truth in the argument put forward by Roscher long before Mr. Longe, that the capital of the employer is not the ultimate source of wages, but only an immediate fund out of which an advance is made, afterwards replaced by the buyers of the commodities produced. Roscher might have added, indeed, that the immediate fund is often not the employer's own capital, but borrowed by him on the credit his sales obtain for him. Yet there remains an important truth in Mr. Mill's proposition, that the funds out of which wages are paid must generally exist before commodities are made, not to say sold. The workmen cannot wait for their wages till the commodities are sold; they may never, indeed, be sold at all, and the employers may be ruined, although workmen have been paid their wages in full. The accumulation, then, of capital on a great scale, either by employers themselves or by lenders, is a pre-requisite to the hire of labour on a great scale. Roscher's tone towards Mr. Mill in this work, it may be observed, is sometimes complimentary and sometimes rather the reverse, the only English economist of whom he speaks contemptuously in it being Mr. H. D. Macleod; though in his 'History of Political Economy in Germany' all Ricardo's followers are slightingly mentioned.

The generalisation which Roscher makes with respect to the successive part played by each of the three great productive agencies—nature, labour, and capital—well deserves the reader's reflection. The history of the economic development of society, he says, divides itself into three periods. In the earliest, nature is the predominant element, affording subsistence almost spontaneously to a scanty population. In the second period, human labour is the chief agency: handicrafts multiply, guilds are established, and a respectable and solid middle class is formed. In the third period, capital predominates, machinery prevails over the manual workman, and the middle class may decline, and colossal wealth be confronted by abject misery. One cannot but admit, in reference to this generalisation, that the disappearance of the small independent craftsman is a deplorable feature of our present industrial economy, even if the condition of the common labourer at the bottom of the scale be less miserable now than it was under an earlier economy; nor does co-operation at present hold out much hope of a remedy.

The historical information and illustrations with which the pages of the book abound may interest many minds to which ordinary economic discussions are repulsive. It should, however, be known that, although a complete work in itself, Roscher's 'Principles of Political Economy' forms part of a more comprehensive scheme. In the preface to the first edition, its author announced that the 'Grundlagen der Nationalökonomie,' or 'Principles of Political Economy,' as Mr. Lalor translates it, was intended as the first part of a complete 'System der Volkswirthschaft,' containing three other parts. Of these, the second, 'Nationalökonomik des Ackerbaues,' has long since been published in Germany. Mr. Alfred Marshall's lectures, and Mr. Joseph Nicholson's essay on Machinery and Wages, afford evidence that a generation of economists is rising who can dispense with the aid of translation to acquaint themselves with German works; but there must always be a large class of readers in this country as well as in America who require it: and Mr. Lalor would enhance the obligation he has already laid them under by translating also the 'Nationalökonomik des Ackerbaues.' It is full of historical learning relating to the history of landed property, and of rural economy in England as well as on the Continent. A fact which English economists should take to heart is, that the only historical treatise on the subject, in relation to England, accessible in the English language, was written by a German (Nasse, of Bonn), not an Englishman, and translated, not by a political economist, but by a cavalry officer, Colonel Ouvry.

XII.

LÉONCE DE LAVERGNE.*

Last year one of the most remarkable Frenchmen of the age that has just closed—for both in England and France a new and more democratic age has begun—passed away almost without remark in this country, although he had peculiar claims to a place in the memory of Englishmen. The name of Léonce de Lavergne was, indeed, better known in England in the days of the Second Empire than during the decade following its collapse, notwithstanding that in the former period he was excluded from public life, while in the latter the curtain which the Empire had drawn over political genius was lifted, and M. de Lavergne was a considerable person in the political world. A younger generation, however, had grown up, and many Englishmen who saw the name Lavergne recur in accounts of French parliamentary proceedings and political parties, were unaware that he had lived, as it were, two previous lives, first, as a rising politician in the reign of Louis Philippe, and afterwards as a distinguished author and economist. Four political epochs—the reign of Louis Philippe, the Second Republic, the Second Empire, and the Third Republic—may be said to have been represented, though in different ways, in M. de Lavergne's career. Two of these epochs were, indeed, for him periods of seclusion and, politically speaking, of obscurity; yet, indirectly, they exercised a powerful influence over the directions of his energies and the tenor of his thoughts. In the preface to the first edition of his 'Essay on the Rural Economy of England' he said: 'Je m'adresse surtout à ceux

---

* *Fortnightly Review*, February 1st, 1881.

qui, comme moi, se sont tournés vers la vie rurale, après avoir essayé d'autres carrières, et par dégoût des révolutions de notre temps.' Repugnance alike to revolution and to despotism not only turned him from politics to country life, but deeply coloured his views of rural economy. His whole career might be shown to throw an instructive light on the part that surrounding social conditions on the one hand, and individual powers and bent on the other, play in determining the pursuits, ruling ideas, and achievements of men of unusual capacity. But the object of this memoir is simply to lay before the reader some account of M. de Lavergne's life, conversation, and work, by one who had the privilege of peculiar opportunities for observation.

Louis Gabriel Léonce de Lavergne was born at Bergerac, in the Department of Dordogne, in 1809, and was educated for the legal profession, but made literature as well as law an early pursuit. He was a frequent contributor to the 'Revue du Midi,' and in 1838 was nominated Professeur de Littérature à la Faculté de Montpellier, but declined the chair. After practising for a short time at the Bar, he took office under M. Guizot, as Sous-Directeur au Ministère des affaires étrangères, and won the entire confidence and warm friendship of his illustrious chief. In 1846 he was elected a member of the Chamber of Deputies, and was soon regarded as one of the most promising of the younger French statesmen. The Revolution of 1848 sent him back to private life and to letters and philosophy. In 1850 he accepted the Professorship of Rural Economy in the Institut National Agronomique; but one of the first measures of the Imperial Government was to suppress that Institute, in order to deprive him, and others whose politics were obnoxious, of their chairs. Special missions, by way of temporary compensation, were offered to the deprived professors. In his zeal for the improvement of French agriculture, which had become his most engrossing object, M. de Lavergne undertook to report on Agricultural Credit in England and Germany. In 1851 he had visited the Great Exhibition and made a tour through Great Britain, and he came again in 1852 and 1853. In 1854 his famous 'Essai sur l'Agriculture de l'Angleterre, de l'Écosse, et de l'Irlande,' was published. In 1855 he was elected member of the Institute of France. In 1857 he issued a volume entitled 'L'Agriculture et la Population.' In 1860 his great work, 'Économie Rurale de la France depuis 1789,' appeared. Two later works, 'Les Assemblées Provinciales sous Louis XVI.' and 'Les Économistes Français du Dix-Huitième Siècle,' brought him additional celebrity. He was the author also of various essays in the 'Revue des Deux-Mondes' and the 'Journal des Économistes,' and of contributions to the Transactions of the Academy of Moral and Political Sciences, which attracted much attention. In 1865 he was elected President of La Société Centrale de l'Agriculture, being now looked up to on all sides as the highest authority in France on all subjects connected with rural economy. It is pleasing to find a French official concerned in the administration of the domains of the State speaking, in one of the Reports of the Enquête Agricole, of 'mon illustre maître, M. de Lavergne,' at a time when it could little conduce to the advantage of a functionary of the Government to profess admiration for an avowed adherent to the Orleanist party, least of all one whose writings had made him an object of especial disfavour in high quarters. Of the public career of M. de Lavergne, after the fall of the Second Empire, something will be said hereafter. To realise what manner of man he was, he should be seen and heard, as it were, in private life and retirement.

The controversy carried on in England in the decade 1860–1870 respecting the comparative merits of *la petite* and *la grande propriété*, and *la petite* and *la grande culture*, deeply interested M. de Lavergne, and having seen an essay of my own on the subject, he invited me to visit him at his country-house in the Department of La Creuse, in Central France. I met him, however, first in Germany, in the summer of 1868. He was already suffering from a gouty affection of the joints, which made the later years of his life a painful struggle between mind and matter, and he walked with difficulty. His frame was large; his face lighted by intellect and strongly expressive of kindness; his manner, while unaffected and gentle, had a natural dignity—one felt oneself in the company of one of the true upper ten thousand of the human race. There was a solidity of judgment, combined with a play of wit, in his conversation that brought to my recollection the observation of Sir Thomas Overbury, nearly three centuries ago, on the character of the Frenchmen of that age: 'For the most part they are all imagination and no judgment; but those that prove solid excel.'* A solid Frenchman is rarer than a solid Englishman; but when a Frenchman is solid, he excels now as he did in the days of Sir Thomas Overbury, because he adds imagination and brilliancy to good sense. M. de Lavergne was a thorough Frenchman, but he had also sober qualities, uncommon in France. The infirmity of most Frenchmen is that they give way too easily to passion; while the Englishman maintains his self-control, and has therefore time for second thoughts and circumspection. Lavergne had the calm of an Englishman.

At our first meeting, M. de Lavergne spoke of his regard and respect for England and English institutions, adding with a smile that his wife, who was present, accused him of Anglomania, and that he in turn charged her with Anglophobia, a charge which Madame de Lavergne did not repel. She was a person of a character and cast of thought unlike his; but they were devotedly attached to each other and inseparable, their differences of opinion only making their society more interesting, and never bordering upon discord. Passages in Lavergne's 'Économie Rurale de l'Angleterre' had left on my mind an idea that some great English landowners had been careful to show him the bright side of England, and of the English land system in particular. He replied to a hint to that effect that, on the contrary, he had declined invitations and letters of introduction in order to see things with his own eyes, but a curious thing had happened in one case. He had gone to see a famous ducal residence and estate, and on arriving at the

---

* *Observations on the State of France under Henry IV.*, 1609; Harl. Misc., viii. 379.

railway station found to his surprise one of the duke's carriages waiting for him. The duke, he was told, was absent, but had given orders that he should be shown every attention, and taken wherever he wished to go. Supposing that some common friend had spoken of his intended visit, and that it would seem ungracious to decline, he accepted the offered civility, and saw more than he could have done had he been left to his own lights. In the end it turned out that there had been a mistake; the duke had given orders about a foreign visitor, and the servants had taken the first foreigner they met at the station.

It was Lavergne's practice, when visiting any new locality, and one which he told me had been very useful to him in his tours in Great Britain and France, with a view to a description of their rural scenery, to survey the surrounding country from some commanding height. He seemed to have the eye, at once of a general, a sportsman, an agricultural expert, and an artist, seizing immediately all the main features of a landscape in every aspect. We were not far from the Rhine, and looking down on it from an eminence, he observed, one day, alluding to a passage in Michelet's picture of France: 'Like Michelet, I fear to look at the heroic Rhine; not, however,' as Michelet says, 'because a lotus-tree grows on its banks, leading me to forget my native land, but because it makes a Frenchman now think of his native land with anxiety and apprehension. I dread a war for the Rhine. It would be either victory for Germany or victory for the Second Empire, and it is hard to say which of the two would be the more injurious to France in the end. Either, moreover, must result in a permanent increase of European armaments, already the curse of our age.'

In the autumn of the same year I was M. de Lavergne's guest at Peyrusse, on the brow of a mountain glen formed by the river Taurion, or Thorion, in one of the most desolate districts of La Creuse, where he had, through his wife, an extensive though not a very profitable estate, mostly in forests, from which immense quantities of wood were annually sold at Limoges, chiefly for use as fuel in the manufacture of porcelain. In his invitation Lavergne had spoken of his residence as 'notre ermitage,' and though he did not lead quite the life of a hermit, since Madame de Lavergne shared his seclusion, and he had a household of servants, no hermit could have desired a wilder solitude. One might wander for hours through his woods without seeing a living creature—unless, perhaps, a serpent, or a she-wolf and her young. On the desert hills in the neighbourhood one might meet a *bergère* tending a few lean animals, but the masculine termination, *berger*, was unknown. The able-bodied men of the department were working as masons in great towns, especially Paris, where the public expenditure on building was enormous, and almost all outdoor work was done by women. One day we drove to a village on a mountain some miles from Peyrusse, where we saw a few women and children; but not a human being was visible on the road or from it, going or returning. 'L'empire, c'est la paix: Solitudinem faciunt, pacem appellant,' said Lavergne. The public expenditure in Paris averaged more than £30,000,000 a-year, draining both money and labour from the rural districts, while, at the same time, the army carried off a percentage of the rustic youth. I remarked that La Creuse owed to the Empire, at any rate, the residence of Lavergne himself for a good part of the year; for were the Orleanist dynasty restored, his political occultation would cease, and he would be resident chiefly in Paris. He replied that the Emperor's policy was to make himself the only conspicuous figure in France, and to allow no lesser light, however faint, to be visible. Napoleonic ambition had always been of the kind denounced in Bacon's essay: 'He that seeketh to be eminent among able men hath a great task, but that is ever good for the public. But he that plots to be the only figure among ciphers is the decay of a whole age.' Lavergne added, however, that he had no personal reason to dislike the Empire, for the peaceful retirement of Peyrusse had great charms for him, and now more than ever, since his health had become far from robust. There had been a time, indeed, when his own farm had been more than a mere amusement. During the scare at the Red Spectre, conjured up to frighten the French nation into regarding Louis Napoleon as the saviour of society, all business in many parts of France had been suspended. Lavergne's own wood could find no market, his tenants could pay only in produce which was unsaleable, and a property he had in the South remitted no income. The want, both of local markets and of cheap communication with distant markets, he continued, which resulted mainly from the monarchical system of concentrating the public expenditure (introduced by Louis XIV., and followed under the Empire), was the principal cause of the perpetuation of the mediæval tenure of métayage. The soil must be made to grow, not the crops for which it might be best adapted, but the necessaries of life for both owner and cultivator—who, accordingly, divided its produce in kind. Lavergne waged an incessant war against the Imperial finance. Both the excessive amount of the public expenditure and its unequal distribution were constantly pointed at in his works as the main obstacles to the economic progress of the Departments of France remote from the capital. He was regarded, accordingly, with an evil eye at the Tuilleries as a rancorous enemy, but there was nothing personal in his antagonism. His motive was not antipathy to the Emperor, but sympathy with the peasant, as the real saviour of French society. 'Dans toutes nos grandes crises historiques,' he eloquently urged, 'le paysan français, si bien personnifié par Jacques Bonhomme, a toujours fini par nous tirer d'affaire. . . . Si les autres classes de la société française, riches, bourgeois, artisans de villes, valaient pour leurs rôles ce que Jacques Bonhomme vaut pour le sien, ce n'est pas l'Angleterre, c'est la France qui serait depuis longtemps le premier peuple de l'univers.'*

Much as M. de Lavergne detested the Imperial system of government, a singularly mild temper and sweet disposition made him incapable of personal resentment, and he never spoke of Louis Napoleon with bitterness. When I applied some strong epithets to the perfidious Coup d'État and the cruelties that followed it, he said calmly, correcting one of my adjectives, 'Non, il n'est pas méchant, il est grand menteur. Voilà

* *L'Agriculture et la Population*, 2nd ed., 342-3.

tout.' Of the falsehood pervading the administration throughout all its ramifications, he gave curious instances. I inquired about Prince * * *, ambassador at the court of * * *. 'He is no more a prince than you or I,' was the answer; 'indeed, even less, for it has never been proved in a court of law that I am not a prince, and I presume it has never been proved that you are not.' In reference to the Coup d'État, he repeated an expression which he had used in Germany, 'Les Anglais sont très indiscrets,' and gave an instance affecting himself. On the very day of it (December 2, 1851), he had paid a visit at the house of a neighbour and political friend in Paris, where he met an English lady, the wife of an English author of great celebrity, herself well known in the literary and social worlds of both London and Paris. Everyone spoke out, as he supposed, in confidence and perfect security. To his dismay, a few days afterwards, he saw an account of the visit in a great London journal. 'Cela pouvait précisément m'envoyer à Cayenne.' Anyone on whom suspicion fell of being hostile to Louis Napoleon's proceedings or plans was liable to be transported to Cayenne without form of trial. In this instance, however, M. de Lavergne appears to have been so far mistaken, that no breach of confidence or discretion was actually committed by the English lady. Her letter, as a recent reference to the file of the journal in question has satisfied me, was not written for publication, and was cautiously expressed; nor was there reason, at the moment at which she described what had passed, to suppose that a mere allusion to M. de Lavergne, in such a way as to identify him, could expose him to danger. The letter was written on the evening of December 2, when some arrests of eminent persons had been made, but before any massacres in the streets or deportations to Cayenne had taken place. It found its way into the 'Times' of December 6, 1851, under the heading 'The following are extracts from a lady's letter.' 'Paris, Tuesday evening, December 2. At about twenty minutes past one o'clock I set forth with Miss B., attended by my two servants on foot. Finding, however, that carriages passed through the Faubourg St. Honoré, we took a remise, and drove to the house of M. de F., near the Madeleine, and went in and found Madame de T. and M. de L. M. de T. was gone out to confer with other members of the Assembly on the occurrences of the morning. M. R., *Conseiller d'État*, joined us, and related some facts, of which the following are the principal.' [The arrests of Lamoricière, Changarnier, and other generals, are described, and some other particulars given.] 'At eleven o'clock all was hushed, and so ended a day pregnant with disquiet and sinister auguries which assuredly have seldom been better warranted, for so monstrous an exercise of brute force on the part of the executive has few precedents in history.' Seeing this letter in the *Times* a week afterwards, when the streets were red with the blood of peaceful citizens, when men were hourly disappearing to be seen no more, and all Paris was quaking, it was natural that Lavergne should have been startled at an allusion to himself as having been in disaffected company. But the writer of the letter could hardly have foreseen such ground for alarm. It is even possible that its publication did more good than harm to M. de Lavergne. The persons carried off to Cayenne were of inferior note, and Louis Napoleon was by no means desirous of raising an outcry from the English press. Looking at all the circumstances, there seems no reason for withholding the name of Mrs. Grote as the English lady of whom Lavergne spoke.

This, however, was only a single instance of English indiscretion in his eyes, from the French point of view. There was the correspondence in the English newspapers during the Crimean war. Mr. Senior's notes of conversations with eminent persons, of whom Lavergne was one, likewise appeared to him a highly characteristic English proceeding. 'But Mr. Senior's notes are not printed,' I suggested. 'No,' he replied, 'but scores of people, I might say hundreds, have seen them, and many more have heard of them. And, doubtless, they will be printed. No Englishman or Englishwoman can keep anything from the printing-press. It is astonishing to me that printing was not an English invention, and that Caxton should have borrowed it from the Continent.' On several occasions he recurred, half in jest, to the English lack of reticence and discretion in relation to printing. I told him, for instance, that I had visited a *ferme école* near Rennes in Britanny, about which he had spoken to me, and on my way back to my hotel, observing a number of women as well as men coming out of a large printing establishment, had asked a question about the employment of women in the business. As the foreman to whom I spoke brusquely refused to answer, I explained that I was a professor of political economy, and therefore took an interest in the subject, as there had been combinations against women in the printing trade in London. Whereupon the man gesticulated furiously, snapped his fingers in my face, and made various other demonstrations of incredulity and hostility. Lavergne tranquilly observed that it must have reached Britanny that the English were very indiscreet, above all in matters of printing. On other points he took a more favourable view of the English than his wife did. He considered them mild and gentle, 'Les Anglais sont très doux.' Madame, on the other hand, maintained that the roughest creature to be seen on the Continent was the British tourist, and that even in good society the English were unmannerly. One instance was, that Lord * * *, whom they had invited to dinner in Paris, kept the company three-quarters of an hour waiting, and, instead of apologizing, coolly said he had been spending three charming quarters of an hour with the Duchesse * * *. Another Englishman had a habit of talking of the Comte de Paris and the Duc d'Aumale as 'Paris' and 'D'Aumale,' without titles—'as if our princes were nobodies,' said Madame de Lavergne. She added that she had seen English ladies and gentlemen crowd round M. Thiers in his salon, and stare at him with a grin, as though he were a monkey performing tricks. Lavergne said he did not mean to pronounce on the manners of the English from an æsthetic point of view, but *au fond* they were the best-tempered nation in Europe. He had never seen a furious quarrel between Englishmen, such as one might see any hour in the streets of a French town. Everything seemed to work smoothly without a hard word. The English railway porter, compared with his fellow in Germany or France, was an angel; the English guard, an archangel. The liberality and courtesy of the Company to passengers on the North-Western Railway had impressed him as one of the most remarkable results of modern civilization. The gentleness of the English might be partly the effect of physical causes, but he attributed it chiefly to a happy political and civil history, and exemption from oppression; the Germans of the same race being irascible and quarrelsome. The Englishman's voice was like that of a bird; it came from the head, instead of from the seat of passion. Madame de Lavergne protested that the Englishwoman's voice was sharp and imperious, while the Frenchwoman's was soft and musical. 'That,' replied Lavergne, 'is because Englishmen are so gentle (doux) that the women have gotten a habit of commanding. The men are under a Queen already; they are going to give the women the suffrage, and they will before long be under petticoat government altogether. The female electors will control the House of Commons.' Madame de Lavergne said the female suffrage movement in England only showed that Englishmen were not the sensible beings her husband imagined. Women would tear each other's eyes out in France, 'elles s'arracheraient les yeux,' if they got the suffrage, and she believed they would do the same in England. I ventured to suggest that men as well as women were more explosive and demonstrative in France than in England; the hero of a French novel generally crying a great deal, whereas no man in an English novel ever sheds a tear. Lavergne said the English were in his opinion certainly more stoical than the French, but he supposed his wife would retort that a Red Indian never weeps. In Campbell's 'Gertrude of Wyoming,' he added, the Christian hero melts into tears, the savage may not give way to them. Although he did not speak English, Lavergne knew the older English poets and novelists well, and in his essay on 'English Rural Economy' has eloquently traced the influences of the love of rural life on the part of the upper classes in England upon English literature. The breath of the country, he there observes, is almost always felt in the English poem or romance of the eighteenth century, while in Voltaire's 'Henriade' there is not so much as grass for the horses.

M. de Lavergne was a very early riser, and at his desk or his books at five in the morning, although I did not see him until breakfast at ten; after which, when his health and powers of locomotion permitted, he walked or drove in a pony-carriage about his demesne and visited his farm. He grew a great variety of plants, not with a view to profit, but to show what could be done by scientific culture in so barren a region. He held that even granite, of which the soil of La Creuse is mainly formed, might be made to produce anything by adding other constituents, and undertook to demonstrate it by experiment. The practical question, however, as he well knew, remained, whether such farming would pay. That, he argued, depended on communication and markets. Accordingly, he had made earnest and not unsuccessful exertions to improve the roads of the Department. Beyond giving general directions, he did not, however, seem to interfere much in the working of his farm; but Madame de Lavergne was not too fine or too Parisian a lady to derive amusement from a daily inspection of what was going on. Both husband and wife had that faculty of being easily amused which seems to distinguish the Latin from the Teutonic nations, and which saves the former from ever feeling bored. One day Lavergne picked up a *bergère's* horn, and proceeded to blow the sheep and cattle calls with great zeal; Madame de Lavergne applauding the performance, which lasted about twenty minutes: 'C'est ça; c'est ça.' Broad and cosmopolitan as his ideas generally were on large subjects, on minor matters they were purely French. He told me more than once, as an amazing instance of the oddity of English ways, that he had seen an Englishman come with his two sons into the Café Anglais at Paris and order nothing but cold meat for lunch, without wine. And he could not get over his astonishment at Lord * * * having asked him to breakfast and given him no wine. It seemed to him quite as odd as it would to an Englishman to be offered only tea and coffee to drink at a dinner-party. Madame de Lavergne was *dévote*, and went on Sundays and Saints' days to a distant church; but Lavergne himself, at least during my visits, remained at home, having, it may be, the excuse of an invalid: yet, in subsequent years, when in more infirm health, he took an active part in the proceedings of the Assemblée Nationale. Politically and socially he was friendly to the Church, but his theological opinions were inscrutable to me. I told him one Sunday, while Madame was at Mass, how a great man in England, when someone wondered that so firm a supporter of the Church was never to be seen inside of one, replied that the buttresses of a church were generally outside. Lavergne smiled, and said every edifice must have an exterior as well as an interior, and sometimes the exterior was the more important of the two. The strength of a palace or a throne depended, not on the number of persons who went to Court, but on the sentiments of the people outside who never went.

On my way back to Peyrusse, in the autumn of the following year (1869), the distance at which its owner lived from his nearest neighbour, and the unbroken solitude of his forests, received a curious illustration. In a railway carriage between Montluçon and Gueret, the chief town of La Creuse, I found myself the object of much surprise and curiosity on the part of a country gentleman of the Department, who said he had rarely seen even a Frenchman from another part of France in it, unless a commercial traveller, and a foreigner never before. In the course of conversation, I inquired whether there were wolves in his neighbourhood. 'Wolves!' he replied; 'there are none in La Creuse.' On my stating that I had myself seen some the year before, he said he had lived fourteen years in the Department since his father's death, and never had heard of a wolf. Where did I imagine I had seen them? 'At Peyrusse.' 'Peyrusse!' was the rejoinder. 'Why, that is M. de Lavergne's place, and he is my nearest neighbour.' I could only retort that I had been M. de Lavergne's guest the year before; that I had first heard of the existence of wolves in his woods from himself; had next been shown one by his steward, and afterwards on several occasions had come upon a she-wolf and her family. On the very day on which I left Peyrusse M. de Lavergne had pointed to one near his hall-door, and I was now going back to Peyrusse, and expected to see another before long. Whereupon my fellow-traveller altered his tone, saying that even nearest neighbours were far apart in La Creuse, and he lived many miles from Peyrusse, and had never been in its forests, which were so extensive, and might contain things not to be found in his own small woods. At midnight we reached Gueret, where the simple honesty of the people, which was one of the attractions of this desert Department in Lavergne's eyes, was exemplified. I had written from Pontarlier to an innkeeper whose name I found in a Directory, to bespeak a room. At the station, late as it was, he met me himself, to explain that his *auberge* was a very humble one, and that he had accordingly ordered a room for me in the principal hotel, and told the conductor of its omnibus to take charge of my luggage. It seemed to me that the poorer the man was the more important it was to him to secure a visitor, and I begged to be allowed to adhere to my original plan. But he was inexorable. Much, he politely said, as he would like to have such a guest, he would be ashamed to take advantage of a mistake on the part of a foreigner. Lavergne, when I told him the story, was much pleased, and, as will be subsequently seen, did not forget it.

When I repeated to him my conversation with his 'nearest neighbour,' he said his steward had killed a wolf only that morning, on account of the loss of two lambs, though it was not his custom to wage war against animals that were not numerous enough to do much harm, and were interesting objects in so lonely a place. He added: 'You have seen things in La Creuse that my neighbour, who lives in it, has never seen. But I dare say, were he to go to London, he might see things that you have never beheld.' I told him I had been lately for some days at Ornans, in the Département du Doubs, which detractors of *la petite propriété* were recommended in his 'Économie Rurale de la France' to visit and be converted. I said I doubted whether the people there would look much about them in London: at least, at Ornans they seemed never to think of anything beyond the little world in which they lived. The wife of one wealthy small landowner, with whose family I became acquainted, had told me she had never been in Switzerland, though she often went to Pontarlier, on its border, to shop, adding: 'Your countrymen go much to Switzerland, do they not? But, then, England is nearer to Switzerland than France is.' Her husband showed no surprise, and quietly remarked: 'Non; l'Angleterre c'est plus loin.' Lavergne said, *la petite propriété* certainly did not teach geography; on the other hand, an English agricultural labourer might know as little about France as the wife of a small proprietor at Ornans did about England, without the compensation of living in a little paradise of his own. Englishmen of a higher class, he continued, seemed generally to know only Paris, not France. Passages from his own works were cited on opposite sides, for and against large and small property, and large and small farms, in a way that showed the controversialists had looked only at books, or they would understand him better. 'After reading one of these controversies,' he continued, 'I feel like the poor man with an old and a young wife, one of whom pulled out the black and the other the grey hairs from his head. I seem to be left bare, without any definite opinion, yet I have expressed very plainly a conviction that there are places to which each system is best adapted; but that, on the whole, the best cultivated parts of France are those where small properties and small farms prevail. What I have sought is to persuade our large proprietors to cultivate their estates as large estates are cultivated in England, and to take the same interest in country life that the English nobility and gentry do.'

We spoke one day of the famous fortress of Phalsburg, which I had lately visited, and where I had a narrow escape of being shot by a French sentry for attempting to take a sketch—one which two years afterwards I finished unheeded under the eyes of German soldiers. Lavergne said it was impossible to say how soon Phalsburg might not have to stand another siege; the only safeguard against a war with Germany was that the French army was absolutely unprepared for it, and the Emperor himself physically incapable of any great exertion. The Emperor, he said, was perfectly aware that systematic peculation went on in every department of the administration, military and civil, and that he was himself daily robbed in his household, but regarded it with apathy and cynical indifference: 'Il méprise tout—même l'argent.' After a duration of nearly twenty years, Lavergne continued, the Empire would be in peril were Napoleon I., in full vigour of mind and body, at its head. 'Le Français est toujours contre le gouvernement qui est là.' That, he said, overturned the government of Louis Philippe, the best France ever had since Henry IV. 'The English, on the contrary, are on the side of what exists, and with them, as they say themselves, nothing succeeds like success. This respect for material success has its bad side, but it has excellent political effects. And, moreover, it proceeds in part from a good quality. The English are not an envious people—they like to see things well done. Their phrase, "Well done!" is characteristic.' M. de Lavergne, it may be observed, did not stand alone in this opinion. I have heard a distinguished diplomatist, who thoroughly knows the continental nations, speak of the English as the only unenvious people in Europe. And the late Professor Adolf Held, of Berlin, whose promising career was cut short by a cruel accident last year, remarked to me in London, not long before his death, 'If you do anything well in England, you are liked for it, and you make friends. If you do anything well on the Continent, you make enemies. The first idea is to pull you to pieces, and to prove that you have done nothing at all.' Envy and jealousy doubtless exist in England, as its statesmen, authors, and professional men are sometimes made to feel; but there is, at least, no disinterested dislike of superiority. Lavergne himself was absolutely free from the smallest tincture of jealousy. I questioned him about every French author whose name occurred to me. The only one of whom he said a disparaging word was Prévost Paradol: 'C'est un enfant;" and even Paradol, he allowed, had great literary talent. Of Emile de Laveleye, though in some degree his own rival as a writer on rural economy, he spoke in enthusiastic praise.

Lavergne's conversation in 1869, and the facts he related with respect to the incapacity of the Imperial administration, the torpor and debility of Louis Napoleon, and the discredit into which he had fallen, left a full conviction on my mind that the Emperor could not maintain his position for twelve months longer, and would be driven to some rash and unsuccessful attempt to recover prestige and power. Of all the schemes open to him he chose the worst. After Sedan, Lavergne wrote repeatedly to me from the south of France, saying that it was the interest as well as the duty of England to come to the rescue of France; referring to Arthur Young's words in a remarkable passage to which he had himself, ten years earlier, drawn attention in his Introduction to Lesage's French translation of Young's 'Travels in France:' 'Suppose the German flag to float over Paris. Where is the security of the rest of Europe? Have we forgotten the partition of Poland? Were France in real danger, it would be the duty and interest of its neighbours to come to its rescue.'* When, more than a year later, I saw Lavergne again, he spoke with a bitterness unusual with him of a want of feeling, as well as of political sagacity, shown by England, which he had always admired and esteemed. At length I observed that I had myself seen enough to assure me that some of his own countrymen took less to heart the loss of territory France had suffered than some of mine did. He asked for an instance. One was a recent one. When on the way to see Phalsburg again, after the long siege it had sustained, I found myself in company with a French party, in a railway carriage from Strasburg to Lützelburg, and in the omnibus thence to the place of our destination. They chatted gaily on other subjects until we came close to the drawbridge of the battered and dismantled fortress, when both ladies and gentlemen burst into a flood of tears. But no sooner had we crossed the bridge, and passed through the *Porte d'Allemagne* into the old town, than all faces brightened, and the party set off to

---

* *Voyages en France*, par Arthur Young; Introduction par M. Léonce de Lavergne, I. xxxvi.

breakfast at the best inn, where presently I heard them give a sumptuous order. Two hours later they emerged with rosy countenances from the inn, and took their seats in the omnibus back to Lützelburg. The town had suffered considerably from the siege, and there was much to be seen, but a cheerful *déjeuner* had engaged their whole time and thought, while the British visitor had gone over every spot, and finished a sketch begun before the war.* Lavergne listened quietly to the story, and then said, with a melancholy smile, that when King David was told his child was dead, he washed his face, and ate and drank, because mourning and tears could not bring back what he had lost. But he never again spoke to me of English want of feeling during the war. He was now a member of the National Assembly, and a leading personage among the party of the Right, while his sagacity, calmness, and moderation gave him also no small influence with a considerable section of the Left. Had his health been good, there was no office in the Republic to which he might not have then aspired. He had at first hoped for a restoration of Constitutional Monarchy; but in 1873 he declared his adhesion to the Republic in a characteristic letter, which produced a great effect, and certainly conduced to the peaceful establishment of a Republican form of Government. 'J'aurais préféré,' he admitted, 'la monarchie constitutionelle et parlementaire, qui est à mon avis le meilleur des gouvernements. Voyant cette monarchie impossible, j'accepte la République.'

In the summer of 1874 I joined M. and Madame de Lavergne at Bourboule, a watering-place in Auvergne. He was at this time very infirm, but took an interest in the life of the place, and was ready to listen to its chatter and gossip, as well as to discuss graver subjects. Every new comer was an object of curiosity to the crowd of visitors. One day the arrival of another *Anglais* was reported, and a story about him, which much amused Lavergne, was brought to us in the evening by a

---

* A fuller account was given by the writer at the time in a letter to the *Daily News*.

young Abbé, who had sat next the stranger at the table-d'hôte. The *Anglais* had inquired eagerly whether Lord . . . . was at Bourboule, or had been there. The Abbé had heard nothing of an English lord, but said there was an *économiste Anglais*, a friend of M. de Lavergne, at the place, and then dining in M. de Lavergne's apartments in the hotel. As the Englishman received this information with perfect indifference, the Abbé continued that he had himself seen and spoken to the economist. 'Je ne m'occupe pas de l'économie politique; cette science ne m'intéresse pas,' replied the Englishman, looking bored, and adding that he had only come to Bourboule to look for Lord . . . , not to learn political economy. 'C'est peut-être le domestique d'un lord,' said the Abbé, imitating the Englishman's voice and accent. Lavergne laughed, and said the stranger seemed to be following a chase which in modern England was called tuft-hunting, but which was an ancient Teutonic pursuit, for the companions of the German *princeps* were tuft-hunters. Yet birth and rank, he continued, had, in some respects, a more unreasonable social influence in democratic France than in England. To be of a noble family was an almost indispensable key to French society. In spite of tuft-hunting, English society was the least exclusive in the world; and most English peers were themselves members of new families. The old families were the untitled landed gentry. On this point he displayed a marvellous knowledge of English pedigrees. When asked how he came to master such details, he replied that he had been led to do so first in his study of English political history, and the part played in it by aristocracy of birth, and afterwards in connexion with English rural economy, and the tendency of new wealth to settle finally in the country instead of the town.

Referring to the decline of aristocracy as a factor in the modern political world, he owned that he was becoming less and less alarmed at the rapid progress of democracy—so far, at least, as socialistic projects were concerned. Dangerous as he had once thought it to give predominant power to the poorest classes by means of universal suffrage, socialism had, in fact, become much less menacing in France. He agreed with Tocqueville that democratic institutions tended to benefit mankind, so far as their material welfare was concerned. As he laid stress on the word 'material,' I asked whether in his heart Tocqueville liked or disliked democracy. 'Il la détestait,' was the emphatic answer. But Lavergne added, that it was in reference to an æsthetic or intellectual standard that Tocqueville in his inmost soul regarded it with repugnance. 'Who in the next century,' he had said, 'will execute a really great work of art for a multitude interested only in buying in the cheapest and selling in the dearest market? Who will spend years on a book for a nation which reads only cheap newspapers? Book-making will become, like everything else, a mere trade.'

Soon after this conversation Lavergne published a letter on universal suffrage in relation to socialism which attracted much attention in both the political and the economic world, and which has its importance still for English readers: who should bear in mind, however, that it was written in a country in which property, as well as political power, is widely diffused. 'Certes, je n'ai pas désiré l'avènement du suffrage universel; je l'ai vu, au contraire, arriver avec inquiétude, mais depuis vingt ans qu'il fonctionne, j'ai appris à le moins redouter. J'ai été surtout frappé de cette coincidence que du moment où il a été institué, le socialisme a commencé à décliner. C'est sous l'empire du suffrage restreint que les utopies socialistes se sont développéés et ont pris de grandes proportions. Je ne puis m'empêcher d'attribuer au suffrage universel une action quelconque sur ce changement. On comprend qu'en effet les faiseurs de systèmes subversifs se forment une arme du suffrage universel pour séduire les ignorants. Si l'on ne met pas nos théories en pratique, peuvent-ils dire, c'est que le pouvoir est entre les mains d'une minorité intéressée à les étouffer. Ce langage perd beaucoup de sa force apparente avec le suffrage universel. Depuis que tout le monde vote, pourquoi les bases de la société n'ont-elles pas changé? Les classes les plus nombreuses sont devenues les plus puissantes; pourquoit n'ont-elles rien fait? C'est qu'apparemment il n'y a rien à faire. Le socialisme est mis au pied du mur; dès qu'on le serre de près il s'évanouit.'

We took long drives about Bourboule, but Lavergne could with difficulty walk a hundred yards, leaning on two supporters. One morning he complained of fatigue, and said he should not attempt to walk that day. 'You would be less tired to-day, sir, if you had walked more yesterday,' said his valet—to whom in that respect he was no hero—'and you will be more tired to-morrow if you don't walk to-day.' In fact, Lavergne was capable of any exertion that his bodily powers permitted for a public object, but was not easily persuaded to take irksome exercise only for the sake of health. Before dinner I found him seated on a bench in front of the hotel, where I had left him at eleven o'clock. 'The spirit was willing, but the flesh was weak,' he observed, alluding to his servant's advice. He liked to be told all that one saw and did, and a little incident connected with my departure interested him considerably. As the diligence from Clermont-Ferrand to Bourboule started at an inconvenient hour, I had hired a carriage, and Lavergne suggested that I might find someone at Mont Dore, another watering-place a few miles distant, disposed to join me in a carriage back—an arrangement which was easily effected. But to get to Mont Dore in the customary carriage and pair was a matter of ten francs, besides a *pourboire;* so I stipulated for a *voiture à un cheval* for six francs, for that part of the journey. After some parley I was promised a *petite voiture à chasse.* When this arrangement was reported to Lavergne, he said it was as hard to change the customs of a French watering-place as to reform the English land laws. Were an English visitor seen in a *voiture à un cheval* it might become the mode, which was not for the interest of the dealers. So he imagined something would happen to prevent the *petite voiture à chasse* from conveying me to Mont Dore. The following morning, at the appointed time, a carriage and pair came to the door. The very man who had struck the bargain with me was on the box, and explained simply that he thought a two-horsed carriage would be 'plus convenable à monsieur.' Lavergne held up two fingers significantly from a window as I drove by. The day before I left Bourboule, he remarked evidently with a practical purpose, that the scrupulous honesty which the innkeeper at Gueret had displayed could hardly be expected at a hotel in a fashionable watering-place, but it was a duty which every visitor owed to others to object to any overcharge—a duty often neglected from false shame.

In the following year (1875) M. de Lavergne was elected by the Assemblée Nationale an irremovable member of the new Senate, and for three years, in spite of bodily helplessness and much suffering, continued to take a part in public affairs. Before his own end came he lost his beloved wife, and during his last months he was afflicted with a nervous disorder which, he wrote to me, left him no rest day or night. 'Il fait des sauts,' said his servant, describing this tormenting affection. At length one of the noblest hearts in France ceased to beat. Léonce de Lavergne became only a name, but one which neither France nor England ought to let die. The present French Constitution was in part his work; but he has left another, and perhaps a more lasting monument, in his work as an author.

M. de Lavergne's chief literary productions are undoubtedly his books on the rural economy of England and France. The main problem in respect of the former was to account for the superior productiveness of English agriculture; and he applied to it what is now called the historical method. It does not appear that he thought of applying a novel method; but his sagacity led him to investigate every subject inductively—that is to say, in connexion with history and surrounding conditions. The superiority of England had not always existed. In the reigns of Henry IV. of France and James I. of England, France was foremost in agriculture, as in other arts. But after the middle of the seventeenth century England steadily advanced under free institutions, while France retrograded under monarchical tyranny and misgovernment until its peasantry sank into the destitution and misery described by La Bruyère and D'Argenson. Investigating further the causes at work on the side of England in his own age, Lavergne laid chief stress upon three: first, the love of country life felt by the opulent classes, leading to the application of wealth and enterprise to the improvement of the soil, while in France the love of the pleasures and excitement of cities caused a constant drain on the country; secondly, the free and orderly spirit of the English people and of their institutions, and the consequent exemption of the island from both military despotism and violent revolutions; thirdly, the immense market for agricultural produce afforded by the development of English manufactures and commerce. Lavergne wrote his 'Essai sur l'Économie Rurale de l'Angleterre,' as Tacitus wrote the 'Germania,' faithful in description of Teutonic manners and institutions, but with a political and social moral in view, and one eye always on his own country. He took for his motto the maxim of Montesquieu, 'Les pays ne sont pas cultivés en raison de leur fertilité, mais en raison de leur liberté.' The Imperialist party in France claimed for the Second Empire the credit of all the prosperity due to science, steam, Californian and Australian gold, and the general progress of the age. The zealous advocate of constitutional and parliamentary government, on the other hand, was disinclined to admit that France had made any real advance under the false splendour of a profligate and corrupting despotism. Hence Lavergne looked at the rural economy of England with somewhat partial eyes. He ignored, or at least left in the background, the fact that English institutions and history had developed a love of rural life and agriculture among only a small minority of the nation. A further reflection, which should not be omitted, is that since Lavergne's famous essay was written a critical juncture has been reached, at which the influence of the expansion of the British market for agricultural produce on British agriculture cannot be clearly foreseen. Lavergne looked chiefly to one side of the market, the side of demand; while the other side, that of supply, is now foremost in importance. The question at present is, whether British agriculture can compete in the British market itself with the foreign supply. This, Lavergne would, indeed, have said, is a question which concerns landlords rather than farmers, 'Pourvu que la rente baisse en proportion de la baisse des prix, le cultivateur proprement dit est à peu près désintéressé.'* Yet the final result may be not altogether in harmony with Lavergne's views. His historical and inductive method of investigation will, however, always remain proof against criticism. In the application of this method he was entirely original. The French statesmen and economists of his age knew nothing of their great countryman, Auguste Comte; and Lavergne was as unacquainted with German political economy as with the positive philosophy. The only German economist, indeed, whose name was known twenty years ago in either England or France, Professor Rau, had followed the old paths, and thrown no new light on the method of economic science.

Lavergne's work on the rural economy of France is in like manner an elaborate application of the inductive, historical method. At a time when economists were accustomed to speak of every country in the lump, and to occupy themselves with generalities and abstractions—such as the wages fund, the average rate of wages, the equality of profits—Lavergne described the actual economy of France in terms before which these crude formulas crumble to pieces. Instead, for example, of 'generalizing the facts of wages,' he showed that the differences in local rates in France were so great that 'the differences resulting from differences of social position were nothing in comparison with those resulting from inequalities of wages.' If the average consumption of meat per head in Paris was ten times as great in Paris as in La Creuse, it was not because Paris had some thousand rich inhabitants, while La Creuse had only a sprinkling of country gentlemen of small fortune, but because a working-man could earn on an average ten times as much in the capital as in a remote rural department.† 'Under an apparent uniformity,' Lavergne says, at the outset of his treatise, 'France is nothing less than an epitome of Europe and almost of the world. Shall we speak first of climate? Nothing can be less alike than the Département du

* *Essai sur l'Econ. Rur. de l'Angleterre*, 4th ed., p. 199.
† *Écon. Rur. de la France*, 4me ed., p. 411.

Nord, which forms one extremity of this vast territory, and the Département du Var, which forms the opposite extremity. Shall we speak of geological constitution? The mountains of the east, the centre, and the south, widely differing from each other, of limestone, granite, and volcanic formation respectively, have nothing in common with the plains at their feet, and which present in turn innumerable diversities. Shall we study moral and political facts? Every province has its history, which has powerfully acted on its economic development; and since they became subject to the same laws, these laws have had a special influence over each. Do we come to systems of husbandry? We find at once every cultivation, every system of working the soil, all degrees in the scale from the extremest poverty to the greatest rural riches. One department is fifty times richer than another department—one canton a hundred times richer than another canton.'*

'Mon illustre maître,' the title given to Léonce de Lavergne by a French official under the Second Empire, is one which every careful student of his works on rural economy ought to feel disposed to accord. The illustrious master of rural economy was also a statesman of first-rate capacity, an accomplished man of letters, a charming member of society, and all this under difficulties and sufferings tasking heroic fortitude to the uttermost.

---

* *Econ. Rur. de la France,* 4me ed., pp. 59, 60.

XIII.

POLITICAL ECONOMY IN THE UNITED STATES.*

The readers who would concern themselves much about the political economy of a foreign country, in order simply to know what doctrines on the subject are taught in its text-books and colleges, are probably few. But when the inquiry is found to include one into the influence of physical geography, history, institutions, moral and religious ideas on economic theory, the curiosity of a class may be excited whose interest in the controversies of economists on their own account is but faint. A wider claim to attention will be established, should it appear that we are engaged in the study not merely of a chapter in the intellectual history of the United States, but of one which elucidates some of the causes determining the directions of the mental energies of nations, their success or failure in various branches of culture, and their fundamental ideas and methods in philosophy. The investigation may likewise help to verify some doctrines generally accepted in England as economic laws, and to ascertain how far they possess the universality or independence of time and place usually attributed to them, or need to be conditioned and qualified, if not abandoned.

America—as for shortness we may sometimes call the United States, though Canada and South America are not included in the present inquiry—is the country above all others to which we might naturally look for original and considerable contributions to the science of wealth through the inductive study of

---

* *Fortnightly Review*, October 1st, 1880.

new facts. The diversity of some of the economic phenomena of this new world from those of the old; the unparalleled rapidity of its material progress, and the novel conditions, physical and political, under which it has taken place; the freedom from the limitations by which the populations of European countries are restricted; the absence of monarchy, aristocracy, and the military element, and of the peculiar direction which they give to production and distribution, seem to open a most promising field of observation. Nor would it seem unreasonable to expect that in a country the most important part of whose economic development has taken place within living memory, some important discoveries might have been reached with respect to the laws of social evolution under which this gigantic growth has been attained. It will presently be seen that American political economy does really exhibit some distinctive features closely connected with the physical character of the region in which it has taken shape, and with the diversity of the material condition of its population from that of any society of the Old World. Yet in America itself, if we except a recent Californian writer, whose claims will be examined, none but the disciples of Mr. Carey would pretend that any considerable discoveries have been made in relation to the natural laws of the production and distribution of wealth, or that any great addition has been made to the stock of economic knowledge. With exceptions and qualifications that will be pointed out, American political economy is in the main an importation from Europe, not an original development; it has made but slight inductive study of surrounding phenomena, and follows, for the most part, the method of deduction from general assumptions; it has hardly attempted to investigate the laws of evolution of which the present economic structure and state of American society are the outcome. In 1876 the 'North American Review' celebrated the centenary of the Declaration of Independence by a number of excellent essays on the progress of the American mind during the century in several directions. In one of these, on 'Economic Science in America, 1776–1876,' Mr. C. F. Dunbar, now Professor of

Political Economy in Harvard College, while admitting the value of some dissertations on special subjects, summed up the history of American political economy for a hundred years in the sentence that 'the United States had done nothing towards developing the theory of political economy, notwithstanding their vast and immediate interest in its practical application.' The qualities displayed in Mr. Dunbar's own essay afford an indication that, if his country has done little for the advancement of his branch of philosophy, it has not been for want of intellectual power, and the works of several of his countrymen in the same field support the conclusion. It is worth notice that practical jurisprudence has long engaged the American intellect with success. Even Franklin seems never to have mastered the elements of economic science; but before the Declaration of Independence, Edmund Burke had noticed the bent of the colonists' mind towards the study of law. 'In no country in the world,' he said, in 1775, 'is the law so general a study. All who read—and most do read—endeavour to obtain a smattering in that science.' Mr. John Stuart Mill, happening to be asked in conversation by the present writer how he accounted for the Greeks doing nothing in jurisprudence when the Romans did so much, answered that 'the question always to be asked was how a people came to do anything? Their doing nothing was easily accounted for.' Like everything Mr. Mill said, the remark was sagacious and instructive. *Vis inertiæ*, routine, the obstacles within and without every man to original intellectual efforts and to their success, account for much being left undone, even by nations possessed of the highest faculties. Yet, in reference to the slight progress of political economy in America, at least down to the last fifteen years, we shall do well not to rest satisfied with the explanation that no explanation is needed.

Mr. Perry, in a chapter in his 'Elements of Political Economy,' on the history of the science, speaks of the circumstances of the United States as having been favourable from the beginning to the cultivation of economic studies, alluding to the resistance to restrictions on trade in which the Revolution began, the various experiments in currency, the discussions excited by tariff after tariff, and the attention directed to the new gold mines. Yet the reader will, we believe, incline to the opposite conclusion, that, down at least to the close of the war between the Northern and Southern States, the circumstances of the country were unfavourable to the cultivation of economic science. The most conspicuous of the causes that have withdrawn the American mind from it may be classed under the head of physical geography, including the natural resources of the Continent, its facilities for internal commerce and migration, and its separation, on the other hand, by two oceans from some of the gravest troubles of the Old World. 'Give me,' said Cousin in his 'Lectures on the History of Modern Philosophy,' 'the map of a country, its configuration, its climate, its waters, its winds, its natural productions, its botany, its zoology, all its physical geography, and I pledge myself to tell you what will be the man of that country, and what place that country will occupy in history.' Had M. Cousin been given only the map and physical geography of North America, it might have puzzled him to say what would be the man of that continent—whether a Red Indian or a Yankee, as the red man pronounced the French name of the Englishman; and what place that continent would occupy in history—whether a place such as it occupied before the age of Columbus, or such as it occupies now. Yet the element on which M. Cousin laid excessive rhetorical emphasis has in reality acted with a potency needing no exaggeration. An English writer, as prone to sweeping generalization as M. Cousin, has referred to America in illustration of a distinction between Europe as the quarter of the globe in which man is stronger than nature, and the other quarters in which man is overpowered and reduced to insignificance by the forces of the external world. Mr. Buckle seems, however, to have had in view only the tropical regions of the New World, where nature, doubtless, is more exuberant, and man less energetic and enterprising, than in its temperate zone. In the latter, man's environment has exercised an influence of the highest importance in relation to the inquiry before us; but it has done so, not by overpowering and crushing, but by stimulating and developing his energies. It has not, however, exercised his faculties equally in all directions. One of the conditions governing throughout the world the occupation and conquests of the human intellect is, that the greater part of the mental power of every people is engaged in the practical business of life, and only a small surplus is anywhere available for the cultivation of science and letters. But two opposite kinds of physical environment tend to restrict, in more than an ordinary degree, the higher ranges of intellectual development. Extraordinary affluence and extraordinary barrenness of natural resources have one and the same tendency to absorb in the pursuit of material welfare the energies of a community. In Lapland and Greenland man's whole strength has been engrossed in supplying his first animal wants. In the United States his activity has been prodigious and many-sided, yet the stock of intellectual power available for achievements of a high order has been small. Production, accumulation, exchange, and consumption, have gone on upon the grandest scale, but they have engaged philosophical observation upon a comparatively insignificant scale.

M. de Tocqueville, in his inquiry into the movement of American intellect, observes that he regards the people of the United States as the part of the English people charged with the mission of subduing a new world, while the rest of the nation, possessing more leisure and less occupied with the material cares of life, is able to devote itself to thought and the development of the spiritual life of humanity. The observation is applicable to political economy in common with other branches of scientific and literary culture; but there are circumstances that have had a special tendency to repress intellectual effort and originality in the direction of economic inquiry. The very causes that were adverted to at the outset, as opening a new field for the economist to explore, have not only tended, in fact, to turn the national mind in other directions, and absorbed it in the actual acquisition of wealth instead of theorising about it, but have prevented the conditions which in Europe chiefly contributed to fasten attention on economic subjects from arising. The problems relating to wealth that have most urgently demanded solution in the Old World have either never emerged or have assumed comparatively little importance in America down to recent years. Without sickness, wounds, and pain, there would have been no physiology, pathology, or science of medicine. It was the distressed condition of Europe in the last century that gave birth to its economic philosophy. Quesnay's motto was, *Pauvres paysans, pauvre royaume; pauvre royaume, pauvre roi.* Adam Smith wrote in a better governed and more prosperous kingdom, and after a generation of unusual plenty; yet his inquiry into the causes of the wealth of nations arose out of their general poverty throughout history and in his own time. The fact that the majority of the population of the whole world stood always on the verge of destitution produced the doctrines of Malthus. The free trade controversy in England grew out of dear bread, depressed trade, low wages, and low profits; and it gave political economy most of its importance in English estimation during the last generation. Had Great Britain been as large, as fertile, and as underpeopled as the United States, Mr. Mill might have made a fortune in a counting-house instead of a reputation as a political economist. America owes doubtless in part to its institutions its exemption from the necessity of attempting a solution of the chief economic problems that have occupied philosophers in Europe. The great writer on American democracy, however, seems to go too far in attributing mainly to it the passion for material welfare and the eagerness and enterprise with which riches are sought in the United States.*

In the most democratic cantons of Switzerland life has been for centuries calm and tranquil enough. It is to the immense prizes that nature offers, rather than to the equality of the conditions of the race, that the ardour of the competitors in the United States is to be ascribed. If democratic institutions be compared with monarchic or aristocratic, abundant proof will,

---

* De Tocqueville, *De la Démocratie en Amérique*, iii. 208-11.

it is true, be found of the superior tendency of the first to diffuse material prosperity throughout the mass of the people. Switzerland is, in all its physical conditions, the antithesis to America: nature has done almost nothing for its inhabitants beyond the immense service, indeed, of interposing barriers between them and the armies of emperors and kings; no road in it leads to great fortunes. Yet, were the conditions of all the countries of Europe as prosperous as that of Switzerland, it may well be that a science of political economy would never have arisen, because no urgent economic problems would have pressed for solution. Switzerland, however, has provided only for its own people. The grand achievement of America is to have provided for all comers, and to have not only rescued from destitution no small part of the population of Europe, but placed them in such affluence that they can endure tariffs which make them buy the produce of their old countrymen at twice its natural cost. This, however, is an achievement not of political institutions but of nature. The maintenance of the American polity with its equality is, moreover, in a great measure due to physical causes. The ocean has kept it aloof from the wars of the Old World, and the configuration of the continent has maintained a single government. Had it been broken up into rival states by deserts and mountain chains, instead of being united by rich plains and noble rivers, it might have been a battle-field. Thrones and military and aristocratic orders might have been founded; a Latin empire in Mexico would certainly have arisen; national debts, war, taxes, and impoverishment, would have followed. That the emergence of these phenomena would have given a stimulus to economic inquiry we have proof, not only in European history, but in the awakening of the American mind itself to the study of political economy since the Civil War, with the burdens and difficulties it entailed.

The inhabitants of the New World have been the more disposed to leave the production of science and literature to the old, that they get their fruits at less than their cost of production by importation; and the absence of a law of international copy-right has in turn been the more unfavourable to American authorship that the rate of remuneration in other occupations has been so high. The Pennsylvanian manufacturer complains that he cannot compete with the cheap labour of England, though freight is added to the prime cost of every pound of English produce imported; yet he is content that the American author should compete with English books for which neither producer nor carrier has been paid. A single copy of Mill's 'Principles of Political Economy,' or Bastiat's 'Harmonies Economiques,' is all the American publisher need buy. No wonder if American economists should be content to take their political economy for the most part ready made from Mill and Bastiat.

It would, nevertheless, be an erroneous conclusion that American political economy has no peculiar features, or that little is to be learned from its study. Besides the perspicuity with which its doctrines are set forth, and the novel illustrations and instances which it affords, it has striking and distinctive characteristics, an examination of the nature and causes of which cannot fail to instruct the English economist. The reader will find in their consideration fresh evidence of the influence, among other conditions, of the physical geography of a country on its philosophy.

American economists have, in the first place, been nearly unanimous in rejecting, or, at least, setting aside as practically unimportant, the Malthusian doctrine of a tendency of population to outstrip the means of subsistence. It is controverted or ignored in all American treatises on the general principles of economics. It is repudiated alike by protectionists and free-traders—by Carey, Thompson, Peshine Smith, and Bowen,* the authors of the chief systematic works on the science which advocate protection, and by Amasa Walker and Perry, the writers of the chief text-books in which the freedom of international trade is supported. Mr. Henry George, the propounder

---

* Mr. Bowen is in error in asserting, in a recent article in the *North American Review* on 'Malthusianism, Darwinism, and Pessimism,' that for the last thirty years English economists have abandoned the Malthusian theory.

of a new theory of the distribution of wealth, and of the causes of poverty, is as zealous in antagonism to it as the writers of American schools, from whom he differs on other fundamental points. The immense resources of the North American continent; the extent of uncultivated land of the highest fertility; the constant movement of agriculture to richer instead of to poorer soils, while the cost of production is further diminished by invention; the actual need of a faster increase of population than the country itself yields; the rapid improvement in the condition of a perpetual influx of emigrants, are enough to account for general scepticism or indifference with respect to the doctrine of Malthus. A comparison of his chapter on the checks to population in France, with its actual movement since his time, shows, indeed, that he much underestimated the force of the preventive check there under institutions conducive to providence; and among the American-born citizens of the United States this check is even stronger than in France. It must be allowed to detract not a little from the practical worth and lasting fame of his doctrines, that Malthus should have shown so little insight into the power of institutions to foster either improvidence or prudence, as to speak of them as in reality light and superficial in comparison with those deeper-seated causes of evil which result from the laws of nature and the passions of mankind. Nevertheless, his fundamental position remains unshaken, that, given the fecundity or power of increase of mankind, or the 'potential rate,' as it has been called, of population, which he assumed, the numbers of any nation must, unless restricted by either preventive or positive checks, soon exceed the means of subsistence. If the 'potential rate' of human increase everywhere and always accords with his assumption that it tends to double in every twenty-five years, the necessity for either positive or preventive restraints to keep population within the limits of subsistence is incontrovertible. Both in America and in England the antagonists to Malthus misapprehend the doctrine they combat, when they point to an actual increase of wealth as well as of population even in old countries.

In neither England nor France has population advanced at the assumed 'potential rate;' it has everywhere been restrained by preventive or positive checks, or by both. But the question follows—Is the potential rate always and everywhere what Malthus supposed? Does it really remain constant, as he assumed?

Mr. Amasa Walker has adduced the following statistics of the proportion of births among American-born and immigrant inhabitants of the State of Massachusetts, merely with the view of proving the strength of the preventive check in a highly civilized and prosperous community, but they suggest something more:—

Native population, ...	970,952
Foreign, ...	260,114
Number of births in native population, .	16,672
,, ,, foreign ,, . .	16,138

The number of births in the native population, as he observes, to be in proportion to the foreign, should have been 60,289, or nearly four times the actual number. 'The grand cause for this remarkable difference,' according to Mr. Walker, 'is to be found in the fact that the foreign population are far less influenced by prudential considerations and social restraint.' They therefore enter the marriage state with less regard to their ability to support a family respectably. 'On the other hand, the resistance to marriage from a more costly style of living is constantly increasing with the native population, among whom the standard of family expenditure rises rapidly with the finer culture, the more elegant arts, and the greater social vivacity of each new year.'* In support of this view the author adds statistics showing that the number of marriages in proportion to population is twice as great among the immigrant as among the American-born inhabitants of Massachusetts. But the proportion of births has been seen to be not twice only but four times as great. Such a decline of births seems to indicate something more than an increased force of the pruden-

---

* *The Science of Wealth*, By Amasa Walker. 7th ed., p. 463.

tial check since Franklin said, 'Marriages in America are more general and more generally early than in Europe; and if in Europe they have but four births to a marriage, we may here reckon eight.' Mr. Walker himself suggests that one cause of the difference is, that 'the foreign population is engaged somewhat less than the native at indoor and sedentary employments, and in so far are likely to be more vigorous.'* He furnishes statistics, too, which prove that the mortality is considerably greater, and the longevity less, among the American-born than among the foreign inhabitants. When to this we add the vastly greater proportion of diseases of the digestive organs in the United States than in Great Britain,† the premature fading of American women, and what dentists report of the frailty of American teeth, the conclusion seems inevitable that a decline in vigour and fecundity is one of the causes of the small families of American-born citizens, and that the 'potential rate' of population is not constant, as Malthus supposed. That climate is not the cause appears from Franklin's statement quoted above. The climate of Lower Canada is healthier than that of Massachusetts, but not sufficiently so to account for the difference in the number of children to a marriage. 'Nous sommes terribles pour les enfants,' said a French Canadian to Mr. Johnston, adding that from eight to sixteen are the usual number of the farmers' families, and naming women who had five-and-twenty children, and threatened *le vingt-sixième pour le prêtre*.‡

The slow growth of the native population of the Eastern States of America seems to lend probability to Mr. Herbert Spencer's doctrine, that the increased cost in nervous structure and function attending the keener struggle for life, as human society advances, entails a diminution in fecundity. And whoever studies Mr. Spencer's arguments, along with facts which may be learned from English physicians, surgeons, and dentists, will find ground for surmising that new elements and

---

* *The Science of Wealth.* By Amasa Walker. 7th ed., p. 463.

† *Notes on North-American Agriculture, Economical and Social.* By James F. W. Johnston, ii. 396.

‡ *Ibid.*, i. 346.

conditions, which Malthus could not foresee, have begun to affect the population of Europe itself. A question, indeed, arises whether Mr. Spencer's view of the matter is not of too optimist a colour; and whether the hurry and anxiety of modern life do not cause more than a mere change in the direction and use of nervous power, and bring with them a decline in physical vigour that takes many painful and distressing forms, and is, in truth, a degeneracy of the race. However this may be, there is much to justify a doubt that Lord Macaulay's prediction will ever be fulfilled, or that American economists will ever be driven to give the theory of Malthus a prominent place in their treatises.

A second marked feature of American political economy is the conspicuousness of a theological element. Mr. Buckle affirmed that in England political philosophy was finally separated from theology before the end of the eighteenth century; and Dr. Roscher speaks of German political economy as having disengaged itself from religion and become an independent science a century earlier. Neither proposition is strictly accurate; but neither German nor English writers on the science have incorporated theology with it, as American economists have habitually done. The assumption of an invisible hand, directing to the general good the efforts of individuals seeking their own gain, appears only in a single passage of the 'Wealth of Nations,' and Adam Smith's economic philosophy could stand without it. He never used his conception of the character and designs of the Deity as a premiss from which to deduce conclusions or laws. Archbishop Whately is the only modern English writer of eminence who has imported theological conceptions into economic discussions: he was a digressive writer, and his introduction of theology is clearly a digression. Of Continental economists, Bastiat is the one in whom the religious element is most prominent; but with him, too, it comes in as an inference, not as a major premiss. The harmony of the economic interests of mankind is not deduced from the beneficence of the Ruler of the Universe, but inferred from economic facts, and applied to confirm the belief in such a ruler. In American treatises, on the other hand, theology becomes the backbone of economic science. Assumptions respecting the Divine will and designs are employed by both protectionists and free-traders in support of their theories. The Malthusian theory is controverted as atheistic in tendency, and contrary to the commandment to replenish the earth. Mr. Perry announces at the beginning of his 'Elements of Political Economy,' which has reached a fourteenth edition, that one of his main purposes is 'an examination of the providential arrangements, physical and social, by which it appears that exchanges were designed by God for the welfare of men.' He bases his theory of value and rent on the proposition that 'God is a giver, and not a seller,' and that 'value has its origin, not in what God has done, but in what man has done.' Children used to have a way of classing books as 'Sunday' or 'week-day books' by looking over the leaves for sacred names. According to this criterion several American treatises on political economy would be set apart as Sunday books. See, for instance, Mr. Perry's 'Elements of Political Economy, pp. 2, 63-5, 131, 238-41; and his 'Introduction to Political Economy,' pp. 29, 73-5, 152, 203.

One cause of this characteristic is the religious origin of the chief American colonies, and the traditional influence of theological tenets over American thought on which M. de Tocqueville lays stress.* The chief American colleges in the Eastern States were, moreover, founded for sectarian purposes, and their original design still exercises a considerable though a declining influence over their systems of instruction and philosophy. At Yale College an attempt was made last year to stop the Professor of Social Science, Mr. W. G. Sumner, whose name is honourably known in this country as well as in his own, from making use of Herbert Spencer's works, and the matter is not yet settled. Down to recent time, also, the lecturers on political economy in American Colleges were for the most part, as many of them still are, ministers of religion. This circumstance is itself connected

* *De la Démocratie en Amérique*, iii. 10, 11.

with a more general cause; for political philosophy has been left to a theological class, who have worked their professional ideas into it, because the laity were engaged in more lucrative pursuits. Again, the prosperity of the American people, and the bountiful aid which human effort receives from nature, are more in harmony than the general condition of European society with assumptions of beneficent design in the arrangements of the economic world. Sentiment has undergone a great change in modern times in relation to this point. In the Middle Ages pain, privation, and poverty were regarded as pleasing to God, and the idea lingered long afterwards. Lord Bacon speaks of times of peace and prosperity as inclining to atheism, 'For troubles and adversities do more bow men's minds to religion.' The feelings of our own day are becoming more and more adverse to such a conception. Mr. Mill's essays on religion leave little room for doubt that had all mankind been as happily circumstanced as the people of the United States, he would have been a confirmed theist. An example of the mixture of national pride in the prosperity of the United States with thankfulness to heaven on the part of its citizens that they are not as other men are, appears in the Secretary of State's letter accompanying the reports of the United States consuls, in 1879, on the 'State of Labour in Europe': 'No American labourer or capitalist,' says Mr. Evarts, 'can read their reports without a feeling of the utmost commiseration for the toiling millions of Europe, and heartfelt pride in and appreciation of the blessings which heaven has vouchsafed to the people of the United States.'

A third characteristic of American political economy is the absence of long chains of deduction, such as English economists have affected, from the assumption that competition equalizes the wages of labourers and the profits of capitalists in different occupations and localities throughout a country. *A priori* one might naturally have anticipated, from the mobility of labour and capital in the United States, that the doctrine of the dependence of prices on cost of production, by reason of the equality of the gains of equal efforts and sacrifices, would have been pushed to its farthest point there. It has been, on the contrary, rejected by some American economists, ignored by others, or greatly qualified, and by none made the foundation of a great superstructure of theory; and two causes seem to have contributed to this:—First, the rapid invention and change in the processes of American industry; for only in a stationary condition of the industrial arts could the value of commodities really depend on their original cost. Secondly, the fluctuation in prices, and the palpable deviation from first cost, resulting from speculation, the manipulation of dealers, and the local variations of demand and supply within the vast area over which American business is carried on. 'The extraordinary fluctuations of the grain and flour market in this country,' says Mr. Bowen, 'American Political Economy,' p. 212, 'are so great as to put all calculations at defiance, and to make the gains of dealers nearly as uncertain as a lottery.' And Messrs. Read and Pell observe in their recent report, 'When we quitted America wheat was $1\frac{1}{2}d.$ per bushel cheaper at Liverpool than New York; and wheat of the same quality was worth almost as much at Chicago, 900 miles from the seaboard.'

A fourth distinguishing feature of the development of Political Economy in the United States is the systematic teaching of protectionism in colleges and text-books as a scientific doctrine. In the United Kingdom only a single professor of the science—the late Isaac Butt, who for a time held the chair of Political Economy in the University of Dublin—has shown any leaning towards protection. In Germany Dr. Schmoller, Professor in the University of Strasburg, supports the present protective tariff, and has some followers. But no regular text-book of the principles of political economy, advocating protection, so far as the present writer is aware, has been published in any country in Europe. In the United States, on the other hand, protection is set forth in formal economic text-books—for example, the treatises of Carey, Thompson, Peshine Smith, Bowen, and Wilson—and taught by the professors of several colleges. Mr. Perry, though himself a zealous advocate of the freedom of trade, in his 'Elements of Political Economy,' describes American economists as falling for the most part into two groups:—'First, those modelled mainly after the ideas of Adam Smith; and, secondly, those modelled mainly after the ideas of Henry C. Carey;' thus recognising the system of Carey and his followers as that of a school of economists. No supporter of free trade, indeed, could be appointed to a chair, or get a class of students, in Pennsylvania. In the other colleges the lecturers in political economy are generally on the side of free trade, yet notable exceptions may be found. In Harvard College Mr. Bowen's chair included economics when his 'American Political Economy' was published, in 1870. The chair has since been divided, it has been said, in consequence of Mr. Bowen's strong protectionist bias; but his successor in respect of economic functions, Mr. C. Dunbar, is reported to be a mild protectionist, though no indication of this appears in the essay above referred to, but only an objection to sudden and violent alterations in tariffs. At Cornell University, Dr. Wilson, who lectures on economic science, has published a manual which shows him to be a protectionist. Physical and political conditions have combined in America to evoke a development of protectionist doctrine. The chief obstacle the manufacturer there has had to combat, in competing with England, has been the superiority of his own country in some of the natural elements of wealth—land and its products, cereals, cotton, tobacco, and the precious metals—creating a scale of wages much above the English rate, and raising the cost of production in industries in which the natural advantages are not so great. The best economy, of course, would have been for American capital to confine itself to the fields in which it had superior productiveness, awaiting a rise of wages and in the cost of coal-mining in England for competition in others. But in some States, Pennsylvania especially, there were rich coal-beds and iron ores; and the owners of these and the capitalists at their side were naturally impatient for an earlier harvest, in reaping which, moreover, they could not, like the English protectionists, be charged with taxing the food of the labourer. The antagonistic feeling towards England of a large section of the Republican party concurred to favour protection. But instead of taking sulk at political economy and turning his back on it, as the English protectionist did, the shrewder American sought a political economy on his own side, advocating a development of all the national resources; and authors and lecturers were soon forthcoming to supply the demand for economic science of this sort.

The professors of political economy in the United States, elsewhere than in Pennsylvania, are, however, for the most part, on the side of free trade. And when it is borne in mind that each of the thirty-six States in the Union has from one to five or six universities or colleges—'university' in the United States means no more than 'college,' and is only regarded as a somewhat finer name—and that there are 287 such universities or colleges, the importance of a decisive predominance of free trade doctrine in academic lectures and instruction is undeniable. Its significance ought not, however, to be overrated. Even in England it was not philosophers and professors, but manufacturers and politicians, who carried free trade: in America the manufacturers and most energetic politicians are against it, and can point to a so-called national system of political economy on their side, while the opposite system labours under the suspicions attaching to a foreign origin.

Economic theories and systems may be regarded in several different lights: (1) in reference to their causes, as the products of particular social, political, and physical conditions of thought; (2) in reference to their truth or error; (3) as factors in the formation of public opinion and policy. It is chiefly from the first of these points of view that American political economy has been considered in this essay; but the other aspects of the subject ought not to be altogether overlooked. The chief different schools of economic doctrine in the United States accordingly call for some notice. On the side of free trade are two schools, of whose leading principles respectively the late Amasa Walker's 'Science of Wealth,' now in its seventh edition, and Mr. Perry's 'Elements of Political Economy' and 'Introduction to Political Economy,' may be said to contain the best expositions. Mr. Walker's treatise fully deserves its popularity and circulation, but is so nearly in accordance with the views of the majority of English economists, unless with respect to population, as to need no special description. Mr. Perry, on the other hand (Professor of History and Political Economy in Williams' College, Massachusetts), claims to belong to a newer school, of which Bastiat is the chief light. The lines of his system seem, by Mr. Perry's own account, to have been somewhat hastily traced in his mind. The study of Bastiat's 'Harmonies Economiques' had, he says, been recommended to him: 'I had scarcely read a dozen pages in that remarkable book,' he adds, 'when, closing it, and giving myself to an hour's reflection, the field of political economy in all its outlines and landmarks lay before my mind, just as it does to-day. From that hour political economy has been to me a new science.' That the clearness with which a conception is entertained gives evidence of its truth is a proposition for which the maxim of an illustrious philosopher might be cited: 'Credidi me,' said Descartes, 'pro regula generali sumere posse omne id quod valde dilucide et distincte concipiebam verum esse.' Modern logic, nevertheless, rejects the presumption, and, as Mr. Mill has observed, no one can have examined the sources of fallacious thought without becoming deeply conscious that a nice coherence and concatenation of our ideas are apt to pass off with us for evidence of their truth. Political economy, in Mr. Perry's view, is simply a science of value, and value is never the result of natural agencies apart from human effort and service, because God's gifts are gratuitous. Rent, accordingly, is a payment, not for the use of a natural agent, but for a service rendered by the owner to the cultivator. To the obvious objection that land varies in value from natural causes Mr. Perry replies, that 'A high degree of natural fertility has been scattered with so bountiful a hand, and lands naturally less fertile have such comparative advantages of another sort, that under a broad view the degree of original fertility becomes a common factor cancelled in price.' In other words, land has everywhere some natural advantage or other of fertility, situation, aspect, climate, water-power, mineral wealth, &c., so that there is a general equality in respect of natural gifts, and land rent is never the price of their monopoly. Mr. Perry has visited the British Islands, and might have learned that even within their narrow compass the gifts of nature are most unequally distributed, and that the barren mountains of Donegal or the Shetland rocks have 'no compensating advantage of another sort' to redress the balance.

A chain of filiation connects Mr. Perry's system with one which, on the question of free trade, is fundamentally opposed to it; for Mr. Perry's doctrines are derived directly from Bastiat; and Carey, not without reason, claimed that Bastiat owed to him his leading ideas respecting the harmony of economic interests, the value of land, and the economic results of the growth of population and civilization. Carey himself owed not a little to Herbert Spencer, though he strangely metamorphosed some of the conceptions he drew from that great thinker's philosophy. A personal element, however, combined to mould Carey's economic ideas. Throughout the history of political economy, indeed, the personal history, education, and character, of particular writers has borne no small part in its developments and forms.* Dr. William Elder, one of Carey's most zealous supporters, remarks that, besides being a philosopher, he was an American and a patriot, and that his passionate hostility to the British system of foreign trade, and to the subsidiary British system of political economy, takes something of the temper and tone of national prejudice.† Dr. Elder adds: 'His father was an Irish patriot and a political exile from the land of his birth. Something hereditary may be detected running with much of the pristine force of blood through the life and character of his son.'‡

* For instances in the cases of Adam Smith, Quesnay, Gournay, and J. S. Mill, see the Essay in the present volume entitled, *The Political Economy of Adam Smith*, pp. 30-34, and also pp. 55–56.

† *Memoir of Henry C. Carey.* By William Elder, Philadelphia, 1880, pp. 30-1.

‡ *Ibid.* Of the fervour of Carey's utterances Dr. Elder says :—'He sometimes clinched his deliverances with expletives and epithets something out of fashion in society.' An English writer who visited him, after favourably describing him on the whole to the writer of this essay, added: 'He is a man of plain speech, and swears like a bargeman whenever Mill's name is mentioned,'

The main doctrine of Carey is, that under a proper national economy all the productive powers of a country and its people are harmoniously developed, and continual progress is achieved both in every branch of production and in the equity of distribution. An industrial nation contains three great fundamental classes: the agricultural, the manufacturing, and the commercial. All three should be developed and exist in equilibrium. In a rude state of the social organism there is no differentiation of functions; every man is warrior, hunter, fisher, builder, and carpenter. In an advanced and harmoniously-developed society all the leading industries are carried on by distinct classes, dependent on each other. Up to this point the advocate of free trade, looking on civilized society as embracing all civilized nations, might concur in the doctrine. The point of separation is, that Carey regarded each nation as a distinct social organism, containing the appointed natural means of independent development. 'No one,' says the chief living expositor of Carey's ideas (Mr. Robert Ellis Thompson, Professor of Social Science in the University of Philadelphia, and editor of the 'Penn Monthly'), 'who believes in the continual government of the world by Divine Will can doubt that nations exist in consequence of that will. "He fixeth the bounds of the nation." Each State, like each man, has a vocation. Every nation is a chosen people. It has a peculiar part to play in the moral order of the world.' Unless in the sense that whatever is is right, and exists by divine ordinance—in which case Carey's followers must concede that free trade itself may be a divine institution—it can hardly be maintained that the boundaries of nations have been providentially ordained. A witty countryman of Professor Thompson has 'guessed' that 'if ever the lion lies down with the lamb, it will be with the lamb inside;' and such is in reality the manner in which the bounds of the nations have for the most part been settled. They have swallowed up their weaker neighbours. History, too, is one long contradiction of the fixity of national boundaries. The limits of no great civilized empire, the United States not excepted, are what they were the year before the 'Wealth of Nations' was published and American Independence declared. How, then, can every State contain within confines which are frequently changed the 'providential' conditions of independent economic existence? Carey argues further that great waste in carriage is saved by bringing the farm and the factory into close proximity to each other, and that a return is thereby made to the soil, which is thus not robbed of its constituents as it is by the exportation of its produce. But in the United States the chief iron and coal mines and factories are at one side of the continent; the richest soils and the most productive farms are many hundred miles off at the other side; considerable cost of carriage is incurred, and no return of constituents is made to the land in the west from produce sold in the east.

Carey's system is, in fact, Pennsylvanian rather than national economy; it is a product of Pennsylvania, like its iron and coal, and has gained little acceptance in its entirety beyond the limits of that State, as may be gathered from the names of its principal supporters. In other States the most popular exposition of economic principles on the protectionist side is Mr. Bowen's 'American Political Economy,' a title assumed on the ground that the system expounded by English writers is really the political economy of England alone, while America needs an American political economy adapted to what is special in its physical conditions and institutions. Yet Mr. Bowen's own system is after all, in the main, English political economy, with an incongruous admixture of Pennsylvanian doctrine in relation to foreign trade. His treatise contains a clear exposition of principles long generally accepted in England, and its protectionism, like an artificial limb, can be detached without hurting or altering the rest of the structure. Mr. Bowen, it ought to be added, pronounces emphatically in favour of a metallic standard, and advocates a resumption of specie payments; while Carey regarded issues of inconvertible paper-money as streams of productive wealth. Carey's followers, in general, have been charged with adhesion to this doctrine, but it is repudiated by Professor Thompson, who advocates convertibility and deprecates an inflation of the currency. Soft money seems to have little support now from any school of economists. Protection, however, has much deeper roots; a majority of the Republican party still leans to it, and the intelligence of the country is to be found chiefly in the ranks of that party. The line between protectionists and free-traders, it should be observed, does not coincide with that between Republicans and Democrats. In Pennsylvania both Republicans and Democrats are protectionists, while in the city of New York many of both parties are free-traders. The most able and energetic supporters of both free trade and protection are Republicans.

Differing on some fundamental points from the systems that have been described is the theory set forth in a work published last year at San Francisco, entitled 'Progress and Poverty,' the author of which, according to the statement of American newspapers, has lately been appointed Professor of Political Economy in the University of California. From a passage in his book it appears that he was formerly a working-man in a trade,* and if this is to be understood in the ordinary sense, his learning and literary power are truly astonishing and admirable. Among other gifts he possesses a fertile imagination, supplying him readily with pertinent illustration. Want of imagination is one of the causes of the inability of many economists to emancipate themselves from old abstractions, generalizations, and formulas. Their minds do not enable them to realize actual phenomena, and to test theories on all sides by a multitude of instances. Mr. George's work, however, calls for notice not only on account of its ability, and because it contains internal evidence of being a product of the economic history of California, but because also of the magnitude of the problem it propounds, and the nature of the solution it proposes. It seeks to discover the cause that makes poverty the constant companion of wealth, and to find at the same time the explanation of recurring seasons of industrial and commercial paralysis and distress. Its author is opposed to protection, and to various notions which, he says, are rapidly gaining ground in the United States, 'that there is a necessary

---

* *Progress and Poverty*, p. 283.

conflict between capital and labour; that machinery is an evil, that competition must be restrained and interest abolished; that wealth may be created by the issue of money; that it is the duty of Government to furnish capital or to furnish work.' He often reasons deductively in the old-fashioned 'orthodox' way, as confidently as Ricardo or Mr. Senior, from the assumption that every man follows his pecuniary interest by the shortest and easiest road. It is surprising to an English reader, accordingly, to find that his main theory is, that the cause of the accompaniment of great wealth by great poverty, and of the succession of commercial depression to commercial prosperity, is the existence of private property in land.

Poverty, Mr. George argues first of all, is never the consequence of either a deficiency of capital or an excess of labourers. The labourer produces his own wages, and is not paid out of pre-existing capital, although the fact is concealed by the separation of employments and the complexity of the process of exchange. When a division of labour first takes place in early society, and, instead of every man as before supplying his own wants, one hunts, another fishes, a third gathers fruit, a fourth makes weapons or tools, a fifth clothing; each really produces his own maintenance, though he exchanges the produce of his own labour for other things. So, in a more advanced stage, an exchange is really going on between the producers in different occupations, and the labourer gets his subsistence in exchange for his own productive work, and does not derive it from capital, though the capitalist conducts the exchange. And an increase in the number of labourers causes a more than proportionate increase instead of a diminution in the rate of production. Twenty men working together where nature is niggardly will produce more than twenty times the wealth one can produce where nature is most bountiful. The denser the population, the more minute becomes the subdivision of labour, the better the economy of work. It is true the growth of numbers necessitates recourse to inferior soils and other natural agents, but the increase of the power of the human factor more than compensates for the decline in power of the natural factor.

The richest countries are not those where nature is most prolific, but where labour is most efficient, not Mexico but Massachusetts, not Brazil but Great Britain. The cause, then, of the depression of both the wages of labour and the interest on capital, and of the growth of poverty, as society advances, is not the increase of population, and does not lie in the conditions of production. It must, therefore, lie in distribution. The rise of rent is the real cause of the fall of both wages and interest, while the productive powers of society, so far from declining, are improving. Where the value of land is low, there may be a small production of wealth, and yet a high rate of both wages and interest, as we see in new countries. In California, where wages were higher than anywhere else in the world, so also was interest higher; but rent was non-existent; wages and interest have since gone down together, while rent has risen with startling rapidity. Where land is free, wages will consist of the whole produce, less the part necessary to induce the storing up of labour as capital. Where land, on the contrary, is all monopolized, wages may be forced down to a minimum. Three parties divide the produce, the labourer, the capitalist, and the landowner. If, with an increase of production, the labourer gets no more, the capitalist no more, but even less, the inference is that the landowner gets the whole increment. It is not the total produce, but the net produce after rent has been deducted, that determines what can be divided as wages and interest. Free trade has enormously increased the total wealth of Great Britain without lessening pauperism, because it has simply raised rent. To extirpate poverty, to make wages what justice commands they should be, the full earnings of the labourer, we must substitute for the individual ownership of land a common ownership: we must make land common property. For this purpose it is only necessary for the State to appropriate rent, not to dispossess the holders of land of its occupation.

Such, in brief, is the substance of Mr. George's argument. And so far as the proposition is concerned, that the labourer produces his own wages, it is true, as an American economist has shown in a work of great ability,* that in new countries labourers are often paid after the harvest, or by the year, and therefore out of the produce of their labour. Even in that case, however, the fund out of which the labourer is maintained while his wages are being earned, though his own, is the produce of past labour, not of the labour he is actually performing. In old countries the majority of the labourers engaged in long operations have not wherewithal to maintain themselves until the product is sold; but if they had, this fund would be a product of previous labour; it would be pre-existing wealth productively employed; that is to say, capital in the sense intended by Mr. Mill in his proposition that industry is limited by capital—a proposition which Mr. George confounds with the doctrine of the wages fund, now rejected by almost all English economists. Piers the Plowman, in Langland's poem, had barely enough food saved from the previous produce of his little farm to keep soul and body together until harvest time, while hired labourers beside him had strong ale and fresh meat and fish, hot and hot, twice a-day, because they were paid out of the savings of their employers. Piers himself could have fared equally well if, instead of waiting on his own crops to dight his dinner as he liked best, he had gone into the labour market for a share of the last year's corn, and of beef and mutton which had taken years to grow. In the England of our own day labourers not only get wages from capitalists long before their own work is finished and sold, but are many of them dead and gone before then. Sometimes the product is destroyed by an accident after the workmen have been paid wages in full, but before the employer has made anything by it. In the agricultural districts of California there was, as Mr. George says, a total failure of crops in 1877; and of millions of sheep, nothing remained but their bones. The farmers, nevertheless, hired labourers for the next crop, and he argues that they could not have done so out of past produce which was lost. The case

* *The Wages Question*, by Francis A. Walker. See an Article by the same writer, *North American Review*, January 1875.

really tells at both ends against Mr. George's conclusion; for it is clear that the labourers who helped to produce the crops that perished were not paid for that year's work, or maintained during it out of its produce; and the funds which the farmers borrowed to resume their operations must have been the produce of previous work, not of work the fruits of which were not yet forthcoming.

The accumulation of capital is, then, necessary for the maintenance of labourers, though it may be accumulated by themselves; and in a country like France, where land is to a large extent held by the productive classes, including labourers, capital is in good part accumulated out of rent. In France, too, rent in the case of a majority of families is an addition to, not a deduction from, wages and interest or profit; and were any government to seek to abolish private property in land, there are several million Frenchmen would 'know the reason why.' Nor is it true that wages and interest uniformly decline as rent advances. All three have been higher during the last thirty years in England than they were a hundred and thirty years ago—a fact which overthrows Mr. George's whole theory. In Holland all three have considerably risen in our own time; and although it is cited by one economist after another as the country where interest is lowest, the rate of interest is now considerably higher than in England, or than it was in Holland itself fifty years ago. A simple illustration will show how this may take place. Suppose a district contains ten million acres, yielding at a low stage of husbandry ten bushels an acre, and ten million acres of better land yielding fifteen bushels an acre, and therefore five bushels per acre as rent. Let agricultural art advance along with population, so as to double the productiveness of the whole district, and the poorer land will now yield twenty, the best land thirty bushels an acre. Ten bushels per acre instead of five will now be payable in rent for the best land; yet the whole labouring population may be better clothed, housed, and fed, in consequence of the improvements attending the division of labour; and the farmer may get a higher return on his capital. The entire amount of rent may also be received by farming and labouring families, whom its very existence may have stimulated to the industry and thrift that led to the increased production. It is overlooked, one may add, by writers who treat the fall of interest as society advances as an established historical fact, that in old times most people could get no interest at all on their savings, and hoarded them for lack of productive investments.

On behalf of abolishing the private ownership of land, and giving an equal share in the bounty of nature to all, Mr. George urges that it is 'but carrying out in letter and spirit the self-evident truth enunciated in the Declaration of Independence, that all men are created equal; that they are endowed by their Creator with certain inalienable rights; that among them are life, liberty, and the pursuit of happiness.' The age of the Declaration of Independence was indeed one in which philosophers believed in inalienable natural rights; and, if we are to be guided by the ideas of its framers, nothing is more certain than that they included among 'natural rights' the right of every man to acquire property in both land and movables. Only by a theory of dynamical inspiration, such as has been applied to the Bible, can we get any other meaning out of the Declaration than its authors intended. Coming down to more recent times, Mr. George cites the actual procedure of the first miners in California, who, he says, falling back upon 'first principles, primitive ideas, and natural perceptions of justice,' declared that the gold-bearing land should remain common property, of which no one might take more than he could use, or hold for a longer time than he actually used it. It may be that the land system of every country calls for reform, but it may be hoped that civilized men will not seek precedents for it in the infancy of the race, or in 'primitive ideas.' Mr. George can but have hastily studied the works of Sir Henry Maine, whom he cites, if he supposes that early communities recognised any common right in mankind, permanent or temporary, to the use of the soil. Each little tribe jealously excluded every other to the best of its power, and recognised no right in a human being, as such, to property of any kind, or even to liberty or life. If, however, the natural perceptions of justice really lead to common ownership, the citizens of California are bound to admit Chinamen without number to a share in the land of the State. Had Mr. George confined himself to contending that the governments of new countries have committed a grievous blunder in allowing their territory to be appropriated in perpetuity by the first comers for a nominal payment, he would have found allies among the advocates of private property in land. Even in old countries like England, whose territory has been appropriated by a small number of owners with the full sanction of the State, and contracts, and dealings, and investments of capital, have gone on for centuries on this foundation, all the requirements of justice and expediency would be met were it enacted that at a remote date—say four generations hence, or in the year 2001—all landed property, both in country and town, shall revert to the State. At that period legislators could decide, with better lights than we now possess, how to dispose of the vast accession to its resources. It would in any case come into a fund which would enable it to extinguish all taxes, and the restrictions to production and commerce they cause. Unhappily, existing generations care little for a distant posterity, and would be too apt, were the project under discussion, to convert it into one for immediate and uncompensated confiscation, such as Mr. George urges with a harshness that might justify a harsher name. His theory bears decisive marks of its growth out of the anomalous history of the marvellous region in which it was published, from the first occupation of the Gold Fields by strangers from every quarter of the globe, down to the sudden impoverishment of San Francisco in recent years by the fall in mining stocks and land values, consequent on rash speculation and imprudent investments. As Carey's system was a product of the mines of Pennsylvania, so is Mr. George's of those of California.

The prospects of political economy in the United States should be augured rather from the capacity shown than from what has been actually done, and in that sense the works of both the writers just referred to afford favourable indications.

Speaking generally, however, the men best qualified to stand in the front rank of American economists are not the authors of systems or general theories, or text-books of principles, but writers on special subjects—David Wells, William M. Grosvenor, Albert S. Bolles, Francis A. Walker, Edward Atkinson, William G. Sumner, C. F. Dunbar, and Simon Newcomb. Only since the Civil War has America begun seriously to apply its mind to economic questions, and the number of powerful intellects it has brought to bear on them is a remarkable phenomenon in the history of philosophy. Many of the best economic essays the last decade has produced will be found in the pages of American periodicals—the 'North American Review,' the 'International Review,' the 'Atlantic Monthly,' the 'Penn Monthly,' the 'Princeton Review,' 'Scribner's Magazine.' Journals like the 'Nation' and the 'Public' discuss economic questions with consummate skill. In the translation of Roscher and Blanqui work has been done by America which England ought not to have left it to do. Two considerable contributions to economic history were made last year in the 'Industrial History of the United States,' and the 'Financial History of the United States, 1774–1789,' by Mr. Bolles. In the perfection of its economic statistics America leaves England behind.

Were we surveying the entire field of political economy, so far as it has been cultivated in both the old and the new world, the question would arise :—How much, beneath what can claim only a local or a temporary importance, possesses universal and permanent value? What problems have been solved for all time? What universal truths have been discovered? How much of the work of Adam Smith, Malthus, John Stuart Mill, Roscher, Knies, Bastiat, Chevalier, Wayland, Walker, Perry, Carey, will remain standing and solid a hundred years hence? The subject of this Essay raises a still more important question : What new economic problems remain? Among them are some, it may confidently be affirmed, which the chief economists of both worlds have never yet raised, and of which they have not dreamt. There is reason to believe that America will take an active part both in bringing them to light and in their solution.

XIV.

ECONOMIC SCIENCE AND STATISTICS.*

ECONOMIC SCIENCE was not formally included within the Statistical Section of the British Association until 1856; and, even since then, addresses of distinguished Presidents of the Section have turned mainly on its statistical functions, and have been devoted principally to an inquiry into the nature and province of statistics. That the inquiry is neither so superfluous nor so easy as might at first appear is sufficiently shown by the fact that there are, according to the great German statist, Dr. Engel, no less than 180 definitions of the term to be met with in the works of different authors. These various definitions may, however, be said to group themselves round one or other of three conceptions, of which one follows the popular view of statistics; the etymological and original meaning almost disappearing in the notion merely of tables of figures, or numbers of facts, of which the chief significance lies in their numerical statement. According to another conception, statistics, following etymology and the signification given to Statistik by the famous Göttingen school, should be regarded as equivalent to the science of States, or political science, but, nevertheless, as confining itself to the ascertainment and collection of facts indicative of the condition and prospects of society, without inquiring into causes or reasoning on probable effects, and carefully discarding hypothesis, theory, and speculation in its investigations. A third conception is, that statistical science aims at the discovery, not only of the phenomena of society, but also of their laws, and by no means discards either inquiry into causes and effects or theoretical reasoning.

* *Athenæum*, September 27, 1873.—Written on the meeting of Section F of the British Association for the Advancement of Science, September, 1873.

It is curious that some who give to statistics the first of these three meanings, and who regard the numerical statement of facts, and the marshalling of tables of figures, as the proper business of the statistician, nevertheless speak of statistics as a science. But, as the eminent economist Roscher has observed, numbering or numerical statement is only an instrument of which any branch of science may avail itself, and can never, in itself, constitute a science. No one, as he says, would dream of making a science of microscopics, or observations made through the microscope. The distinguished English statistician and economist, Mr. Jevons, has likewise condemned the misconception of statistics and the misuse of the term we refer to in language worth recalling:—'Many persons now use the word statistical as if it were synonymous with numerical; but it is a mere accident of the information with which we deal that it is often expressed in a numerical or tabular form. As other sciences progress, they become more and more a matter of quantity and number, and so does statistical science; but we must not suppose that the occurrence of numerical statement is the mark of statistical information.'

The doctrine that the consideration of causes and probable reasoning are excluded from the province of statistics, and that statisticians should confine themselves to the ascertainment of facts, is hardly more satisfactory. No branch of science, no scientific body, confines itself to the observation of phenomena without seeking to interpret them or to ascertain their laws. It is not, indeed, possible, at present, to explain all the phenomena which come within the observation of the statist, or to connect them with any law of causation; and even naked collections of statistical facts may be useful as aids to further inquiry, or as supplying links in the chain of observed effects. But serious error, and even practical mischief, have followed from attention merely to the recurrence of statistical facts without inquiry into their causes. A theory of a decennial recurrence of commercial crises, for example, was based on the occurrence of crises in 1837, 1847, and 1857. Had the causes of commercial crises been examined, it would have been discovered that they are extremely various and uncertain in their occurrence; that a war, a bad harvest, a drain of the precious metals, anything, in short, which produces a panic, may cause a crisis; and as there is no decennial periodicity in the causes, there can be none in the effects.

These considerations lead us to adopt the third conception noticed above, namely, that statistical science investigates the laws of social phenomena as well as the phenomena themselves; and, if not co-extensive with sociology, or the science of society—because not going so far back in its researches, and confining itself to the phenomena of modern society—yet employs all available methods, inquiry into causes, theory, and probable reasoning for the interpretation of the facts it discovers. But it is not easy to give to a word a signification other than the one which long usage has put upon it; and, unfortunately, to the majority of persons the term statistics denotes simply dry figures and tabulated facts. The Statistical Section of the British Association has found a means to escape from the difficulty, in a great measure, by allying itself formally to Economic Science. It thus embraces definitely and expressly the whole economic side of the science of society, including the investigation of laws of causation, as well as the observation of facts, and employing all the methods of scientific investigation and reasoning. But if it deals in this manner with economic facts, it can hardly fail to do so likewise with the other classes of social phenomena which it approaches. And thus, however narrow may be the sense in which the term statistics may be elsewhere employed, the Statistical Section of the British Association is free from all trammel, and unfettered by any exclusion of theory, or even speculation, in its investigation of political and social problems.

The formal incorporation of economic science with statistics has another great advantage: it tends to correct the error to which economists as well as that to which statisticians are specially prone. If the latter have been apt to think only of facts, it has been the besetting sin of the former to neglect facts altogether; if statisticians have often been content to collect phenomena without heed to their laws, economists more often still have jumped to the laws without heed to the phenomena; if statistics have lain chiefly in the region of dry figures and numerical tables, economics have dwelt chiefly in that region of assumption, conjecture, and provisional generalization, which other sciences, indeed—geology to witness—have not escaped, but from which they are triumphantly emerging by combining the closest observation of phenomena with the boldest use of speculation and scientific hypothesis.

We may thus look for considerable benefit to both political economy and statistics from the combination of the methods to which the followers of each have been specially addicted. The subjects which occupied the principal place in Mr. Forster's address, and in the attention of the Section, conspicuously illustrate the importance of combining statistical with economic inquiry, and the characteristic defects of the economic and statistical methods hitherto commonly followed. Take, for example, the question of wages. The relations of capital and labour, and the causes determining the rates of wages, are not to be summed up or disposed of in any brief formula or so-called 'economic law.' But much might have been done, by the collection of statistics and careful inquiry into facts, towards obtaining much closer approximations to truth than the generalizations which take the name of 'the wages fund,' 'the equality of profits,' 'the average rate of wages'—generalizations of which the world generally has grown a little doubtful and not a little weary.

Economists have been accustomed to assume that wages on the one hand and profits on the other are, allowing for differences in skill and soforth, equalized by competition, and that neither wages nor profits can anywhere rise above 'the average rate,' without a consequent influx of labour or of capital bringing things to a level. Had economists, however, in place of reasoning from an assumption, examined the facts connected with the rate of wages, they would have found, from authentic statistics, the actual differences so great, even in the same occupation, that they are double in one place what they are in another. Statistics of profits are not, indeed, obtainable like statistics of wages; and the fact that they are not so, that the actual profits are kept a profound secret in some of the most prominent trades, is itself enough to deprive the theory of equal profits of its base. Enough, however, is known or discovered from time to time, by the working men in particular trades, to justify them in the conclusion, on the one hand, that profits will bear a reduction, and that wages may consequently receive an augmentation; and, on the other hand, that competition has not produced, and will not produce, those results. When, therefore, Mr. Forster assumes that the majority of working men are now disposed to admit, as fundamental truths of economic science, that the remuneration of labour can be raised only in three ways—by the increase of capital, the diminution of the whole labouring population, or the participation of labourers in capital—we are reminded that not a few working men in certain trades believe there is another mode by which their remuneration might be raised, namely, by a participation in profits, which are enormously high; and that they believe, too, that this participation can be secured only by combination, not by competition. Not quite consistently with his own statement, that one of the methods by which wages may be raised is a diminution of population, Mr. Forster pointed to the increase in the population of England and Wales from 16½ millions in 1831 to 21½ millions in 1871, simultaneously with an increase of general prosperity, as militating against the theory of population advocated by Malthus and Mr. Mill, and the necessity those great writers contended for, of a prudential check to the potential rate of births. An unrestrained potential increase would have doubled the 16½ millions about 1856; at the present time there would, at the same rate, be about 50 millions of people in England and Wales; and, before the end of the century, the population of that part of the United Kingdom would exceed 100 millions. Either, therefore, the prudential check has been firmly opposed by some classes of the population to the potential increase, and has permitted that increase of prosperity which Mr. Forster assumes; or other checks, in the shape of death and infirmity, have acted instead of the prudential check, and demonstrated the urgent necessity for it. Another point, in connexion with wages, on which Mr. Forster's reasoning seems to need some explanation, relates to the agricultural labourers. He seems to throw out an opinion that there is yet another source, besides those which have been named, from which the wages of labour may be raised, namely, rent; but his language on the subject leaves much to be desired, to use a Gallicism, on the head of clearness. He says it is well there is here 'a third class, namely, the landlords, who are able to enter into the question, and to act as mediators.' But then he adds that a Paper might well be devoted in the Section to the question, how far the rent paid for land affects the question of wages. The innuendo would appear to be that an increase of rural wages may be brought about by an abatement of rent; and we fail to see how that prospect places the landlords in a position to qualify them for the position of impartial mediators between farmers and men. Another important subject discussed in the Section, the treatment of which was not exhaustive in respect of either the economic or the statistical methods employed, was that of prices, and the rise in the cost of living. Mr. Levi took the prices of the Metropolitan Meat Market for his measure with respect to that article, adding, indeed, the expression of an opinion, that the rise has been greater in the chief towns than in other parts of the kingdom. The fact is, that the diffusion of steam communication in the last twenty-five years has raised the price of meat in country places and remote parts of the kingdom much more than in the chief towns, because it has raised it from a much lower point in the former to something like the same price as in the latter localities. In many parts of Ireland and Scotland, where, thirty years ago, the price of butcher's meat averaged 3*d*. a pound, it is now not much below the London price; and this equalization of prices, where the means of communication have been equalized, is connected with the distribution of money over the world, in a manner very necessary to be borne in mind in estimate both of past and probable future changes in the cost of living. The prices of the Metropolitan Meat

Market afford, for another reason, insufficient indications of what has actually taken place in respect of the purchasing power of money. The price of mutton per pound in that market has risen from 6·37, in 1863–7, to 7·62, in 1873. But in the same period the price of a mutton chop in a London railway refreshment-room has risen from 6*d.* to 1*s.*; and, in fact, the rise in retail prices, on which the cost of living really depends, is more accurately indicated by the latter figures than by those which Mr. Levi has cited. It is obvious, too, that the rise in wages is to a very large class, who have to pay servants' wages—an addition, and not a counterpoise, to the increased cost of living arising from the rise of commodities. Mr. Levi, we might add, seems to have caused some confusion of ideas, if he did not fall into it himself, with respect to the effect on the price of necessaries and ordinary comforts of an increased expenditure on luxuries. The consumption of better qualities of food and clothing would naturally tend to raise the cost of the particular articles on which the increased outlay took place. But an increased expenditure on luxuries, such as seal-skin jackets, carriages, wine, tobacco, would, *cæteris paribus*, diminish the outlay on other things, and would tend to a corresponding fall in the prices of the latter. Had we, however, much fuller statistics than are forthcoming respecting the changes in prices throughout the United Kingdom, we should still be unable to form a sound judgment respecting the most important part of the question, namely, the probable future range of prices, without a mass of additional information respecting the causes which have acted on the supply of each article, and on the distribution of money as well as on its amount. And we have in this matter an illustration of the defective character of that kind of statistical inquiry which confines itself to the collection of a multitude of instances of facts, without reference to causes. It must be allowed that the principles laid down by the illustrious Quetelet rather tend to foster the error to which we advert. He assumed that by enlarging the number of instances we eliminate chance, and arrive at general and stable laws or conditions. But a great number of instances does not give us their law, or justify us in any positive conclusion respecting the future. New conditions, for example, have been acting on prices during the last two years, and mere tables of prices for the last twenty or ten years confound years in which those causes were in operation with years in which they were not.

We cannot close these few remarks and suggestions without thanking Mr. Forster, the eminent President of Section F, for the just, but not the less generous, tribute which he paid to the great leader of economic science, whom the world has lately lost in Mr. John Stuart Mill.

XV.

ON THE PHILOSOPHICAL METHOD OF POLITICAL ECONOMY.*

Adam Smith called his famous treatise an inquiry into the nature and causes of the wealth of nations. Mr. Senior defines political economy as the science which treats of the nature, the production, and the distribution of wealth. The definition in Mr. Mill's 'Principles of Political Economy' is similar, though broader: 'Writers on political economy profess to teach or to investigate the nature of wealth and the laws of its production and distribution, including, directly or remotely, the operation of all the causes by which the condition of mankind, or of any society of human beings in respect to this universal object of desire, is made prosperous, or the reverse.'

These definitions sufficiently indicate the character of the problem of political economy, namely, to investigate the nature, the amount, and the distribution of wealth in human society, and the laws of co-existence and sequence discoverable in this class of social phenomena. The solution offered by the method hitherto chiefly followed by English economists—known as the abstract, *a priori*, and deductive method—may be briefly stated as follows:—The nature of wealth is explained by defining it as comprising all things which are objects of human desire, limited in supply, and valuable in exchange. Of the causes governing its amount and distribution, the chief exposition is, that the desire of wealth naturally leads, where security and liberty exist, to labour, accumulation of capital, appropriation of land, separation of employments, commerce,

* *Hermathena*, vol. ii., 1876.

and the use of money; whence a continual increase in the total stock of wealth, and its distribution in wages, profit, rent, and the prices of products, in proportion to the labour, sacrifice, amount of capital, and quantity and quality of land, contributed by each individual to production. It is added that, inasmuch as human fecundity tends to augment population in a geometrical ratio, while the productiveness of the soil is limited, the proportion of rent to wages and profit tends to increase in the progress of society.

This theory, it is here submitted, is illusory, as a solution of the problem. It throws, in the first place, hardly any light on the nature of wealth. There is a multitude of different kinds of wealth, differing widely in their economic effects. Land, houses, furniture, clothing, implements, arms, ornaments, animals, corn, wine, money, pictures, statues, books, are but a few of the different kinds of wealth; and of each kind there are various species. No inconsiderable part of the present wealth of the United Kingdom consists of intoxicating drink. Wealth, moreover, undergoes great changes in kind in different states of society, and one of the most important features of economical history is the evolution of new kinds, profoundly affecting the material as well as the moral condition of nations. The wealth of Rome under the Cæsars differed from its wealth in the first age of the Republic, in quality as well as quantity; and there are essential differences, as well as resemblances and historical relations, between the constituents of mediæval and modern wealth. Some of the fundamental distinctions between Oriental and European wealth have been vividly brought before us in the last few months. One of these is, that the movable wealth of rich men in the East consists chiefly of precious stones, gold and silver ornaments, and splendid apparel. An English writer long ago described a religious ceremony in Turkey, at which a prince of eleven years old 'was so overloaded with jewels, both on himself and his horse, that one might say that he carried the value of an empire about him.' That is to say, the wealth that might have made a territory prosperous, and been distributed in wages through many hundreds of families, was concentrated on the bodies of a child and a horse. The correspondent of the 'Times' recently remarked on the appearance of the officers of an Indian municipality: 'It would have rather astonished the members of an English town council to have seen these Punjabees in turbans of the finest tissue, gold-brocaded gowns and robes, with coils of emeralds, rubies, and pearls round their necks finer than any Lord Mayor's chain.' This allusion to the surviving finery of English official dress illustrates a change which has taken place since the French Revolution in the ordinary dress of men in Western Europe. Another description of a reception of native chiefs at Calcutta a few months ago seems to give indication of the beginning of a similar change in India. While one Maharajah, 'dressed in black satin and silver lace, wore a cap which was literally covered with diamonds, said to be worth £100,000,' and another was 'resplendent in a dress of mauve, embroidered with gold,' Holkar and Sir Salar Jung 'presented a striking contrast from the extreme simplicity of their attire.' It is no unimportant example of the mutation in the nature of wealth, in the progress of society, that diversities exist in Western Europe, in respect of splendour and costliness of apparel, between masculine and feminine wealth, which did not manifest themselves conspicuously before the present century. The accounts of the dresses of the princes and nobles of India, during the Prince's visit, read like one of the dresses of a number of great ladies at a London ball; but even in England the fashion of wearing silks, satins, velvets, diamonds, and jewels, was formerly not confined to one sex. There was a time when men 'wore a manor on their backs.' The remark of Addison in the 'Spectator' that 'one may observe that women in all ages have taken more pains than men to adorn the outside of their heads' is inaccurate. An Eastern prince still sometimes wears precious stones on his turban to the value of half a million; and probably no lady ever wore such a weight of diamonds as the Shah of Persia displayed in London. It is at least conceivable that the attire of an English lady may one day rival in simplicity and inexpensiveness that of a gentleman. The wealth of all but the stationary part of mankind of both sexes undergoes various changes in the nature as well as in the number of its constituents; and the differences and changes in the character of Eastern and Western, mediæval and modern, masculine and feminine wealth, of which some indications have been given, ought surely to meet with investigation, as regards both cause and effect, in a true Science of Wealth. The definition already referred to, that wealth comprehends all things which possess exchangeable value, is a mere abstraction throwing no light on these differences and mutations, or on the laws of society and social evolution by which they are governed. It originated in opposition to the Mercantile theory, and amounts in fact to little more than a negation of the doctrine, erroneously imputed to the Mercantile School, that money only is wealth. What that school really taught was that money is the most durable and generally useful kind of movable wealth, and their chief error lay in the measures by which they sought artificially to increase its amount. Money really had acquired great additional usefulness by its substitution for barter and payments in kind, and by the extension of international trade; and money is one of the kinds of wealth the invention and variations of which form a most instructive chapter in economical history. Adam Smith, it should be observed, did not fall into the error of later antagonists to the Mercantile theory. His doctrine was that wealth consists chiefly, not in money, but in consumable commodities; in the necessaries, conveniences, and luxuries of life. Although he did not systematically investigate the subject, he has in several passages indicated important differences in the economic effects of different sorts of wealth, and pointed out some essential changes which have taken place in its component elements, in the progress of society.

Closely connected with the illusory exposition of the nature of wealth to which attention has been drawn is the doctrine of abstract political economy, that the mental principle which leads to its production and accumulation 'is the desire of wealth.' No other branch of philosophy is still so deeply tinctured with the realism of the schools as economic science.

A host of different things resemble each other in a single aspect, and a common name is given to them in reference to the single feature which they have in common. It is, properly speaking, only an indication of this common feature, but it puts their essential differences out of mind, and they come to be thought of in the lump as one sort of thing. The desire of wealth is a general name for a great variety of wants, desires, and sentiments, widely differing in their economical character and effect, undergoing fundamental changes in some respects, while preserving an historical continuity in others. Moralists have fallen into a similar error, though from an opposite point of view, and, in their horror of an abstraction, have denounced, under the common name of love of wealth, the love of life, health, cleanliness, decency, knowledge, and art, along with sensuality, avarice, and vanity. So all the needs, appetites, passions, tastes, aims, and ideas which the various things comprehended in the word 'wealth' satisfy, are lumped together in political economy as a principle of human nature, which is the source of industry and the moving principle of the economic world.* 'That every man desires to obtain additional wealth, with as little sacrifice as possible, is in political economy,' says Mr. Senior, 'what gravitation is in Physics, or the *dictum de omni et nullo* in Logic, the ultimate fact beyond which reasoning cannot go, and of which almost every other proposition is merely an illustration.' The division of labour, the process of exchange, and the intervention of money, have made abstract wealth or money appear to be the motive to production, and veiled the truth that the real motives are the wants and desires of consumers; the demands of consumers determining the commodities supplied by producers. After all the reproach cast on the Mercantile School, modern economists have themselves lapsed into the error they have imputed to it. If every man produced for himself what he desires to use or possess, it would be patent and palpable how diverse are the motives summed up

* Many years ago I endeavoured to draw attention to the error of both economists and moralists on this subject, in an Essay on the Love of Money, reprinted at the beginning of the present volume.

in the phrase 'desire for wealth'—motives which vary in different individuals, different classes, different nations, different sexes, and different states of society. Hunger and thirst were the first forms of the desire of wealth. A desire for cattle is its principal form at the next social stage. A desire for land comes into existence with agriculture; but the desire for land is itself a name for different feelings, aims, and associations, in different ages, countries, classes, and individuals, producing at this day widely different effects in two countries so close to each other as England and France. Adam Smith's historical and inductive mind here again preserved him from the realistic error. He has even attempted to indicate the actual order in which the desires of wealth succeed one another in the progress of history; and although his generalizations on this point are scanty and inaccurate, they ought to have suggested a fruitful line of investigation to his followers, and doubtless would have done so but for the dominion over their minds which the abstract method acquired. His illustrious successor, John Stuart Mill, has indeed made some instructive observations on the point in the Preliminary Remarks of his 'Principles of Political Economy,' but he had been brought up in the straitest sect of the abstract economists, and his method was formed before his mind was matured; so that there is no systematic application of historical and inductive investigation in his treatise, although it abounds in luminous suggestions, and corrections of the crude generalizations of the school in which he was taught. An investigation of the diverse and varying desires confounded in the phrase 'desire of wealth' would be requisite, were we even, with some of that school, to regard Political Economy as a mere theory of exchanges and value. For the value of commodities rises and falls with changes in the degree and direction of these desires. Both in England and France, the love of land, for example, raises its price out of proportion to the income it yields; but this may not always be, as it has not always been, the case; or, on the contrary, it may display itself hereafter in increased price. At this day it is a national passion in France, but felt only by a limited number in England. Works of art, again, undergo extraordinary variations in value with the currents of fashion and taste; and diamonds would lose almost all their value were the indifference towards them, already felt by one sex in this country, to extend to the other, and to become general throughout the world.

It is true that a love of accumulation or of property, an acquisitive propensity, a desire for wealth apart from its immediate or particular uses, is a principle of social growth of which the economist must take account. But this principle opens up another neglected chapter in the science of wealth, for the love of property, or of accumulation, takes very different concrete forms in different states of society. Were there no division of labour, it would take forms—land, cattle, houses, furniture, clothing, jewels, &c.—determined by the existing or anticipated wants of the accumulator himself, or his family. In the actual commercial world in which we live its forms are determined, either by the wants and demands of other consumers, or the accumulator's own desires, anticipations, and associations. The holder of a share in a mine may never see his investment, and may have no desire for the coal, iron, or silver it contains, yet the form of his accumulation is determined by the demand for these particular kinds of wealth on the part of surrounding society.

The questions we have been discussing are immediately connected with the conditions which govern the amount of wealth. The abstract theory on this subject is of the most fragmentary character. It exists only in the form of a few propositions and doctrines, such as that, under the influence of the desire of wealth, human energy and effort are constantly devoted to its acquisition; that its amount is largely augmented by the division of labour; that of the three great instruments of production, the supply of two—labour and capital—tends to increase, but that of the third—land—remains stationary, while its productiveness tends to decrease with the growth of population; that wealth is increased by productive and diminished by unproductive expenditure and consumption. The first of these propositions really throws as little light on the amount as on the nature of wealth. The desire for it is by no means necessarily an incentive to industry, and still less to abstinence. War, conquest, plunder, piracy, theft, fraud, are all modes of acquisition to which it leads. The robber baron in the reign of Stephen, and the merchant and the Jew whom he tortured, may have been influenced by the same motives. The prodigal son who wastes his substance in riotous living is influenced by the same motives—the love of sport, sensual pleasure, luxury, and ostentatious display—which impel many other men to strenuous exertion in business. Good cheer, meat, beer, and tobacco, are the chief inducements to labour with the majority of working men, and to beggary and crime with another part of the population. Unproductive expenditure and consumption, on the other hand, do not necessarily tend to diminish wealth. They are the ultimate incentives to all production, and without habits of considerable superfluous expenditure, as Mr. Senior himself has observed, a nation would be reduced to destitution. Moreover, the effect of expenditure on the amount of wealth depends on the direction which it takes, for example, whether of services and perishable commodities, or, on the contrary, of durable articles. Here, once more, Adam Smith opened the way to a line of investigation which abstract political economy afterwards closed. He observed that a man of fortune may spend his revenue, either in a profuse and sumptuous table, or in maintaining a great number of menial servants and a multitude of dogs and horses, or in fine clothes, or in jewels and baubles; or, again, in useful and ornamental buildings, furniture, books, statues, pictures. 'Were two men of equal fortune to spend their revenue, the one chiefly in the one way, the other in the other, the former would, at the end of the period, be the richer man of the two: he would have a stock of goods of some kind or other. As the one mode of expense is more favourable than the other to the opulence of an individual, so is it likewise to that of a nation. The houses, the furniture, the clothing of the rich become useful to the inferior and middling ranks of the people.' Consumption and expenditure in abstract political economy have become misleading terms.

Both have come to denote the using up and destruction of things, whereas expenditure properly denotes simply the purchase, and consumption simply the use, of the article in question. If the things purchased be of a durable kind, unproductive consumption so called may amount in reality to a form of accumulation. It was, in fact, one of the chief forms down to recent times. In the fifteenth century, and long afterwards, one of the chief modes of laying by for a man's wife and family was the purchase of plate, furniture, household stuff, and even clothing. Some modes of expenditure, although intended simply as such, may be actually productive, as in the case of articles which, like rare works of art, or lands for purposes of enjoyment and amusement, acquire increased value with time and the growth of surrounding wealth. Even a stock of wine in a private cellar may, on the death of the owner, prove to have been a good investment for his family. The main questions respecting the influence alike of the 'desire of wealth' and of expenditure and consumption are: To what kinds of wealth, what modes of acquisition, and what actual uses do they lead in different states of society, and under different institutions, and other surrounding conditions? To what laws of social evolution are they subject in the foregoing respects? On these points we learn nothing from abstract political economy. A distinguished English economist and man of science has lately admitted, in the following passage, the absolute necessity for a true theory of consumption: 'We, first of all, need a theory of the consumption of wealth. J. S. Mill, indeed, has given an opinion inconsistent with this. "Political economy," he says, "has nothing to do with the consumption of wealth, further than as the consideration of it is inseparable from that of production, as from that of distribution. We know not of any laws of the consumption of wealth, as the subject of a distinct science; they can be no other than the laws of human enjoyment." But it is surely obvious that economics does rest upon the laws of human enjoyment, and that if those laws are developed by no other science, they must be developed by economists. We labour to produce with the sole object of consuming, and the kinds and amounts of goods produced must be determined with regard to what we want to consume. Every manufacturer knows and feels how closely he must anticipate the tastes and needs of his customers : his whole success depends upon it, and in like manner the theory of economics must begin with a correct theory of consumption.' * No such theory, however, respecting the effect of consumption on either the nature or the amount of wealth, can be forthcoming without a study of the history and the entire structure of society, and the laws which they disclose.

But further, in order to form any approach to an adequate estimate of the influence of human desires on the amount of wealth, it must surely be evident that we need an investigation, not only of the motives and impulses which prompt to the acquisition of wealth, but also of those which withdraw men from its pursuit, or give other directions to their energies. What abstract political economy has to teach on this subject is stated by Mr. Mill in his Essay on the Definition and Method of Political Economy, and also in his Logic, as follows:—

'Political economy is concerned with man solely as a being who desires to possess wealth. It makes entire abstraction of every other human passion or motive, except those which may be regarded as perpetually antagonizing principles to the desire of wealth, namely, aversion to labour, and desire of the present enjoyment of earthly indulgences. These it takes to a certain extent into its calculation, because these do not merely, like other desires, occasionally conflict with the pursuit of wealth, but accompany it always as a drag or impediment, and are therefore inseparably mixed up in the consideration of it.' Abstraction has here clouded the reasoning of the most celebrated logician of the century. Had Mr. Mill looked to actual life, he must have at once perceived that among the strongest desires confounded in the abstract 'desire of wealth' are desires for the present enjoyment of luxuries; and that the aversion to labour itself has been one of the principal causes of inventions and

* *The Theory of Political Economy.* By William Stanley Jevons. 2nd ed., pp. 42, 43.

improvements which abridge it. Frugality, as Adam Smith has observed, has never been a characteristic virtue of the inhabitants of England; commodities for immediate consumption and luxuries have always been the chief motives to exertion on the part of the bulk of the English population. The love of ease is the motive which has led to the production of a great part of household furniture, and is one of the chief sources of architecture.

'A great part of the machines,' says Adam Smith, 'made use of in those manufactures in which labour is most subdivided, were originally the inventions of common workmen, who naturally turned their thoughts towards finding out easier and readier methods of performing it. . . . One of the greatest improvements (in the steam engine) was the discovery of a boy who wanted to save his own labour.' By what logical principle, moreover, can economists justify the admission of 'two antagonizing principles' into their theory while excluding or ignoring others? In fact, no economist has ever been able to limit his exposition in this manner. Mr. Mill, in his own 'Principles of Political Economy,' follows Adam Smith in including in his doctrine of the causes which govern the choice of occupations and the rates of wages and profits, many other motives, such as the love of distinction, of power, of rural life, of certain pursuits for their own sake, of our own country, the consequent indisposition to emigrate, &c.

The real defect of the treatment by economists of these other principles is, that it is superficial and unphilosophical; that no attempt has been made even to enumerate them adequately, much less to measure their relative force in different states of society; and that they are employed simply to prop up rude generalizations for which the authority of 'laws' is claimed. They serve, along with other conditions, to give some sort of support to saving clauses—such as 'allowing for differences in the nature of different employments,' '*cæteris paribus*,' 'in the absence of disturbing causes,' 'making allowance for friction'—by which the 'law' that wages and profits tend to equality eludes scrutiny. Had the actual operation of the motives in question been investigated, it would have been seen to vary widely in different states of society, and under different conditions. The love of distinction or social position, for example, may either counteract the desires of wealth, or greatly add to their force as a motive to industry and accumulation. It may lead one man to make a fortune, another to spend it. At the head of the inquiry into the causes on which the amount of the wealth of nations depends is the problem, What are the conditions which direct the energies and determine the actual occupations and pursuits of mankind in different ages and countries? A theory surely cannot be said to interpret the laws regulating the amount of wealth which takes no account, for instance, either of the causes that make arms the occupation of the best part of the male population of Europe at this day, or, on the other hand, of those which determine the employments of women.

Enough has been said in proof that the abstract *a priori* and deductive method yields no explanation of the causes which regulate either the nature or the amount of wealth. With respect to distribution, it furnishes only a theory of exchange (or of wages, profits, prices, and rent), which will be hereafter examined. The point calling for immediate attention is, that such a theory, even if true, must be altogether inadequate to explain the distribution of wealth. One has but to think of the different partition of land in England and France, of the different partition of real and personal property in England, of the different partition of both between the two sexes, of the influence of the State, the Church, the Family, of marriage and succession, to see its utter inadequacy. Take land, for example. Sir Henry Maine has justly observed that exchange lies historically at the source of its present distribution in England to a greater extent than most modern writers on the subject seem aware. The purchase and sale of land was active, both in the Middle Ages and in the age of the Reformation; and the original root of the title of the existing holder, in a vast number of cases, is a purchase either in those ages or since. But it is only by historical investigation that we can mount up in this manner to purchase; and the present distribution of land, descending from such a source, is none the less the result of another set of causes, among which that great historical institution, the Family, which has never ceased to be one of the chief factors in the economy of human society, holds a principal place.

The truth is, that the whole economy of every nation, as regards the occupations and pursuits of both sexes, the nature, amount, distribution, and consumption of wealth, is the result of a long evolution, in which there has been both continuity and change, and of which the economical side is only a particular aspect or phase. And the laws of which it is the result must be sought in history and the general laws of society and social evolution.

The succession of the hunting, pastoral, agricultural, and commercial states is commonly referred to as an economic development; but it is, in fact, a social evolution, the economical side of which is indissolubly connected with its moral, intellectual, and political sides. To each of these successive states there is a corresponding moral and intellectual condition with a corresponding polity. With the changes from savage hunting life to that of the nomad tribe, thence to fixed habitations and the cultivation of the soil, and thence to the rise of trade and towns, there are changes in feelings, desires, morals, thought and knowledge, in domestic and civil relations, and in institutions and customs, which show themselves in the economic structure of the community, and the nature, amount, and distribution of its wealth.

The celebrated German economist, Wilhelm Roscher, has remarked that every economical system has a corresponding legal system as its background; but the more general proposition may be advanced that every successive phase of social progress presents inseparably connected phenomena to the observation of the economist, the jurist, the mental, the moral, and the political philosopher. The same institutions—marriage, the Family, landed property, for example—may be regarded from a moral, a legal, a political, or an economical point of view.

Both an intellectual and a moral evolution is visible in the successive modes of satisfying human wants—by hunting and cannibalism; by the domestication of animals, with slavery instead of the slaughter of captured enemies; by agriculture, with serfdom gradually superseding slavery; and by free industry and commerce, instead of conquest and piracy. And it may be affirmed that the means by which wealth is acquired in successive states of society are subject to regular laws of social evolution, as a whole, although only in the earlier stages is their operation easily traced. Slavery would exist in England at this day but for the co-operation of moral and political, with what are specially termed economical, causes. The successive evolution of the hunting, pastoral, agricultural and commercial states is intimately connected with 'the movement from status to contract,' to employ Sir Henry Maine's appropriate formula; one which affords striking evidence of the indissoluble nature of the connexion between the moral, intellectual, legal, political and economical phases of social progress. Sir H. Maine has considered it chiefly in its legal aspects, but it is easily shown to involve the other aspects referred to. To that primitive state in which there are no individual rights, in which the legal position of every one—law then appearing in the embryo form of usage—is determined by blood, birth, and sex, there is a corresponding polity, that is to say, a rude tribal organization, not without analogy to that of a herd of wild animals; and there is a correlative economic structure, limiting individual possession to certain articles of personal use, recognising no property in land, making sex and age the sole basis of division of labour, and leading to no exchanges between individuals. The moral condition is of a corresponding type. Communism in women is one of its original features; another is an entire absence of the feeling of individual responsibility. Tribes and groups of kinsfolk collectively are responsible for offences.

The intellectual state is strictly analogous. There is no mental individuality, no originality, or invention; all think as well as act and live alike. The savage is a savage in his intellectual development and ideas, as in his morals, his institutions, and his economy. The movement from status to contract, on the other hand, evolves not only individual property from communal ownership, and rights based on individual agreement from the transactions of whole communities of families, but also individual responsibility and individuality of thought and invention. It is likewise inseparably connected with a political development, with the gradual growth of a central government, and the substitution of the control of the State for that of the family or kindred. Every institution relating to property, occupation and trade, evolved by this movement, is an economic as much as a legal phenomenon. Changes in the law of succession, the growth of the testamentary power, the alienability of land, its liability for debt, are economical, as well as juridical facts; they involve changes in the economical structure of society, and in the amount and distribution of wealth. And every successive intellectual discovery, every new employment of the mental energy, has its part in determining the economical condition of the nation. *A priori* political economy has sought to deduce the laws which govern the directions of human energies, the division of employments, the modes of production, and the nature, amount, and distribution of wealth, from an assumption respecting the course of conduct prompted by individual interest; but the conclusion which the study of society makes every day more irresistible is, that the germ from which the existing economy of every nation has been evolved is not the individual, still less the mere personification of an abstraction, but the primitive community—a community one in blood, property, thought, moral responsibility, and manner of life; and that individual interest itself, and the desires, aims, and pursuits of every man and woman in the nation have been moulded by, and received their direction and form from, the history of that community.

Both the desires of which wealth of different kinds is the object, and those which compete with them, are in every nation the results of its historical career and state of civilization.

What are called economical forces are not only connected, but identical, with forces which are also moral and intellectual. The desires which govern the production, accumulation, distribution, and consumption of wealth are passions, appetites, affections, moral and religious sentiments, family feelings, æsthetical tastes, and intellectual wants. The changes which Roman wealth underwent after the conquest of Asia Minor represent moral changes; the new desires of wealth which became dominant were gluttony, sensuality, cruelty, and ostentation. These moral changes, again, were inseparably connected with the political history of Rome, and they had intellectual aspects which the author of the 'Dialogus de Oratoribus' has vividly portrayed. Allusion was made in an earlier page to the passion for jewels which distinguishes the men of the East from the men of the West, and this form of the desire of wealth has sprung mainly from the absence for many ages of the conditions essential to general prosperity, economic progress, and the accumulation of wealth in really useful forms. Where insecurity has long prevailed, not only are those aims and distinctions which take the place, with the growth of civilization, of personal display, prevented from emerging, but a desire is generated for the kinds of wealth which contain great value in a durable and portable form, and are easily hidden, easily removed in flight, and nothing the worse for being buried for months or years. The wealth of England at this day, it should be observed, although dissimilar in some essential respects to that of Asia, ancient Rome, and mediæval Europe, displays also features of resemblance, alike to oriental, to classical, and to mediæval wealth—for example, in architecture, both ecclesiastical and civil, in the structure of landed property and the associations surrounding it, and in the surviving passion in women for jewellery—which are, in fact, historical features. Our wealth is historical wealth, has been made what it is by historical causes, and preserves visible traces of its history. How long a history lies behind the feelings with which land is regarded, and its price in the market, as well as behind its existing distribution! Our whole national economy is a historical structure, and in no other manner to be explained or accounted for.

Recent apologists for the *a priori* and abstract method of economic reasoning feel themselves constrained to confine its application to the most advanced stage of commercial society; they seem even prepared to concede its inapplicability to every country save England, and to confine it to the latest development of English economy. The position which they take up seems to be, that the social evolution, already referred to as a movement from status to contract, issues in an economy to which the assumptions and deductions of abstract theory respecting the tendencies of individual interest fit. In modern England, they say, there is such a commercial pursuit of gain, and such a consequent choice of occupations, as to effect a distribution of the produce of industry to which the doctrines of Ricardo respecting wages, profits, prices, and rents may be fairly applied. They thus abandon at once the claim formerly made on behalf of political economy to the character of a universal science founded on invariable laws of nature. 'Political Economy,' said Mr. Lowe only six years ago, 'belongs to no nation; it is of no country: it is founded on the attributes of the human mind, and no power can change it.' It is now restricted by Mr. Bagehot to 'a single kind of society—a society of grown-up competitive commerce, such as we have in England.'* The economic society which we behold in England, and which is the result of the social evolution referred to, is, however, one which displays on every side the influence of tradition, custom, law, political institutions, religion and moral sentiment; it is one in which the State, the Family, and even the Church, are powerful elements directly and indirectly, and in which the pursuits of individuals, the nature and value of different kinds of wealth, the structure of trades and professions, are incapable of explanation apart from history. It is one in which, as Mr. Bagehot himself has remarked, 'there are city families, and university and legal

* *Economic Studies*, p. 17

families—families where a special kind of taste and knowledge are passed on in each generation by tradition'; and in which the system even of banking and the money market is the product of a peculiar history. Not even looking exclusively to the purely commercial side of the English economical structure; not even as a mere analysis of 'business' or 'commerce,' in the narrowest sense, is the abstract theory which used to claim rank as a Science of Wealth able to hold its ground. It is, in fact, as inapplicable to the most advanced stage of commerce as to that primitive state of nature from which Ricardo deduced it by a process which deserves a high place in the history of fallacies, and which was not present to Mr. Mill's mind when arguing that 'no political economists pretend that the laws of wages, profits, values, prices, and the like, set down in their treatises would be strictly true, or many of them true at all, in the savage state.'* The principal foundation of Ricardo's theory of value, prices, wages, and profits, is the assumption that 'in the early stage of society the exchangeable value of commodities depends almost exclusively on the comparative quantity of labour expended on each. Among a nation of hunters, for example, it is natural that what is usually the produce of two days', or two hours', labour should be worth double of what is usually the produce of one day's or one hour's labour.'† The minor premiss in his syllogism is the assumption that it is 'natural' that in a tribe of savages things should exchange in proportion to the labour required to produce them; the major premiss is, that what is natural in the earliest must be natural in the most advanced state of society. The minor involves a *petitio principii*, and one entirely at variance with fact, for savages work only by fits, and have no measures of labour and sacrifice. The produce of the chase is determined largely by chance. Such exchanges as take place are of the

---

* *Auguste Comte and Positivism.* By J. S. Mill, p. 81.

† 'That this is really the foundation of the exchangeable value of all things, he continues, 'excepting those which cannot be increased by human industry, is a doctrine of the utmost importance in Political Economy.'—*Ricardo's Works*, Ed. M'Culloch, p. 10.

special products of different localities, and between groups or communities, not individuals. If any exchanges took place between individuals within the community, they would obviously be governed, not by cost of production, but like the exchange between Esau and Jacob, by the urgency of the respective needs of the parties. The major premiss, on the other hand, involves the fallacy of undistributed middle, the two states of society being entirely dissimilar. Thrown into a form less unfavourable to Ricardo's conclusion than the one he has himself given to it, his argument is, that in a small and stationary community—in which employments are few and simple, and every man knows all his neighbours' affairs, how much they make, how they make it, and can transfer himself to any more gainful employment than his own—the values of commodities and the earnings of individuals depend on labour and sacrifice; and therefore, in a great commercial nation in which there is an infinite subdivision of labour, an immense and ever-increasing variety of occupations, incessant change in the modes of production and in the channels of trade, constant fluctuations in speculation, credit and values, and in which each man has enough to do to mind his own business—wages, profits, and prices, and the distribution of the gains of production, are determined by the same principle, namely, the labour and sacrifice undergone by producers. It is the conclusion thus arrived at by Ricardo which Mr. Bagehot sets forth as the first fundamental assumption of abstract political economy, applied to advanced commercial society, though with an exception with respect to one sex which illustrates its essential weakness. 'The assumption,' he says, 'which I shall take is that which is perhaps oftener made in our economical reasonings than any other, namely, that labour (masculine labour, I mean) and capital circulate within the limits of a nation from employment to employment, leaving that in which the remuneration is smaller, and going to that in which it is greater. No assumption can be better founded, as respects such a country as England, in such an economical state as our present one.' It is an assumption equally ill-founded with respect to both the extremes of economical progress, the earliest and the most advanced;—to the former, because there is no regular labour, no calculation of gain, and no exchange between individuals; to the second, because each of a vast multiplicity of occupations needs unremitting attention, and exchanges are infinitely numerous, and subject to perpetual variations in the conditions affecting them. Ricardo ignored both the homogeneousness of primitive, and the heterogeneousness of advanced, society; Mr. Bagehot ignores the infinite heterogeneousness of the latter. The assumption really made its only approach to truth in the intermediate economical stage to which Adam Smith expressly limited it, when he restricted it to well-known and long-established employments, in the same neighbourhood, undisturbed by speculation or other causes of fluctuation, and between which there is perfect facility of migration*—in other words, to a small and stationary world of trade. Consider the complexity of the causes which, in the modern commercial world, affect the price of a single commodity, and judge of the possibility of estimating the relative profit to be made by the manufacture and sale of every article. The following passage, written by one of the most eminent living philosophers, with no reference to political economy, will enable the reader to form some conception of the demand which the abstract economic assumption makes on his faith:—'The extreme complexity of social actions, and the transcendent difficulty which hence arises, of counting on special results, will be still better seen if we enumerate the factors which determine one single phenomenon, the price of a commodity—say cotton. A manufacturer of calicoes has to decide whether he will increase his stock of raw material, at its current price. Before doing this, he must ascertain, as well as he can, the following data:—Whether the stocks of calicoes in

---

* In order that this equality may take place in the whole of the advantages and disadvantages of the different employments of labour and stock, three things are requisite, even where there is the most perfect freedom. First, the employments must be well known and long established in the neighbourhood; secondly, they must be in their ordinary or natural state; and thirdly, they must be the sole or principal employments of those who occupy them.—*Wealth of Nations*, Book i., c. 10.

the hands of manufacturers and wholesalers at home are large or small; whether by recent prices retailers have been led to lay in stocks or not; whether the colonial and foreign markets are glutted or otherwise; and what is now, and is likely to be, the production of calico by foreign manufacturers. Having formed some idea of the probable demand for calico, he has to ask what other manufacturers have done and are doing as buyers of cotton—whether they have been waiting for the price to fall, or have been buying in anticipation of a rise. From cotton-brokers' circulars he has to judge what is the state of speculation at Liverpool—whether the stocks there are large or small, and whether many or few cargoes are on their way. The stocks and prices at New Orleans and other cotton ports have also to be taken note of; and then there come questions respecting forthcoming crops in the States, in India, in Egypt, and elsewhere. Here are sufficiently numerous factors; but these are by no means all. The consumption of calico, and therefore the consumption of cotton, and the price, depend in part on the supplies and prices of other textile products. . . . Surely the factors are now all enumerated? By no means. There is the estimate of mercantile opinion. The views of buyers and sellers respecting future prices, never more than approximations to the truth, often diverge from it widely. . . . Nor has he got to the end of the matter when he has considered all these things. He has still to ask, what are the general mercantile conditions of the country, and what the immediate future of the money market will be, since the course of speculation in every commodity must be affected by the rate of discount. See, then, the enormous complication of causes which determine so simple a thing as the rise or fall of a farthing per pound in cotton some months hence.'* To admit the assumption on which the abstract doctrine of the equality of profits rests—and on which, again, the doctrine of indirect taxation is based—one must be prepared to admit that men in business are able to make, and do make, similar calculations respecting every other commodity,

* *The Study of Sociology.* By Herbert Spencer, pp. 18–19.

and thus are enabled to estimate the relative profits of different businesses.

The only verification adduced in support of the assumption is, that capital and labour desert employments known to be comparatively unremunerative for those which are known to yield better returns. Even this proposition is far from being universally true, and, if it proved the conclusion, would prove that the migration of labour from Europe to America must long ago have equalized European and American wages. Mr. Mill, in stating the doctrine, has granted that individual profits depend, among other things, 'on the accidents of personal connexion, and even on chance,' adding, 'that equal capitals give equal profits, as a general maxim of trade, would be as false as that equal age or size gives equal bodily strength, or that equal reading or experience gives equal knowledge.' He supposed, however, that bankers and other dealers in money, by lending it to the more profitable trades, put the various employments of capital 'on such a footing as to hold out, not equal profits, but equal expectations of profit.' In like manner, Mr. Bagehot argues that 'the capital of the country is by the lending capitalists transmitted where it is most wanted.' If individual profits vary to the extent which Mr. Mill admitted, since there are no means of knowing what individual profits really are, it is hard to imagine how bankers and bill brokers can gauge the existing profits of different trades, and still harder to imagine how they can foreknow them. How much they really know of the matter has been recently exemplified by the transactions of banks and bill brokers in the cases of Messrs. Overend and Gurney, and Messrs. Collie and Co.* Mr. Bagehot himself, writing on the money market and joint-stock banks, has observed: 'The old private banks in former times used to lend much to private individuals; the banker formed his judg-

* On the failure of these firms a commercial writer observes: 'The nation entrusted most of its floating capital to the bill-brokers, and the public found that they had no check on their indiscretion. . . . Bankers took the bills as security because bill-brokers did, and hardly stopped to test the bills or to study their nature.'—*The Rationale of Market Fluctuations*, pp. 52-3.

ment of the discretion, the sense, and the solvency of those to whom he lent. And when London was by comparison a small city, and when by comparison everyone stuck to his proper business, this practice might have been safe. But now that London is enormous, and that no one can watch anyone, such a trade would be disastrous; it would hardly be safe in a country town.'*

If there is one lesson which the history of trade and the money market in the last ten years ought to have brought home to us more clearly than another, it is that both the lending and the borrowing capitalists, both bankers and traders, are singularly ill-informed and short-sighted with respect even to the condition and prospects of their own business. The Deputy Governor of the Bank of England told a meeting of Turkish bondholders, a few months ago, that he had gone into these bonds largely himself, and had advised others to do so. A man of business, of considerable experience, had asked my own opinion, as an economist, of that very security, and afterwards complained that I had dissuaded him from a good investment.

Such is the stability of the main proposition of abstract political economy. The nature of the superstructure built on it may be judged from the doctrine that all special taxes on production fall, not on the producer, but on consumers, the former receiving the tax with 'average' profit on its advance; although, in fact, the producer may make no profit, may never sell the articles taxed, may even be driven from the trade and ruined by the impost, as the last load which breaks the back of the camel, for taxation has notoriously contributed to drive the smaller capitalists from several branches of business—for example, distilling and brewing. I must leave it to physicists, geologists, and naturalists, to judge of the analogy for which Mr. Bagehot contends, of reasoning of this kind to the processes by which their sciences have been built up; nor may I attempt to pass judgment on the sufficiency of the method which Mr. Darwin, in particular, has followed. But when it is urged that

---

* *Lombard-street.* By Walter Bagehot. 6th ed., p. 251.

the abstract economist, like Mr. Darwin, reasons deductively from 'one *vera causa*,'* the rejoinder is obvious that the 'desire of wealth,' which in abstract political economy occupies the place of gravitation in astronomy, and of natural selection in Mr. Darwin's theory, so far from being a *vera causa*, is an abstraction, confounding a great variety of different and heterogeneous motives, which have been mistaken for a single homogeneous force; and that Mr. Darwin's hypothesis was based on many previous inductions, and followed by minute and elaborate verification, for which the sole substitute in political economy has been an *ignoratio elenchi*. Mr. Cairnes, indeed, emphasizes in italics the proposition that 'the economist starts with a knowledge of ultimate causes; † adding: 'He is already, at the outset of his enterprise, in the position which the physicist only attains after ages of laborious research. If anybody doubts this, he has only to consider what the ultimate principles governing economic phenomena are.' First among these 'ultimate principles' he places 'the general desire for physical well-being, and for wealth as the means of obtaining it.' Yet the desire for physical well-being is so far from being identical with the desire of wealth, that they are often in direct antagonism to each other. And the title of such an abstraction as the desire for wealth to rank as an ultimate principle has been, it is hoped, sufficiently refuted.

The abstract *a priori* method, it ought not to be overlooked, has almost entirely lost credit in Germany, and has never had undisputed possession of the field in either England or France. It is repudiated by M. de Laveleye, and by some of the most eminent economists in Italy. Malthus and Say, the two most eminent contemporaries of Ricardo, emphatically protested against it. Mr. J. S. Mill's treatise on the 'Principles of Political Economy' often departs from it, and in his later writings he showed an increasing tendency to question its generalizations. Nor did the founders of political economy, either in England or France, intend to separate the laws of the

---

* Bagehot, *Economic Studies*, p. 13. † *Logical Method, &c.*, p. 75.

economical world from the general laws of society. Their error lay in the assumption of a simple harmonious and beneficent order of nature, in accordance with which human wants and propensities tend to the utmost amount of wealth, happiness, and good. Mercier de la Rivière, whom Adam Smith calls the best expositor of the doctrines of the Economistes, entitled his work 'L'Ordre Naturel et Essentiel des Sociétés Politiques'; and with Adam Smith himself political economy was part of a complete system of social philosophy, comprising also natural theology, moral philosophy, and jurisprudence. He regarded the economical structure of the world as the result of a social evolution, but the dominant idea of a natural order of things disposed him to dwell chiefly on 'the natural progress of opulence'; and led him to regard its actual progress as 'unnatural and retrograde' wherever it diverged from the imaginary natural order, in place of being the result of the real laws of nature at work. He followed, nevertheless, the historical, as well as the *a priori*, method, the latter being simply an offshoot of the eighteenth century theory of Natural Law; and the same language may be used in reference to political economy, which Sir H. Maine has employed in describing the influence of that theory on jurisprudence: 'It gave birth or intense stimulus to vices of mental habit all but universal, disdain of positive law, impatience of experience, and the preference of *a priori* to all other reasoning. . . . There is not much presumption in asserting that what has hitherto stood in the place of a science has, for the most part, been a set of guesses, the very guesses of the Roman lawyers.'*

Ricardo's fundamental assumption is a 'guess' respecting the natural principle regulating value and the distribution of wealth in the early stages of society, or in a state of nature; and he proceeds to determine by the same process the 'natural' course of wages, profits, and prices in advanced society. In proof that every improvement in the processes of manufacture which abridges labour is attended with a corresponding fall in

* *Ancient Law*, pp. 91–113.

the price of the product, his argument is: 'Suppose that, in the early stages of society, the bow and arrows of the hunter were of equal value and of equal durability with the canoe and implements of the fisherman, both being the produce of the same quantity of labour. Under such circumstances, the value of the deer, the produce of the hunter's day's labour, would be exactly equal to the value of the fish, the produce of the fisherman's day's labour. The comparative value of the fish and the game would be entirely regulated by the quantity of labour realized in each, whatever might be the quantity of production, or however high or low general wages or profits might be.' To prove that profits are equalized in the modern world by the flow of capital into the more profitable trades, he resorts, in like manner, to a 'guess':—'It is perhaps very difficult to trace the steps by which this change is effected: it is probably by a manufacturer not actually changing his employment, but only lessening the quantity of capital he has in that employment.' How far this conjecture was well founded appears in his own words in the same chapter. 'The present time appears to be one of the exceptions to the justice of this remark. The termination of the war has so deranged the division which before existed of employments in Europe, that every capitalist has not found his place in the new division which has now become necessary.'

Mr. Cairnes defines political economy as 'the science which traces the phenomena of the production and distribution of wealth up to their causes in the principles of human nature and the laws and events, physical, political, and social, of the external world.'* This process has been exactly reversed by the *a priori* and deductive method. The economist 'starts,' according to it, with the assumption of a 'knowledge of ultimate causes,' and deduces the phenomena from the causes so assumed. What has still to be done is to investigate the actual phenomena, and discover their ultimate causes in the laws of social evolution and national history. The bane of political economy

* *Logical Method of Political Economy*, 2nd ed., p. 57.

has been the haste of its students to possess themselves of a complete and symmetrical system, solving all the problems before it with mathematical certainty and exactness. The very attempt shows an entire misconception of the nature of those problems, and of the means available for their solution. The phenomena of wealth may be made the subject of a special inquiry by a special set of inquirers, but the laws of coexistence and sequence by which they are governed must be sought in the great Science of Society, and by the methods which it holds out. And that science itself is still in its infancy. Auguste Comte's 'System of Positive Philosophy' (not his 'System of Positive Polity') is a work of prodigious genius, yet it did but suggest and illustrate, it did not create, the science—that could not be done by a single mind, nor in his time; still less did it work out the connexion between the economic and the other phases of the social evolution. If Political Economy, under that name, be not now bent to the task, it will speedily be taken out of the hands of its teachers by Sociology.

Inadequate as is the exposition contained in this Essay, it is submitted as establishing, on the one hand, that the abstract and *a priori* method yields no explanation of the laws determining either the nature, the amount, or the distribution of wealth; and, on the other hand, that the philosophical method must be historical, and must trace the connexion between the economical and the other phases of national history. As regards the nature of wealth, it has been shown that essential differences in its kinds and constituents, profoundly affecting the economical condition of mankind, manifest themselves at different stages of progress, and that their causes must be sought in the entire state of society—physical, moral, intellectual, and civil. The amount of wealth has been proved to depend on all the conditions determining the direction and employments of human energies, as well as on the state of the arts of production, and the means of supply. And the distribution of wealth has been shown to be the result, not of exchange alone, but also of moral, religious, and family ideas and sentiments, and the whole history of the nation. The distribution effected by exchange itself demonstrably varies at different stages of social progress, and is by no means in accordance with the doctrines of *a priori* political economy. Every successive stage—the hunting, the pastoral, the agricultural, the commercial stages, for example—has an economy which is indissolubly connected with the physical, intellectual, moral, and civil development; and the economical condition of English society at this day is the outcome of the entire movement which has evolved the political constitution, the structure of the family, the forms of religion, the learned professions, the arts and sciences, the state of agriculture, manufactures, and commerce. The philosophical method of political economy must be one which expounds this evolution.

XVI.

POLITICAL ECONOMY AND SOCIOLOGY.*

Philosophical, like religious and political history, is the history of change and reform, of the decline of old and the rise of new systems, and the reformers encounter the same opposition in the world of philosophy as in that of religion and politics, being accused of attempts to destroy what they seek to regenerate and preserve. Those whose interest or pride is on the side of the old system resist the new one as an attack on themselves, but they call it an attack on religion, on the constitution, on science, or on some venerable name. The upholders of an ancient worship did not cry publicly that their craft was in danger to be set at nought, but 'Great is Diana of the Ephesians.' So a cry is now heard in reply to Mr. Ingram from an old sect of economists of the greatness of Adam Smith. And it is well that the cry is now for him instead of Ricardo. Not long ago Adam Smith's name was seldom heard; his reputation was eclipsed by Ricardo's; the 'Wealth of Nations' was treated as almost obsolete. A sort of mythical glory surrounded Ricardo, and we may realize in his instance the process by which the ballads of a number of singers came to be ascribed to one bard, and the exploits of a line of chiefs and warriors to a single hero. A theory to which a contemporary of Adam Smith was led by his own experience and observation of farming in Scotland, and which was afterwards reproduced

* *Fortnightly Review*, January 1, 1879.—In connexion with this Essay, and the controversy referred to in it, see *The Present Position and Prospects of Political Economy*, by John K. Ingram, F.T.C.D., and an article in the *Nineteenth Century*, November, 1878, entitled 'Recent Attacks on Political Economy,' by the Right Hon. Robert Lowe, M.P. (Lord Sherbrooke).

by two contemporaries of Ricardo, came to be called 'Ricardo's Theory of Rent,' in spite of his own acknowledgment in his preface and elsewhere that he took it from Malthus and West, and of the fact that only the exaggerations and inaccuracies were his own.* Mr. Mill's theory of international values has in like manner been traced to Ricardo, contrary to its author's own statement in his Autobiography of its independent origin. Mr. Mill himself, indeed, though he so qualified and amended the doctrines of his predecessor that the latter could scarcely have recognized them, and brought new elements and conditions within the field of political economy, sometimes spoke with the piety of a disciple, and has been represented by some of his own followers as little more; the giant thus standing on the shoulders of the dwarf to see over his head. It is a sign, then, that Ricardo has lost ground when his adherents fall back on Adam Smith, just as a victory was gained when theologians could no longer oppose a new doctrine as contrary to the Fathers, and were driven to contend that it was against the Bible, which they had before kept in the background. A bold attempt may be made now and then hereafter to rehabilitate Ricardo, but practically he is given up. It is to be noted that the phrase 'desire of wealth,' which with some of his successors is made to bear the whole weight of political economy, was not used by Ricardo. But that is only because he dispensed altogether with psychology, and with all inquiry into the mental forces at work; setting out with naked assumptions, such as that it is 'natural' that the value of things should be proportionate to the labour of producing them, and that the 'natural' rate of wages is the price of the labourer's subsistence. These nebulous assumptions are not only both false, but also contradictory; for if the cost of the labourer's subsistence determined the rate of wages, it could not vary in different occupations with the nature

* 'In all that I have said concerning the origin and progress of rent, I have briefly repeated and endeavoured to elucidate the principles which Mr. Malthus has so ably laid down, on the same subject, in his *Inquiry into the Nature and Progress of Rent*, a work abounding in original ideas.'—*Ricardo's Works*, M'Culloch's ed., p. 374. Compare the preface to Ricardo's *Principles of Political Economy and Taxation*.

of the work. A deduction from the assumed relation between wages and food, on which much of his system was built, was that a tax on corn could not fall on the labouring class, and this doctrine, as both Cobden and Sir Robert Peel have borne witness, was the main cause of the Corn Law. His theory, that no improvement or economy in production can augment profit unless it lowers wages, has in like manner done incalculable harm. 'It has been,' he says in his treatise, 'my endeavour throughout this work to show that the rate of profits can never be increased but by a fall of wages.' Had he been an English Lassalle or Karl Marx, and his main object to sow enmity between capital and labour, he could not have devised a doctrine better adapted to the purpose. The notion, too, which his language did much to establish, that all wealth, including capital itself, is the produce of labour, in the sense of manual labour, exclusive of the capitalist's enterprise, invention, trouble, and abstinence, is actually the corner-stone of the creed of the German 'social democrat.' Political economy is, then, emerging from a cloud of *petitio principii*, bad generalization, and mischievous fallacy, when the controversy turns on the system of Adam Smith. It reminds one of the contest between the spirits of darkness and light for the body of Moses, to find the followers of Ricardo claiming Adam Smith for their prophet, and seeking to make his shrine the prop of a falling superstition.

The real issue, of course, is not what Adam Smith's system was, but what is the true one; the two questions, however, are not unrelated. 'Whom ye ignorantly worship, him declare I unto you,' the true disciple of Adam Smith may say to those who raise altars to his name, but to whom he is virtually an unknown being. Not only is the phrase 'desire of wealth' not to be found in the 'Wealth of Nations,' and Adam Smith guiltless of a vicious abstraction that has done much to darken economic inquiry; he introduced into his theory of the motives to exertion and sacrifice various desires and sentiments besides those which have wealth for their object. A writer from whom something more may be learned than was known in the days of Plato respecting the philosophy of society, history, and law, has observed, with respect to the deductive economists' practice of setting aside a number of forces as 'friction,' that the best corrective would be a demonstration that this so-called friction is capable of scientific analysis and measurement.* Friction is not, one may remark, a very appropriate or an adequate term, indicating neither the strength nor the mode of operation of the forces included under it. It would hardly seem correct to say that the earth is prevented by friction from falling into the sun. The motives, too, 'eliminated' in this fashion act in opposite ways, sometimes counteracting and sometimes stimulating by an additional object the love of gain. But Adam Smith was so far from 'eliminating' them, that he has set the example of an attempt to carry out Sir Henry Maine's idea of subjecting them not only to analysis, but to measurement. The assertion of a recent advocate of the *a priori* and deductive method, that the whole science of political economy is based on the desire of wealth and aversion from labour, is contrary not only to the spirit but to the letter of Adam Smith's 'Wealth of Nations.' It is characteristic, indeed, of the laxity of the deductive method, in spite of its pretence of rigorous logic, that immediately after laying down the foregoing proposition Mr. Lowe drops one of the two abstractions contained in it, and affirms that Adam Smith's method was successful because the subject admitted of the elimination of all motives save the single one of pecuniary interest. And at the centenary of the 'Wealth of Nations' he pronounced that 'the result of Adam Smith's investigation amounts to this, that the causes of wealth are two, work and thrift, and the causes of poverty two, idleness and waste'; adding that, in his own opinion, no more need be known, or perhaps could be known, on the subject. Nearly three thousand years before Adam Smith, Solomon had said as much; summing up in his proverbs on the subject the results of sagacious observation and induction, while men in general sought to grow rich by shorter methods, such as prayer

---

* *Village Communities in the East and West.* Third Edition, p. 232.

to their gods, as in later times by the aid of human protectors.

But to set aside all other motives to exertion besides riches is quite opposed to Adam Smith's *rationale* of the choice of employments, and the different rates of wages and profit. Observing that these were everywhere in Europe extremely different in different occupations, he traced the diversities to various circumstances 'which, either really or in imagination, make up for a small pecuniary gain in some, and counterbalance a great gain in others'—the desire, for instance, of credit, distinction, or health, the love of independence, power, or country life, the interest in certain pursuits for their own sake, the dislike of others on various accounts. The cases in which such influences come into play in his system are by no means abnormal or uncommon. He examined their operation in many of the ordinary employments of life—the farmer's, the weaver's, the smith's, the collier's, the carpenter's, the painter's, the butcher's, the jeweller's, the soldier's, the sailor's, the barrister's, the author's; and sought to measure them by a pecuniary standard. Honour, he said, formed a great part of the reward of all honourable professions. The farmer's profit was lower than the merchant's or the manufacturer's in proportion to the other attractions of his business. So far from building a science of the production and distribution of wealth on Mr. Lowe's two abstractions, the famous tenth chapter of his first book involves a complete refutation of such a system; as it does also of the assertion that its leading principles were not obtained by induction. The notion of evolving from his own consciousness the circumstances and motives that diversify the employments of a nation, and the remuneration obtained in them, would be preposterous, even if Adam Smith himself had not expressly stated at the beginning of the chapter that he had gathered them from observation. His exposition of the causes that lead men to accept a comparatively low rate of profit in farming shows both the closeness of that observation, and the delicate analysis to which he subjected influences which have been either disregarded altogether, or lumped together as 'friction' or 'disturbing causes' by the deductive school of his successors. The beauty of the country,' he said, 'besides the pleasures of country life, the tranquillity of mind which it promises, and, wherever the influence of human laws does not disturb it, the independence which it really affords, are charms that more or less attract everybody, and in every stage of his existence man seems to retain a predilection for this primitive employment.' Mr. C. S. Read, speaking the other day from practical knowledge, and without thinking of Adam Smith, of the reasons why men continue to hold farms at rents that leave little or no profit, fell into nearly similar language. The fact that Mr. Lowe, with Adam Smith on his tongue, can think of no incentive to exertion save pecuniary gain, is enough to prove the inadequacy of the method he follows, of deducing the laws of political economy from his own mind, instead of from careful induction. Even Mr. Senior, though ambitious to construct the science from the fewest possible principles, laid down several besides the two jumbled into one in his treatise, as a desire to obtain wealth at the least possible sacrifice. Among these additional principles is that of population, and Mr. Lowe's mention of Malthus among the successors of Adam Smith might have suggested to him the insufficiency of the foundation on which he builds a science of the production, accumulation, consumption, and distribution of wealth, as he defines political economy. Among the chief motives to production, the most powerful of all to accumulation, and deeply affecting consumption and distribution, are conjugal and parental affection. The family finds no place in a system which takes cognizance only of individuals, and of no motive save personal gain. Yet without the family, and the altruistic as well as self-regarding motives that maintain it, the work of the world would come almost to a standstill; saving for a remote future would cease; there would be no durable wealth; men would not seek to leave anything behind them; the houses of the wealthiest, if there were any houses at all, would be built to last only for their own time. In order to solve the problem of political economy, Mr. Lowe assures us that 'all that is wanted is the knowledge that the ruling passions of mankind are wealth and ease.' It does not appear whether, like Mr. Bagehot, Mr. Lowe excludes women from the sphere of the science; but the exertions of that hardest-worked of all labourers, the poor man's wife, can hardly be explained by the love of wealth and ease. Had not more than one of Mr. Ingram's opponents contended that the scientific character and the complete success of the method of eliminating all other motives, is demonstrated by its enabling the economist to predict, it would seem too plain to need statement that just the opposite is the truth. If you know all a man's inclinations and motives, and their relative force, you may foretell how he will act under given conditions. But if you set aside all save the desire of pecuniary gain and aversion from labour, you will to a certainty go wrong about human conduct in general; you will not be right about even the miser, for he has sometimes some human affections, and, on the other hand, thinks nothing of trouble. Mr. Jevons, though favourably disposed by philosophical culture and tastes towards historical investigation in economics, has urged, on behalf of deduction from the acquisitive principle, that even the lower animals act from a similar motive, 'as you will discover if you interfere between a dog and his bone.' A bone fairly enough represents the sort of wealth coveted by a dog, who has a comparatively simple cerebral system, and few other objects. Yet you cannot predict the conduct even of a dog from his love of bones, or not one would be left in the butchers' shops. The dog has a regard for his master and a fear of the police, and he has other pursuits.

All men, it may be said, desire health, 'and in the absence of disturbing causes' will seek it. But can a science of health be based on this assumption, or the conduct of mankind be predicted from it? Everybody, it might be affirmed, loves vritue 'in the abstract,' and 'in the absence of disturbing causes' would be virtuous; yet, policemen, prisons, and the Divorce Court show that no theory of morals, much less absolute predictions, can be drawn from this abstract principle. That the *a priori* method in political economy renders positive prediction possible is indeed contrary to the doctrine of its most eminent expositors. Mr. Mill, though he subsequently much enlarged the scope and system of economic investigation, was in his earlier years an advocate of the *a priori* method; yet in the well-known essay in support of it he emphatically insisted that the conclusions deduced from it are 'true only in the abstract,' and 'would be true without qualification only in purely imaginary cases.' Mr. Cairnes, in like manner, says, 'it is evident that an economist arguing from the desire of wealth and the aversion to labour with strict logical accuracy may be landed in conclusions that have no resemblance to existing realities'; adding that 'the economist can never be certain that he does not omit some essential circumstance, and it is indeed scarcely possible to include all; therefore his conclusions correspond with facts only in the absence of disturbing causes, and represent not positive but hypothetic truths.'*

The more sagacious adherents to the mere deductive method will therefore probably decline to accept Mr. Lowe as their representative, but his exposition is a *reductio ad absurdum* of their own system. He is only more thoroughgoing—one cannot say more consistent or logical, for he sometimes includes and sometimes discards the dislike of labour—in his elimination of all principles save the desire of wealth, which is the real backbone of their theory as well as his. The other motives and forces to which they nominally concede a place are only admitted at the outset for form's sake, to be afterwards set aside as 'disturbing causes' in a manner without precedent or analogy in physical science. The last thing an astronomer would dream of is, that having admitted in general terms the existence of other forces besides those that were taken account of by the earliest observers, he need not concern himself with them further, and may calculate the movements of the heavenly bodies without reference to them. Nor is this the only fundamental objection. No such principle as 'the desire of wealth,' in the sense of a single, universal motive, whose consequences are uniform and can be foreseen, really exists.

---

* *Logical Method of Political Economy*, p. 49.

Adam Smith does not use the phrase, and his doctrine respecting the nature of wealth shows the impossibility of using it as a key to the movements of the economic world. Wealth, he says, 'consists not in the inconsumable riches of money, but in the consumable goods annually reproduced by the labour of the society.' It includes therefore food, drink, clothing, houses, furniture, plate, ornaments, books, works of art; in short, necessaries, comforts, luxuries, in all their varieties, and all the productions of nature or of human exertion and skill to be had in the market. It includes things which vary in different countries and different ages, and have very different economic effects; and which are objects not only of different but of antagonistic desires. The love of gin is the love of one kind of wealth which too often competes in the mind of a poor man with the love of a decent dwelling. There is a saying about a four-footed animal not without firmness of character but of limited ideas, between two bundles of hay both soliciting his choice. The decalogue shows that this animal was one of divers things which the Israelites were prone to covet. The ox, to which allusion is also made, in the commandment, was, as Sir Henry Maine has explained, the kind of wealth most valued by early agricultural communities; yet even they desired some other kinds, and sometimes the reason why a man was without an ox for his plough, was that he was too fond of strong drink. In modern society there are countless varieties of wealth. Adam Smith has made some excellent remarks on the difference, in respect both of its amount and its distribution, of expenditure on different sorts. But expenditure is simply the method of acquisition by which, under a division of labour, the desires of men for different things are satisfied. Were there no such division, some would build houses and make clothes for themselves, while others in nakedness or rags distilled spirits or brewed ale in mud hovels or caves.

One of the most important economic inquiries relates to the changes which take place in the direction of the chief wants of mankind, and the species of wealth which they call into existence. The main object of industry and accumulation on the part of the French nation is landed property; the chief impulse determining the national economy is the desire of it: in England this desire is absent among the nation at large, and the one which takes its place with no small number of Englishmen is the love of beer. Happily in England there is a still more general object of desire in the house, and the house owes its structure, perhaps its very existence, to the institution of the family. Even in the matter of dress, the changes in the nature of the things constituting wealth deeply affect its economic condition. Richard II. wore a coat which cost more than £20,000 in modern money; the Prince of Wales would not take £20,000 to wear it. The stronger passion of women than men in our time for personal decoration is the result not of an original difference in the mental constitution of the two sexes, but of a different social and political history. The formula of demand and supply is still supposed by some economists to explain everything fully, but both demand and supply have in every case a long history. The demand for duelling swords and pistols in France is such that the supply makes no inconsiderable figure in the inventory of French wealth. Were they used only in duels, there would probably not be two swords or a brace of pistols in England. It is a misrepresentation of the Mercantile System that its adherents considered nothing but money as wealth, still they did attach undue importance to it; and the consequence of the excessive estimation in which they held it demonstrates the absurdity of basing either the economic prosperity of nations or economic science on the abstraction which is the corner-stone of both in the deductive system. The other principle which Mr. Lowe associates with it, the dislike of labour, involves an equal confusion. One might ask, when it is maintained that we can predict the conduct of mankind from these two principles, in what proportion are we to mix them for the purpose? The Jews were always a wealth-loving nation, and many of them industrious, yet there seem to have been not a few sluggards in Solomon's time who would go to no trouble to get it. Can employers tell whether higher weekly earnings or fewer hours of work will be the principal object of their workmen a year hence? The savage has a dislike for regular labour which only some form of slavery can overcome, but with the progress of civilization a love of exertion for its own sake grows up, and employment becomes necessary to the happiness of a great number of men. We are told somewhat abruptly in the Psalms that a man was famous according as he had lifted up axes on the thick trees, yet the most celebrated woodcutter of that period perhaps felled no more trees in a week than Mr. Gladstone will do for mere recreation. The German emperor replied to a deputation that he had felt the pain of his wounds less than the abstinence from his ordinary activity which they compelled. The love of several occupations for their own sake is one of the causes by which Adam Smith explains the small profit to be made in them. Had Mr. Lowe ever watched a French peasant at work in his vineyard, he could hardly have made a universal dislike of toil one of the two pillars of political economy.

Other motives, which eminent advocates of the deductive system propose to take into account, vary in like manner in force, direction, and consequence. Mr. Cairnes refers to the love of men for their own country as the main cause of the diversity of the rates of wages and profit in different countries, and it is a highly complex feeling, varying greatly in strength in different nations and ages. The Fleming was the great emigrant of the middle ages; now he can hardly be got to migrate to an adjoining province for double wages. Patriotism did not exist in England some centuries ago. Different races, nations, and clans had been too recently blended under one government for a strong feeling of nationality; a man belonged to his township, his borough, his guild, not to his country. Had Englishmen been as patriotic as they were brave, William of Normandy might never have got the title of Conqueror. The Germans when they invaded the Roman Empire knew no common fatherland. In 1870 they left lucrative employments in all parts of the world for a soldier's perils and pay, in a manner that shows how much there is on earth that is not dreamt of in Mr. Lowe's philosophy. And this is far from exhausting the principles entitled, even on the admission of distinguished adherents of the deductive method, to a place in the science of wealth. Mr. Cairnes asks, for example, 'How far should religious and moral considerations be admitted as coming within the province of political economy?' His answer is that 'They are to be taken account of precisely in so far as they are found, in fact, to affect the conduct of men in the pursuit of wealth'; and one need only allude to the influence of mediæval religion on both the forms and the distribution of the wealth of the community, the changes in both with the change in religion after the Reformation, in proof of the impotence of the *a priori* method to guide the economist in relation to this class of agencies. Yet a few pages after recognising their title to investigation, Mr. Cairnes argues that induction, though indispensable in physical, is needless in economic science, on the ground that 'the economist starts with a knowledge of ultimate causes,' and 'is already, at the outset of his enterprise, in the position which the physicist only attains after ages of laborious research'.* The followers of the deductive method are, in fact, on the horns of a dilemma. They must either follow Mr. Lowe's narrow path, and reason strictly from the assumption that men are actuated by no motive save the desire of pecuniary gain, or they must contend that they have an intuitive knowledge of all the moral, religious, political, and other motives influencing human conduct, and of all the changes they undergo in different countries and periods.

Shut out by their own method from the investigation of the true problems of political economy, the deductive school have devoted themselves to a fictitious solution of others which the ablest among them have nevertheless admitted to be insoluble. 'If you place a man's ear within the ring of pounds, shillings, and pence, his conduct can be counted on to the greatest nicety,' according to Mr. Lowe. Mr. Cairnes on the other hand, as we have seen, concurs with Mr. Mill that positive, unconditional conclusions are beyond the reach

* *Logical Method of Political Economy*, p. 75.

of the economist, since he does not take into account, or even know, all the forces at work, much less can measure them with precision. An entire lecture in Mr. Cairnes' 'Logical Method of Political Economy' is devoted to proof that quantitative exactness is unattainable in the science, and that its conclusions being only hypothetically true, and representing only several tendencies 'in the absence of disturbing causes,' ought not to affect the semblance of numerical exactness. Mr. Lowe's proposition is nevertheless true in the sense that the deductive system does affect the power not only of absolute prediction but of prediction with mathematical accuracy. Take any treatise following the deductive method, and it will be found to consist mainly of propositions respecting wages, profit, prices, rent, and taxation, which profess to determine with arithmetical exactness on whom a given tax, say on a box of lucifer matches, will fall, how much it will add to the price of the box, and what profit both the manufacturer and the retailer will net on its advance. In a previous article* the present writer has exposed the fallacies involved in the whole chain of reasoning, and shown that it cannot be foreseen whether a trader will ever recover a so-called indirect tax at all; that it may be a direct tax on himself, may drive him and all other small capitalists from the business, and ultimately give a lucrative monopoly instead of 'average profit' to a few great capitalists—half-a-dozen distillers and brewers, for example. The deductive theory of wages, profits, prices, rent, and taxation, is substantially a set of predictions respecting the distribution of wealth, which affect to foretell exactly the gain in every business, and the rates at which goods of every kind may be sold. It has been well said that before predicting the future, we must learn to predict the past; and before predicting the past, it might be added, we should learn to predict the present, by studying the forces at work in the world around us, the conditions under which they operate, and their actual results. A striking instance of the failure of

* 'The Incidence of Imperial and Local Taxation on the Working Classes.' *Fortnightly Review*, February 1st, 1874. (Reprinted in the present volume.)

the deductive economist to predict even the present, is Mr. M'Culloch's assertion in several editions of the 'Wealth of Nations' that the local inequalities of wages, of which Adam Smith spoke, had almost disappeared with the improvement in the means of communication. In point of fact, they had greatly increased; agricultural wages varying from 6*s.* to 16*s.* a-week when his first edition was published, and from 9*s.* to 22*s.* at the date of the last, varying, too, from causes which inductive investigation had enabled Adam Smith to discover, namely, the unequal local development of manufactures, commerce, the greater demand and competition for labour in some places than in others, and the obstacles to its migration.

The history of the last few years gives disastrous proof of the falsity of the predictions of both present and future involved in the theory of the equality of profits, which assumes that the gains in different employments can be foreseen with a close approximation to accuracy, and that competition accordingly keeps them nearly at a level. If there was a man in the country who might have been supposed capable of foresight in such matters, by reason of the widest information and great financial skill, it was Mr. Gladstone, when a few years ago he described the trade of the country as advancing by leaps and bounds. Did he see that they were leaps in the dark? Did the capitalists who rushed into the businesses in which prices and profits were trebling see that they were bounds that would end in a fall on the other side? Have the capitalists in other businesses, who were heavily mulcted by the rise of coal and iron, recovered their losses 'with average profit'? Adam Smith, reasoning from observation, rigorously and emphatically confined the tendency of profits to equality to long-established well-known trades in the same neighbourhood, unaffected by new discoveries, by speculation, fluctuations of credit, accident, or political events, carried on, not by directors and shareholders with other business to mind, but by persons whose sole occupations they were. In other words, from an induction he predicted inequality where the deductive economist predicts equality. Mr. Cairnes, indeed, though adhering to the general truth of the doctrine of equality, was of opinion that the new gold would, by its unequal distribution over different trades, disturb the level of profits for many years. The actual course of the distribution was, however, very different from that which *a priori* reasoning led him to predict, the chief rise of prices being in foreign countries, where railways, industrial progress, and the opening of the English market raised them suddenly from a low scale towards the English range.* The new gold was only one of many new conditions of modern trade. In an age of companies there is a very imperfect division of labour: credit and speculation have made trade a lottery, in which 'the absurd presumption of every man in his own abilities, and the still more absurd presumption in his own good fortune,' of which Adam Smith speaks, have full play.

The recurrence of commercial crises alone defeats all attempts to predict the course of prices and profits, and would do so even if the doctrine of decennial cycles had a solid foundation; for if the periods of inflation and depression could be foretold, and the occurrence of each crisis timed with precision, the particular movements of credit, speculation, and prices, and the gains and losses in each business, could not. The theory of a decennial cycle, like that of the equality of profits, and the whole *a priori* system, with its seeming simplicity, symmetry, and roundness, owes its attractions to that idol of the tribe which, as Bacon says, leads the spirit of man to suppose and feign in nature a greater equality and uniformity than is in truth, and to mark the hits of his system, but not the misses. An ingenious attempt has lately been made to account for the imaginary decennial cycle by the supposition that about every ten years there is a change in the management of business through a younger generation taking the place of the older, as though the commercial world

* An example of this was cited lately by the eminent French economist, M. Leroy-Beaulieu, in the *Économiste Français*, from statistics compiled by Mr. Newmarch, showing that between 1830 and 1870 the price of corn fell 14 per cent. in England, while it rose 17 per cent. in France, 88 per cent. in Belgium, 133 per cent. in Hungary, 142 per cent. in Austria.

were composed of successive ranks of men born together at the beginning of successive decades, and all in each rank reaching sixty, and retiring together. But the commercial class, like the army, the bar, and the whole nation, is recruited with fresh blood every year, not only every tenth year. Lord Bacon himself showed a strong tendency to believe in both a political and an economical cycle, and supposed his own age of the world on the descent of the wheel, though he judiciously thought it 'not good to look too long on these turning wheels of vicissitude, lest we become giddy.' Adam Smith, too, leaned to the notion of a code of nature regulating the movement of the economic world with perfect equality and uniformity. Perhaps, therefore, one need not wonder that Mr. Jevons, whose philosophical powers have enabled him to make real discoveries, should be fascinated by the idea of commercial cycles recurring with the regularity of astronomical phenomena, and traceable to astronomical causes. But one is driven to suspect that Mr. Lowe can never have made a discovery, when he argues that Adam Smith's method was wholly deductive, because in the 'Wealth of Nations' he puts his conclusions first; supporting them afterwards by the instances which he deems most convincing, instead of setting before his readers a vast number of historical and statistical facts, and working out the principle which they establish under their eyes. A library would not contain the books he would have written, had he attempted to convey to other minds by such a method the knowledge he had himself reached by long and laborious investigation. A discoverer would be avoided like a pestilence or the ancient mariner, were he to relate all the steps by which he got to his journey's end, after many misfortunes and failures, it may be, and often burning his fingers in the crucible. Results, it is well said, not processes, are for the public eye. How little Adam Smith was disposed to publish all his processes appears from his direction to Hume, in 1773, to burn all the papers, with one exception, found in his house at his death, and from his own destruction of them a few days before his end. The advantage of the division of labour—to which Mr. Lowe refers as a proof that he proceeded by assumption, because the number of examples he gives is small—was not a new doctrine; but his chapter on its limitation by the extent of the market bears all the marks of wide research and induction. The work of induction in relation to the division of labour is, moreover, by no means complete. There are plain symptoms in modern economy of tendencies to an amalgamation, instead of a division, of occupations. And the most arduous problem respecting the separation of occupations has never even occurred to the deductive school—namely, What are the causes governing its actual course, determining the directions of the national energies, the employments of different classes and of both sexes, in different countries and ages?

The human being or 'individual' from whose assumed tendencies the conclusions of the deductive system are drawn, and its predictions made, is a fiction, not a reality—a personification of two abstractions, the desire of wealth and aversion for labour—feelings differing, as has been shown, in different countries, ages, and persons—differing much, for example, in men and women. Mr. Bagehot felt so strongly the inapplicability of the assumptions of the system to the greater part of the world, that he actually limited political economy to England at its present state of commercial development, and to the male sex in England. Such a limitation involves a complete surrender of the position that the system is based on universal laws or principles of human nature; it involves also an admission that it is only by inductive investigation that we can determine what the actual economy of society is, and what the causes that govern its structure and movement. Enough has been said, too, to show that the fundamental assumptions of the deductive economist are really as fallacious in reference to modern Englishmen as to Frenchmen, Germans, Asiatics, or Africans. The economy of English society can, no more than that of any other nation, be explained by assuming that Englishmen are personifications of the love of wealth and ease. But this is only one of the fundamental shortcomings of the system. Looking only to the assumed motives of individuals, it ignores altogether the collective agency of the community, through its positive institutions as an organized political body or state, its history and traditions, and the social environment with which it encompasses every man and woman within it, from the cradle to the grave.

Adam Smith's philosophy was not, like the little system that pleases some of his successors, if I may use a Horatian phrase, 'complete in itself, smooth, and round.'* There was, it is true, in his mind an ideal order of things which he called 'natural,' as being that which would take place if certain tendencies of human nature were allowed to operate without interference. Even in this ideal world, however, he saw that there must be laws relating to property, succession, tenure, and other subjects, although, in accordance with both the political and the theological philosophy of his time, there was a 'natural' type to which these institutions ought to conform. Mr. Macleod has urged, on behalf of confining the scope of political economy to commercial exchange, that the 'distribution' of wealth contemplated by the French Physiocrates was that effected by exchange, or by the process of distribution as distinguished from that of production. The Physiocrates, it may be observed, were not the first to use the term in this sense; it was so employed by English writers on commerce a hundred years earlier. But one might as reasonably exclude all agencies save water from geology on the ground that Werner did not take them into account, as limit the investigations of the economist to the mode of distribution taken cognizance of in either the seventeenth or the eighteenth century, in either England or France. The very word 'distribution,' moreover, which Adam Smith applies in his first book to the partition effected by exchange, is in his third book applied to that effected by succession; though in both cases we may perceive the influence of the ideal code of nature on his opinions and language. Long before his time, indeed, the term was applied to the distribution of wealth by law, as the Statute of Distribu-

* 'In se ipso totus, teres atque rotundus.'—Hor.

tions shows. He sets before us both the 'natural,' as he called the ideally best, order of things, and the actual order resulting from positive institutions, historical events, and the constitution of human nature with its various and conflicting propensities; among which, as he points out, the love of dominion is apt to prevail over the desire of gain. The third book of the 'Wealth of Nations' is mainly an investigation into the action and reaction of political and economic history, the progress of agriculture, manufactures, and commerce, and of the different classes of society in both country and town, until out of mediæval Catholic and feudal Europe had issued the Europe of his own time with an economy moulded and fashioned by centuries. The word 'evolution' had not come into use in Adam Smith's day, and social philosophers did not call the historical order of events the natural order, or the actual sequences resulting from the whole constitution of human society and the surrounding world the results of natural law: the word 'Nature,' in their terminology, having a purely ideal meaning. Yet in substance Adam Smith shows that the economic condition of the nations of modern Europe was the outcome of a long historical evolution, and could not otherwise be accounted for or understood, although a better state of things, which in the language of his time he called the natural state, would have resulted from better human government and institutions. Whoever compares the last three books of the 'Wealth of Nations' with the announcement, at the end of the 'Theory of Moral Sentiments,' of the author's intention 'in another discourse to give an account of the general principles of law and government, and of the different revolutions they have undergone in different ages and periods of society, not only in what concerns justice, but in what concerns police, revenue, arms, and whatever else is the subject of law,' will find evidence that political economy was not the only branch of political science in which Adam Smith had advanced beyond Plato, in whose days Mr. Lowe affirms that knowledge in all other branches of moral and political philosophy came to a standstill. Adam Smith saw that 'the revolutions of law and government' had followed a determinable order; that the whole movement of society, including even that of positive law, was subject to law in the scientific sense of regular and intelligible sequence; and that the economic state of a nation at every period of its history was only a particular aspect of the whole social development. This is the fundamental conception on which the Science of Society rests, although the modern social philosopher calls the actual succession of social phenomena the natural one, while Adam Smith used the word 'natural' in a different sense.

'In love, or war, or politics, or religion, or morals,' Mr. Lowe argues, 'it is impossible to foretell how men will act, and therefore it is impossible to reason deductively;' whereas, 'in matters connected with wealth, deviations arising from other causes than the desire of it may be neglected without perceptible error.' The truth is that all these causes—war, love, religion, morals, and politics—do profoundly influence the conduct and condition of mankind in relation to wealth, and the economic structure of society. It is one of Mr. Buckle's incorrect generalizations that in the middle ages there were but two engrossing pursuits—war and religion—and only two professions—the church and the army. It is, on the other hand, a no less superficial philosophy that overlooks the influence of war and religion on the economy of modern Europe, the occupations of its inhabitants, and the nature, amount, distribution, and consumption of their productions. At no period of the middle ages was so large a proportion of the population of the Continent trained to war as at the present day. An immense part of the wealth of modern Europe, England included, consists of weapons, warlike structures and stores, and the appliances of armies and fleets. What would be the worth of a treatise deducing the economy of Germany from the assumption that every man is occupied solely in the acquisition of wealth, 'the actual deviations being so slight that they may be treated as practically non-existent?' Were astronomers able to discover certain indications of human life in another planet, on Mr. Lowe's principle we should know all that need interest or could instruct us respecting the economy of the planetary world from 'the two ruling passions of mankind—wealth and ease.' Would not the questions arise :—'Does war exist, and if so, is every man a soldier, or is there a distinct military profession?' 'Have the inhabitants of the planet any religion, and if so, is there a wealthy priesthood?' 'Are the institutions of marriage and the family established?' 'What are the checks to the increase of population?' 'Is land held in common, or does private property in it exist?' 'What are the laws and customs with respect to succession?' 'Have the people of this planet the same kinds of wealth as those of the earth, and have different countries in it different kinds, as in our own world?' It has been shown that the mundane economist possesses no such powers of prediction as Mr. Lowe ascribes to him, just because politics, war, religion, morals, and love, do all powerfully affect human conduct in matters connected with wealth. Nevertheless, the philosophy of society is not so undeveloped that no regular sequence or natural law is discoverable in these very influences, or prediction altogether impossible in relation to them. It can be foretold, with a close approximation to accuracy, how many marriages there will be between the 1st of January, 1879, and the next census. A well-known economist is said to maintain that marriage is nothing but a commercial contract; but Edmund Burke's complaint that the age of chivalry was gone, and that of economists and calculators had succeeded, was not quite so well grounded. Love, chivalrous sentiment, morals, religion, do still deeply affect marriage, even among a nation of shopkeepers; and it is because they do that we can nearly foretell the number of such unions, and the number of children born and reared. We should be altogether without data for calculating the advance of population, the supply of labour, the movement of rent, the accumulation of capital, and its distribution by marriage and succession as well as exchange, if men and women, or even men alone, were influenced by no other than mercantile motives.

The economic structure of any given community, the direction taken by national energies, the occupations of the different classes and of both sexes, the constituents and the partition of movable and immovable property, the progressive, stationary, or retrogressive condition in respect of productive power and the quantity and quality of the necessaries, comforts, and luxuries of life, are the results not of special economic forces, but of all the social forces, political, moral, and intellectual, as well as industrial. The very wants and aims summed up in 'the desire of wealth' arise not from innate, original, and universal propensities of the individual man, but from the community and its history. Hunger and thirst, desire of shelter from cold and heat, are probably the only forms of the economic impulse that a human being isolated altogether from social influences would feel. The very kinds of food sought in civilized society are determined by a long national history, and are not the same in England and France. The predominant form which the love of wealth takes in the last country is, as already said, the love of landed property, a form non-existent in primitive humanity, and which in civilized countries is so much the result of national history, that it is extinct in our own as a motive to labour and thrift on the part of the nation at large, though once widely diffused through all classes in both country and town.

Political economy is thus a department of the science of society which selects a special class of social phenomena for special investigation, but for this purpose must investigate all the forces and laws by which they are governed. The deductive economist misconceives altogether the method of isolation permissible in philosophy. In consequence of the limitation of human faculties, not that the narrowing of the field is in itself desirable or scientific, it is legitimate to make economic phenomena, the division of labour, the nature, amount, and distribution of national riches, the subject of particular examination, provided that all the causes affecting them be taken into account. To isolate a single force, even if a real force and not a mere abstraction, and to call deductions from it alone the laws of wealth, can lead only to error, and is radically unscientific. The development of the positive law of a nation, for example, is in all its bearings on industry, commerce, accumulation, and the distribution of property, a subject demanding the economist's investigation. The primitive ownership of things in common, the evolution of the separate possession of both chattels and land; of slavery, serfdom, and free labour; the changes in the law of intestate succession; the growth of the testamentary power, and of the law of contract in its different forms, are at once jural and economic facts, which the jurist regards from one point of view and the economist from another. The field of human society is so large and complex, man's capacity so limited, that it is by a number of investigations in relation to different aspects of the subject, that the science of society, as a whole, is most likely to be advanced, and its ultimate generalizations and laws at last reached. The history of political economy is a warning against all attempts to reach them *per saltum*, and to construct at once a complete and symmetrical system. A radical error with respect to the history of both science in general, and political economy in particular, lies at the root of Mr. Lowe's notion, that 'science means knowledge in its clearest and most absolute form, the test of which is prediction'; and that the fabric of economic science, under the hand of Adam Smith, 'rose up, like Jonah's gourd, in a single night.' If science meant only knowledge in its clearest and most absolute form, no science could have a beginning or a youth: it must spring into life fully grown and armed, like Minerva from the head of Jove; and only a science founded, like deductive political economy, on fiction, could do so. Had political economy grown up, like Jonah's gourd, in a night, it would like it have perished in a day, and could not have borne the light. A long line of inquirers had preceded Adam Smith, to some of whom he has acknowledged his debt. Nearly a century before the publication of the 'Wealth of Nations,' Dudley North, himself a merchant, had expounded the policy of commercial liberty, going on some points even beyond his illustrious successor. Adam Smith's own language respecting the French economists answers a question raised by Auguste Comte's remark, that he made no pretence of founding a new and special science of wealth. He did not pretend to be its founder, but he did regard such a science as not only founded, but far advanced, by Quesnay and his followers, whose system of political economy he describes as, 'with all its imperfections, the nearest approach to perfection that had yet been made in that important science.' At the same time, like his French contemporaries, he regarded it as a branch of a wider science, which they called Physiocratie, or the science of the government and laws of nature, and which he called Moral Philosophy.

Science is patient and progressive, never, therefore, reaching perfection; its essence consists in a right method of investigation more than in the extent of its progress. The same misconception that leads Mr. Lowe to admire the *a priori* political economy, with its fictitious completeness, symmetry, and exactness, and to deny a science of society, because it is yet in an inchoate state, shows itself in his assertion that no more is known now in psychology, morals, or politics, than was known in the days of Plato. No such realistic abstraction as the 'Ideas of Plato' now deludes the psychologist, though something akin to it lingers in the deductive economist's notion of 'the desire of wealth.' The association of ideas is a psychological law which alone places mental philosophy far beyond the point it had reached with the Greeks; and the change in the course of social progress, on the one hand, and the inheritance, on the other, of cerebral qualities can hardly be known to Mr. Lowe, or he could not refuse to admit a great recent advance in our knowledge of the laws of the human mind. In the science of law and politics the superiority of Adam Smith himself over Plato is evident. His remarks on the Athenian tribunals show that he could have saved Pericles from a blunder which not only deprived Athens of a system of jurisprudence, but did much to corrupt and undermine the State; yet Plato failed to discover it, though its consequences were under his eyes, and the constitution of courts was one of the subjects that engaged his attention. And the perception of revolutions in law and government following a regular sequence, and evolving successive economic as well as political states, to which Adam Smith attained, not only never dawned on Plato's mind, but may be said in itself to be a long step towards the foundation of a true science of society. The attempt to raise a prejudice against such a science, on account of the difficulty of naming it otherwise than sociology, a compound of Latin and Greek, is not only captious and frivolous, but displays an extraordinary forgetfulness of scientific nomenclature. To say nothing of the admission of such combinations in Germany, the fatherland of philology, in words such as *Socialpolitik*, English philosophical terminology itself abounds in them. Natural philosophy, moral philosophy, are names compounded of Latin and Greek, which, according to German usage, would be written in one word, like *Socialpolitik*; and the term 'natural law' is a mixture of Latin and English. One wonders, indeed, that Mr. Lowe, who is so shocked at sociology, does not shudder at the name of Adam Smith, as a combination, not from cognate tongues like Latin and Greek, but from Hebrew and English.

Yet, although neither the objection that sociology has not attained to the perfection of astronomy, nor that it is a hybrid word, is entitled to a serious consideration, it would be a grave error to regard it as otherwise than a science still in its infancy. Its students should take warning from the history of political economy against hasty induction, and attempts to rise at once to the deductive stage. Two men of extraordinary genius, Auguste Comte and Herbert Spencer, though differing considerably on some points, have struck out some luminous generalizations and *aperçus*; but great circumspection and caution are needed in their application: they cannot safely be made to support trains of deduction, still less can they be treated as constituting the supreme inductions and fundamental laws of a science of society. Mr. Spencer's theorem, for example, that 'a movement from the homogeneous to the heterogeneous characterizes all evolution,' in both the physical and the social world, is true in a number of instances; and he has connected it with *veræ causæ*, with ascertained natural forces and conditions, indubitably creating diversity where there had been similarity, and evolving new kinds and species of phenomena. Yet it is not a universal law, or an invariable truth from which inferences respecting the course of social development can with certainty be drawn.* The movement of language, law, and political and civil union, is for the most part in an opposite direction. In a savage country like Africa, speech is in a perpetual flux, and new dialects spring up with every swarm from the parent hive. In the civilized world the unification of language is rapidly proceeding; probably no Celtic tongue will be spoken in any part of Europe, Brittany or Wales not excepted, in a few generations. The diversities of English speech were so great four hundred years ago, that Caxton found them a great obstacle to printing; four hundred years hence the same English will be spoken over half the globe, and will have few competitors, there is reason to believe, over the other half. The movement of political organization is similar; already Europe has nearly consolidated itself into a Heptarchy, the number of States into which England itself was once divided; and the result of the American war exemplifies the prevalence of the forces tending to homogeneity over those tending to heterogeneity. Two systems of civil law, again—the French and the English—now extend over a great part of the civilized world; and Sir Henry Maine has established many grounds for the proposition that 'all laws, however dissimilar in their infancy, tend to resemble each other in their maturity.' In customs and fashion civilized society is likewise advancing towards uniformity. Once every rank, profession, and district had a distinctive garb; now all such distinctions, save with the priest and the soldier, have almost disappeared among men; and among women the degree of outlay and waste is becoming almost the only distinction in dress throughout the West. In the industrial world a generation

* [In an article published in the *Academy* of October 23rd, 1880, Mr. Leslie wrote as follows:—

'The movement of society, designated by Mr. Herbert Spencer as from "the homogeneous to the heterogeneous," is highly important in its economic aspects; and the present writer acknowledges that Mr. Spencer's recent reply"—(Appendix to *First Principles*, dealing with criticisms)—"to some comments of his own on the doctrine so formulated is in the main substantially just and sufficient.']

ago a constant movement towards a differentiation of employments and functions appeared; now some marked tendencies to their amalgamation have begun to disclose themselves. Joint-stock companies have almost effaced all real division of labour in the wide region of trade within their operation. Improvements in communication are fast eliminating intermediate trades between producers and consumers in international commerce; and the accumulation and combination of capital, and new methods of business, are working the same result in wholesale and retail dealing at home. Many of the things for sale in a village huckster's shop were formerly the subjects of distinct branches of business in a large town; now the wares in which scores of different retailers dealt are all to be had in great establishments in New York, Paris, and London, which sometimes buy direct from the producers, thus also eliminating the wholesale dealer. These changes are among the causes that baffle the supposed prevision on which the doctrine of the equality of profits rests.

In the early stages of social progress, again, a differentiation takes place, as Mr. Spencer has observed, between political and industrial functions, which fall to distinct classes: now a man is a merchant in the morning and a legislator at night; in mercantile business one year, and the next perhaps head of the navy, like Mr. Goschen or Mr. W. H. Smith. There is even a strong tendency to sink the representative into the delegate, and to give every male householder a direct and immediate part in the government of the country. Improvements in both manufactures and the art of war seemed to Adam Smith, with good reason, to necessitate a separation between the military and industrial occupations: now every able-bodied man is a soldier on the Continent. And here one of Auguste Comte's great generalizations also comes into question. Were a tendency to division of labour and differentiation of functions still to display itself on all sides, it would not give us a fundamental law determining the directions of human energies and their actual occupations. To take the case of another planet inhabited by human beings, astronomers might conceivably discover marks of a diversity of employments, and yet get no clue to the nature or course of the division of labour. We should need to know, for example, whether war and religion had any influence on their occupations. One of Comte's inductions affords an example of the kind of fundamental law needed to give us an insight into the causes and directions of the movement. Theology and war, according to Comte, are the ruling powers governing, in the early stages of society, human energies and employments; science and industry the chief powers in the more advanced stages. Undoubtedly the grounds on which this induction rests go to the root of the matter, and bring some great changes in the political, moral, and economic state of society under scientific law. Theology has long been a declining force, and, though its indirect influence is still great, has now little direct control over the economic structure of Western society. But the military element is more powerful now in Europe, and its power rests on less accidental causes than in Auguste Comte's own day. The very improvements in manufacture and the military art which tended, in Adam Smith's view, to wean the mass of mankind from war, the very agencies represented by steam and gunpowder, to which Buckle triumphantly traced its extinction in the civilized world, have brought nations so close together, and armed them with such deadly weapons, that every man may almost be said now to sleep with arms at his side, ready to do battle in the morning. Science and industry themselves, along with pacific tendencies, have others of the opposite character, both in the effects already referred to and in the higher pride, rivalry, ambition, and patriotism of nations, developed by intellectual and industrial progress. When Buckle pointed to the Russians as the only warlike people in Europe, except the Turks, because the least civilized, they were really a most unwarlike people under a warlike government. Now a military spirit is fast rising among them. Who shall say, too, that when the people of the United States have fully assimilated their present territory, and are at the same time brought into close proximity to the old world, their energies may not take a military direction for a time? 'The Americans,' said Tocqueville, 'have no neighbours, consequently no great wars to fear; they have almost nothing to dread from military glory.' When they are within four days of Europe they may find they have neighbours beyond sea; but, without crossing it, the whole continent north and south of the isthmus may tempt their ambition. Although a fundamental truth underlies the generalization referred to, it is not, then, a law from which deductions can be made. There are, moreover, diversities in the course of social evolution in different countries, which must be closely investigated before the sociologist can be in a condition to lay down universal canons; and after these are reached, much will remain for inquiry respecting the special development of particular races and nations.

A science of society thus does not exist in the sense of 'knowledge in its clearest and most absolute form, of which the test is prediction.' That, however, is not a scientific definition of science, and the sociologist may answer it with Bacon's words, *prudens interrogatio dimidium scientiæ.* Nor is it the science of society in its entirety only that is yet in its youth, and has a long and arduous future before it; it is so also with the department of it relating to the economic condition of mankind in different countries and ages. The labourer in this field, too, must go to work in a modester frame of mind than that of 'the Political Economist,' as he called himself in capitals, of twenty years ago. Mr. Lowe arrogates 'triumphs' for his own economic method: those he refers to were achieved by the opposite method of reasoning from observation and experience. But the scientific spirit is not a triumphant and boastful one, fired with a sort of intellectual Chauvinism, seeking polemical distinction and a path to promotion in the field of party war. A cavalry officer of the period before the Crimean War, when that branch of the army was distinguished by the glory of a moustache, used to say that no man could conceive the pitch to which human conceit could soar unless he had served in a light dragoon regiment. He was, however, mistaken. There was a being yet more elate with a sense of superiority over his fellow-creatures in the economist who had Bastiat at his fingers' ends, and who looked on political economy as a weapon by which he could discomfit political adversaries, and on free trade as a personal triumph; though he had as much claim to renown for it as a passenger in a Cunard steamer to the fame of Columbus.

Some of the earlier economists—Adam Smith, Malthus, Tooke, and John Mill—had a true claim to honour and reputation as discoverers. But the generalizations and conceptions that do credit to one period may discredit the next, just as it would disgrace the navigators of our time to follow the same course, and sail in the same kind of ship, as Columbus. The deductive economists of the present generation have contented themselves with the repetition of doctrines and formulas which once caused the light of science to dawn where all had been confusion and darkness. Clouds of abstraction and *a priori* reasoning nearly extinguished the promise of day; but fresh light is beginning to break. A few years ago Mr. Ingram's Address could hardly have been delivered, and the 'orthodox' economist, who now receives it with sullen respect, would have scoffed at it. It is suggested, indeed, by way of diminishing its effect, that its author is a follower of Auguste Comte; but it expresses the views of many who, like the present writer, are not, however highly some of them, like him, may think of Comte's genius.

XVII.

THE KNOWN AND THE UNKNOWN IN THE ECONOMIC WORLD.*

THE most characteristic feature of the commercial situation for more than a year past has been not so much the depth of the depression—for there have been worse times in that respect; or its extent—for the stagnation was as general throughout Europe, and much more widely felt throughout France thirty years ago—as the sense of being in the dark, and surrounded, as it were, by the unknown. Yet it is the consciousness only of not seeing their way on the part of people that is new. Trade has long been carried on blindly, and people as little knew what was before them when it was said to be advancing by leaps and bounds as they do now that these are found to have been leaps in the dark. Temporary circumstances have added to the gloom and uncertainty, and it is ascribable in part to a false economic theory; but to get a ray of light we must first recognize that the obscurity of the present crisis has arisen in a great measure from causes inherent in the constitution of the modern economic world. It is not the writer's purpose to inquire whether, in the most vital sense, the present depression is temporary or permanent. Our manufactures and commerce may or may not recover their vigour and supremacy; our agriculture may or may not be overborne finally by American competition. The chief point to which attention is sought here is that, even in the most favourable event, elements of disorder, difficulty, and recurring disaster, which have been growing

---

* *Fortnightly Review*, June 1st, 1879.

with the growth of our trade, will remain, unless new sources of light can be discovered. Another point that should not be left unnoticed is, that the economic world is not bounded by its trade, and has other regions in which to add to the known and diminish the unknown ought to be the economist's aim.

The full knowledge and foreknowledge lately claimed for political economy in modern commercial society can exist only at an opposite stage of development, at which human business and conduct are determined, not by individual choice, or the pursuit of wealth, or commercial principles, but by immemorial ancestral custom. All that relates to the occupations and movements of a nomad tribe in Central Asia is known and foreknown by all its members, who possess the power of prediction, which Mr. Lowe calls the test of science. 'Every tribe and every awl,' says a recent traveller among the Kirghis, 'follows year after year the same itinerary, pursuing the same paths, stopping at the same wells as their ancestors did a thousand years ago. No awl ever mistakes its way. The regularity and exactitude of the movement is such that you can predict to a day where, in a circuit of several hundred miles, any awl will be at any season of the year.' At the more advanced stages of early agricultural society the power of prediction continues, and is not destroyed by disturbing causes of a more abnormal and violent character than the follower of the *a priori* method of political economy has in view in the phrase. Dynasties rise and fall, conquerors come and go, empires are shattered above the head of the village community; yet it survives unchanged. The village itself may be burned, its lands laid waste, the inhabitants driven away for a generation; but another generation returns and resumes the old life, each man following the occupation of his fathers, pursuing the same methods, and seldom being either richer or poorer than they. It is in what Mr. Bagehot called a pre-economic state, though it is more properly regarded as an early state of the economic world among stationary communities—'where the thing that hath been it is that which shall be, and that which is done is that which shall be done, and there is no new thing under the sun'—that 'knowledge in its most perfect form, as tested by prediction,' exists. And just in proportion as the stationary passes into the progressive condition, as industry and commerce are developed, does the social economy become complex, diversified, changeful, uncertain, unpredictable, and hard to know, even in its existing phase, at any given time. In the primitive village community the prices of commodities and the gains of producers are not only known, but foreknown, because they are customary prices. But when a market grows upon the border, when dealings with strangers are unrestricted by the tie of kinship or community, or by usage, the prices at which things are bought and sold can no longer be known beforehand, and are not even necessarily known to everyone afterwards. Another element of uncertainty, introducing itself so soon as traffic with the outer world begins, is that production can no longer be exactly adjusted to consumption, supply to demand, both the number and the means of customers from without being unknown. And as industrial development proceeds; as labour is subdivided, and occupations multiply, and the methods of production improve; as commerce enlarges its borders and changes its paths, the unknown more and more takes the place of the known. The desire of wealth, or of its representative—money—instead of enabling the economist to foretell values and prices, destroys the power of prediction that formerly existed, because it is the mainspring of industrial and commercial activity and progress, of infinite variety and incessant alteration in the structure and operations of the economic world. For more than a hundred years before Adam Smith's birth the rate of wages might have been nearly foretold throughout most of Scotland, and in parts of the Highlands down to the time when the 'Wealth of Nations' was written. But so soon as commercial activity began to stir in the Lowlands, the price of labour became variable and uncertain. The Philosopher relates: 'In the last century the most usual day-wages of common labour through the greater part of Scotland were sixpence in summer and fivepence in winter. Three shillings a-week, the same price very nearly, still continues to be paid in some parts of the Highlands and Western Islands. Through the greater part of the low country the most usual wages of common labour are now eightpence a-day; tenpence, sometimes a shilling, in the counties which border on England, and in a few other places where there has lately been a rise in the demand for labour—about Glasgow, Carron, &c.' Had Arthur Young foretold the rates of agricultural wages in England in 1868 from those which he found prevalent in 1768, the prediction would have proved nearly correct in the stationary southern counties, though utterly false in the mining and manufacturing counties north of the Trent.

It is thus a fundamental error of the *a priori* or deductive political economy that it takes no cognizance of the cardinal fact that the movement of the economic world has been one from simplicity to complexity, from uniformity to diversity, from unbroken custom to change, and, therefore, from the known to the unknown. The origin of the error is in part traceable to the extreme slowness and almost imperceptible character of the movement down to the age of steam. Adam Smith's own theory of wages, profits, and prices, rested on the assumption that employments in general were long established, well known, and undergoing no change, and was expressly restricted to such. The immobility of the world he lived in shows itself in an observation of his great contemporary, Hume:—'In five hundred years the posterity of those in the coaches and those on the boxes will probably have changed places.' Hume seems to have taken for granted that five centuries after his time the same sort of coaches would travel on the same sort of road, the only change being in the places of the passengers inside and out. An age of iron, however, succeeded to his age of wood; the age of iron is already giving place to an age of steel; and who now attempts to forecast the modes of conveyance five centuries, or even five generations hence? 'De minimis non curat lex,' said Mr. Mill in the House of Commons, citing the legal maxim adroitly in reference to the small importation of meat little more than a decade ago. Now, nearly one-fourth of the animal food consumed in the kingdom comes from abroad, and even live beasts are largely imported. The extension, again, of the area of trade has brought with it liability to countless unforeseen and sudden changes, rendering it impossible to adjust supply to demand. Not only a great war, like the Franco-German, disturbs the calculations of merchants and manufacturers; the outbreak of the present Zulu war led to the sudden countermanding of large orders for sheep-shears, wire-fencing, and edge-tools for the Cape. Credit adds another unknown quantity. It springs from the growth of confidence between man and man, and of foresight in one sense; yet it greatly augments the uncertainty of trade, the difficulty of anticipating the future, and the chance of expectations being frustrated by fraud. So long as goods are sold only for cash, prices are fixed by the pecuniary means of purchasers, and are subject to comparatively little variation of demand; as soon, too, as the sale is effected, the amount of the seller's profit is certain. But when once promises to pay acquire a purchasing power, the fluctuations of prices have no assignable limit, and a promised payment may never be made; so that after parting with his goods the producer's profit still remains doubtful. Not only the future, but even the present, becomes inscrutable in a highly advanced community. The number of employments is so great, each of them is so intricate a business, and affected by such a variety of conditions, the fortunes of the individuals engaged in them are so diverse, that no one dreams of surveying the entire field; he often cannot tell even how the people he deals with himself, and to whom he is perhaps making large advances, are doing. The banker of fifty years ago, in Mr. Bagehot's words, 'formed his judgment of the solvency of those to whom he lent. And when London was by comparison a small city this practice might have been safe; but now that London is enormous, and that no one can watch anyone, such a trade would be disastrous: at present it would hardly be safe in a country town.' In the same work, 'Lombard Street,' Mr. Bagehot lays stress on the extent, beyond the conception of our ancestors, to which English trade is carried on by borrowed capital. It is a surprising instance of the force of a foregone conclusion that this acute thinker did not see how inconsistent this fact was, by his own showing, with the doctrine of an equality of profits, to which he adhered :—'A new man, with a small capital of his own, and a large borrowed capital, can undersell a rich man, who depends on his own capital only. The rich man wants the full mercantile rate of profit; but the poor man wants only interest on much of what he uses.' The man who trades with his own capital thus can no longer count on what Mr. Bagehot calls 'the full mercantile rate of profit.' But the new system introduces much else that disturbs the old order of things. Did 'the new man' take as much care of the capital he borrows as if it were his own, he would not treat the whole surplus of his gross profit above interest, as at his disposal, either to lower prices or to spend. He may be unexpectedly called on to refund what he has borrowed; his credit may be shaken; a hundred unlooked-for events may subject him to pressure; his position is far more precarious than that of the man with funds of his own; and he ought to provide an insurance fund in proportion. But he risks other people's money—not his own; if he loses it all, he is, at the worst, no poorer than when he began, after, perhaps, living like a lord in the meanwhile; and it will go hard with him if he does not save something out of the fire for himself. At a much earlier stage of the economic world a man ran some risk of being robbed of all his money; but he seldom ran any of losing it in a trade speculation. We talk of modern security of property in comparison with the middle ages; yet it would be much to say that the wealth of a modern capitalist is as secure as that of a stout franklin in the worst days of the Plantagenets.

Professor Nasse of Bonn, replying, in a recent essay, to the socialistic doctrine that, under State regulation, production might be so adjusted to consumption, and supply to demand, as to render industrial crises impossible, observes that such an adjustment, without individual freedom in respect either of production or consumption, is not inconceivable, though on terms involving the destruction of civilization and all that makes life worth having. 'But to reconcile it with individual freedom is a problem comparable only with the quadrature of the circle. All the operations of fixed capital—ships, railways, factories, mines—involve production for the future; but how is the future to be foreseen?'* One may add that the 'orthodox' theory of prices and profits is as inconsistent as the socialistic programme with individual liberty. It is a curious characteristic of the deductive political economy that, in spite of its show of logic, its followers have never firmly grasped either their own premises or their conclusions. With Mr. Senior and Mr. Lowe they suppose, for the most part, that the assumption on which their theory of value rests is a universal desire of wealth. Indeed, some who no longer contend that the whole economic world can be isolated, for the investigation of its laws, from the moral and political world, are still disposed to hold that there is a department of economic phenomena, namely, that of commercial exchanges, values, and prices, the laws of which may be deduced from the single motive of pecuniary gain. No theory whatever, nevertheless, is deducible from that motive alone. You may know that everybody you meet between Belgrave-square and the Bank loves wealth of some sort, and money, as the means of purchasing all sorts; but what can you infer from that with respect to anyone's part or conduct in either production or distribution? Can you infer, either, that the Duke of Westminster will, or that he will not, sweep a crossing for sixpence? The late Lord Derby is said to have replied to an engineer who urged that a particular line of railway would add ten thousand a-year to his rental—'How do you know that I care to have ten thousand a-year added to my rental?' The economist, however, need not ascend to too lofty a region, or perplex himself with so transcendental a question. He may take it for granted, like the engineer, that people do care for ten thousand a-year. Mr. Lowe's doctrine is not wholly unfounded, that the general love of money enables the economist to foretell human conduct. Just as from the strength of the impulses to marriage,

---

* *Ueber die Verhütung der Productionskrisen durch staatliche Fürsorge.* Von Dr. Erwin Nasse. Holtzendorff-Brentano. Jahrbuch III. i.

together with observations of their consequences, you may predict that, other circumstances remaining the same, nearly the same number of young men in business will marry this year as last; so from the strength in this country of pecuniary interest, and the course of conduct it has been found for centuries to lead to, you may predict that, if business does not greatly fall off, about the same number of young men will go into it this year as last. For fresh youth recruits the commercial world every year—not every tenth year, as a cyclical theorist naively persists. But you can no more predict from their love of money what prices and profits the young men will get in their business than from their love of fair women what fortune they will get with their wives. And you might as well assume that, allowing for difference of age, looks, family, and other attractions, the fortunes the wives bring will be equal, as that, allowing, according to the orthodox formula, for differences in the nature of their employment, they will make equal rates of profit on their capital. Here the real main postulate of the deductive economist comes in. They cannot, he says, make a higher rate of profit in one business than in another, because other people will not allow that if they know it, but will cut in at once. And he assumes that they do know it. He assumes that the choice of occupations and investments, and the movements of labour and capital, are determined by knowledge so accurate that the result is the same percentage of profit on capital all round, and a scale of comparative prices in proportion to the quantity and quality of the labour and sacrifices required to produce commodities, or their comparative cost of production. He predicts, in short, that the price of any given article will be such as to give average profit to its producers, after paying the labourers average wages. If you object that prices fluctuate in the most unforeseen manner—that producers, so far from all getting 'average' profits, meet with the most different fortunes, some being ruined, and some becoming millionaires—his excuse is ready. Political economy, he tells you, with an air of offended dignity, is a science of tendencies in the long run, and in the absence of disturbing causes; it does not predict in individual cases. A great general used to say that a man who was good at excuses was never good for anything else; and nearly as much may be said of a theory. But the deductive economist has really no title to the excuse, such as it is. His theory of profits and prices, when examined, will be found to claim to be true, under all circumstances, in the case of every individual in trade and of every particular article, and to foretell the exact rates at which goods will be sold. His theory of taxation is an application of his theory of profits and prices; and it proceeds on the assumption that prices will actually conform to the cost of production, so nicely in every particular case, that every special tax on any commodity will be recovered by the producer from the consumer, with a profit on the advance. No one was less disposed than Mr. Mill to strain the orthodox system till it cracked; and in his chapter on the relation of cost of production to value it is somewhat vaguely laid down that, as a general rule, things tend to exchange at such value, that is, to sell at such prices as will enable each producer to be repaid the cost of production with ordinary profit. But when he comes to taxes on commodities he affirms, in accordance with the orthodox theory, that 'there are but two cases in which duties on commodities can, in any degree or any manner, fall on the producer.' The excepted cases do not concern the question; and in the case of customs and excise duties, trade licenses, and various stamp duties, taxes, and rates, the strict theory is, that a producer recovers all special taxation with a profit in every particular instance. No disturbing causes can be pleaded, nor can the trader obtain a postponement of taxation until it becomes certain that he will be recouped by his customers.

The orthodox, *a priori*, or deductive system thus postulates much more than a general desire of wealth. It postulates, also, such full knowledge of the gains in different employments, and such facilities of choice and change of employment, that any special tax can be evaded or shifted. A case where the conditions seem sufficiently realized will illustrate the matter. Indoor and outdoor servants meet in the same establishments, and are in the closest relations; they know each other's wages, perquisites, and circumstances exactly; and the classes recruiting them both are the same, and equally well-informed. The son of the gamekeeper, gardener, coachman, or groom, knows as well as the butler and footman how the indoor servants are off; and he knows that, if the duties were abolished, the condition of outdoor servants and labourers, who buy their own tea and beer, would be improved. It is therefore a reasonable inference that masters who supply these articles to their indoor servants give, or may give if they like, lower wages in consequence of the duties, and that indoor wages would rise if the duties were taken off, so that their real incidence may be said to be on the servants. To confound this case with that of indirect taxes in general, as a recent writer has done,* is to fall into the fundamental error of the *a priori* system of confounding the unknown with the known in the economic world. The farmer, the merchant, the manufacturer, the innkeeper, the grocer, the tobacconist, the publican, do not know the profits of other businesses, and are, to a very small extent, recruited from the same classes. Farmers, for instance, as Mr. Bear says, 'as a rule do not go out of farming until they are ruined.' Most of them know no other means of getting a living, without sinking into the position of stewards and bailiffs—a class far too numerous already. Again, the master can stop the amount of the duties at the time he pays his servants their wages, whereas a trader's premises may be burnt down, or he may become bankrupt a week after his rates and taxes are paid, and before the sale of any part of his stock: the payment, indeed, may be the last straw that breaks an overburdened back. Many men in trade, during the last four years, have failed to recover their taxes in prices, because they have failed altogether.

Adam Smith's economic theory was mainly a theory of production and abundance, or, in his own words, of 'the great multiplication of the productions of the different arts in consequence of the division of labour, which occasions that universal

* Mr. H. Sidgwick, *Fortnightly Review*, February, 1879, p. 304.

opulence which extends itself to the lowest ranks of the people.' With distribution by means of exchange he was concerned chiefly as promoting the division of labour, and thereby the plenty and variety of commodities. With Ricardo distribution, as he states in his preface, became the chief problem, and he elaborated a theory of exchange values, wages, profits, and prices, irreconcilable with the fundamental principles of Adam Smith's theory of production. Industrial liberty and the division of labour, the two pillars of Adam Smith's system, produce an economic world, the vastness, complexity, and incessant changes of which are absolutely incompatible with the main postulates of the Ricardian theory, that the advantages and disadvantages of all the different occupations are known, that competition equalizes the rewards of both labour and abstinence, and that the prices of commodities therefore are determined by the respective cost of production. The whole deductive theory of distribution rests on that postulate. It is, indeed, because so much has been built on it that scrutiny of the ground it stands on is resisted and resented. The system rests on the wrong end, the superstructure supporting the foundation. For though it is true in logic, as in mechanics, that nothing is stronger than its weakest part, it is not so in matters of opinion, whether in politics, religion, or philosophy. A seemingly symmetrical system has in itself charms for many minds, and the interests bound up with orthodox economics are various and strong. The opponent of direct taxation, for instance, is well pleased with a system which teaches that taxes on trade and commodities fall with perfect equality; and had not their inequality been thus put out of sight, Mr. Gladstone could hardly have dreamt of the enterprise of abolishing the income tax.

In Adam Smith's time a revolt against the blundering interference of the State led by reaction, in both England and France, to an overweening trust in the enlightenment and sagacity of individual interest, with which the notion of keen insight into the condition of every employment was in harmony. But there was also in a comparatively small, simple, and stationary economic world better reason to assume the existence of such insight. It might, for example, be not irrationally conjectured that in a little village at the present day every man knows all his neighbours' affairs. To jump from that to the conclusion that everybody in England knows the affairs of everybody else is the leap that Ricardo and his followers have made. The present writer, after personal inquiry some years ago in villages and small towns within the United Kingdom and on the Continent, was led to doubt that even in a modern village is there such a knowledge of profits as the deductive economist assumes. The village innkeeper, publican, or shopkeeper, who is making a small fortune, does not invite competition by telling his neighbours of his profits; and the man who is not doing well does not alarm his creditors by exposing the state of his affairs. If you take a whole country like England, it becomes a matter of accident, situation, and personal history and connexion, what a man knows about the state of any particular business. There are people in London and elsewhere who know more about the state of trade and the openings for capital and enterprise in California, China, and Japan, or some South American State, than in their own country, and who could more easily make their own way, or push on their sons or their nephews, in a place some thousand miles off, than in their own town. The distinction which Mr. Mill has drawn between international trade and home trade, in respect of the transferability of labour and capital and the equalization of wages and profit, if it had once some foundation when trade at home was simpler and better known, and when foreign countries were almost wholly unknown, cannot now be sustained. Not that the doctrine of the equality of profits and of the determination of comparative prices by comparative cost of production is now applicable to both, but that it is applicable to neither. It was a step in the right direction to recognise its inapplicability to the exchanges between different countries, but the further step is now required of abandoning it altogether.

In both home trade and international trade the migration of

labour and capital has some effect on wages and profits, and the comparative cost of producing different commodities some effect on their comparative value and price; but in both cases the effect is uncertain, irregular, and incalculable. In neither case is there an equalization of either wages or profits; in neither case do prices conform to the Ricardian law of cost. If a particular business is known or believed to be flourishing, capital flows into it; but it also flows into businesses that are, in reality, very unprosperous. One has only to keep one's eyes open in the streets of London to see, year after year, shops fail, disappear, and reappear with another name over the window, though the locality evidently does not support them. Save in so far as the prosperity of their own business depends on that of others, the people in one trade know little or nothing of the condition of other trades, or no more than the newspapers tell them. So far, too, is the producer of one article from knowing the cost of every other, that often he does not know what the cost of his own commodity is to other producers in the same business. That varies with the method they follow, their situation, connexion, and the rapidity of their returns; the solvency of the people they give credit to, and the number of bad debts; their own credit; the economy, the skill, care, and invention exerted by both themselves and those under them; luck, and many other conditions. Ricardo and his followers have assumed labour to be the only element in the cost of production, and the only productive power: and the notion has had pernicious consequences. Capitalists have been led by it to look to reduction of wages as the only means of keeping up profit, and labourers to suppose that every increase of profit must have arisen from their own work, and be at their own cost. All the sophistry in the literature of Socialism has not given birth to a more mischievous fallacy than that contained in the Ricardian dogma: "The rate of profit is never increased by a better distribution of labour, by the invention of machinery, or by any means of abridging labour, either in the manufacture or the conveyance of goods. These are causes which operate on price, and are beneficial to consumers; but they have no effect whatever on profit. On the other hand, every diminution in the wages of labour raises profit.' * A capitalist, no less than a statesman, may, by taking thought, add a cubit to his stature. He may diminish his outgoings and augment his returns without lowering wages. The soil, the seed, the animals, the coal, the machinery, the chemical agents that capitalists employ, have productive powers; their own brains have productive powers; and all these forces may be made, by skill and economy, to produce more at less cost. Mr. Mill made, doubtless, an important correction of Ricardo's language in saying that the rate of profit depends, not on wages, but on the cost of labour; but the cost of labour is only one of several conditions affecting the result.

What is or may be known generally, with respect to commodities, is not the cost—still less the profit—of producing them, but their actual market price. People in a particular trade may further know what profit a particular price yields to themselves, though the same price may give very different profits to different producers. People outside the trade, again, may know whether the present prices of the things produced in it are above or below the usual level. But not even the people in the trade can know what the price will be six months hence. When the price of an article—say coal or iron—is above the usual level, capital is attracted to its production, and bills increase in the business; but no examination of the entire field of employment is known or attempted. In truth, the choice of employment runs in a very narrow groove. There is, no doubt, a tendency of trades to localize themselves, like cotton manufacture in Lancashire, in the places with the best natural aptitudes for them. But in the degree and manner in which this localization takes place it is largely the result of want of information, and want of originality and enterprise, and is far from effecting the best distribution of industry. Men follow each other, like sheep, in flocks, though the sheep are not wise in

* Ricardo's *Works*, ed. M'Culloch, p. 49.

inferring that wherever there is enough good grass for a few, there must be plenty for the whole flock that goes after them. Belfast is well situated for the manufacture of linen, and has a trained population, with hereditary aptitudes; but that is far from affording adequate reason for the fact that almost everyone there with capital has, for the last two generations, gone into linen; for the place and people have capacities for other manufactures. The Belfast people have put almost all their eggs in one basket. There has been a great over-production of linen; and the case is only one of many, showing that Chancellor Oxenstiern's saying, 'Quantula sapientia regitur mundus,' is as true of the commercial as it is of the political world.

Instead of the world of light, order, equality, and perfect organization, which orthodox political economy postulates, the commercial world is thus one of obscurity, confusion, haphazard, in which, amid much destruction and waste, there is by no means always a survival of the fittest, even though cunning be counted among the conditions of fitness. 'The race is not to the swift, nor the battle to the strong, nor yet riches to men of understanding; but time and chance happeneth to them all.' The part of chance in the matter is really so great, the venture so often chiefly at other people's risk, and the ramifications of commercial relations and credit, the sudden changes in the activity of business and in demand, the fluctuations of prices, make the trader's future dependent on so many other conditions than his own skill and care, that not a few hardly try to exercise judgment or foresight. The Duke of Wellington is said to have replied to a lady who besought him to tell her how the Battle of Waterloo was won: 'Well, madam, we pounded and they pounded, and we pounded the hardest.' If the story is correct, the Duke probably thought no better account of a battle intelligible to a woman; but many men nowadays seem of opinion that the only way to succeed in the battle of life is to pound the hardest as long as they can, especially if they can do so with metal from other people's magazines. The very word 'speculation' has undergone a perceptible change of meaning, denoting something much nearer gambling than it once did.

Adam Smith spoke of certain employments in his day as lotteries—'the lottery of the law,' 'the lottery of the sea,' for example—and of the absurd presumption of mankind in their own good fortune in respect of such lotteries. Now almost every trade has become a lottery, and human presumption has in no respect diminished.

The ignorance and blindness with which modern trade is carried on are, as the foregoing pages have shown, partly inevitable and irremediable, resulting as they do, to a great extent, from the consequences of industrial and commercial progress on the one hand, and the limitations of human faculties on the other. So much could never be known, in a free and progressive world, of the condition and prospects of every employment, nor could the transfer of labour and capital become so easy, as to produce an approximation to the equality in the rate of profit imagined by the orthodox economist. His system has, indeed, done much to defeat itself and to aggravate the obscurity, disorder, and inequality. By assuming that the laws determining profits, prices, and the division of employment, are fully understood, and pursuing the method of deduction from arbitrary assumptions to the neglect of the investigation of facts, he has left us in darkness with respect to many matters as to which the economic world might be less unknown than it is. Arthur Young's 'Tours,' Tooke's 'History of Prices,' Porter's 'Progress of the Nation,' Thorold Rogers' 'History of Agriculture and Prices,' Caird's 'English Agriculture in 1850,' the so-called 'Domesday Books'—inaccurate as they are—the 'Agricultural Statistics,' and those relating to trade and to income, together with the Reports of many Parliamentary Committees, afford an example of the facts that might be gathered, marshalled, and sifted. We might by this time have an almost complete industrial and commercial map of the kingdom, showing, for the last forty years, the distribution of trades, the changes in the methods of both manufacture and farming, the migration of their sites, the new employments invented, the number of persons in every employment in each successive year, the fluctuations in the prices of both commodities and labour, not in the chief markets only, but in every town and parish, and the main changes that have taken place in the nature, amount, and distribution of national wealth, and other causes. Mr. Bagehot, criticising the plea of a German economist and statist, Dr. Gustav Cohn, for a close investigation of all facts relating to banking and other departments of industrial and commercial economy, called it, by way of disparagement, 'the all-case method,' affirming that no discovery was ever so made. It would be nearer the truth to say that no discovery was ever made by the no-case method. To imagine that a clever man, with his eyes shut, can think out the laws of the economic world is as reasonable as to suppose that he could, in the same manner, discover the laws of the physical world. In chemistry, in natural history, in physiology, in physical astronomy, discoveries are made every year by the all-case method—by neglecting no phenomenon as unworthy of observation, and investigating every case that presents itself, with a view to ascertaining its causes and laws. The economist might acquire by this method something of the faculty of prediction which Mr. Lowe claims for him. The relation, for example, between the economy and the law of a country, and between the movements of both, is one of the cases in which a power of prevision may be acquired by the inductive method. When Mr. Lowe affirms that political economy is the only department of political and moral science in which prediction is possible, he forgets that all the laws of civilized society are based on the assumption that the conduct of the great majority of its members can be foretold, that they will obey the laws, and that certain consequences, moral, political, and economic, will ensue. Were it otherwise, the desires of which the various kinds of wealth are the objects would lead, not to industry and commerce, but only to plunder and theft. In relation to the present depression of trade, an instance may be given of the power of prediction the lawyer possesses. As Auguste Comte well said, 'to predict the future you must be able to predict the past, where your predictions can be verified and your method put to the test.' The following prediction of the past, proving a power of predicting the future, is in point. Not long ago, an eminent economic authority, Mr. Jevons, referred, in a letter in the 'Times,' to the number of bankruptcies in the United States in 1878, in support of his theory of a decennial solar cycle, resulting in regular periods of depression and commercial crises. An eminent legal authority, on the other hand, Mr. Francis Reilly, observed at once to the present writer, that Mr. Jevons should have inquired whether anything besides the number of sun-spots had changed, adding, that the American bankruptcy law varied, and as in this country the number of bankruptcies varied with the law, he believed it would be found to be so in the United States. Soon afterwards facts were published, proving that this prediction of the past was well-founded, that the great number of American bankruptcies last year arose from the desire of debtors to take advantage of an expiring Act—too liberal to defaulting traders—and that Mr. Reilly might draw an Act that would much diminish the number of fraudulent bankruptcies in England, and possibly baffle Mr. Jevons' solar cycle in 1888.

Again, although the modern commercial world is, by its nature and constitution, by the ever-increasing extent of its area, not only one of perpetual change, but liable to sudden and unforeseen disturbances, yet the very perception of this fact and of its causes gives a power of prevision. A curious and instructive example of the error of the *a priori* economist on this point will be found in Ricardo's chapter on natural and market price. He could not shut his eyes altogether to the fact that there were fluctuations in prices and profits, disturbing the order and equality his theory assumed, and was compelled to admit that the termination of the great war with France, for example, had deranged the previous distribution of employments in Europe, and destroyed some of the occupations of capital.* But he proceeded at once to set aside such changes in his exposition of the laws of wages, profits, and prices, on the assumption that they were equally operative in all states of society—an assumption absolutely false in itself, and assuredly

* Ricardo's *Works*, ed. M'Culloch, p. 48.

not a reason for leaving the phenomena in question out of consideration, had it been true. 'Having,' he says, 'fully acknowledged the temporary effects which, in particular employments, may be produced on the prices of commodities, as well as on the wages of labour and the profits of stock, by accidental causes, *since these effects are equally operative in all states of society*, we will leave them entirely out of our consideration, whilst we are treating of the laws which regulate natural prices, natural wages, and natural profits.'* That is to say, in discussing the natural as distinguished from the positive laws governing the distribution of wealth, he ignored the essential difference between stationary and progressive society—between the ancient economic world, with its simple and customary methods and prices, and the modern, with its vastness, complexity, incessant movement, and sudden vicissitudes and fluctuations. The changes which he set aside as the results of 'accidental causes' were mainly the natural and inevitable consequences of the constitution and course of the economic world in which he lived. But even disturbances which arise from political and other causes of a different nature ought to be taken into account by both the theoretical economist and the practical man of business, as inseparable from the world and the age in which we live. The present depression of trade has been attributed to various temporary causes—the Franco-German War and its consequences, the war in Turkey, the immense military expenditure through Europe, the demonetizing of silver, a succession of bad harvests at home, and famines in India and China. These are not, in truth, the only causes of the depression which has arisen in a great measure, as already explained, from conditions inherent in modern economy; but even the temporary occurrences referred to have nothing really abnormal in their character: they are natural incidents of the world and the age, and as such should have been included in the speculations of both economists and men of business. It is written, indeed, that 'he that observeth the winds shall not

* Ricardo's *Works*, ed. M'Culloch, p. 49.

sow, and he that observeth the clouds shall not reap;' but he is a poor husbandman who reckons on nothing but fine weather.

The present article has kept the industrial and commercial side of the world chiefly in view; but it would be a fundamental error to regard the economical world as bounded by commerce and industry, or as containing no other phenomena whose laws it is the object of political economy to investigate. The desires for various kinds of wealth are not the only motives on which the production and distribution of wealth depend; the economist must penetrate even into the most romantic passions and sentiments of the human heart. There, too, all is not unknown, or beyond scientific, or even commercial, prevision. No writer of his time had a keener insight into the secret springs of the movements of society, when he was not in economic leading-strings, than Mr. Bagehot, who has finely observed that 'the range and force of some of the finest impulses and affections of young hearts enter largely into the calculations and anticipated profits of the speculative builder.' Stop for a twelvemonth marriages of the most sentimental order—those of pure love—and many builders and house-owners will be ruined; many clergymen, lawyers, and doctors impoverished; and a generation hence it will be felt in the labour market, and in every trade and profession. But marriages for love will not stop for a twelvemonth; the calculation of the Registrar-General will not be defeated; clerical, legal, and medical functionaries will be employed, and five-and-twenty years hence sons of this year's lovers will be found in every vocation. A critic has severely rebuked the writer for having, in a previous article, controverted Mr. Lowe's proposition that the desire of wealth is the single motive in human affairs on which predictions can be founded, and that 'in love, war, and politics, prediction is impossible.' 'He actually,' the critic says, 'adduces the fact that we can predict, within a certain small limit of probable error, the number of marriages, for any year, as a proof that economic phenomena do not depend on the operation of a single motive. He could not have chosen a more unlucky example; for the merest tyro in statistical inquiry is aware how closely the number of marriages is connected with the price of grain, and this in all countries. No one can possibly look at the curves representing these two facts without seeing that the price of grain determines the movement of the marriages.'* The critic would appear to hold that the single motive to marriage is to go share in a big loaf. But it is true that, although only the poorest class is restrained by the price of corn, when bread is dear many poor persons are unable to marry for love. The curious thing is that in England, among a nation of shopkeepers, marriages are more commonly for love than in France, where the tender passion is supposed to be more easily excited; and that if the love of money be anywhere the single motive from which transactions in the matrimonial market can be foretold, it is at the other side of the Channel. In all countries, however, the forces by which the economic world is moved are many and complex; and it is only by a searching investigation of its actual movements that the laws by which these movements are governed can be known.

It is not meant that deduction has no place in economic science; every inference from, or application of, a general principle is a deduction. What is meant is, that political economy has not reached the stage of a deductive science; that the fundamental laws of the economic world are still imperfectly known; and that they can be fully known only by patient induction. The aphorism of Bacon, moreover, respecting the application of human laws, should be constantly present to the mind of the student of economic laws:—'Consequentiae non est consequentia; sed sisti debet extensio intra casus proximos: alioqui labetur ad dissimilia, et magis valebunt acumina ingeniorum quam auctoritas legum.' The theory of profits, prices, and taxation, referred to in a previous page, affords an instructive instance. That everyone desires money is a consequence of the fact that money is the common medium of exchange, and purchases everything. But every subsequent link in the chain of circumstances deduced in the orthodox theory is defective—that there is a consequent equality of both

---

* The *Statist*, January 4th, 1879.

wages and profits; that prices are, therefore, in proportion to cost of production; and that a tax on any special trade or commodity falls necessarily on the consumer, and cannot fall on the producer. Small capitalists have been driven out of several trades by taxation, and it is thus possible that in particular cases so-called indirect taxation, by ruining producers, may cause the stock-in-trade to be sold at a sacrifice to consumers.

Two conclusions at least, it is hoped, many readers will concur in—that the economic world is still, in a great measure, an unknown one; and that to know it economists must explore it, as geographers have explored the world of physical geography.

XVIII.

THE HISTORY AND FUTURE OF INTEREST AND PROFIT.*

The history of interest, which involves that of profit, is connected with fundamental changes in human society, and in the ideas and feelings on which it rests. It raises, too, economic and social problems of no little importance for the future of the civilized world. Once it was a question wholly of moral and religious sentiment, at length embodied in positive law, whether interest were permissible, and, if so, what rate should subsist. A generation ago in this country all restraint of its rate, together with all other interference on the part of society at large, or the State, with pecuniary dealings between adult men, seemed definitely abandoned. But on the Continent of Europe the legitimacy of interest is vehemently disputed by the adherents of Socialism ; a feeling against it is growing up in the United States ; and even in England, although no special question about interest has been raised, there are indications of a tendency to revert to ancient ideas on kindred subjects.

The mediæval reprobation of interest under the name of usury has often been ascribed to the Christian Church, but its origin may be traced to a much earlier stage of society. Churchmen and canonists, doubtless, appealed to Christian doctrine, as well as to Aristotle's doctrine, that interest is unnatural, because money, unlike corn and cattle, is barren and cannot beget money ; and since nothing is lost by the loan of an unproductive commodity, they argued that the lender was

---

* *Fortnightly Review*, November 1st, 1881.

in equity entitled to no recompense. But Aristotle himself unconsciously sought to justify a notion inherited from prehistoric times, when the members of each community still recognized each other as kinsmen; when communism in property existed, at least in practice, and no one who had more than he needed could refuse to share his superfluous wealth with a fellow-tribesman in want. Tacitus, who remarks that usury was unknown to the ancient Germans, tells also that anyone might enter the house of a German, and ask for what he pleased: receiving it as a matter of course, and placed under no obligation by the gift. Describing, in like manner, the ancient customs of the Eskimo, Dr. Rink says that if anyone had anything to spare, it was ranked among goods that were possessed in common; and if a man borrowed the boats or weapons of another, he was not bound to give the owner any compensation for damage or loss. The usages and sentiments of archaic communism survived in various forms long after private property, even in land, had grown up. Far down in the middle ages, the rich man who closed his hall-door, and dined in a private room with his family, was a byword for extraordinary selfishness and meanness. Many other mediæval customs and opinions had their original source in pre-historic tribal and family ideas, and in the practices of a stage of social evolution when each little community deemed itself one in blood and ancestral gods, and individual proprietary rights were most imperfectly developed. The maxim 'Natura non facit saltum' is true of the social as of the physical world. The structure of English mediæval society, especially on its economic side, had throughout a foundation of which the original type must be looked for in archaic kinship. The guild was a brotherhood bearing all the marks of deriving its organization and fundamental ideas from the ancient joint family. The township or village community had been constituted either by actual kinsmen or by a body of men organized as such. The typical town was an expansion of the township. The nation was an amalgamation of tribes whose tribal ideas survived in various forms. On all sides social structures, practices, and notions existed, descending from a time when neighbourhood was scarcely possible without blood relationship or formal adoption, unless in the case of the conquered serf. The feeling of actual kinship might have disappeared in that of membership of a local community bound together by ancient customs, rights, and obligations, but neither townsmen nor countrymen could have conceived individuals dwelling in the same place, without bond, connexion or reciprocal duties, each pursuing what life and occupation he thought fit, controlled neither by his neighbours, nor by ancient local usage. The theory of mediæval prices had grown out of the archaic idea that the vendor of a commodity or the labourer for hire in a neighbourhood was either a member by descent or adoption of the local community, or its servant, and in either case bound to conform to its usages, to render to it honest and loyal service, and to accept customary or equitable remuneration. And the connexion is close between the prohibition of interest and the penalties in the early statutes against forestalling, engrossing, and regrating. The forestaller was regarded as seeking an exorbitant profit, not by honest work, but simply out of the necessities of a neighbour, who stood in the shoes of the ancient kinsman, and had inherited, as it were, the moral rights of one. A man was held entitled to a fair price, determined commonly by custom or authority, for work or produce, but not to a profit on buying or storing up things of which his fellow-townsmen stood in need. Dr. W. von Ochenkowski, in a recent work of merit, 'Englands wirthschaftliche Entwickelung im Ausgange des Mittelalters,' lays too exclusive a stress on the duty which the mediæval citizen owed to the State. That duty plays an important part in mediæval economy; but Dr. von Ochenkowski overlooks the nearer duty which the burgher owed to the civic body, and the inhabitant of a township or manor to the little village community and its lord.

The fundamental idea of modern English economy—that every man should be free to follow his own pecuniary interest as he thinks fit without fraud—does not distinctly emerge until the sixteenth century, in which Shakespeare deplored the decline of the loyalty of the antique world, 'when service sweat for duty, not for mead.' Yet we may detect in commercial towns an earlier break with antiquity in respect of dealings between lenders and borrowers. Two opposite practices in relation to the payment of interest co-existed in the fourteenth century, one descending from social infancy, the other developed in the progress of intercourse between mercantile people—among whom, moreover, the clergy were in no great esteem—by experience of the needs of trade. There were ordinances of the Mayor of London against usury, but they were rarely enforced, and seem to have been chiefly aimed against foreigners and the high rate of interest they exacted. The civic authorities formally sanctioned in the case of citizens what would now be regarded as an enormous rate of interest, and passed accounts in which it was charged, as in accordance with 'the custom of the city.' The city records show that the fortune of a ward was customarily intrusted to his guardian to employ in his own business, paying interest at ten per cent. Thus, in 1374, the account of a mercer was duly presented respecting '£300 belonging to a minor, son of a late citizen, and delivered to the mercer to trade with.' The mercer 'charges himself with £300 so received, and with the increase by way of profit, four shillings being paid yearly for the use of every pound according to the custom of the city, of which he asks that he may be allowed two shillings in the pound for his trouble, according to the custom of the city.'* The customary rate of profit is here computed at twenty per cent., the customary interest at ten per cent., or half profit; the rate of profit being 'double interest,' as Adam Smith says it was in his time, four hundred years afterwards. The Act 37 Edward III., c. xi., which puts merchants, citizens, and burgesses with a capital of £1000 on the same footing in point of expendible income as landowners with £200 a-year, proves that twenty per cent. was then considered the customary rate of profit in the commercial towns of the kingdom. It is observable, too, that ten per cent., the customary rate of interest among the tradespeople of London in Edward III.'s reign, is

* Riley's *Memorials of London*, p. 378. Compare a fishmonger's account, *ibid.*, pp. 446, 447.

the rate permitted by the Act of Henry VIII. in A.D. 1546, which first legalized interest, so that it seems to have been still regarded at the latter period not only as the traditional rate, but also as moderate and reasonable.

We must not, indeed, take the profit and interest customary in commercial towns in the reign of Edward III. as representing rates current throughout the country. The profits of agriculture after the pestilence in the middle of the fourteenth century, lowered as they were by the rise of wages consequent on depopulation, could not have borne a rate of interest approaching to ten per cent. on the capital engaged in ordinary farming. Outside of the region of town trade no regular or customary rate prevailed. Unless among townspeople, money in the Middle Ages was usually borrowed not to make profit, but because the borrower was in need, and the interest was often extortionate. In many cases the penalties on usury prevented loans altogether. The amount of accumulation, moreover, in the Middle Ages was small, and but little of it took the form of coin, the only loanable form of capital, even townspeople commonly investing their savings in land, cattle, sheep, plate, household stuff, and clothing. The amount of capital that could be put into trade was limited in various ways, and, save in trade, loans for interest were surrounded with danger, discredit, and trouble. Money, too, that is to say coin, was scarce. The English silver mines had become exhausted in the fourteenth century:* the Papal See caused a constant drain of treasure; foreign war was another source of pecuniary loss; and base money from abroad supplanted the sterling coin of the realm. Monasteries and great landowners not unfrequently raised loans, but there was so little lending throughout the country, that we may confine our attention to the towns.

Several questions arise with respect to interest and profit in the towns. How did so high a rate of interest as ten per cent. come to subsist in mediæval trade? Why did it continue

---

* See Dr. Georg Schanz's excellent work, *Englische Handelspolitik, gegen Ende des Mittelalters*, i. pp. 492–494.

at the same rate, neither fluctuating from time to time, nor declining on the whole, as it has done in modern times? How was a customary profit of twenty per cent. established? The high rate of interest in the Middle Ages has often been ascribed to the insecurity of capital. But unless in foreign commerce—which as yet was chiefly in foreign hands, and in which there was danger of both piracy and shipwreck, and great gains and great losses were made—trade risks were less in the Middle Ages than they are now. Trade, in general, was carried on in a small, customary, circumspect way, regulated by guilds and civic authority; demand and prices could generally be estimated beforehand; and there was little or no speculation. The rate of commercial interest was not determined by the demand for, and supply of, money; had it been so, it would have varied from time to time, instead of remaining steady at ten per cent. Its explanation must be sought, first of all, in the rate of profit. Modern economists have for the most part assumed that competition proportions prices to cost of production and equalizes profits. Mediæval economy was based on very different principles, yet it brought about a much closer approximation of profits to equality, and a much closer correspondence of prices with outlay, labour, and sacrifice. The mediæval theory was, that the trader owed to the community to which he belonged good articles for reasonable and moderate remuneration, and should not seek his own 'singular profit;' while he was, on the other hand, entitled to such profit and prices as yielded a sufficient livelihood to himself and his family—the family forming an important unit in the social economy. In Elfric's 'Colloquy of the Eleventh Century,' the Merchant says, 'I say that I am useful to the King and to ealdormen and to the rich and to all people. I ascend my ship with my merchandise and sail over the sealike places, and sell my things, and buy things which are not produced in this land.' To the question, 'Will you sell your things here as you bought them there?' he answers, 'I will not, because what would my labour benefit me? I will sell them dearer here than I bought them there, that I may get some profit to feed me, my wife and children.'

Anything above a fair profit was regarded, like extortionate interest, as usurious, because out of proportion to labour and cost. Thus the 'Ordinances of the Plumbers,' approved by the Mayor and Aldermen of London in the thirtieth year of Edward III., ordain 'that everyone of the trade shall do his work well and lawfully, and that for working a clove of lead for gutters or for roofs of houses, he shall take only one halfpenny, and for working a clove for furnaces, belfrys and conduit pipes, one penny. Also that no one for any singular profit shall engross lead coming to the said city for sale, to the damage of the commonalty, but that all persons of the said trade, as well poor as rich, shall be partners therein at their desire.' There were many ordinances, both royal and municipal, in the fourteenth century for the sale of various commodities 'at reasonable prices.' The general standard of 'reasonable' or fair price and profit was custom. Where the seasons, as in the case of food, or other circumstances made a customary price impossible, the local authorities or the central government itself intervened to prevent sellers from taking advantage of the necessities of buyers. There was abundance of self-seeking and greed of lucre, as well as of hypocrisy, in the mediæval world, but they worked not through competition, but through combination; towns, guilds, companies, classes, grasping at exclusive privileges, monopolies, and gains. Men pursued their prey, as it were, in troops and packs. What was sought was not the gain of individuals as such, but of communities, corporations, fraternities, and orders.

The causes determining mediæval profit may then be easily understood. Its high rate was not the result, as in new countries in modern times, of a great productiveness of labour and capital, aided by prolific natural agents. In a small, and, compared with our own, a nearly stationary commercial world—where the number of persons engaged in each trade was limited by guild ordinances, or by the governing body of the town; where every business was carried on in accordance with usage or rule, even the amount of capital or work being often restricted; where prices were controlled by custom, public opinion, authority, or positive law—the ordinary rate of profit might be without difficulty measured, indirectly regulated, and kept at a high level. Twenty per cent. came accordingly to be the customary rate of profit in the fourteenth century, and seems to have continued so long afterwards. Again, the customary rate of interest in mediæval trade was half profit, or ten per cent., not because the competition of lenders and borrowers resulted in such a rate—for competition would have produced a fluctuating, not a stable or customary rate—but, it may be reasonably conjectured, on the same principle that prevailed in the common European tenure of metayage, that the person furnishing the capital should get half of the produce, and the person performing the labour the other half. Throughout the greater part of Europe down to the sixteenth century the prevailing rate of interest was ten per cent., and twenty per cent., or double interest, appears to have been the customary profit, at least in common opinion.

The statute of Henry VIII.'s reign (37 Henry VIII., A.D. 1546), which legalized interest at ten per cent., though prohibiting higher rates as usurious, opens a new epoch in the history of the subject. Interest was now distinguished from usury. The same cause that had led the civic authorities of London two centuries earlier to sanction trade loans at that rate, now acted on the Legislature with respect to all loans. Economic considerations prevailed over early moral ideas and later theological dogmas. The extension of manufactures and commerce called for an extension of credit, and interest was the foundation or *raison d'être* of credit. The change was connected, too, with the Reformation and the decline of ecclesiastical authority, while the position and influence of merchants and citizens had risen. There was, at the same time, a general tendency of legislation towards a relaxation of restraints on the disposition and use of property, of which the Statutes of Fines and of Wills are instances; commercial policy and the dictates of experience superseding the notions of both archaic and feudal society respecting the inalienability of family property. Theology recovered ground for the moment in Edward VI.'s reign, when 'a Bill against Usury,' in 1552, enacted that the late statute sanctioning interest should be 'utterly abrogate, void, and repealed.' But in 1571, an Act of Elizabeth, following that of Henry VIII., again legalized interest at ten per cent. Thenceforward the Legislature intervened only to lower the legal rate, which early in the seventeenth century was reduced to eight, afterwards to six, and in the middle of the eighteenth century to five per cent. These reductions might appear at first sight like attempts to tighten restrictions on dealings between lender and borrower; but they simply followed at a distance a fall in the market rate, which always averaged below the legal maximum. During Elizabeth's reign, though the Queen herself, at her accession, had borrowed at twelve per cent. on account of the supposed insecurity of her throne, the market rate sank far below the lawful ten per cent. Throughout the seventeenth century the usual rate was five per cent. In the eighteenth century the interest on the National Debt stood at one time so low as three per cent. The immense loans contracted by the Government during the long war with France afterwards caused a considerable rise; but the permanent tendency of the rate in modern times, amid frequent fluctuations, has been to decline. In the later Middle Ages it stood, as we have seen, at ten per cent.; while in the present year, according to the price of the Funds, it has kept close to three per cent. What have been the causes of this fall? What conditions now govern the rate of interest? How are its incessant fluctuations on the one hand, and its decline in the long run, on the other hand, in contrast with its stationary rate in former years, to be explained? Is a continuous fall to be looked for in the future?

Many eminent writers before Adam Smith supposed that the fall in the rate of interest after the middle of the sixteenth century had been caused by the change in the purchasing power of money, consequent on the influx of silver from America. Money, they said, was worth less, and therefore less was given for the use of it. But, as Adam Smith has replied, the change in the purchasing power of money affected both interest and principal alike, and could not alter the proportion. Yet the writers referred to were not wrong in ascribing the reduction of interest mainly to the increase of money, though mistaken in their view of its mode of operation. It was by augmenting, not the sums of money in the market for commodities, but the stocks of money entering the loan market, that the new silver lowered interest. The sudden descent in the market rate in Elizabeth's reign, already alluded to, may be traced mainly to two causes—the increase of silver in Europe after 1545, when the mines of Potosi were discovered, and the new coinage under the great queen. In 1523, it had been computed in Parliament that the total amount of money in the kingdom did not exceed a million. Elizabeth's mint coined more than five millions. Old men, says Harrison, in his description of England in her reign, could remember when it was rare for a farmer to have so much as six shillings in hand; whereas, when he wrote, it was common for one to have as much as six or seven years' rent by him, though rents had enormously risen. Little of the coin thus accumulated in the country was put out at interest; but in London and other commercial towns stores of money did not lie idle.

The steadiness of the mediæval rate of commercial interest has already been accounted for by the steadiness of the rate of profit on the one hand, and the fact that half profit was accounted fair interest on the other, in conformity with the principle commonly followed in farm tenures throughout Europe—that the person advancing the capital was entitled to half the produce. According to Adam Smith, interest in his time bore the same proportion to profit. 'Double interest,' he says, 'is in Great Britain what the merchants call a good, moderate, reasonable profit—terms which, I apprehend, mean no more than a common and usual profit.' Whether this estimate was strictly accurate may be questioned. The rate of profit was no longer as certain as it had been under the mediæval system. Nevertheless, the philosopher lived in an age in which custom was still 'the principal magistrate of man's life.' Trade was carried on in the main by customary methods. In old and well-known employments, to which he limited the doctrine of the equality of profits, the rate may have been tolerably well ascertained and uniform; and the steadiness of profit tended to make interest steady. Some of Adam Smith's fundamental ideas—such as the correspondence of price with cost of production, the equality of profits, and that ordinary profit was double interest—had come down from an earlier economic world, many of whose usages and traditions survived. He referred phenomena, which were really vestiges of an old stationary economy, to a new and progressive one slowly emerging, under which free competition was about to supersede custom, law, and official control, and to transform a standstill and uniform world into one of infinite diversity, and change, and incessant movement. His own observations show that industrial and commercial progress was already creating wide divergence of prices, profits, and interest from old standards. The period was one of transition, which at length brought the old economic *régime* to a close, and established one of which production on a large scale, speculation, unlimited competition, and ceaseless fluctuations of prices, profits, and interest are essential features. We are thus brought back to the questions, What are the modern conditions determining the rate of interest, and whether its continuous decline is an inevitable consequence of social progress? These inquiries involve topics transcending the province of economics; but even those that are strictly within it deeply concern the future of the civilized world.

Why, then, is the rate of interest on the best security only three per cent. in Great Britain, while it is higher in the United States, and even in Holland, formerly the stock example of low interest? The answer which a chapter of Mr. Mill's 'Political Economy' suggests, and which is true so far as it goes, though inadequate, is that the desire and the means of accumulation have led in this country to the existence of a quantity of capital which its owners are led by the preference of other pursuits, or of ease and leisure, above commercial business, to lend instead of personally employing; while there is, on the other hand, a demand on the part of people engaged in trade for loans. The consequent equation of demand and supply results in a rate of commercial interest which indirectly governs the price of the funds and the income from such investments, trade being the chief competitor with Government stock and similar securities for loanable capital. In connexion with this explanation, it should be borne in mind that the increasing accumulation is not the only cause that has vastly augmented the supply of loanable capital. The greater part of the movable and immovable property accumulated in a country, in goods, machines, materials, cattle, buildings, and soforth, never directly enters the loan market; and in former times such accumulations would not have affected the rate of interest even indirectly. But banking and credit have rendered the intervention of money no longer necessary to effect loans, unless in a panic. A vast quantity of wealth, not itself directly loanable, is practically converted by credit into productive capital, of which borrowers get the command. The manufacturer and the merchant obtain, through the intervention of banks, advances of the fixed or circulating stock they stand in need of. In former times they must first have obtained a loan of money in sterling coin. Credit, though unfortunately called money in city phraseology, is neither money nor capital, but it acts as the representative of both in the loan market, and has virtually multiplied beyond calculation the supply of loans. Yet, vastly as it has augmented the supply, it has not tended only to lower interest, for it has also vastly augmented the demand. The holder of goods can get advances on his stock, and is often a borrower. The operation and activity of modern credit are, moreover, connected with a system of industrial and commercial enterprise which creates a prodigious need of the loan of capital to carry it on. It is impossible, accordingly, to lay down any general proposition respecting the effect of credit on the rate of interest. At one time it augments chiefly the demand for loanable capital, and at another time the supply. The difficulty is thickened by the close connexion between the action of credit on capital on the one hand, and on the circulation and prices on the other. When credit expands in the loan market, it is active also in the market for commodities, and prices rise, giving promise of profit; when it collapses in the former, it contracts in the latter, and prices fall, to the discouragement of enterprise. The chief fluctuations of both interest and prices thus find their explanation in credit, which is not, like coin, a given quantity, but subject to sudden expansion and contraction.

When all this has been said, we are still far from an adequate view of the movements of interest. The supply of capital and the demand for it determine the shares of lenders and borrowers in the revenue derived from its employment in business, but do not determine the revenue to be shared. The price of stock and the rate of interest on such securities are governed by the competition of investments, of which trade is the chief; and the terms which trade can offer must depend on the expected profit. If the rate of profit anticipated in business be twenty per cent. at the least, a much higher rate of interest will evidently follow a given state of supply and demand in the loan market, than if no higher profit than ten per cent. could be looked for. Interest fluctuates from causes independent of the rate of profit, and bears no fixed proportion to it—sometimes varying in an opposite direction when the immediate need of loans is urgent. But only high profit can permanently support high interest, and low profit can afford only a low recompense to the lender of capital. The rate of profit determines in general both the maximum and the minimum of interest; the maximum must be below it, or the borrower would make nothing, and the minimum must not be so low as to drive the owners of capital to employ it themselves, instead of lending it, or to spend it. Thus before we can adequately explain the causes governing interest, we must ascertain those determining profit. For the like reason we can make no answer to the inquiry whether interest tends to rise or to fall in the progress of society, until we have learned the tendency of profit in that respect. In speaking of profit, however, it is not meant here that there is in modern trade any customary, equal, or average rate, such as is talked of in text-books. The mediæval rate of profit was a customary one, and the commercial rate of interest was then a customary one likewise. Now profit is uncertain, variable, and speculative; nevertheless, interest still bears an essential relation, though not a fixed proportion to it, being higher when and where high profits are frequent and probable, than where the returns are commonly small. The rate of profit can no longer be described as 'double interest,' but unless the returns to capital ordinarily exceeded bare interest, and afforded remuneration for its active employment, borrowing in business would cease.

The inquiry whether the rate of profit necessarily declines as the world grows older has a double claim to attention, possessing an intrinsic importance apart from its relation to the future of interest. Historical and surrounding facts seem at the first view to support the doctrines of those economists who regard a tendency of profit to a minimum as an inevitable consequence of social progress and an established economic law. The actual fall of interest from ten to three per cent. seems presumptive evidence of a fall of profit on the whole hitherto, since interest bears always a relation to profit. And though individual traders now sometimes make more than the ordinary mediæval profit of four shillings in the pound, no one supposes that, gains and losses together, profit approaches an average of twenty per cent. on all the capital in trade. In Adam Smith's time the market rate of interest was generally below five per cent., yet merchants thought double interest good profit. The economic world of his day, it is true, resembled the mediæval more than the modern world in the narrow dimensions of trade, the lack of movement and change, and the influence of custom. Yet there were essential differences. Prices and profits were not artificially kept to a certain standard by guilds, civic authorities, and laws. A natural tendency of profit to decline from age to age could hardly, therefore, be inferred from its lower level in the eighteenth century than in the fourteenth. *A fortiori* no such inference can be drawn from a comparison of mediæval profit with its rate under the industrial and commercial system of our own time. In the middle ages each trade was in the hands of a limited and organized body; capital, competition, and production were subject to various restrictions;

prices were customary, or regulated; the total amount of profit was accordingly small, but the rate was high. Under unlimited competition, unrestricted production, and uncontrolled prices, had the state of society permitted of such a system, profit would have varied much in individual cases and in different employments; its aggregate amount might have been much greater, because the amount of capital would have been so, but the mean rate would in all probability have been considerably lower.

If from historical we turn to surrounding facts, the state of trade and agriculture in this country during recent years is regarded by many as indicating more than a temporary fall in the profit of British capital. The novel feature of reduced assessments to the income-tax, especially under Schedule D, and diminished proceeds of the legacy and succession duties, exhibit a retrogression only partially accounted for by diminished incomes, expenditure, and savings of landlords and farmers. But the most prosperous countries, the United States and France for example, have their unprosperous periods. The tendency towards more stringent protection abroad is not to be regarded without anxiety; yet our trade statistics prove that an immense market is still open to our productions, and that British energy hitherto has surmounted opposition. A falling-off in the foreign demand for British produce, such as is sometimes argued from the small proportion of exports, would have the opposite effect of diminishing the proportion of imports, by altering the equation of international demand to the disadvantage of Great Britain. A diminution of exports might result from hostile tariffs, but imports would fall off more. A good market abroad for our exports raises their value measured in foreign commodities, and swells the amount of goods given for them; while a declining demand in foreign countries would compel us to give more for our imports; the ratio of exports would increase, exporters would sell at ever-increasing disadvantage and diminishing profits. Yet even in such an event it could not be inferred that the advance of society lowers the returns to capital, but only that national ignorance and international jealousy may do so in commerce as well as in war. The chief unsoundness in the actual state of matters, and the most threatening indication for the immediate future, lie in two circumstances independent of foreign countries, namely, that our trade is carried on in uncircumspect, over-speculative, and haphazard manner, and that the immense fabric of our system of credit rests on so narrow and precarious a basis that it might suddenly be overthrown altogether. The gradual and spontaneous growth, however, with better communication and commercial information, of a better organization of our industrial economy, is not to be despaired of. With respect to agriculture, on the other hand, it is not enough to say with Mr. Bright that adverse seasons have caused the depression of the profits of British farming and the ruin of many farmers. Farming that pays only in fine seasons must be a losing business in such a climate as ours. It is no mere question of sunshine; nor will five thousand or more miles, at which engineers will smile in spite even of Lord Derby, protect the British corn-grower from loss in competition with American produce under present conditions. Cereals, however, play a minor and diminishing part in British rural economy, and even as regards them, the exhaustion of virgin soil and the increase of population may alter the terms at which the Transatlantic grower can hereafter sell. On the whole, the present situation forebodes no lasting depression of the profits of British capital.

But the question as to the tendency of profit to fall is not to be answered by reference to the particular case of Great Britain, still less its state at this moment. It involves a consideration of the general causes on which profit depends, and the conditions under which they will operate as ages advance and capital accumulates. Adam Smith thought that the mere growth of capital necessarily entailed a fall of profit. 'When,' in his words, 'the stocks of many rich merchants are turned into the same trade, their mutual competition tends to lower profit; and when there is a like increase of stock in all the different trades carried on in the same society, the same competition must produce the same effect in them all.' Were this reasoning correct, profit must inevitably decline in every prosperous country. But there is a flaw in the argument. When in a single trade alone the goods for sale increase, the competition of the sellers may force them to accept reduced prices and lower profits, because the general produce and revenue of the country may not have increased in proportion. But when capital and production take larger dimensions in all businesses alike, all producers have more to exchange, the general revenue is greater, and no class need get less for its goods in the market. It might even be that no increase of capital or production in any pre-existing employment would follow an augmentation of the total amount. A new trade was a rare thing in Adam Smith's days; now scores grow up every year, and new trades may both absorb much new capital and create new markets for the produce of old trades. If the growth of capital lower profit, it must be either by raising wages or by forcing resort to inferior or more costly instruments of production.

A later theory of a tendency of profits to a minimum is that an increased cost of subsistence follows the advance of population; so that, to obtain a sufficient supply of labour when capital is increasing, employers must raise wages and submit to a decrease of profit until a stationary state is reached, at which the further increase of capital is arrested. This theory is defective in two opposite ways. On the one hand, it omits all but one of the causes tending to a depression of profit; on the other, it overlooks both counteracting agencies, and the possibility of a change in the fundamental conditions determining the movement of population. The soil, in the first place, is not the only natural agent whose productiveness diminishes. Mines of all kinds would be exhausted even by a stationary population, whereas the productiveness of agriculture would increase with agricultural skill, were the number of consumers to remain constant. The cost of land, too, rises for all purposes of production, and not in agriculture alone. Many employments again besides agriculture yield diminishing returns to successive applications of capital, because the best places are taken by the first-comers, and those who come later must work in worse situations. The first roads, canals, and railways in a country are usually those, as M. Leroy-Beaulieu has observed, between the chief centres of population, wealth, and business, and traverse the districts where traffic and movement are greatest, later lines of communication running through poorer and less populous localities. The best sites for docks, wharves, warehouses, shops, and other places of business are, for the most part, the first occupied. When any new and lucrative enterprise is started, or any invention or novel production is introduced, a crowd of competitors follow, and profits fall off. Nor is an increased cost of food the only cause tending to raise wages; it is not the cause that has raised them in England during the last twenty years. Facilities for migration, emigration, and combination, together with greater intelligence, knowledge, and self-respect on the part of the working classes, have produced the rise.

Yet there is another side to the subject. The rate of profit depends on the ratio of the gross returns to the total outgoings—on the cost and efficiency of all the instruments of production, not of labour alone. Given the entire produce of the capital, labour, and natural resources of a country, in order to ascertain how much is profit, we should know not only how much falls to the share of human labourers, but also how much must be applied to the maintenance of fixed and circulating capital, including animals, seed, materials, fuel, machinery, buildings; how much, too, must be paid as rent for the use of natural agents; and how much is to be deducted in taxation and legal expenses, or what is the cost of protection and of the other advantages of government. In a country whose natural resources are abundant and prolific, efficiently co-operating with capital and labour at small cost, and whose government and legal system are inexpensive, both wages and profit may be high. If the soil and climate be favourable, mines of all kinds rich and easily worked, the structure of the country lending itself to cheap and rapid locomotion, taxes and law costs small, it is plain that the return to capital, alike in agriculture, manufactures, and commerce, may give a large surplus in profit, although at the same time the reward of labour is abundant. And what the bounty of nature may effect may be effected by the art of man. Better machinery may be applied at once to the factory, the farm, and the locomotive: while chemistry cheapens and improves the cultivation of the ground, it may do like service in every branch of manufacture. Less costly and more efficient means of heating and lighting every place of production and business may be discovered. The general rate of profit might thus be sustained by the progress of science, though population were advancing. No speculation respecting the economic future of the civilized world which does not take account of the inexhaustible resources of science, and of the progressive development of the human faculties for discovery and invention, has now much claim to attention. Labour, in the narrow sense, is not, as political economists as well as 'social democrats' have assumed, the sole cause of profit. There might be production and profit without the employment of a single human labourer, and profit in that case would be greater or less, according to the qualities of the other agents, and the manner in which they were used. A company in a new colony, where hired labour was not to be had, might carry on a great business by the aid of animals, machines, and natural agents; the profit depending partly on the cost, partly on the powers of these animate and inanimate coadjutors. And the progress of industrial art constantly augments the number and efficiency, and diminishes the expense, of some of these auxiliaries. The fact that the best steam-engines still waste the greater part of the fuel is enough to show that the field for economic invention in mechanics is immense. Again, if it be true that the first railways are the best situated, and bring in the largest returns, it is true also that commerce and industrial movement have a constant tendency to spread, and to create markets and traffic where there had been stagnation. The tendency of many great enterprises, like the Suez Canal, is to become more remunerative. Fifty years ago the farthest-seeing mind could not have formed a conception of the profitable occupations that steam would provide for fresh accumulations of capital, and steam is perhaps a feeble agent compared with some future sources of power. The facilities for the migration and emigration of labour may tend to raise wages at the expense of profit; but they are connected with causes which constantly enlarge the sphere for capital in the application of neglected or imperfectly developed resources, both in old and new regions. The overflow of British capital to foreign countries has two aspects. Mr. Mill has contemplated it as a sign of the fall of profit in old countries; but it may be regarded also as an example of the tendency of social progress to find fresh fields of employment for their accumulations. Students of Mr. Herbert Spencer's works know, moreover, that there is reason to question the undiminished fecundity of the population of the civilized world, which the theory of a decline of profit assumes. Civilization makes constantly greater demands on the nervous system, enlarges the brain, and multiplies its expenditure of physical power, thereby diminishing the quantity expendible on the increase of the race, while at the same time raising the standard of wants, and augmenting prudence. One and the same cause—the increase of cerebral force and activity, and therewith of science, foresight, and adaptation of means to ends—tends to add to the industrial productiveness of the people of the West, and to slacken the growth of their numbers, although a different future may be before the people of the East. The time must indeed come, after countless ages, when the decline of solar and terrestrial heat shall arrest the mental advancement of the human race, and make the returns to capital and industry dwindle. But within economic as distinguished from astronomical and geological periods, there seems no ground for concluding that in the more civilized parts of the globe man must press constantly closer and closer on the means of subsistence, and thrift and enterprise consequently obtain a decreasing reward. Were population stationary, it may perhaps be argued, the price of labour would rise to such a pitch from the accumulation of capital as to leave little or no profit. The answer is, that the accumulation would not take the form of wages, but of new mechanical and other agencies for aiding production, which would benefit the labourer as a consumer without raising the cost of his services. One remote difficulty, indeed, raises a formidable, and at present insoluble problem, namely, What is to be done for coal and iron when the mines become exhausted? Yet the men of a former age might have regarded the disappearance of forests, and the consequent rise in the cost of wood, with equal embarrassment. It is at least certain that the earth contains resources now undreamt of, which science is sure to reveal; or, rather, which the mind of man, the real cause of all wealth and profit, is sure to discover. Some of the chief sources of modern profit must ultimately fall short; but food is not likely to be among the number, because the number of human beings can be kept within bounds—as it is already in France and among the old American families in the States of New England—and substitutes for those which must fail may be in the womb of time. No certain conclusion respecting the future of profit can be reached, but the theory of its tendency to a minimum has no claim to the character of a law of social progress, ignoring, as it does, some of the chief results of that progress, and its chief cause—the constant improvement of human faculties. Profit may uniformly fall from its first high level in new countries like the Western States of America, yet may not continuously decline in old countries. The rate will probably vary from time to time in the future as it has done in the past.

If profit, then, be subject to no law of inevitable decline, can interest be so? It is almost needless to say that no inference can be drawn from its lower level in modern times than in the Middle Ages, since the mediæval rate of profit was fixed, and interest bore a fixed proportion to it. Now, profit is indeterminate and fluctuating; interest, too, fluctuates from causes independent of profit, affecting the loan market, such as the state of credit, the foreign exchanges, the movements of bullion actual or anticipated, the harvests, Government and foreign loans, and political events and prospects. The movement of interest in trade may consequently be different from, and even opposite for the moment to, its movement in respect of other investments. The price of Government stock might be high, and interest on such securities falling, while the rate of discount showed that men of business were eager for loans, either because credit had been shaken, or because a shock to it or a scarcity of money was apprehended, or, on the other hand, because a speculative mania had arisen. Or again, people in trade might be slow to accept short loans on very favourable terms, because waiting for a turn in commercial affairs, while stable and permanent investments like the funds or land mortgages returned a high interest. Yet the main cause determining, throughout the whole field open to capital, the general tenor of the movement of interest, is the rate of commercial profit. Let new channels of trade offer bountiful returns for a series of years, and the savings of the country would flow into them, the price of Consols would fall, and mortgagors would pay dearly for loans. The main reason why the rate of interest has been constantly higher in the United States than in England is that the prolific natural resources of America have afforded a richer field for the employment of capital than was found in this island. The chief cause of the rise of interest in Holland is that Dutch capital has found in colonial undertakings, American investments, foreign commerce, and husbandry at home, more profitable employment than lay open to it a century ago. And the stationary state ultimately reached by the whole civilized world may possibly be that of a stationary population, whose savings are more productively employed than those of the present generation, and yield a higher interest.

We have yet to consider how profit is distributed between lenders and borrowers of capital, and what proportion falls to the share of the former. Gross profit, according to Mr. Mill, is made up of three elements:—interest, or the reward of simple abstinence; insurance, or the compensation for risk; and the remuneration for superintendence or management. This analysis however, errs in treating insurance as a constituent of profit. The sum spent in insuring the goods of a manufacturer or merchant against fire or shipwreck forms part of his outgoings, not of his profit upon them. He may spend what he receives both as interest and as recompense for management, but what comes to him as insurance should be laid by to provide against accident or loss, and is not expendible income. It is true, since losses and accidents may be escaped, that men in a trade exposed to them who do not insure may get a higher profit from the higher prices caused by the risk. They have played double or quits, and have won. But if all risk in trade, and therefore insurance, could be extinguished, the total amount of profit would not be diminished, as it would be by the extinction of interest, or of the earnings of management. On the contrary, were the same amount of insurance required in all trades alike, its elimination would be a saving, and a source of additional profit all round. The mistaken classification of insurance with the elements of profit, instead of with those of cost of production, is connected with the common inaccuracy of treating interest as higher in proportion to risk. Interest proper is net income, and safely expendible as such; the provision against loss of the principal is not so. As in the case of profit, however, particular lenders may be gainers by the risk of losses which do not actually befall them, though nothing may be gained from it by lenders all round. How far risk attracts or repels capital depends indeed partly on national character and the temper of the age. But the presumptuous trust in their own good fortune, which Adam Smith imputes to the greater part of mankind, tends to make the losses resulting from risk exceed, on the whole, the indemnity.

Profit, then, includes two elements only—interest for the mere loan of capital, or an equivalent where the capital is the employer's own, and the additional return resulting from its active employment in production. This second element is not happily called wages of superintendence or earnings of management. Regarding it in that light, Mr. Alfred Marshall and some eminent foreign economists consider it simply as a species of wages, determined by the same causes that govern the recompense of skilled labour in general, such as the rarity of the faculties and acquisitions required, and the amount of toil undergone. Were there no other constituent than this, in addition to interest, in gross profit, interest would absorb a greater share of profit than it does, and therefore be higher than it actually is. The surplus above interest arising from the active employment of capital is in proportion, not to the difficulty and trouble of management, but to the amount of the capital. If two companies, one employing twice as much capital as the other, can make a good profit by selling at a particular time or place, the gain of each will be in proportion to the business done and the amount of the sales; and one will make twice as much as the other, although the skill and exertion required to conduct the operations in the two cases may be the same. There may be a manager of each company who gets a fixed salary, and this, doubtless, is wages; but the profit on the transaction will be so much per cent. on each company's capital, and may far exceed the manager's pay. The shares of interest on the one hand, and of the return for the employment of the capital on the other hand, are determined by the supply of and demand for it in the loan market. The proportions will vary in different countries and ages, according, in a great measure, to the attraction or repulsion that active trade has for the owners of capital. The rate of interest, in short, is determined by no invariable rule; but, like that of profit, seems subject to no law of inevitable decline—at least until great astronomical and geological changes supervene, and the whole solar system begins to approach the end of its career.

So far the future of interest and profit has been considered with reference to economic conditions alone. But is it certain that economic conditions exclusively will henceforth control them? The policy of society in reference to both has been determined by various conceptions. Archaic notions and feelings founded on kinship, Greek philosophy, Roman law, Christianity, Catholic theology, commercial ideas, the modern regard for individual liberty, political economy, have all played a part in their history. Other sources and modes of thought have yet to be reckoned with—democracy, the views of the working classes, German and French Socialism, the subtler shapes of

Socialism which ostensibly seek only to enlarge the intervention of the State in the economical sphere, and new conceptions of moral and social duty. The authority of the economic theory hitherto dominant with respect to individualism, competition, and non-interference, is visibly shaken even in England. The notion that all capital should belong to the State for the benefit of the working classes has many strenuous adherents in Germany and France, notwithstanding the wide distribution of property in those countries, but for which it would have already overcome all opposition. The favour with which Mr. Henry George's 'Progress and Poverty' has been received in the United States makes a curious revelation of the tendencies of educated thought in a country where individual energy has worked under the most propitious conditions. Mr. George, indeed, proposes to confiscate land-rent only without compensation; but rent in a vast number of cases is virtually a form of interest, being the return to an investment by purchase or outlay. Protection, again, is a revival of the mediæval regulation by law or authority of trade, prices, and profit; and the policy of most civilized countries is protective. In England, a generation ago, when at length Bentham's 'Defence of Usury' had led to the abolition of a legal limit to interest, much more seemed to be swept away. The change apparently formed part of a wider and deeper change in social opinion and legislative policy, and belonged to a general movement of thought, emancipating human conduct from a multitude of ancient restraints in the name of morality or religion. Yet, little as people are dreaming of it at present, there are indications of a tendency on the part of English society to slide back to the mediæval system of regulating contracts, bargains, pecuniary dealings, and prices by authority. Fair wages, fair profits, and fair rents are now objects more or less distinctly conceived by many who, ten years ago, regarded buying in the cheapest and selling in the dearest market as the sole rule in all questions of contract. No one, perhaps, in England at this moment thinks of controlling interest; yet propositions are now often put forward respecting wages and profit involving the regulation of both, and indirectly, therefore, of interest, which follows the movement of profit. Ten years ago no English statesman would have listened to a proposal to regulate rent in any part of the United Kingdom by statute or judicial decision. Yet the principle of the Act by which judicial rents are now introduced into Ireland is no other than that of the mediæval law against usury, that the owner of property should not be permitted to take advantage of his neighbour's necessity to extort a high price for the loan of it. The establishment of rings and corners, and of bulling and bearing in English trade, might considerably alter public opinion with regard to the mediæval laws against forestalling and engrossing. Democratic legislation will assuredly intervene in directions not in accordance with the doctrines that have commended themselves hitherto to the minds of great capitalists or landowners. Ideas of moral and social obligations, too, seem likely to play a greater part in the commercial sphere than they have ever done since Adam Smith based a complete economic code on the desire of every man to better his own condition, and some of these ideas may make light of that code.

The misfortune is that great general principles, like that of the freedom of contract, are now abandoned in a moment to promote a particular measure, perhaps expedient or necessary in itself and defensible on special grounds, like the Irish Land Act. Mediæval economy has been ignorantly decried; there was much in it that was good in design and suited to the time; yet let us not ignorantly go back to it from a notion that we are following new and advanced guides. Let us look steadily before us; and if we are to revert to an ancient system which tolerated no individual liberty in production or exchange, let us, at least, do so advisedly and deliberately, not sliding back into it unconsciously.

XIX.

THE DISTRIBUTION AND VALUE OF THE PRECIOUS METALS IN THE SIXTEENTH AND NINETEENTH CENTURIES.*

It seems to be still a matter of doubt with many whether the new mines have actually diminished the purchasing power of gold, or have only contributed the additional currency required by the increase of the world's commodities and trade. Fortunately for those who care to pursue the inquiry, the very causes which, by their complexity and fluctuating character, make it vain to seek an exact measure of the effect of the new gold on prices, are in themselves subjects of great interest; for the history of prices is interwoven with the history of the progress and fortunes of mankind. Several writers on the gold question have drawn conclusions from the fall in the value of both the precious metals after the discovery of America; but, without a careful comparison of the economical conditions of that epoch and the present, no sort of inference can be rationally made; and the comparison—one might say the contrast—abounds in instruction apart from the light it throws on the monetary problem. The proper region of money is the region of industry, roads, navigation, and trade; and prices tend to approach to equality as these are improved, as men become equally civilized, and as political disorders cease to interrupt human intercourse and prosperity. At this day, in the most civilized countries, the precious metals serve two masters—war and commerce; but in those least civilized they serve none. The currents from the mines may vibrate through a third of the

* *Macmillan's Magazine*, August, 1864.

habitable globe, but they have no conductors through more than half of Asia and South America, or through almost the whole of Africa. In the sixteenth century, the bulk of the people of Europe itself could seldom, if ever, have touched a coin from the mines of Mexico or Peru. There was no even distribution through Christendom of the treasure which the Spaniards tore from the New World ; and on this and other accounts prices rose unequally in different places, and not at all in some. In the chief towns of Spain they seem to have risen even before the fifteenth century had closed ; and in the Netherlands their ascent was much earlier than in England, where the state of the currency before 1560, and the drain consequent on its debasement, together with the foreign expenditure of the Government, both retarded and concealed the first symptoms of the falling value of the precious metals. During the first sixteen years after the mine of Potosi was opened,* although prices measured in base coin rose rapidly in England, they rose in no proportion to the increase of silver and gold in the world. There was, as it were, a hole in the English purse ; and the ancient fine coin of the realm ran out into the foreigner's hands as fast as the new base coin was poured in (just as eagles and dollars have been driven from the American States by the issues of paper). Moreover, war with France and Scotland drew much money out of England, and most of the treasure netted upon trade was hoarded, or made into plate. But with Elizabeth came peace with France and a reformation of the currency : silver flowed fast into the Royal Mint ; old fine coin returned into the market ; and prices, instead of falling in proportion to the improvement of the currency, continued to rise, because the new issues exceeded the old, and the increase of commodities, great as it was, did not keep pace with the increase of money and men in the most prosperous parts of the country. Prices depend on the quantity of money in proportion to commodities—not on its quality—whether it be made of

* In 1545. The increase of the precious metals before that year was not considerable.

metal or paper. Prices accordingly in England, before 1560, rose in proportion to the increase of base money, and not in proportion to its baseness. One Englishman alone, however, down to 1581, seems to have connected the phenomenon of extraordinary dearness in the midst of extraordinary plenty, which was the common complaint, with the mines of the New World.* With others it was a cry of class against class, for covetousness, extortion, extravagance, and luxury; and of all classes against the landlords for exorbitant rents and enclosures. The complaint against enclosures, that they fed sheep instead of men, was no new one; it had been a popular grievance for more than a century, and a subject of legislation before the discovery of America. A recent writer, nevertheless, supposes that at the period of Stafford's 'Dialogues,' 'the foreign demand springing from the increased supply of the precious metals fell principally upon wool. The price of wool, accordingly, rose more rapidly than that of other industrial products in England; the profits of sheep-farming outran the profits of other occupations, and the result was, that extensive conversion of arable land into pasture which the interlocutors in the Dialogues describe, and which was undoubtedly the proximate cause of the prevailing distress.'† But the truth is, that corn was not, as this theory assumes, at once comparatively scarce and comparatively cheap: the real paradox is, that it was, like other articles of food, extraordinarily plentiful in the country, and extraordinarily dear in and near the capital

* William Stafford, the supposed author of the famous 'Dialogues,' published in 1581. He says:—'Another cause I conceive to be the great plenty of treasure which is walking in these parts of the world, far more than our forefathers have seen. Who doth not understand of the infinite sums of gold and silver which are gathered from the Indies and other countries, and so yearly transferred into these coasts?' &c. &c.—See *Harl. Misc.* vol. ix.

† *Political Economy as a Branch of General Education.* By J. E. Cairnes, Esq. It is immaterial to the point in question above, but not to the monetary history of the period, to observe that unmanufactured wool was then far from being the chief export from England, and that the loom was then, as now, England's chief mine. But had the price of wool been disproportionately high, and led to the growth of sheep in place of corn, the price of mutton should have been comparatively low, whereas its price, like that of beef, was extravagantly high in comparison with all former rates.

and chief towns.* England had become rich, both in money and in commodities, but not in roads and means of carriage; and wool had risen only with all other produce of the realm within reach of the chief markets. The gains of the wool-grower were not greater than those of the clothier, the hatter, the shoemaker, the blacksmith, the butcher, the baker, or the tillage farmer, in most places near the chief centres of increasing population and trade.† Before the New World was discovered, and down to the eve of Elizabeth's reign, the extension of pasture had caused much real distress. But, for a generation before the 'Dialogues,' tillage had increased and prospered; and the popular charge against the landlords had become an anachronism. Poverty and suffering, it is true, still existed side by side with rapidly-increasing wealth, but not through the scarcity of corn. Food of all sorts, though abundant in the country, was dear beyond precedent in and around the places where the population had multiplied fastest. The old feudal and ecclesiastical economy of society had broken up; monasteries and noble houses no longer maintained swarms of serfs, and paupers, and waiting and fighting men; the nobility and gentry were deserting the country for the town; a long peace, while it had swelled the general numbers of the people, had extinguished

---

* 'Albeit,' says a historian of that age, 'there be much more ground eared now almost in every place than hath been of late years, yet such a price continueth in each town and market that the artificer and poor labouring man is not able to reach unto it, but is driven to content himself with horse-corn: I mean beans, peas, oats, tares, and lentils.'—Harrison's *Description of Great Britain.* And again, 'There are few towns in England that have not their weekly markets, whereby no occupier shall have occasion to travel far off with his commodities, except it be to seek for the highest prices, which commonly are near unto great cities.' And the knight in the *Dialogues* says:—'I say it is long of you, husbandmen, that we are forced to raise our rents, by reason we must buy so dear all things we have of you, as corn, cattle, goose, pig, chicken, butter, and eggs. Cannot you, neighbour, remember that I could, in this town, buy the best pig for fourpence, which now costeth twelvepence? It is likewise in greater ware, as beef or mutton.'

† One cause of corn being cheap in some places was that the gains of the farmer had stimulated agriculture and produced unusual abundance. Harrison accordingly says:—'Certainly the soil is now grown to be much more fruitful than in times past. The cause is that our countrymen are grown to be much more painsful and skilful through recompense of gain than hitherto they have been.'

the calling of the soldiers; and labourers seeking bread were gathering to the chief centres of employment and wealth. The dearness of provisions in and within reach of the markets where the competition of mouths was thus greatest was caused, not by a decrease of tillage, nor yet by the increase of money alone, but in part by the fact that the increasing supplies which were wanted were drawn at an extravagant cost of carriage from limited districts, pack-horses being the principal means of land transport from the country to the town. For a similar reason food is now extravagantly dear at the mines of British Columbia, and not merely on account of the plenty of gold, for it is cheaper at San Francisco than in London. The price of meat was even more unequal than that of bread in town and country generally, because there were few roads by which cattle could be driven to market. Corn was, as it still is, more portable than fresh meat; but the means of carrying even corn were so scanty and costly that it was often at a famine price in one place and cheap in another not far off. Wool, again, was more portable than corn, and might be sent to market with profit from districts too remote to supply corn or fresh meat. These circumstances explain the inconsistency of statements in the 'Dialogues,' and other writings of that period, respecting the prices of corn and meat, and the numbers of the population. Cheapness and dearness, plenty and scarcity, of corn and other food, depopulation and rapidly increasing numbers, really co-existed in the kingdom. There were places from which the husbandman and labourer disappeared, and the beasts of the field grazed where their cottages had stood; and there were places where men were multiplying to the dismay of statesmen. There were places where corn was above the labourer's reach, and places where it had come little or not at all within the waves of the monetary revolution about all the chief centres of traffic. In every locality, and with respect to every commodity, the range of prices was determined by the quantity of money circulating there on the one hand, and the quantity of commodities, or their cost of production, on the other; and these proportions varied in different places, in different years, and with respect to different commodities. In the very year after Stafford's tract was published, 'all the commodities of Greece, Syria, Egypt, and India, were obtained by England much cheaper than formerly,'* by a direct trade with Turkey, which saved the charges of the Venetian carrier. Nor was the rise of corn or meal general throughout the country, for the cost of carriage cut off the remoter places altogether from the markets in which the new gold and silver abounded. Most writers, from Adam Smith downwards, have taken the price of corn in or near the principal markets of the most opulent and commercial countries as the measure of the effect of the mines in the sixteenth century, and have treated the fall in the value of money as general and uniform over Europe. Mr. Jacob, for example, came to the conclusion that 'in England and the other kingdoms of Europe, within the first century after the discovery of America, the quantity of the precious metals had increased nearly fivefold, and the prices of commodities had advanced nearly in the same proportion.' Most subsequent writers have followed in Mr. Jacob's steps. It generally happens that, when a man gains the position of an authority on a question, all that he says is accepted in a lump, and his errors and oversights take rank with his best-established conclusions. One recent inquirer, however, has pertinently asked whether prices were really trebled or quadrupled (some economists have said more than decupled), even in all the chief cities of Europe. 'And what was the extent in Muscovy and Poland, or in the Highlands of Scotland and the West of Ireland?'†

The inquiry is important apart from the bare question of depreciation to which it refers, for the answer goes far to give a measure of the progress and civilization of the different districts of Europe. Two centuries and a quarter after the mine of Potosi had begun to affect the value of money, Arthur Young compiled a Table of the comparative prices of provisions at different distances north of London. Within fifty miles of the

---

* Macpherson's *Annals of Commerce*, A.D. 1582.

† Letter in the *Times*, by W. M. J., September 3, 1863.

capital he found the price of a pound of meat in several places fourpence—at greater distances, in several, only twopence. 'The variations in the prices of butcher's meat,' he observed, 'are so regular, the fall so unbroken, that one cannot but attribute it to the distance, nor can any other satisfactory account be given of it.' It was not, however, the mere difference of distance from London which made prices so unequal; for in the southern counties Arthur Young himself found them more uniform. Distance, both north and south, operated on prices through the cost of carriage; and, when the distance was short, the result was the same as if it were great, where access to good markets was hindered by the badness of the roads. There were, both north and south of London, lower prices than any tabled by Arthur Young. About the time of his tours the price of mutton at Horsham, in Sussex, was only five farthings a pound,* or, allowing for the difference in the standards, little higher than what seems to have been a common price in England before the conquest of Peru.† In Scotland, again, down to the Union, there were, as Adam Smith relates, places where meat, if sold at all, was cheaper than bread made of oatmeal; and he speaks of a village in his own time in which money was so scarce that nails were carried to the alehouse. At a later period, indeed, in many parts of the Highlands, men were their own butchers and brewers, and no money passed from the right hand to the left. In Ireland, in like manner, until the famine of 1846, there were districts in which not a coin from the American mines was in circulation; the labourer was hired with land or potatoes, and paid his rent in turn, and bought his clothes, with labour. Neither in the British Isles, nor in any continental country,

---

* See Porter's *Progress of the Nation.* Ed. 1851, p. 296. 'The only means,' says Mr. Porter, 'of reaching the metropolis from Horsham was either by going on foot, or by riding on horseback. The roads were not at any time in such a state as to admit of sheep or cattle being driven to the London market, and for this reason the farmers were prevented from sending thither the produce of their land, the immediate neighbourhood being, in fact, their only market.'

† In 1527 the pound weight of silver was coined into £2; and about that time the price of mutton seems to have been generally three-farthings a pound. At the period referred to above the pound weight of silver was coined into £3.

was the money from the mines of the West spread over all localities and commodities alike. Much that was grown and manufactured in every State was both produced and consumed at home, gave money no occupation, and absorbed nothing of its power. Had every Englishman in the reign of Elizabeth bought and sold as he does now, the money which the Queen coined could not have raised prices through the kingdom, as it actually did in the chief towns. Nor did the new streams of silver penetrate into the remoter and more backward districts of the Continent. The trade of the Low Countries, then the distributors of the precious metals, with Denmark, Sweden, Norway, Russia, and Poland, was almost entirely a barter of Oriental luxuries and Western manufactures for the raw produce of those countries. The price of the bulky merchandize of the north and east of Europe in Western markets was principally freight, which the Western merchant got; what balance there was for the remote producer was usually paid in kind. In Guicciardini's Tables of the exports of the Netherlands to the countries named above the precious metals are not named; and Raleigh, in the 17th century, lamented the small English trade with Russia, because 'it was a cheap country, and the trade very gainful.' Less than a hundred years ago, an English traveller found the price of a pound of meat at Novgorod three-halfpence; but it was much cheaper, or without a price, in the forest and the steppe, and is so in some such places still. Adam Smith, it is true, has asserted that, although Poland was, in his time, 'as beggarly a country as before the discovery of America, yet the money price of corn had risen, and the value of money had fallen, there as in other parts of Europe.' But this opinion must have been founded on the price of a small part of the produce of Poland, in foreign markets, for the chief part of the produce of the country was not sold for money at all. Down to our own time, the bulk of the people of Eastern Europe have lived for the most part on their own productions, or on a common stock; their few exchanges have commonly been performed in kind; what little money they have gotten from time to time has been hoarded and not circulated; and prices have not risen where there have been no prices at all. Nor did prices rise in all the secluded inland towns and villages of France, as they did in Paris, and near the ports of commerce with the Netherlands, England, and Spain. From the prices of corn in Paris, a French economist concludes that prices generally in France were twelve times higher in 1590 than in 1515, owing to the American mines. But the true history of the Paris market itself cannot be learned from naked figures of the prices of a single commodity. The movements of the city and surrounding population, the harvests in the neighbourhood, and the means of carriage from a distance, political and military events, and many other circumstances, besides the bare fact of the increase of silver in Europe, must be taken into account. Prices are the abstract and brief chronicles of the times, but they are often too concise for clear interpretation, and many leaves are missing. And the Paris prices of corn are so far from giving the average of prices generally throughout France, that, as we shall presently see, a great inequality of prices in different parts of the country continued down to the era of railways, and the contemporary influx of gold from the new mines; and the market of the capital exercised, until recent years, little or no influence upon the produce of the remoter rural districts.

Although, then, there is evidence of a great fall in the purchasing power of money in Europe in the 16th century, it was unequal in point of time and place; it was a partial and irregular depreciation, and one which cannot be measured with any approach to arithmetical precision. There were still, when it had reached its lowest point, millions of men, and the cattle on a thousand hills, fetching no more money than before; and the change would have been much less than it actually was at the centres of commerce, had the sums collected there been spread over all the people and produce of this quarter of the globe. The most of the money was expended in a few particular places—those most commercial and advanced—in which other causes besides the fertility of the new mines contributed to raise the price of the very commodity, corn, which has been commonly referred to as an accurate measure of the force of the metallic cause alone. Such rise of prices as really took place was almost confined to the neighbourhood of the chief seats of wealth and traffic ; but there, certainly within a few years from the first arrival of silver from Potosi, it was rapid, evident, and in respect of nearly all commodities, raw and manufactured, domestic and foreign. Is any such phenomenon discernible now in Europe, and in the chief towns of Europe in particular, after the lapse of a similar interval from the first discovery of mines of extraordinary fertility ? The same economic laws still govern prices. Different countries, now as then, share unequally in the new treasure, according to their produce, situation, and the balance of their trade ; and its expenditure must have different effects in different markets and on different articles, according to the local supply of goods as well as money. Now, as then, it is a question, not as to the total increase of the stock of gold and silver in the world at large, but as to the addition to, and the local distribution of, the currency of each country, compared with the quantity forthcoming of each sort of commodity on which more money is spent than formerly. According as the supply of each sort of thing has increased as fast as, or not so fast as, or, on the contrary, faster than, the increase of money expenditure upon it in each place, its price should evidently have remained stationary, risen, or, on the contrary, fallen there. In the 16th century the things on which the new money was poured out were not only comparatively few, but comparatively cheap, even in the dearest markets ; so that a small sum made a large addition to their price. Sixpence more doubled the price of a pair of shoes in an English town at the beginning of Elizabeth's reign ; another penny doubled the price of a chicken, and a shilling trebled that of a goose or a pig. In the four and forty years of her reign, Elizabeth coined little more than five millions of money, but that was nearly five times as much as was current before ; and the things on which the additional money was laid out were, after all, but a scanty assortment. The modes of manufacture were little improved, and the greater supplies of raw produce required in the principal towns were carried to market at increasing expense. The new money of this age, on the contrary, while very much greater in amount, has been spread over a far wider area, and a much larger stock of goods; and it found on its arrival a much higher level of prices in the principal markets than that which the silver from Potosi disturbed. The period of the new gold mines, moreover, is one in which several other new agencies have been at work, tending on the one hand to counteract to a great extent the effect of the circulation of more money in the markets previously dearest, and tending on the other (by contrast to what happened at the earlier epoch) to raise most considerably the price of the produce of some of the more remote and recently backward countries and districts. The bare question of the rise of prices is in itself, and so far as merely relates to the change in the value of money, of comparatively little importance. Its chief interest lies in the test the inquiry may elicit of the pace and direction of industrial and commercial advancement. For, in proportion to improvement in the processes of production and the means of importation, the monetary power of the mines is counteracted at the chief seats of industry and commerce by the contemporary increase of commodities; while again, in proportion to the improvement of the methods of locomotion and the extension of trade, prices are brought nearer to equality over the world, and the more distant and undeveloped regions gain access, at diminished expense, to the markets where prices have been hitherto highest. Hence, by a seeming contradiction, it is a sign of great progress in commerce and the arts, in the places farthest advanced in civilization, if the prices of commodities are found slowly advancing in the face of an uncommon abundance of money; while it is, on the contrary, usually a sign of the growing importance and economic elevation of the poorer and cheaper, and hitherto backward localities, if prices are rising in them. By reason of their previous poverty and remoteness from good markets, and consequent cheapness, the pecuniary value of the produce of the latter sort of places suddenly rises when they are brought into easy communication with the former; and the rise is a mark of improvement in their commercial position and command over distant markets and foreign commodities. The sort of produce in which undeveloped regions are naturally richest—the produce of nature—is the sort for which the population, capital, and skill of the wealthiest and most industrious communities have created the most urgent demand; and it is the sort which, in many cases, derives the greatest additional value from cheap and rapid modes of conveyance. The cheapest land-carriage, less than ninety years ago, of two hundred tons of goods from Edinburgh to London, would, we are told by Adam Smith, have required 100 men, 50 waggons, and 400 horses, for three weeks. A single engine, twenty trucks, and three men, would do it now in a day. All the ships of England, again, would not have sufficed, in Adam Smith's time, he tells us, to carry grain, to the value of £5,000,000, from Portugal to England. In 1862, we imported grain to the value of nearly £38,000,000—most of it from a much greater distance. And the extension in the last fifteen years (the very period of the new gold) of the best means of land and water carriage to many distant and formerly neglected and valueless districts has brought about, both in international trade, to a great extent, and in the home trade of many countries, the sort of change which Adam Smith perceived in the last century, to some extent, in the home trade of the United Kingdom—a change, however, which, even in the United Kingdom, has only very lately become anything like general and complete. 'Good roads, canals, and navigable rivers,' said the philosopher, 'by diminishing the expense of carriage, put the more remote parts of the country more nearly on a level with the neighbourhood of the towns.' Railways and steam navigation have done more to equalize the conditions of sale through the world, since the new mines were discovered, than all preceding improvements in the means of communication since the fall of the Roman Empire and the ruin of its roads.

Immediately after the Californian discoveries, a Russian economist predicted that, if a fall in the value of gold should ensue, England must be the first country to feel it;* and an English economist more recently argued that a greater rise of prices had, in fact, taken place in England than anywhere else, save in the gold countries themselves and the States of America.† Looking back, however, at the situation of England since the opening of the new mines, it is easy to see several agencies tending to counteract the effect upon prices here, some of which tended, on the contrary, to turn their chief effects upon prices abroad. Our vast importations of food and materials, through recent legislation, aided by steam, have, thanks to the gold mines, been easily paid for, but they have made foreigners the recipients of the bulk of the new treasure;‡ and, while tending to lower the price of the produce of our own soil, they have added to the price of the foreigners' produce sent to our market at diminished expense, owing both to the reduction of duties, and to cheaper and faster means of transportation. Corn was,

---

* M. De Tęgoborski: *Commentaries on the Productive Forces of Russia* (Eng. trans.), vol. i., p. 208.

† J. E. Cairnes, Esq.: *Dublin Statistical Journal*, 1859; *Fraser's Magazine*, 1859 and 1860; and letters to the *Economist* and *Times*, 1863.

‡ Mr. Cairnes reasons that England, in consequence of the greater amount of its trade with the gold countries, must receive much more gold than other countries, and that the gold it receives must act more powerfully upon prices because of the activity of credit in the English system of circulation. But the comparative increase of the precious metals in England, or any other country, depends, as Mr. Mill has pointed out, not on the comparative amount of its trade with the mining regions alone, but on the comparative balance of its whole foreign trade and expenditure. The general course of international demand and transactions may be such that a couutry may even part with all, or more than all, the bullion it imports. Such, in fact, has been the situation of England in several years past. In the four years, 1859–1862, the exports of specie exceeded the imports according to the returns, and there is reason to think the balance was more against England than appears by the official accounts. What bullion we got in those years went from us at once into foreigners' hands; and much of the money we get for our manufactures abroad is always in reality partly the price of the foreign materials of which they are made, and the articles of foreign production which the makers consume. Again, although speculative credit often raises prices for the moment above their natural level, representative credit, which merely saves the expense of coin, is only a substitute for it, and not an augmentation of the currency, and the prices it fixes are not higher than would prevail under a metallic system. Moreover, a given addition to prices here would make less change than in previously cheaper countries. And there have been, lastly, peculiar circumstances, pointed out in the text, tending to cheapen prices in the English market.

therefore, less likely to rise in Great Britain than in many other regions; and the improvement in our manufactures generally surpassed the production of gold until the failure of cotton from America. About six-sevenths of the exports of Great Britain are manufactured commodities, and accordingly the productions of this country, which first felt the influence of the new money, generally fell instead of rising in price. Nine-tenths of our imports, on the contrary, are unmanufactured commodities, and the things which have really risen most in our markets are, consequently, to a large extent, foreign commodities; as to which it is important to notice that comparative Tables of past and present prices in England do not measure the change in prices abroad. Even a low price of wheat, for example, to the buyer in London may be a high price to the grower in Poland or Spain; and the French peasant may be trebling the price of his eggs and his butter, when the Londoner pays little more for those articles than he did before French railways and free trade. In fact, the chief monetary phenomenon of this epoch is the rise of prices in remote places, put suddenly more nearly on a level with the neighbourhood of the great centres of commerce as regards the market for their produce. And the Tables by which Mr. Jevons has attempted to measure the change in the value of money fail on this very account to exhibit the real extent of the change even in the United Kingdom itself, to which his researches have been confined. They give comparative prices in England of several sorts of country produce for some years before and since the opening of the gold mines; but they are the prices of the capital and chief towns, not of the remote places of the kingdom. Beef, mutton, veal, butter, eggs, and poultry, for example, have risen about twenty-five per cent. in the London market; but they have risen a hundred per cent. above their rates a few years ago in the inland parts of Ireland and Scotland on the new lines of railway. The common price of meat in the towns in the interior of Ireland before they were connected with the ports and the English market by railways, was from 3½*d.* to 4*d.* a pound, and now is from 7*d.* to 8*d.* The rise of wages, again, in the agricultural districts of England falls far short of the rise from a much lower level in the rural districts of Ireland, suddenly brought into easy and cheap communication with both England and America. The complete revolution which has thus taken place in the scale of local prices in the United Kingdom itself renders all arithmetical measures of the change in the value of money, founded on the rates in a few particular markets, altogether fallacious. The truth is, that the change has been unequal in different years and different places, and in respect to different commodities. Measured in corn, the value of money in these islands is much greater now than it was during the Crimean War; measured in cotton, the value of money is much less than before the war in America. Speaking generally, however, the monetary movement of the sixteenth century has been reversed, and the rise of prices has been much greater in Ireland and the north of Scotland than in England, and greater in the remote parts of the country than in the capital. This contrast illustrates the general distinction already pointed out between the commercial and monetary phenomena of the former and the present metallic epochs. At the former period the change in the worth of money was greatest in the country receiving its supplies directly from the mines, and next at or around the chief centres of commerce, such as Antwerp and London, and moreover, in what had been the dearest markets before, or the towns as compared with the country. Now, it will be found most conspicuous in many of the ruder and remoter localities, where prices were previously lowest.

Not one-tenth of the general produce of the mines of the world, since the new gold was discovered, has been finally allotted by the balance of trade to Great Britain, and some signs of the presence of the remainder might naturally be looked for in places having little or no direct dealings with the mining countries themselves. The new gold regions have, for example, added a much larger amount to the treasure of France than of England. From the returns of the French Custom-house, it would appear that bullion to the value of nearly £100,000,000 had been added, by the end of 1862, to the metallic stock of France; but the issues of gold coin from the French Mint since

1848 greatly exceed the declared imports of that metal. And we are not without evidence of perceptible effects of so vast an addition to the French currency upon the market of the country. In 1848, the French Government revised the official scale of prices, based upon a scale of 1827, and found that prices generally (inclusive of raw produce) had fallen in the interval. Since then the current and the ancient money values of all commodities, imported and exported, have been set down year by year; and it appears from their comparison that, in 1852, a change took place. Prices, instead of falling, began to rise, and, down to the end of 1861, ranged generally much above the old valuation, in spite of an enormous increase of importation and production. But these statistics, like those of Mr. Jevons for Great Britain, afford no real measure of the actual changes which the purchasing power of money has undergone throughout France; for, wherever railways have intersected the country, they have carried up prices towards the metropolitan level; and the advance upon former rates has been much greater in France than in England, because of the previous inferiority of the former in the means of locomotion, and the more backward condition of the places farthest from the capital.* In France, as in England, there has been some controversy respecting the influence of the gold mines on prices; but there too writers on both sides have overlooked the effect of railways upon the distribution of the national currency and the prices of country productions. The writer on the Precious Metals, for example, in the 'Dictionnaire Universel du Commerce,' simply pronounces that provisions and raw materials are rapidly rising in price, but manufactures tending rather to fall. But in the article on Railways, in the same work, it is remarked that prices have risen enormously in the districts they traverse, and that 'one hears every day, in some place where people lived lately almost for nothing, that the passage of a railway has made everything dear.' The rise of prices in the provincial towns and rural districts forms the most prominent subject in most of the reports of the Britsh Consuls

* See on this subject, *Les Chemins de Fer en* 1862 *et* 1863, par Eugène Flachat.

in France for several years past.* In each locality, special causes are commonly assigned by persons on the spot, for 'the dearness of living;' but how is it that the same phenomenon presents itself in so many different localities—in the capital, the provincial town, and the agricultural district? How is it, if railways have raised wages, prices, and rents, that the rise has taken place at both ends of and along their lines? How is it, if labour and produce are rising in the country, because they are carried off to the town, that they are rising also in the town? And how could the prices of things, for the most part increased greatly in quantity, have risen prodigiously throughout France, if there were no more money than formerly circulating through it? Many persons seem to imagine they have accounted for a rise of prices, without reference to the influx of money from the mines, when they have pointed out how the additional money has been actually laid out, and through whose hands it has most recently passed. Unless they see the miner himself, they will not believe that he is the prime agent in the matter, although it is commonly only being brought by other hands than his own, that his gold can raise prices at a distance. An interesting German writer has reproduced one of the popular theories of

* Thus the Consul at Nantes, in his Report for 1862, observes: 'The market prices of goods have been greatly increased by the railway communication between Nantes and Paris, while house rent has risen to a price almost equal to Paris.' The Consul at Bordeaux, in his Report for 1859, says: 'For a while the hope was entertained that the establishment of railways would realize the problem of cheap living; but this has proved a fallacy, for the facility of transport and increased demands of the capital have created a drain in that direction. House-rent has within the last few years doubled, if not trebled.' In his Report for 1862, the same Consul says: 'With the exception of bread, the price of every commodity remains excessively high; and, though wages have risen in proportion, there does not appear to be any marked improvement in the state of the lower classes. It cannot be denied, however, that the progress of civilization has gradually created among them a tendency towards more expensive habits, and that what formerly were esteemed luxuries have now become indispensable wants.' There are similar reports from the Consuls at Havre and Marseilles. Nor is it only in the provincial towns that this monetary revolution has taken place. The cultivators of the soil, although they sell their produce at much elevated rates, complain bitterly of the increased cost of rural labour. The rise of house-rent in the towns is, no doubt, due in part to the concentration of the population; but this would not, if there were not more money in general circulation, raise wages and commodities both in town and country.

Elizabeth's reign—that luxury, ostentation, and expensive habits among all classes are the causes of the modern dearness of living, and not the abundance of money.* There cannot, however, be more money spent, if people have no more to spend than before. A mere change in the ideas and desires of society would add nothing to the number of pieces of money, and could not affect the sum-total of prices. If more money were spent upon houses, furniture, and show, less would remain, if pecuniary means were not increased, to be spent upon labour and food, and the substantial necessaries of life; and, if the former became dearer, the latter would at the same time become cheaper. But, when people have really more money than formerly to spend, they naturally spend more than they formerly did, and their unaccustomed expenditure is considered excessive and extravagant. And, when an increase in the pecuniary incomes of large classes arises from, or accompanies, greater commercial activity and general progress, there commonly is a general taste for a better or more costly style of living than there was at a lower stage of society. There is always, it is true, much folly and vanity in human expenditure; and masses of men do not become philosophers of a sudden because they are making more money, and their state is improving upon the whole. But their state is improving on the whole when their trade is increasing, and the value of their produce rising to a level with that of the most forward communities, and when the lowest classes are breaking the chains of barbarous custom, and furnishing life with better accommodation than servile and ignorant boors could appreciate. It is better to see German peasants building chimneys and embellishing their houses than burying their money, even if we find them copying their superiors in non-essentials and in finery, as well as in the plain requisites of civilization. The greater expense of ordinary life in North than South Germany has been cited as positive proof that the growing dearness of living on the Continent comes not from the plenty of money, but from the costlier habits of the people; and there

* See the chapter headed 'Der Geld-preis und die Sitte,' in Riehl's *Culturstudien.*

may be much that is wasteful and silly in modern German fashion, as well as much that is uncleanly and unwholesome in what is called ancient German simplicity. But the chief reason why South Germany is comparatively cheap is, that there is really less money in circulation; partly because it has more recently been opened up by railways, and still remains farther from the best markets of Europe; and partly because a greater proportion of the money actually gotten is hoarded*—which is a sign of comparative backwardness, and illustrates the connexion between progress and ascending prices noticed already. Wherever backwardness is changing into progress, and stagnation into commercial activity, it will be found that cheapness is changing into dearness, and that something like English prices follow hard upon something like English prosperity. Thus the British consul at Bilbao reported lately: 'The increased trade and prosperous condition of the country have drawn numbers of families to Bilbao. As a result of this the cost of living has risen enormously, and Bilbao, long one of the cheapest towns in Europe, has become a comparatively dear place.'† To Spain, which in the sixteenth century robbed the treasures of the New World directly from their source, gold now comes by honest trade, and the miner is hidden behind the merchant.

---

* The following passage is taken from the *Revue Germanique* for October, 1863, in which it forms part of a translation from an article which appeared in 1857 in a German Quarterly:—'La population de scampagnes a été dans les huit dernières années comme une éponge qui s'est gorgée d'argent. Des statisticiens ont calculé que dans un seul canton à blé de l'Allemagne du sud, lequel ne compte que quelque milles carrés, on a thésaurisé dans le cours des dix dernières années au moins un million de florins d'argent comptant, qui n'est pas rentré dans le commerce.'

† The Consul gives the following comparative Table of Prices in 1854 and 1860:—

	1854.				1860.			
	£	£	s.	d.	£	£	s.	d.
Houses and apartments,	15 to	30	0	0	50 to	80	0	0
Beef (per pound),		0	0	2½		0	0	4
Mutton, ,,		0	0	2½		0	0	4¾
Veal, ,,		0	0	3¼		0	0	8
Bread, ,,		0	0	1		0	0	2
Potatoes (per stone),		0	2	0		0	3	7½
Eggs (per dozen),		0	0	3¾		0	0	7½
Wine (two quarts),		0	0	7½		0	1	3¼

Unaccustomed streams of money are flowing, not only into the towns of Northern Spain, but through all the more fertile districts of the Peninsula near the new lines of railway. And the sums by which prices have been raised in Portugal and Spain could evidently not have been drawn from England and France without a corresponding fall of prices in those countries, had their coffers not been replenished from a new source. It is, too, in regions like the great corn-district of Medina del Campo, poor lately in money, but rich in the wealth of nature, that prices must rise fastest when they are brought into easy communication with the markets where money abounds, since the money is both attracted by their cheapness, and produces the more sensible change on account of it. It is in such places also that the unwonted abundance of such treasure, and the rise in the pecuniary value of the labour and produce of the people, are to be regarded as signs of rise in the international and economical scale, and of the obstacles being at length overcome which for centuries prevented them from contributing their natural resources and energies to advance the general prosperity and happiness of mankind. Thus the trade of the Swiss, shut out by their own mountains from the principal markets of Europe in the last century, now reaches to the farthest regions of gold; the merchant and the traveller pour the precious metals into their lap; and a country, not long ago scantily furnished with a base native currency, is now flowing with money from the mints of the wealthiest States. In the north and east of Europe we likewise find the range of prices indicating the course of local fortunes, and the share of remote places in the increased currency of the world depending on the improvement of their means of intercourse and trade with the more forward regions and their general progress. In Norway—which, with a population about half of that of London, is, in respect of its commercial marine, the fourth among maritime powers—the wages of seamen rose at a bound to the British level on the repeal of the navigation laws; and no sooner did Australian gold appear in Europe than the Norwegian currency swelled to an unprecedented balance, and prices rose to a pitch unknown before.* In Russia, a commodity which, a few years ago, was worth to the producer in the interior only a fourth of the sum it would sell for in the capital, may now be carried thither at comparatively trifling cost in fewer days than it might formerly have taken months to perform the journey; and the producer gains the difference. Such a burst of traffic ensued upon the new means of locomotion that the receipts of the St. Petersburg and Moscow Railway for the carriage of goods in 1859 are said to have equalled those of the best railways in England; and in the summer of the previous year 300 steamers plied the waters of the Volga, where only ten could be counted in 1853. This rapid growth of trade was accompanied, as the British Secretary of Legation reported, by a great improvement in the condition of the people, increased demand for labour, and higher wages, better food, and the exchange of the sheepskin for cloth. The exports of Riga, again, are of the very class which benefited most by the alterations in the English tariff, and which rose the most in the English market immediately after the influx of new gold began; and at Riga the same monetary revolution has ensued which Bilbao and other Western towns have experienced. In his report for 1859 the British Consul says:—'A fact which seems rather to weigh against Riga is the rapid increase of late years in the cost of living in this port. The necessaries of life have doubled in ten years; labour has risen in proportion.'† It would, however, be an inference wide of the truth, that the whole Russian Empire exhibits similar indications of a rise towards the Western level. Great part of it is hardly better furnished with the paths of traffic than before the discovery of America; the carrier in

* British Consul's Report for 1852–3. The Consul at Gottenberg, in Sweden, reports for 1855:—'The year 1855 has been most prosperous. Notwithstanding that most articles are now admitted free of duty, provisions of every kind are excessively dear, many articles having, within the last few years, advanced to treble, and in no instance to less than double in price. This may be attributed to the general prosperity, and consequent increased consumption of better food, among the working classes.'

† A part of this rise is attributable to the depreciation of the paper rouble, but this was not considerable at the period referred to.

many places leaves the cultivator little or no surplus; and the resources of a teeming soil and the industry of an ingenious people are imprisoned and valueless. There is, in fact, still great inequality of prices, as of opportunities of progress, in different parts of Europe; but there is evidence, nevertheless, of the presence of a new money power in parts of every European country since the new gold first glittered in the market, and the Englishman has had, in his own quarter of the globe, many successful competitors for a share in the treasure, some of whom have been realizing prices much more above the ancient level than those which have ruled in the wealthiest towns of this island. Different countries—different localities—by reason not only of the inequality of comparative progress, but also of the vicissitudes of the seasons and political affairs—have participated unequally from time to time in the general enlargement of the circulating medium of Europe. One prevailing tendency is, however, discernible in the commercial movement of this age—to reverse the monetary order of the 16th century, and to raise most, in relation to money, the produce of places where money was scarcest before. Is it so in Europe only? On the contrary, the most remarkable contrast between the former and the present epoch in the history of the precious metals lies in the share allotted to Eastern countries, and the rise of Eastern industry and productions in international value, as measured by the universal standard of money. From 1500 to 1595 the Portuguese monopolized the maritime trade with the East Indies; and the cargoes of Asiatic merchandize which arrived in Europe, few and small in the first half of the century, declined in the latter half; nor does Mr. Jacob estimate at more than fourteen millions the entire amount of treasure which moved to Asia from the West in the first 108 years after America was discovered. In the last fourteen years, India has netted a balance of about a hundred and fifty millions. For upwards of two years the scale has been loaded in favour of India with money lost to the American States by the war—a fact which illustrates the connexion with the fortunes of nations of the movement of the precious metals. This influx into India began, however, with the increase of their quantity in the world,* following the general law of the period of the attraction of money to cheap and fertile places with which communication has been improved, and in favour of which international trade must be redressed. The money has flowed into India, it is true, not only in the immediate purchase of its commodities, but also in loans, public works, and investments of English capital—a fact, however, springing from the same general cause, and tending in the same direction. It is a fact of the same order with the gradual rise of the country to an economic level with the earlier elevated towns which struck the sagacious mind of Adam Smith. 'Everywhere,' he said, 'the greatest improvements of the country have been owing to the overflowing of the stock originally accumulated in the towns.' The ruder and remoter regions are at length, if commerce be allowed its natural course, brought into neighbourhood and fellowship with the regions more advanced and endowed with the same advantages, especially with that advantage to which the latter mainly owed their earlier progress, the advantage of a good commercial situation, which steam navigation, railways, and roads, are giving to many districts in India, rich in the food of mankind and the materials of industry, but until lately unable to dispose of their wealth, unless upon beggarly terms. There are some who view the accession of metallic treasure to such countries as a burden and a loss to them—who maintain that the money exported to India, for example, abstracts a proportionate sum of commodities from the consumption of the natives, and then disappears in useless hoards or frivolous ornaments, adding little or nothing to its industrial spirit and power, or to the pecuniary value and command over foreign markets of its produce. As to the actual use of the new treasure in India, the truth is, that there, as in Egypt, and every continental country in Europe, it has been both hoarded and circulated. Even in England there is always

---

* The bullion imports of India in 1852–3 exceeded five millions sterling; in 1855–6 they rose nearly to eleven millions and a-half; in the year 1856–7, the year before the mutiny, they reached £14,413,690.

a considerable quantity of money lying temporarily idle in the purse of the people too poor to keep bankers; and we shall see reason to believe that the amount of hoarding in India is by no means so great as some English writers assume. Almost all the gold, however, or rather more than a third of the whole treasure lately imported into India, has certainly been either hoarded or made into ornaments. By reason of gold not being legal tender in India, the gold mines have added only indirectly to its currency—adding not gold but silver money. In the West the new gold has taken the place of silver; the greater part of the silver set free has been, finally carried to India, where it has a purchasing power—which gold—a far more portable, convenient, and economic medium—has unfortunately been denied. Even the hoards and ornaments in India, however, are not to be regarded merely as waste. They are not only as legitimate pleasures and uses of wealth as many of the modes of expenditure common in the West, but they are also the private banks and insurance offices of the Indian natives.*

The total coinage at the three Indian Mints, including an insignificant quantity of copper and gold, since the discovery of the gold mines, amounts to about a hundred millions of English money; and, in considering the effects of so great an addition to the coinage, it is material to observe that prices had generally been falling in India for more than five-and-twenty years previously. During that period the balance of treasure netted by India had not been large, owing to the slow development of its export trade, and the considerable remittances of specie to

---

* It may not be considered out of place here to notice a misconception which seems to exist with respect to the effect on prices of the large portion of the annual supplies of silver and gold made in all countries, not into money, but into articles of use or ornament. Some writers treat this portion as having no effect at all on prices; others make calculations in which the whole additional stock of the precious metals from the new mines is counted as money. But, when the precious metals are converted into articles other than money, and sold and circulated as commodities, they tend not to raise, but to lower, the general level of prices, by absorbing a portion of the currency in their own circulation; for money cannot be in two places or doing two things at the same time, and the quantity engaged in buying plate, watches, ornaments, &c., is withdrawn from the market of other commodities. Hence the whole addition to the stock of the precious metals in

England. On the other hand, the production of commodities increased from internal quiet, and the work to be done by the circulating medium of the country was multiplied not only by the increase of ordinary traffic, but also by the adoption under British rule of payments in money for taxes and other purposes, where payments in kind and barter had been customary before. The amount of the currency had in consequence become insufficient; the natives were often inconvenienced, and sometimes even ruined by its scarcity; and the labour and commodities of India were bought cheaper and cheaper by other countries. In fact, the price of labour and of many commodities was lower in India in 1845 than in England when the mine of Potosi was discovered three hundred years before, and we have seen how the previous cheapness of the English market contributed to the monetary revolution which followed the first considerable influx of silver from the New World.

But it would be an error to look for a rise of price in all commodities and localities alike in India on the augmentation of its currency. The apparent effect of an expanded currency is sure in any country to be magnified in the case of some commodities, and diminished in the case of others, by extrinsic causes. The additional money is, in the first place, not laid out on all things or in all places equally—on some there may be no additional expenditure at all; and it raises more, or less, or not at all, the prices of the things on which it is expended, according to the supply forthcoming in each case to meet the increased pecuniary demand. Thus, for example, the paper price of different commodities at New York had arisen above their level a

---

England since the discovery of the new mines has not only not tended to raise the prices, but a portion, and probably a very considerable portion, has really acted in the contrary direction, having been made into articles which added to the stock of commodities to be circulated. The consumption of gold and silver in the useful and ornamental arts in England, for watches, plate, jewellery, and decoration, must be very great. In Adam Smith's time the value consumed in the town of Birmingham in plating and gilding alone was estimated at more than £50,000 (*Wealth of Nations*, Book I. ch. xi.); and last year it was stated, in the Campden House case, that 'a single artist had received from the proprietor of a single house no less a sum than £1000, not for the work of gilding generally, but for the actual gold to be used in the process.'—*Times*, Sept. 5, 1863.

year before in different degrees from 10 to 220 per cent.* In India prices have varied much in different places, and in different seasons, partly through the unequal distribution of the new money through the different localities, and partly on account of local inequalities in the supply, not of money, but of commodities. The defect of means of internal communication, more than any other circumstance, has contributed to cause great local inequalities in Indian prices in the last ten years.† It throws some light upon the English prices in the 16th century to read that, in the North-west Provinces during the famine which followed the Mutiny, 'while in one bazaar prices of 4 rupees per maund might be ruling, in another not far off the price would be R. 1·8; yet no flow could take place from the full to the ex-

---

* See a table of prices of fifty-five commodities in the New York Market.—*Economist*, March 28, 1863.

† The effect of the increase of money in India cannot be measured by the rates at which Indian products sell in the English market. Prices are very unequal in different parts of the East, and our imports may come from the cheapest places. Moreover, prices may be actually rising at the place of exportation, while falling at the place of importation, and the very cause of a fall at the latter may produce a rise at the former. Thus, the price of rice has been low of late years in the English market, because of large importations from the cheap Burmese provinces, where, however, the price has risen in consequence. For the same reason, together with the abundance of the crops on the spot, the price of rice has latterly been low in some districts of Bengal in which prices generally have been high. Thus, at Dacca, the price of rice was not higher in 1862 than in 1854; it was, however, 30 per cent. higher at Berhampore, and 100 per cent. higher at Cuttack. The exports of India—coffee, cotton, grains, hemp, hides, indigo, jute, oils, opium, saltpetre, seeds, shawls, silk, sugar, tea, wood, wool—have almost all risen greatly even in foreign markets. Nevertheless, the prices in Mr. Jevons tables of 'tea, sugar, rice, foreign spirits, spices, seeds,' have been referred to by an able writer as confirming his conclusion that prices have risen less abroad, and especially in India, and Eastern and tropical countries generally, than in England. But English prices are not foreign prices. Of the commodities just named, rice has greatly risen in most parts of India; tea has risen considerably even in the English market, but much more in India; and sugar has risen in India (more than 100 per cent. in some places), but it has fallen in Europe for several years, owing to the enormous increase of the produce of Cuba and Porto Rico, and of beetroot sugar on the Continent. Foreign spirits (except brandy, which has much risen) have fallen in England, in common with British spirits, by reason partly of the immense production of rum in the West Indies, and partly of diminished consumption in England and Ireland. Spices have been falling in the British market ever since the cessation of the Dutch monopoly, owing partly to the immense increase in the sources and amount of supply, partly to the extent of adulteration, and partly to the

hausted market, because roads were not in existence.'* Before the Mutiny the prosperity of these provinces had steadily increased, and labour bore a price in them from 1854 to 1857 that it had never borne before. Then came destruction and famine; and while the price of labour fell, that of food increased—just as, in the winter of 1586, food bore an enormous price at Antwerp and Brussels, not because the new mines were prolific—for the plenty of money had disappeared—but because the Spaniards had stopped cultivation.† In the adjoining provinces of Holland, on the contrary, prices at the same period were high, though every commodity abounded in the market, because American silver abounded there too; so likewise in India, while famine prices reigned in the North West, there were other provinces in which things were at once abundant and dear, because the harvest of money as well as of food had been rich; and the same may be said of the North West itself for two years past. During the famine years in the North West, the enormous rise in prices, generally in the Lower provinces of Bengal, was not attributable exclusively to the operations of the Indian Mints; but in 1862 and 1863 plenty reigned all around, and yet prices ranged far above their level in 1854, with striking inequalities in the rise in different districts in different commodities, varying from above 300 per cent. to less than 20. Sugar, for example, was only 25 per cent. higher at Dacca in 1863, but at Patna and Dinapore it was 130 per cent. higher than in 1854. Rice is almost the only native product in any part of the Lower provinces of Bengal which did not sell much higher in 1863 than before the drain of silver to the East, which the gold mines made possible; and the rare exception is accounted for not only

---

alteration in our tastes and customs of cookery, through which the demand has not increased with the supply. Oil seeds have risen enormously in India. Opium (to which the writer quoted has not referred) is the only Indian export of importance which has fallen in India itself; the causes of the fall being, first, a great increase of production since the Government raised the price to the cultivator, in order to drive rivals from the Chinese market; and, secondly, the late monetary crisis at Calcutta.

* Colonel Baird Smith's *Report*.

† Motley's *United Netherlands*.

by splendid crops upon the spot, but by the diversion of a part of the demand to the Burmese rice-grounds. Corn, in like manner, is as cheap in the London market now as it was a hundred years ago, because the supply of last year has outgrown the money demand. But rice sold in 1863 for double its ancient price in many parts of Madras, although cultivation had extended, and the two last harvests had been good, while the importations of food had increased, and its exportation diminished. In the interior of Bombay such unprecedented prices have been latterly witnessed that the natives (who seem to be equally blamed whether they save or spend) have been accused, in an official Report of 'playing with their money like the Californian gold-finders in the first days of the diggings.' In this novel profusion of expenditure, in the new comforts and luxuries with which the natives of India are filling their houses, in the new and more numerous exchanges which money performs in the interior of the country, and the larger sums necessary to perform them at rates enormously higher than formerly, we have the real account of much of the money supposed to have been hoarded because it has not found its way back to the bankers in the chief towns. The peasantry of the poorest districts in Ireland, in the late famine of 1847, were, in like manner, supposed to be hoarding the silver introduced by the Board of Works, because it did not return to the banks: the true explanation being that barter had ceased, and the coins which had disappeared were busy performing common exchanges, which had never been performed by money before. It is no slight advantage to the Indian natives to have their industry excited, and their traffic facilitated by the unwonted abundance of the currency, and it liberates the ryot from the cruel exactions of the money-lender. It raises the value of Indian commodities in the market of the world, and the Hindoo is no longer forced to sell cheap and buy dear, in international trade.* It is in the rate of wages, perhaps, that the most remarkable proof is afforded of the elevated rank

---

* The disadvantage to which a country is exposed in international trade from a lower range of prices than obtains in the countries with which it trades, is wel

of the Indian people in the scale of nations; for the comparative powers of production and purchase of different nations are measured by the average pecuniary earnings of labour in each. The rise of money-wages in England is seldom computed at so much as 20 per cent.; but the localities are now few in India where the labourer cannot earn more than twice the sum he could have done twelve years ago, and there are many in which he can earn more than three times as much. The railways, and new public works, and the emigration of Coolies to Ceylon, Mauritius, and the West Indies, have, along with the European purchases of cotton, contributed largely to this result; but a fact is not explained away by showing how it has come to pass. The better market for the industry of the Hindoo, the expenditure of unprecedented sums upon it, and its extraordinary rise in price, are the very things spoken of. All the silver sent to the East could not add a rupee to the price of its produce and industry unless it were expended; the railways, public works, and the payments for cotton, are among the channels of expenditure; but the true sources of the money, though it be nearly all silver, are the new gold mines, for the silver could not have been spared from the West, had its place not been supplied by new gold.

There is, then, upon the whole, incontrovertible evidence of a great change in the value of the precious metals in the world, far more extensive than occurred in the 16th century, and upon a different ground-plan; but, like that earlier monetary revolution, it has been neither universal nor equal where it has occurred. It has not been universal, for the Egyptian is almost

---

explained in the following answer of the Doctor to the Knight in the old *Dialogues* referred to in the early part of this article:—

'*Knight.*—Yea, but, sir, if the increase of treasure be partly the occasion of this continued dearth, then by likelihood in other our neighbours' nations, unto whom yearly is consigned great store of gold and silver, the prices of victuals and other wares in like sort be raised, according to the increase of their treasure.'

'*Doctor.*—It is even so; and, therefore, as I account it a matter hard to revoke all our English wares unto their old prices, so do I not take it to be either profitable convenient to the realm, except one should wish that our commodities should be uttered cheap to strangers, and on the other side be dear unto us, which could noc be without great impoverishment of the commonwealth.'

the only African enriched; China has netted nothing on the balance of its trade for many years, and the cattle wandering in the pampas of La Plata soon leave the golden circle. Nor has it been equal, for the change has been greater in cheap markets than in dear. But the immense rise of prices in many of the former has been balanced by no corresponding fall in any of the latter markets, and a great diminution in the value of money, on the whole, is therefore clear, though to attempt to measure it with precision is vain, and to talk of it in terms of arithmetic is an abuse of figures. The only reasonable conclusion on the subject is, that money has for the present lost much of its purchasing power in the general world of trade—a conclusion by itself little to be desired. To load the exchanges of men—to alter the terms of agreement, and disappoint just expectations—to make landlords unwilling to grant leases, and all classes doubtful about contracts for time and thrifty investments—were a calamitous result of the enterprise and toils of the miners. And some evil of this kind has undoubtedly been done. The first consequence, too, of the discovery of the new mines was a diminution in the production of commodities. In 1851, half the male population of Victoria deserted their occupations for the diggings. In 1850, when the population of the colony was only 76,000, more than 52,000 acres were under cultivation. In 1854, when the population amounted to nearly 237,000, only 34,657 acres were cultivated. In 1860, this very colony imported from the rest of the world consumable commodities to the value of more than fifteen millions, and gave commodities in exchange to the value of only four millions and a quarter. British Columbia to this day has produced little but gold, and has levied a continual tribute upon the food, clothing, and implements of the rest of the world. Nevertheless, the good and the gain which have accompanied the evil and the loss are infinitely greater. The new gold has not only founded commercial nations of great promise round its sources, and enabled our own nation to work out (not only without a paralysing monetary drain, but with triumphant success) the problem of free trade, and to purchase in most critical times the material of our manufactures; but it has assisted many backward communities to rise rapidly in the scale of civilization, and 'wandered heaven-directed to the poor.' The rapid rise in the pecuniary value of the labour and produce of several such communities, of which evidence has been given, is not merely a sign and effect of their growing prosperity and elevated commercial position; it has also helped to conduce to their progress. The new money has obtained the immediate execution of great works such as a long line of ancient Egyptian tyrants could not have compelled;* it has been a stimulus to the cultivator's industry and to the merchant's activity; and it has substituted to a considerable extent a civilized medium of exchange for the barbarous and obstructive contrivance of barter.

So much the increase of the precious metals may be said to have accomplished. What more in their future increase they may accomplish it is not in the province of political economy to forecast. They may become a curse instead of a blessing; they may turn the reaping-hook into a sword, and become the sinews of war in Europe, when the sinews of war are exhausted in America. In Asia they may be buried out of the reach of the merchant by rebellion and anarchy, and prices may rise although

* 'An extraordinary revolution is rapidly proceeding in this country (Egypt). Europe has finally understood the immense future of Egypt, and is eager to develop her yet budding resources. Every steamer is pouring a new population and a golden stream on our shores; energy and capital are taking possession of the land, and urging it forward in the path of civilization and wealth. Not only are the cities of Alexandria and Cairo receiving so great an influx of inhabitants that, although whole quarters are rising on every side, house-room is still insufficient, and rents are always increasing; but the inland towns and villages are overrun, and factories with high chimneys and long lines of black smoke cut the sky of our flat landscape through the length and breadth of Lower Egypt. Gradually, but surely, the tide is creeping upwards, and will soon people the shores of the Thebaid. Englishmen, I am glad to say, are not behind in the race, and their numbers must always increase in a corresponding ratio to the amount of machinery employed. The effect of all this is telling on the natives. I lately heard that Halim Pacha, in conversing with his farm labourers, had found the intellect of the lads who have grown up since the introduction of the new mechanical appliances was greatly in advance of that of the men who had reached manhood under the former primitive system of cultivation, when the ox was the all-in-all to the fellah, and when his mind had no stimulus and no cause for thought or inquiry.'—*Times*, March 28, 1864.

money is scarce, because food is scarcer still. But, should both hemispheres be blessed with peace, their hoards as well as their mines may pour their contents into the lap of trade, and a new use may be found for all. The emancipation of the Russian serfs affords, in the payment of wages it involves, an example of the useful employment which the progress of civilization may provide for an increase of silver and gold in the world. The history of the last fifteen years bids us believe that, if the sword can be kept in its sheath, the precious metals will become less precious, chiefly in places where they are too precious at present; that prices will rise fastest where they are now lower than they should be, or could be, if commerce had convenient pathways; and that commodities will finally be multiplied as much as pieces of money on the market. Given the fertility of the mines and the total quantity of money in circulation, prices in the aggregate must be lower through the world as a whole, in proportion to the general industry and skill of mankind, and the extent and facility of their trade; but in the same proportion they must also be nearer equality in different markets; and the rise of prices in cheap places to the level of the dearest is a sign of advancing civilization and prosperity. If prices were at a perfect equality in all places, it would prove that even distance as well as war had ceased to separate mankind. Although the literal attainment of a perfect monetary level is, therefore, manifestly impossible, the history of prices proves that, while many obstacles to human fellowship remain, more has been done since the new gold mines were discovered to make the world one neighbourhood than was done in 300 years before.

XX.

THE NEW GOLD MINES AND PRICES IN EUROPE IN 1865.*

On the discovery of the new gold mines, under the name of the Gold Question, an economic inquiry, unconnected with party politics, for the first time gained the ear of the public at large. Yet public interest has been languid, in comparison with the real importance of the monetary problems involved. The chief reason for this is perhaps the diffusion of an opinion, that the effect of the increase of money upon prices practically concerns persons alone whose pecuniary incomes are fixed: an opinion which would be sufficiently true if prices were everywhere uniformly affected, and with respect to all things alike. But the fact is, that the scale of relative incomes, and of relative prices, in different places, and with respect to different commodities, has been so altered, that the old level of profits in different employments, and the old rates of expenditure in different situations, have been permanently disturbed, and new elements must be imported into all calculations respecting the best markets to buy and sell in, the cost of living in different localities, the outgoings and returns in different trades, and the rates of interest which different investments will yield. Those who omit to take these new elements into account may find that their expenses, both as producers and consumers, are largely increased, while the prices of their own productions are not higher than formerly; or they may find themselves buyers in markets in which prices have unexpectedly and enormously risen, and sellers where they

* *North British Review*, June, 1865.

have risen in no such proportion; or again, they may miss investments which would yield extraordinary gain. The British farmer complains that while labour and many of the requisites of production are dearer, he gets no more money than formerly for his wheat, and the migration of population from the country to the towns, and the production of animal food instead of corn, are among the results of changes in relative prices at home. Most writers on the effects of the Mines have confined their observations to changes in prices at home. The truth, however, is, that changes in prices abroad are of equal importance even to Englishmen, not for the purpose of theoretical instruction alone, but even with a view to pecuniary saving and gain. Every day people are making speculations and entering into transactions—in emigration, in foreign trade, and in foreign loans and undertakings—the prudence of which depends upon the movements of prices abroad. Great undertakings by Englishmen abroad, in fact, have been based upon estimates which have proved fallacious, because they made no sufficient allowance for the effects of an extraordinary increase of money in remote places. Chairmen of Indian Railway and Irrigation Companies, for example, have reported in London that the rise of prices in India had falsified all their calculations, and entailed the heaviest losses on contractors. Nor is it in production alone that the unequal alteration of prices has made itself felt, for consumers have been very differently affected according to the place of their residence and the things they are accustomed to use. The class of British holders of fixed incomes, who have really been the chief sufferers from the increase of money in other hands than their own, are not fundholders and Government servants in Great Britain, who are generally placed first in dissertations on the subject, but military and civil servants of the Crown in India, who are confronted by a rise of prices to which there has been nothing similar in England since the reign of Elizabeth. Even in England itself, consumers are differently affected, according to their class of life and habits, and the localities they live in. To the agricultural labourer the price of grain is the chief matter, and grain is cheap; he suffers comparatively little from the dearness of butter and meat, and nothing from the dearness of service, now pressing so hard on the poorer gentry and tradesmen, especially in the parts of the country where such things used to be cheapest. It depends entirely on the localities men buy and sell in, and the things they buy and sell in them, how they are affected by the greater amount of money in the world; and statistical averages of prices in general are not only fallacious in principle, but misleading in practice. The additional money has been unequally distributed by the balance of trade to different countries, and very unequally shared by different classes in the countries receiving it; again it has been spent by the classes receiving it, not upon all commodities alike, but unequally, and the supply of some things upon which there has been an additional expenditure has increased very much more than that of others. Moreover, a low range of prices is raised more by a given addition to money than a high one, which is one reason why the change has been greatest in places once remarkable for their cheapness.* And from what has been said, it is plain that a change in comparative incomes and prices would have been caused by the new gold alone, since it would increase the incomes and expenditure only of the classes, beginning with the miners, to whose hands it successively came. But the new gold has by no means been the only new agency at work; an altered distribution of money through the world has been brought about by more general and permanent causes. And at a time like the present—a time of doubtful markets and hesitating trade—it is peculiarly desirable to lay hold of the

---

* The greater effect on low prices of an additional sum of money is a matter of considerable practical importance, which may be illustrated in this way. Let us suppose that the price of common labour was formerly 1*s*. 6*d*. a-day in England, and 1*d*. a-day in India, and that the increased demand for labour has added a sixpence to the rate of daily wages in both countries, raising the rate from 1*s*. 6*d*. to 2*s*. in England, and from 1*d*. to 7*d*. in parts of India. Wages would then have risen 33 per cent. in England, and 600 per cent. in India; and whereas a contractor could only hire three men in England for the sum with which he could formerly have hired four, in India he could only hire one man for the sum with which he could formerly have hired six.

fundamental causes at work, because, although the fortunes of individuals here and there may depend on the momentary condition of things, to the bulk of society the permanent agencies which prevail in the end, and the permanent rates they tend to establish, are the objects of greatest importance. Commerce and enterprise may pause and falter for a few weeks or months; a transitory disturbance originating in America may possibly agitate all markets; but such possibilities only make it of greater importance to know what to look forward to afterwards, and to distinguish between permanent and temporary changes of prices and of the profits of production in each place and with respect to each sort of thing.

The general principle determining the distribution of the precious metals is, that money is spent by those who receive it on the things they want most for production or consumption, and in the places where those things can be procured at the smallest expense. To buy in the cheapest and sell in the dearest market is the policy of trade; and a combination of causes has latterly given, and is continually giving buyers, on the one hand, access to cheaper places of production for many commodities, and the sellers of the produce of such places, on the other hand, easier access to the markets where their value is greatest. But this necessarily leads to a change in the seats of production and in relative prices, the tendency being always towards the production of everything in the places within reach where its cost of production is least, and towards an equality in the prices of portable goods over the area of cheaper and closer commercial intercommunication. Producers in particular occupations and particular places, accordingly, have not only obtained no share in the new treasure, getting no additional custom either from the mining countries or from the countries these deal with, but have even found the demand for their produce decreasing, and transferred to other localities; and capital and industry are in a course of migration, not only because extraordinary profits are offered in new regions and new employments, but also because ordinary profits are no longer to be made in old places and old employments.

The great gold movement itself—that is to say, the production and distribution of the new gold—is only a part of a much larger movement, resulting from the new facilities of producing many things, gold among the number, in cheaper places than formerly, and disposing of them more readily in the places where their value is the highest, and the enterprise with which such facilities are being turned to account. The mines of California and Australia, for which older mines were forsaken,* are only a particular class of new sources of production from which the markets of the world are being supplied, and their rapid development is only a particular instance of the energy with which cheaper and better sources of supply are sought and developed. The bent of the industrial and commercial movement of our times is, above all things, to discover and put to profitable use the special resources, metallic and non-metallic, in which each region excels, to seat every industry in the places best adapted for it, and to apply the skill and capital of old countries more productively in remote places with great natural resources. 'The first phenomenon,' Mr. Patterson observes, 'attendant upon the gold discoveries, has been the great emigration—the transfer of large masses of population from the old seats to new ones, the vast and sudden spread of civilized mankind over the earth. The countries where these gold-beds have been found are in the utmost ends of the earth, regions the most isolated from the seats of civilization. Of all spots on the globe, California was the farthest removed from the highways of enterprise. Not a road to it was to be found on the map of the traveller; not a route to it was laid down in the charts of the mariner. Australia was, if possible, a still more isolated quarter of the globe.' This migration to the remote regions of the new gold is not, however, a singular and isolated movement of industry. We shall find, on the contrary, that the key to the principal permanent changes in prices which have followed the

* 'The product of gold in the Atlantic States has fallen off since the discoveries of gold in California.'—*Preliminary Report on the Eighth Census of the United States*, p. 63.

path of the new gold through the world, is to be found in the fact that remoteness is no longer the obstacle it was to the best territorial division of labour, and that buried natural riches and neglected local capabilities are obtaining, in a thousand directions at once, a value proportionate rather to their actual quality than to their nearness to market, and attracting capital and skill by high profits to their development. For the same reason, and by the same aids to industrial enterprise which have brought miners and merchants to cheaper places for gold, cheaper places for the production and purchase of many other things have been contemporaneously found, and the distribution of the new gold and its effects upon prices have been very different from what they would have been, had the fertility of the new mines been the only altered condition of international trade. The general principle which regulates the distribution of money through the world is, as we have said, that those who receive it naturally spend it on the things they want most, and in the places where such things can be had cheapest; but they have of late years obtained access to markets not formerly within reach, and much of the new money has been absorbed in new regions, and in the circulation of produce not before in the market. The world may at present be divided into three classes of regions: first, those in which prices were formerly highest; in the second place, those in which the new movements of trade have already raised prices towards the level prevailing in the former regions; and, thirdly, the places not yet within the influence of the new means of commercial intercommunication. The first and second class of regions may be said to be fast merging into one, with pecuniary rates approaching to equality, while the third class is also, in numerous directions, on the point of assimilation. A permanent change is thus taking place in the conditions which govern comparative prices in different markets, and one the more worthy of notice, since, in the earlier years after the discovery of the new mines, there was, both in the gold countries themselves, and in the chief markets of Europe, an abnormal, and in a great measure, temporary elevation of prices, which, although not in reality principally due to the increase of gold, led to mistaken conclusions respecting its real effects.

The first rise of prices in California and Australia, from which M. Chevalier and other eminent writers were led to apprehend a proportionate fall in the value of money throughout Europe, was, in fact, as Mr. Newmarch has shown,* both temporary in degree and partial in extent; those things alone rising in price which were in demand with the classes whose pecuniary incomes were increased. While, for instance, the coarser sorts of clothing adapted to life at the diggings were fetching extraordinary prices, the best quality of cloth for a time was almost unsaleable. Moreover, the early rise in prices in the gold countries was not only partial, but only partially caused by the new gold. In the face of a rapidly increasing population, there was an actual decrease in the supply of labour and many of the necessaries of life. Farms and pastoral settlements were forsaken; the crops in many places were lost for want of hands; all building ceased in Melbourne at the very time that crowds were arriving; and the vessels coming from Europe were too full of emigrants to have room for considerable cargoes. So far, too, as the rise of prices was really caused by the increase of gold, and not by the scarcity of commodities, it should be taken into account that a great part of the gold current at first came not from the new, but from the old mines of the world, brought by immigrants who did not come empty-handed, and who were driven to spend a good deal of old money before they could make any new, or even get to the mines. Hence the first fall in the value of money in the gold countries was in a great measure due to a temporary and abnormal condition of things, and not to the fertility of the mines. In 1854, prices in Victoria were already much lower than during the two years before, and the following Table of prices, published by the Registrar-General of the colony, shows their continuous descent in subsequent years:—

---

* *History of Prices,* vol. vi., Appendices xxx. and xxxii.

ESTIMATED WEEKLY EXPENDITURE OF AN ARTISAN, HIS WIFE, AND THREE CHILDREN.

	1854.			1857.			1861.		
	£	*s.*	*d.*	£	*s.*	*d.*	£	*s.*	*d.*
Bread, 28 lbs., . . .	0	12	6	0	6	8¾	0	5	3
Beef, *or* mutton, 21 lbs., .	0	15	9	0	12	3	0	6	10
Potatoes, 21 lbs., . .	0	5	10½	0	2	10½	0	1	0
Flour, 5 lbs., . . .	0	2	2	0	1	2¼	0	1	0
Tea, 1 lb., ...	0	2	0	0	2	6	0	2	9
Sugar, 6 lbs., . . .	0	3	0	0	2	6	0	2	3
Soap, 3 lbs., . . .	0	1	0	0	1	0	0	0	9
Candles, 2 lbs., . . .	0	1	6	0	1	4	0	1	2
Milk, 7 pints, . . .	0	7	0	0	3	6	0	2	4
Butter, 2 lbs., . . .	0	9	0	0	5	6	0	3	0
Firewood, ¼ ton, . .	0	12	6	0	6	0	0	4	0
Water, 1 load, . . .	0	10	0	0	5	0	0	2	0
Rent of cottage, per week, .	2	0	0	0	10	0	0	6	0
Clothing, ...	0	15	0	0	10	0	0	6	0
School fees, . . .	0	3	0	0	3	0	0	3	0
	£7	0	3½	£3	13	4½	£2	7	4

The reader will perceive in these figures a proof of the error of a method by which some writers have attempted to measure the permanent effect of the new mines on the value of money—that, namely, of taking an average of prices one year with another since their discovery. An average of prices for a succession of years hides the material point whether prices have continuously risen, or, on the contrary, have latterly fallen—a point of great practical importance, since, as already observed, the general movement of prices has been very different in different places. As an illustration of this we beg attention to the following Table of prices at Bilbao, in contrast with the previous Table of prices at Victoria:—

	1854.*	1860.	1864.
	£ s. d.	£ s. d.	£ s. d.
Mutton, per lb., . .	0 0 2¼	0 0 4¾	0 0 8½
Beef, do., . . .	0 0 2½	0 0 4	5*d.* to 8*d.*
Veal, do., . . .	0 0 3¼	0 0 8	8*d.* to 10*d.*
Butter, do., . . .	0 0 5	0 0 9½	0 1 3
Eggs, per doz., . . .	0 0 3¾	0 0 7½	0 0 10
Bread, per lb., . . .	0 0 1	0 0 2	0 0 2
Common wine, two quarts,	0 0 7½	0 1 3¼	0 0 10
Rent, ...	£15 to £20.	£50 to £80.	£30 to £80.

It is evident, from a comparison of the two Tables, that persons intending to trade with, or settle at, either Melbourne or Bilbao, would make a serious mistake in averaging prices one year with another. The average would give a range more than three times too high at one of the places, and nearly three times too low at the other. Prices in Australia in the first years after the derangement of industry by the mines, and prices in Spain before the new gold had found entrance, are so far from affording a basis for calculations respecting the future probable value of money, that they ought rather to be excluded from the estimate. The contrast, however, between the descending movement of prices at one place, and their ascending movement at the other, indicates an important practical distinction. The causes which raised prices so high in Australia from 1852 to 1854 were in a great measure transitory and local;

* Prices in 1854 were the average prices of a long period anterior. The very nigh price of wine in 1860 was in part occasioned by scarcity; not so with the other articles. The harvests have been good, and although bread was at the same price at Bilbao in 1864 as in 1860, in consequence of railway communication with the interior, its price rose in the interior between those years.

but those which have raised them in Spain are fundamental and permanent in their character, and extend in their operations over the whole area of commercial intercommunication. Mr. Windham has left the following note of Dr. Johnson's conversation on the effect of turnpike-roads in England:—'Every place communicating with every other. Before, there were cheap places and dear places; now, all refuges are destroyed for elegant and genteel poverty. Disunion of families by furnishing a market for each man's ability, and destroying the dependence of one man upon another.' The train of consequences described in these sentences has, with extraordinary rapidity, followed the recent increase in the communication between distant parts of the world, created by the knowledge and enterprise of our times, as well as by its better means of locomotion. Wherever these causes have acted may be seen the equalization of prices, the disappearance of comparative cheapness, the opening-up of new markets for the special capabilities of each place and its inhabitants, and the rupture of ancient bonds of local dependence, of which Dr. Johnson saw, eighty years ago, almost the beginning in England. It is curious to observe how writers, at places the most remote from each other, fall naturally into the use of the very same words in describing the changes taking place under their eyes. Of Bilbao, the British Consul, four years ago, when prices had not reached their subsequent pitch, reported:—'The cost of living has risen enormously; and Bilbao, from being one of the cheapest towns in Europe, has become a comparatively dear place.' From Yokohama, in Japan, the Consul writes:—'From being one of the cheapest places in the East, it has become second only to Shanghai in expensiveness.' And from Alexandria we hear:—'Egypt, which a few years ago was one of the cheapest countries, is fast rising to the Indian scale of prices.'

The rising prices in such places indicate, it should be particularly observed, not a mere fall in the local value of money, but a rise in the general as well as in the pecuniary value of their produce. If all the cattle in the pastures of South America could be carried rapidly and cheaply to Europe, their value in money might be more than decupled; but the change would not be a depreciation of money; for, on the contrary, money would have found an additional demand. Less than a generation ago, the *Landes* of the Gironde were a pestilential waste, covering 300,000 hectares, and valued at 900,000 francs on the whole, or three francs a hectare on the average. Partly by being brought nearer to markets by railways, partly by the mere fact of their capabilities becoming known, partly by drainage and cultivation, and partly, no doubt, through the general increase of money in France, the price of the *Landes* has risen in the extraordinary manner described in the British Consul's report, and more in detail by M. About, who relates that the tobacco crop of a single hectare was lately sold for more than a thousand francs, and that the wood alone, on a plot of 500 hectares, only partly in plantation, will, in less than twenty years, be worth a million francs, being more than the worth of the whole territory of the *Landes* about the time that the mines of California were discovered. M. About adds:—'This enormous territory, which did not figure for a million francs when I was at College, will be worth six hundred millions in 1894.' In the same work from which these figures are taken,* M. About graphically describes some of the causes of the enormous advance in prices in Paris. It denotes, he observes, that Paris has become the metropolis of the business as well as of the fashion of the Continent; and rents are trebled, because shops and hotels are crowded, and Paris is a city frequented by the rich. So far as it goes, this description is true, though it fails to allow both for the immense influx of gold shown in the official accounts of the foreign commerce of France, and for the expenditure in the metropolis of vast sums lent to the Government from the old hoards of the people. But we must differ entirely from M. About where he says that, while Paris has become a place only for the rich, there remains, and will always remain, a refuge for poverty in the country. 'If the rise of prices in Paris terrifies you, there is the railway;

* *Le Progrès*, 1864.

it not only brings people to Paris, but takes them away. Live in the country.' We affirm, on the contrary, that, just because the railway brings people and things from the metropolis as well as to it, it brings metropolitan prices into the country, and far more effectively than the old turnpike-road realizes Dr. Johnson's opinion of the results of easy communication between place and place: 'Before, there were cheap places and dear places; now, all refuges are destroyed for elegant and genteel poverty.' The price of eggs a few years ago at Bayonne was six or seven sous a dozen; now, you will not get as good a dozen for fourteen; and the price of boarding in a pension at the same place has exactly doubled in the same period. In formerly less accessible places than Bayonne, the change in the cost of subsistence has been greater; and one cause of the concentration of the population of Europe in large towns—which is a fact of immense political significance in our times—is not only that access to them is easier, and employment in them is greater, but that railways are making the country as dear as the town. M. About recommends the country to the poor for its healthfulness and beauty as well as for economy; but modern means of locomotion, and the movement of which they are both cause and effect, tend to give all the advantages of each place a pecuniary value in proportion to their real utility and rarity, and to turn them to the utmost commercial account, thus finding new markets for the produce of the mines in the Pyrenees and the Alps. The same general tendency towards the commercial development of the natural wealth of such regions, which led to the production of the new gold, governs its distribution and effect upon prices. Buyers on the one hand, and sellers on the other, have gained, and are constantly gaining, access to new markets. The necessary consequence is to bring money in unusual abundance to places where prices were formerly low, and on the other hand, to bring the cheap produce of such places to the markets previously dearest, and to counteract more or less in the latter the fall in the value of gold which the increase in its quantity would otherwise have produced. And thus it is that stationary prices of commodities in general are the best marks of prosperity in one class of localities, namely, those in which money has always abounded, and where cheapness indicates improvement in production at home, and access to cheaper places of production abroad; while, in another class of localities, rising prices indicate improved means of exportation, better markets, and inducements for the ingress of capital and skill as well as money. For the rate of profit on capital and skill employed in the development of their resources, and bringing their produce cheaply to market, is in proportion to the increase of the quantity and price of the produce. If people can sell for £100 what cost them but £50, their profit in money is 100 per cent.; and the high profits and interest latterly yielded on capital employed in foreign trade and investments has arisen mainly from obtaining a share in the rising pecuniary value of the productions of regions whose commercial situation has been improved. This movement certainly tends to destroy the refuges of poverty, but it tends, on the other hand, to destroy poverty itself by 'furnishing a market for each man's ability.' It brings with it hardship to those whose condition is stationary, but it makes the condition of many progressive. A few years before Dr. Johnson's remarks on the effect of roads, Goldsmith made those excursions through the country which resulted in the poem of the 'Deserted Village,' in which the features of the landscape, and something of personal incident, were drawn from his native village in Ireland; but the picture of the intrusion of the wealth of towns and 'trade's unfeeling train' into remote parts of the country, was taken from England. The poet saw only the privation to the parson, who 'remote from towns' had been 'passing rich at forty pounds a-year,' and the sorrowful side of the migration of the peasantry; Dr. Johnson saw also the market opened for each man's capacity by the union of localities, and the liberation of individuals from hereditary restraints and family dependence. This is exactly the movement which a philosophical jurist has pronounced to be the chief characteristic of progressive societies. Their movement is uniform, says Mr. Maine, in the substitution of the commercial principle of contract for the ancient family bond as the principle which associates men, and the amalgamation of isolated original groups into larger communities connected by local proximity.* This theory is equally true of the economic and of the legal and political framework of civilized society; the migration of labour to new fields of employment, and of capital and wealth into the inmost recesses of the country or remoter regions, and of both money and commodities to new markets, are incidents of the better division of labour in which it results, by which the majority of men must be gainers; and the working of the new gold mines is only a particular instance of the rapid development of the natural resources of each place, which must result in a vast increase of the aggregate of human wealth, although involving loss to particular classes. Considerable misapprehension has arisen with respect to the effects of the new gold, by attributing to it changes in prices due mainly to different causes. M. Levasseur, for example, concluded in 1857 that the mines had caused a monetary revolution in Western Europe very unfavourable to the well-being of the labouring classes. In the mining countries themselves, he observes that labouring men were the first to receive the gold, and the price of labour rose before that of commodities: the latter rising only in consequence of the increased expenditure of the labouring class. But in countries like England and France, the new treasure was first received in exchange for commodities; the price of which consequently, according to this able writer, rose before labour; high profits preceded increased wages; the manufacturer, the merchant, and the farmer were gainers, but the labouring classes were losers. This, he says, is a repetition of what happened in the sixteenth century after the influx of money from the mines of America, when the labourers incessantly complained of the insufficiency of their wages. Happily, however, the historical parallel fails, for wages in the sixteenth century were kept down by law; and the modern changes in production and trade, of which the new gold is only an instance, tend rather to lower than to raise the price of corn in England

* Maine's *Ancient Law*, pp. 132, 168–170.

and the districts of France in which it was formerly dearest. 'As commerce extends,' says Mr. Mill, 'and ignorant attempts to restrain it by tariffs become obsolete, commodities tend more and more to be produced in the places in which their production can be carried on at least expense of labour and capital to mankind.' We get corn from America and Russia for the same reason that we get gold from California and Australia, instead of from our own rivers and mountains—although there is gold in every stream that flows and on the side of nearly every hill —namely, that we seek the cheapest places for everything, and have access to cheaper places than formerly for many things, corn and gold included. Bad harvests, the Russian war, and speculation, and not the cheapness of gold, were the chief causes of the dearness of corn, and of several other important commodities, in England and France from 1853 to 1857. We have here another example of the error of measuring permanent prices by averages of foregoing years, without regard to their ultimate range and the permanent or temporary character of the causes of a rise. It is on the reasons for prices, and not on mere prices themselves, that producers should found calculations for the future; and a farmer would be greatly in error in taking the price of corn from 1853 to 1857 as a safe basis for calculating the future profit and loss of its growth. The harvest of 1853 was almost the worst for a century throughout Western Europe; that of 1855 was very deficient; that of 1856 was under an average, while the war with Russia still farther shortened supply, and added to the cost of importation; and the scarcity of corn, and not the abundance of money, was the cause of the sufferings of the labouring classes during the period. The relative price of labour and bread in both countries has really undergone an alteration in favour of those who purchase the latter by the sale of the former. Thus in France, while corn has considerably fallen, money wages have greatly advanced both in country and town, and the advance has been constant. In 1860, the average of wages in Paris was 4 f. 55 c., and is now computed at 5 f.; and the pay of agricultural labour in the country around Bordeaux has risen in the same time from

40 to 50 sous a-day. In the United Kingdom, money wages have also considerably risen; and the rise in the price of animal food, though greater in remote rural districts than in the large towns, and considerably greater on the average than is shown in any statistics on the subject, but little affects the bulk of the rural population, since agricultural labourers have never been accustomed to consume much of it. In towns, on the other hand, money wages have risen fully as much as the price of meat, the rise of which is, in fact, mainly due to an increased expenditure of the working population; and, accordingly, it is pork, and the inferior qualities of mutton and beef, which have risen most. The very causes which tend to raise wages and to cheapen corn, tea, sugar, and clothing, evidently tend to raise the price of animal food, by leaving the bulk of the people more to expend on it; it being a thing of which there are not the same means of increasing the supply as of clothing and corn. We cannot, indeed, exempt the owners of land from blame in respect to the dearness of meat and dairy produce, since the uncertain duration of tenure has been, along with some unfavourable seasons, an obstacle to the increase of the domestic supply, on which its price must chiefly depend. But the change in the relative prices of corn and fresh animal food, and the change in husbandry it is leading to, are mainly to be traced to the general movement of commerce, which it is the endeavour of this article to explain, and which is one certainly far from injurious to the labouring classes in its general results. The movement tends, as we have seen, to the production of everything, money included, in the cheapest accessible places, and its sale in the dearest accessible markets, and hence to equalize prices approximately in cheap and dear markets brought closer together, thereby raising considerably the price of each class of commodities in the places connected, in which it was previously lowest, and, on the contrary, counteracting the effect of the increase of money in those in which it was previously highest. The price of corn has accordingly risen in many distant places nearly to its level in England; but in England its level has not been raised. But just as the improvement in communication

is not the same between all parts of the world alike, and the equalization of prices is not universal for any commodities, so the improvement is not equal for all classes of commodities alike; and the price of commodities, such as fresh butter and meat, which are portable only for a limited distance, has been equalized over a much smaller area than that of corn. The cheaper places to which London has access for fresh animal food, are only the remoter parts of the kingdom itself and the nearest parts of the Continent. Improvements in communication produce an approximation to equality in the prices of portable goods only in proportion to their portability, and hence a double change in relative prices ensues. In the first place, the prices of easily portable articles approach to a level in cheap and dear markets; but, secondly, as all things are not equally portable, a change is produced not only in comparative prices in different places, but in the comparative prices of different commodities; and both changes result in a disturbance of the profits of different occupations, and a change in the places of different industries. The same general cause tends to raise the price of meat at Athlone almost to the price it fetches in London, and to lower the price of corn in London almost to its price at Odessa. And the consequence is, that since labour and capital desert the occupations in which money returns are declining and stationary, for those in which they are increasing, the production of animal food is taking the place of the production of corn in this kingdom, and shepherds are increasing, and agricultural labourers decreasing, in number.

But this internal change in our industrial economy is a small part of the change in the territorial division of labour which the changes in relative prices in the world of commerce are producing. For the very same reasons that the price of meat has risen in England, but not that of corn, and that the former has risen more in the remoter parts of the country than in the capital, and again, that the change in prices is producing the changes in the occupations of the people just stated, prices in general have rapidly risen in many foreign countries, and

British industry and capital have been attracted from domestic to foreign employment. The pecuniary value of the produce of cheap places rises in proportion as they are brought within reach of the best markets; and capital employed in the improvement of their commercial situation, the development of their resources, and the transport of their produce, obtains an extraordinary profit from sharing in the increase of its money value. If, for example, a cwt. of goods is worth £1 at one place, and only 5*s.* at a distance for want of communication, a railway company making the line of connexion may charge more for the carriage of goods, and buy the land and unskilled labour they require for its construction very much cheaper than if prices were near an equality at the two places already.

The great rise of prices in India and the enormous growth of its trade are regarded by many as passing results of the American war. And it is desirable, with reference to the future not only of India but of many other places under the same economic conditions, or which will soon be brought under them, and also with reference to the future outlets both for English capital and enterprise, and the produce of the new mines, to ascertain whether we ought really to regard the increase of money in India, and of English capital engaged in its foreign commerce or internal improvement, as a fortuitous and transitory event, or, on the contrary, as the result of permanent causes, which, upon the one hand, are continually investing with additional value the capabilities and productions of places circumstanced like India, and, on the other hand, are finding food and materials from the cheapest accessible quarters for countries like England, and new and remunerative employment for their accumulated capital and skill.

That the stream of the precious metals to India, and the rise of prices ensuing, are not solely attributable to the payments for cotton caused by the American war, is clear from the facts that the bulk of the treasure was imported before 1861, and that the balance of imports of specie above exports, reached fifteen and a-half millions sterling in the year 1859–60, and has not reached twenty millions a-year as the average since the war.

It is an error to suppose we have paid the new cotton countries sums of money proportioned to the price of cotton in our markets, part of which has gone to our own merchants and carriers, and part has been paid in our own manufactures. The balance of trade is always considerably more in our favour than appears in the official reports of the value of our imports and exports, respectively. We are ourselves the chief carriers both of our exports and imports, and foreign countries really pay more for our exports, and we pay them less for our imports than appears by our Custom-House valuation, since we receive ourselves a great part of the freight of cargoes both outwards and inwards, and of the mercantile profit on the exchange. The balance of trade, however, has been largely in favour of India for many years past, and the rise of prices was anterior to the war. In a speech at Calcutta, in February, 1860, Mr. Wilson, after referring to the rapid growth of Indian commerce, observed: 'It is notorious how much the price of all country produce has increased of late years, in consequence of the demand for exportation. I am thankful to know that the benefits thus conferred by our commerce upon the land have extended in no slight degree to the labourer. It is no exaggeration to say that the rate of wages has risen in many districts twofold, and in some threefold, during the last few years. In the face of evidence of this kind, can anyone doubt that all classes in India are in a state of prosperity, unparalleled in any former time?'* A very different view of the matter has latterly been taken by

* *Economist*, March 31, 1860. The following Table of prices of the chief articles of daily consumption in the 'Statement showing the Material and Moral Progress of India for 1860–61, pursuant to Act 21 and 22 Vict., c. 10, sec. 53,' shows the great rise of prices in Bengal before the cotton drain began :—

	1849.			1859.			March, 1861.		
	R. A.		R. A.	R. A.		R. A.	R. A.		R. A.
Grain, . .	1 2	to	1 4	1 11	to	2 2	2 6	to	2 7
Urrur Dhol,	1 7	,,	1 10	2 2	,,	2 12	2 8	,,	2 9
Paddy, . .	0 7	,,	0 11	1 2	,,	1 4		——	
Ghee, . .	15 8	,,	21 8	23 8	,,	27 8	28 0	,,	28 8
Oil, . . .	6 12	,,	7 0	9 4	,,	9 6	17 0	,,	28 8
Tobacco, .	2 10	,,	6 0	5 0	,,	5 8	4 8	,,	6 8

several writers, who regard the rise in the price of all Indian produce as a calamity to India resulting from the growth of cotton for Europe instead of food for the natives. The real increase in the cultivation of cotton in India has, however, been immensely exaggerated on the one hand, and the increase in the cultivation of crops for native consumption in numerous districts, has on the other hand been left out of sight. Our import of cotton from Bombay, Madras, and Bengal, amounted in 1860 to 570,000 bales, and in 1864 to 1,398,000; but the bales in 1864 were considerably lighter than in 1860, and a great part of their contents was not an additional growth, but cotton withdrawn from native manufacture and the markets of China. And there is copious evidence, that except in particular and exceptional localities, the dearness of food has not arisen from scarcity. In one of the principal new cotton districts—the Nagpore country, in the lake region of which 300,000 acres were under cotton—Mr. Temple's report on the trade and resources of the central provinces of India for 1863–4, states that 'agricultural produce abounds of all descriptions common to India.' General Mansfield, in his Minute on the Currency of India, March 8, 1864, observes: 'One great reason of the rise of prices in all descriptions of food, is the greater disposition to consume. The people, being richer, actually eat more than they did in the days of their poverty. Great tracts of land which for ages had lain waste, are being daily brought into cultivation.' In the 'Papers relating to a Gold Currency for India,' lately published by order of the House of Commons, there is a Memorandum by the Board of Revenue at Madras which states: 'Agriculture is extending everywhere. There is a great demand for cotton, and indeed for every product of the field. Prices are at the same time exceedingly high.' And the Madras Athenæum, not many weeks ago (March 4, 1865), contained the following explanation of the rise of prices in that Presidency: 'The rise in the price of provisions has succeeded a general rise in the price of labour, skilled and unskilled. Men engaged in mercantile pursuits, from the lowest ryots and coolies, have been making money, and this has caused everything to be dear to those whose salaries were fixed in the good old times. Mutton is not dear solely because pasturage and grain are more costly, but because it has been eaten very much more largely. People took to it as soon as they could afford it. It has often been thought that religious prejudices among the natives would always preserve animal food for the Englishman at a cheap rate. But religious prejudices succumb under the influence of rupees, as they are dispelled by the light which rupees throw on the question.'

It is true that in particular places the dearness of the necessaries of life is partly the result of a failure of the crops, and is so far a misfortune; and in Bombay the late exorbitant prices of cotton have really led to a diminished production of food, and to a rise of general prices which cannot be regarded as entirely of a durable or beneficial character. But taking the upward movement of prices over India as a whole, we cannot consider it as otherwise than both beneficial and durable, and as being, like the rise of prices in the *Landes* of the Gironde and at St. Nazaire,* the result of a permanent improvement in commercial position, and in the means of turning to profitable account the great natural resources of the country and industrial powers of the people. In a speech at the opening of a railway two years ago, Sir Bartle Frere, the remarkably able Governor of Bombay, said:—'We all know what vast sums, chiefly of English capital, have of late years been spent in this country. Let us consider for one moment what has been the effect of giving a fair day's wages for a fair day's labour. As a rule, this was unknown before the railway period. Not only were wages in most parts of the country fixed by usage and authority, rather than by the natural laws of demand and supply, but the privilege of labour was in

* 'St. Nazaire, a small fishing-town seven years since, has attained a prodigious development, equal to any American city. France, a short time since, did not possess a commercial port over an extent of 500 miles of coast washed by the Atlantic. The manufacturers of that part of France were consequently placed in a disadvantageous position in consequence of having no seaport whence to ship their produce. The population has kept pace with the traffic. The value of ground has risen with the population. Ground sold formerly for sixpence the square yard is now worth almost £8.'—*Times*, April 29, 1865.

general restricted to particular spots, and nothing like the power of taking labour to the best market practically existed. The result was that the condition of the labourer was wretched in the extreme, and Government could do little to raise him above the status of a serf of the soil. All this has now changed, and for the first time in history the Indian coolie finds that he has in his power of labour a valuable possession, which, if he uses it right, will give him something better than a mere subsistence. As a general rule, the labourer works far harder and better, and acquires new and more civilized wants in proportion to the wages he receives.'

The whole population of India by no means indeed immediately shares in the gains arising from access to better markets and the ingress of European inventions, which on the contrary tend to deprive some classes of their former means of subsistence. 'The native handloom is collapsing in every part of India. The best wares of English manufacture are getting possession of the market, and in the form of utensils for cooking, eating, and drinking, are passing from luxuries into necessaries. Even Cheshire salt is supplied at prices which are obtaining for it a wide field of consumption in Northern India.'* This is part of the general change in the relative profits of different occupations and the seats of different industries attending the altered distribution of money, produced by closer international commerce and the tendency of all things to be bought and produced in the cheapest and sold in the dearest places. Europe can now manufacture cheaper than Asia, which was once the manufacturer for Europe; the steel of Sheffield has supplanted that of Damascus; and the looms of Asia Minor and India are constantly decreasing in number. The same cause, however, which diminishes the earnings of Hindoo weavers increases the money incomes of the Hindoo population as a whole; for in proportion as they are enabled to buy and sell in the best markets, they get better prices for the numerous productions in which they excel. Mr. Senior pointed out that the comparative number of ounces of silver or gold the Indian and the Englishman can earn

* *Papers relating to a Gold Currency for India*, p. 74.

in a year depends on the comparative productiveness of their industry in exportable commodities. But an Indian labourer earned, when Mr. Senior wrote, only a ninth of the money earned by an English one, not because his labour was really less productive in that proportion, but because his means of exporting the produce were greatly inferior. The price of Indian cotton may decline; Bombay may cease to be England's principal cotton field; yet may it be safely predicted that the capabilities of India and its people for numerous other productions are such that, with the means of exportation henceforward at their command, prices in the three Presidencies will never subside to their former beggarly level. Future candidates for appointments and undertakers of industrial enterprises in India, would do well to include this result of the improved commercial situation of India in their calculations.

The monetary future of India has a more general practical importance for Englishmen. Mr. Fawcett remarked two years ago, that the question of a future depreciation of money in England, supposing the increase in the supplies from the mines to continue, is substantially a question as to the continuance of the drain of the precious metals to the East. We would expand Mr. Fawcett's proposition into the wider one, that it is a question as to the continued absorption of money in places in all quarters of the world, including Europe itself, in which the amount hitherto current has not been in proportion to their powers of production. India is only a representative of a large class of localities, whose industrial resources are providing new markets for the produce of the mines. In India itself, the Governor of Bombay observes in a Minutere commending a gold currency: 'Great quantities of silver absorbed in remote parts of the country go to furnish a currency where no general medium of exchange before existed. There can be no doubt rupees are now found in hundreds of small bazaars where all trade used to be conducted by barter.'*

* *Papers relating to a Gold Currency for India*, p. 9. In page 89 of these Papers the following passage occurs:—'Partly owing to the change from a native to a European form of government, partly to the substitution of money

Adam Smith has observed that the difficulties of land traffic are such that commerce settles first on the borders of seas and rivers, and is long before it penetrates into the inland parts even of the most opulent and mercantile countries. And notwithstanding the immense improvement in the means of land carriage, it is still true, not only of Asia, but even of the most civilized countries in Europe, that there are inland districts in which prices are far below the surrounding level, because they cannot or do not sell in the best markets, or on the same terms as their neighbours. While some French writers expatiate on the rise of prices in the parts of France intersected by railways, others complain that in a country whose institutions are intended to favour equality, the railways promoted by Government have created a shocking inequality in local incomes and prices, by giving some places the power of transporting their produce cheaply to the capital, while others are not nearer to good markets than before railways were invented. A railway map of the world enables anyone to predict that prices must rise greatly and soon in a vast number of places. However obvious the remark, it is one of great practical importance in trade, speculation, emigration, the purchase of land, and industrial enterprises of a hundred different kinds, that the price of labour and produce will eventually rise wherever the soil is productive, and the means of locomotion are defective; and will rapidly rise wherever those means are suddenly and greatly improved. But physical obstacles to traffic are by no means the only causes of low prices; ignorance is often the mountain to be removed, and it is one which still divides England itself into regions with different monetary rates. Mainly from the want of agricultural statistics, the differences in the wages of farm-labourers, the profits of small shopkeepers, and the prices of produce in different counties are surprising. An excellent authority on this subject drew attention last winter to the fact that, while in

---

for barter in remote districts, but chiefly to the general increase of prices and wages, and the vastly augmented amount and numbers of transactions, the requirements of India for coin are only beginning to be felt.'

some counties the farmers were paying ruinous prices for fodder, in others, hay, straw, turnips, mangolds, and carrots were selling at much the usual rates.* But these are inequalities which cannot continue; and the fact of their present existence enables us to foresee in a great measure the future movements of money and prices, and the most profitable places for the investment of capital. Knowing the places where prices will rise as soon as their resources are turned to account, and their markets frequented, the capitalist knows places in which he can get a large return for the expense of assisting to develop these resources, or carry the produce to the best buyers. For example, a considerable part of the enormous prices paid in Europe for cotton imported from the East has really been received by our own merchants; and the fact serves to explain the discrepancy between our own official accounts of the value of our imports from India, and those of India itself as to the value of its exports to us. And the enormous profits which have been made of late years in our foreign trade, and upon various investments of capital in regions the pecuniary value of whose produce has rapidly risen, is one principal cause of the high rates of interest latterly prevailing. A high rate of interest, like a high scale of prices, may arise from several causes. It may arise from a scarcity of capital, a great demand on the part of unproductive borrowers, or high profits which enable producers to borrow on liberal terms to the lender. Governments may pay a high interest out of taxes, but mercantile men can only pay it out of profits, and the maximum of profit fixes the maximum permanent rate of interest in trade. Mr. Mill is of opinion that the new mines have tended to lower the rate of interest. 'The masses of the precious metals which are constantly arriving from the gold countries are, it may be said, wholly added to the funds that supply the loan market. So great an additional capital tends to depress interest.'† And there can be no doubt that a great portion of the new gold

---

* *Daily News*, November 19, 1864.

† *Principles of Political Economy* (sixth ed.), Book iii., chap. 23.

received in this country did at first enter the loan market, and tended to make interest low. The subsequent distribution of the precious metals, however, seems to us to have tended in the opposite direction. Money spent, for example, in improving the *Landes*, in building at Bilbao or St. Nazaire, in cultivating cotton in Egypt, and cotton, tea, oil-seed, and other productions in India, and in carrying such productions to the markets of Europe, has reproduced itself with extraordinary profit, and could be borrowed with profit at higher than ordinary interest. In the future distribution of the precious metals, in like manner, over markets in which prices will rise—thereby investing with considerable pecuniary value resources which now have scarce any pecuniary value at all—we may reasonably foresee a source of high profit and interest for a long time to come. The very spirit of mingled economy and enterprise, which adds to the quantity of the capital in the loan market, by attracting hitherto unemployed funds from the hoard, the till, and the private account at the bank, tends to provide more profitable employment for the capital seeking investment. 'It is,' in Mr. Patterson's words, 'the utilization of hitherto useless things which peculiarly characterizes our times. It is the utilization of neglected resources, the accumulation and concentrated appliance of a thousand forces or savings, which is the basis of our extending power. We are economizing our money like everything else; and this economy of capital, almost as much as the new gold mines, is the agency which is giving to commerce its enormous expansion.'* In the production of gold in mines utterly valueless less than a generation ago, and now worth twenty millions a year—in the reclamation of waste lands and waste substances at home and abroad—in trade with new markets and industrial enterprise in new regions—in the collection and subsequent diffusion of formerly unemployed money, the same principle is operative throughout: a principle on which we may rely to find profitable use for the fresh produce of the mines, and for the savings of our incomes for an indefinite period.

---

* *The Economy of Capital.* By R. H. Patterson.

The same economical movement has brought petroleum*—to take one of the latest examples of the redemption of wealth from the regions of waste—and the new gold into the market, and the former is a new demand for the latter. In every neglected or undervalued resource in the natural world or in human capacity there is a profitable investment for money, and commercial enterprise is constantly finding fresh employment for money, both in the purchase of new articles of value, and in higher prices for things of which the value is enhanced by improvement. Speaking of the *non-valeurs* (a term for which we have no exact English equivalent) which still abound even in the most civilized countries, M. About remarks that among them should be classed, not only things absolutely wasted and worthless from neglect, but also things whose value is only partially realized, like land under corn, which would fetch more under grass. Such things M. About designates as *non-valeurs relatives*, including among them all the insufficiently exercised powers of humanity. An entire half of the French nation, he adds—the whole female sex—belongs to the category of *non-valeurs relatives*. But if women were enabled, by both custom and law, to realize the full worth of their powers, the higher prices their industry would obtain would denote, not a fall in the value of money, but a rise in the value of women. So the increase in the money earnings of coolies and ryots in India, and fellahs in Egypt, denotes not a mere doubling or trebling of counters of payment, but an elevation of the commercial status of two nations. There is thus an important distinction between the significance of a rise of prices in Calcutta and in London; in the latter it signifies generally either a scarcity of commodities or a depreciation of money, but in the former it signifies trade on better terms with the world, as well as a change in the local value of money.

---

* 'Though petroleum has been but four years an article of commerce, it has already assumed the second place among the exports of the United States, and now ranks next to breadstuffs. In 1860 scarcely any was exported; last year the exports amounted to 32,000,000 gallons, while the domestic consumption was even greater.' —*Times*, April 27, 1865.

The question whether the new mines have lowered the value of money in England is one the more difficult to answer with precision, since, in addition to the absence of perfect statistics, causes, such as bad seasons and the Russian and American wars, have temporarily affected the prices of great classes of goods. Setting aside these disturbances, the truth seems to be, that while, on the one hand, such important commodities as corn, sugar, and coal* are cheaper than formerly, and the wholesale prices of textile manufactures, although higher than during the depression of trade, for some years before 1851, remained nearly stationary from that year until the American war,—on the other hand, the prices of animal food, of land, and of metal manufactures, have considerably risen; and the result would appear to be, that in wholesale trade the general value of money was not sensibly altered in England before the American war. But, speaking of retail prices, into which higher rents, wages, and prices of animal food more or less enter, we should say that the cost of subsistence is decidedly greater to all classes, except agricultural labourers, whose chief expenditure is on bread, sugar, and tea; and that fixed incomes by no means buy as much as they used, especially in remote parts of the country. We believe, too, with an eminent economist, that the real rise of prices to consumers is partially disguised in a deteriorated quality of many things. The disguises which the fact that people are really given less for their money may assume are numberless. For example, the prices were the same at the bathing establishments of Biarritz last autumn as in former years, but the visitor could often get nothing but a wet and dirty bathing dress for his sous. French gloves, again, are not only dearer than formerly, but seem made in order to tear; and both in England and France washerwomen are apt to spoil linen now for the prices at which they used formerly to dress it.

But the effects of the new mines upon prices are far less obscurely and far more satisfactorily discernible in countries

* 'Average shipping price of Newcastle coal:—1841, 10*s.* 6*d.* per ton; 1850, 9*s.* 6*d.*; 1860, 9*s.*'—*The Coal Question*, p. 61, by W. S. Jevons.

like India, where they have directly or indirectly furnished the means of raising the remuneration of industry, and circulating produce which had formerly little or no circulation. The result of this influx of money into India is by no means merely the trouble of carrying and counting more coins to do the same business as formerly; and so far as there has been such a result, it might have been in a great measure avoided had the Government allowed gold to pass current as money. By the exclusion of gold, India has been obliged to fetch a much bulkier material for its currency from a far greater distance, and to incur an unnecessary loss, first, on the freight from abroad; next, on the coinage at the mint; thirdly, on the carriage through the country; and fourthly, on the wear and tear of so many more new coins. The great mines of Australia seem to have been specially designed to provide, at a comparatively small cost, the additional money required by the increased trade of India, and its Government, too, have resolved to defeat the economy of nature. In contending, however, for all possible economy in the monetary system of India and every other country, we cannot adopt the opinion Mr. Patterson appears to entertain, that the economy might be carried so far as to dispense with the cost of metallic currencies altogether. Coin is better fitted for rough work and for the labourer's pocket than bank-notes. It cannot, like paper, be eaten by ants in the East, and is safer from water and fire. Nor can we conceive that a currency would be safe from depreciation by excess, unless based upon things possessing intrinsic value like silver and gold. Mr. Patterson argues that the value of money depends simply on its conventional use and acceptance. But limitation of supply is in all cases an indispensable condition of value; and the history of assignats in France, and greenbacks in America, shows that negotiability does not constitute the determining element of the value of a currency.* And taking this view of the monetary use and

* Mr. Bonamy Price says in a recent article:—' The peculiarity of this commodity (gold) consists only in this, that every man agrees to take it in exchange for his goods. The general consent to make gold the medium of exchange consti-

importance of the precious metals, it seems to be a question worth considering, whether the future supplies are likely to be sufficient to supply money enough for the rapid progress of the backward parts of the world, and the immense development their resources seem sure to obtain. Mr. Maine has remarked that investigators of the differences between stationary and progressive societies must, at the outset, realize clearly the fact that the stationary condition of the human race is the rule, the progressive the exception; and, when this reflection was made, the condition of the greater part of Asia and of Northern Africa might even have justified the proposition that a retrograde condition of the human race was the rule. In the wildest regions frequented by the nomad hordes of Central Asia, the traveller discovers the vestiges of former cultivation and wealth. But he can now perceive in such regions that while he stands on the grave of an old civilization he stands also on the borders of a new one. It seems certain, at least as regards Asia, which contains the bulk of the human race, that not only the stationary, but the retrograde communities will become progressive—will be reached by roads, railways, river navigation, and Western commerce, and obtain the aid of Western capital and skill. And it seems equally certain that the pecuniary value of their produce will immensely increase; that they will need vast quantities of coin for its circulation; and that the question

---

tutes the precise demand for gold, just as the general consent to make shoes of leather constitutes the demand for leather.' But the social compact to wear shoes does not determine what they are worth; that depends on the supply of leather and competent shoemakers. The public consents to take shillings as well as sovereigns; but it is not their consent that makes a sovereign worth twenty shillings, which it would not be if gold were as easy to get as silver. So the public may consent to take pieces of paper for coins, but how many must be given for a horse or a cow or a loaf depends on the comparative scarcity of each. We make this comment merely to illustrate the principle that the value of money depends on its rarity, and not on convention and custom; for we confess we do not see the drift of Mr. Price's arguments. He refutes some fallacies of the old mercantile school which hardly required fresh refutation, and which are not supported by any of the writers on currency he refers to. But he by no means makes it clear whether he objects only to the particular provisions of the Bank Charter Act, or to a metallic standard altogether, and to Sir Robert Peel's definition of a pound.

is one of importance, whether coin enough for the purpose will be easily obtained. The steady decline of the produce of some of the new gold mines might seem to justify a doubt on the subject. But from Mexico and South America additional supplies may be expected. Of Peru the British Consul says: 'Peru is one vast mine which the hand of man has only hitherto scratched.' To the produce of the mines must be added the vast sums that the progress of commerce will restore to circulation from the hoards of Asia and Europe, which, even in such places as Lapland, are great. Large sums of Norwegian money are said by Mr. Laing, in his 'Journal of a Residence in Norway,' to have disappeared in Lapland; the wealthiest Laplanders having always been accustomed to live, like the poorest, on the produce of the reindeer, and to bury the money coming to them from Norway in places where their heirs often fail to discover it.

The movement we have discussed is one which tends to bring all buried and neglected riches to light; and we anticipate from it both an ample provision of money and an increasing demand for it; although temporary fluctuations in both may cause changes in prices.

XXI.

PRICES IN GERMANY IN 1872.*

The theoretical principles involved in what is called the gold question are matters, for the most part, about which little controversy exists, although there may be much respecting their application to facts, from the difficulty of ascertaining the real facts. The effect on prices of a great increase in the quantity of the precious metals in the world depends on their distribution; on the proportions converted into money on one hand, and articles of use or ornament on the other, the latter constituting, in the hands of dealers, an addition to the demand for money, not to the supply of it; on the activity of the part converted into money, and the degree to which the volume of metallic circulation is swollen by instruments of credit; and, lastly, on the course which the additional expenditure takes in each country, and the conditions affecting the supply of the things on which it is laid out. The mere statement of these conditions shows such a multiplicity of agencies at work that the necessity of proceeding by observation to determine the actual movements of prices is evident; indeed, extensive and careful observation on the part of many inquirers is likely, after all, to leave us in ignorance or doubt on some points, but it cannot fail to afford much information, especially as foreign countries must be the principal field of inquiry. On the distribution of the precious metals, first of all, and the opening up of new channels for the new streams of treasure, hang the gravest issues affecting the classes with stationary incomes in this country. The rise of prices has for some months attracted

---

* *Fortnightly Review,* November 1, 1872.

considerable attention in England, and with good reason; but in many parts of the Continent it has been for more than a decade the subject of remark and complaint, and in the earlier attention to it abroad one may perceive the main reason why it has received comparatively little at home until now. A much more rapid fall must have taken place in the value of money in England had there been no considerable fall in other parts of the world, had the chief part of the additional gold which has come into circulation in the last twenty-two years been poured into English markets: a matter in itself sufficient to show how deeply we are concerned in its distribution, and in the movement of prices in other regions. The movement in Germany in particular deserves investigation, as a country which has undergone great economic as well as political changes in the period of the new gold, and one in which several of the conditions determining its action on prices can be most advantageously studied. German statistics afford fuller information respecting local prices than are obtainable with respect to England or any other great country. But in every country the real movement of prices has been a number of different local movements, and in Germany we can trace the causes governing the modern changes not in German prices only, but in prices throughout the world. Wide miscalculations respecting the effects of the American silver mines on the value of money in the sixteenth and seventeenth centuries arose from attending only to some statistics of prices in a few principal markets. Even two centuries after the discovery of the American silver mines prices had not risen all over Europe in the manner commonly supposed. It was a partial, local, and irregular rise over a limited area, whence the prodigious effect of the streams of additional money in the localities which actually received them; prices rising enormously in London, for example, while wholly unaffected in part of the Highlands of Scotland and of the west of Ireland, and but little affected even in some parts of England itself not far from the metropolis. The monetary phenomenon which now first strikes the eye on an inspection of German statistics is the extraordinary inequality of local prices, and it is one which throws a flood of light on both the past and the probable future distribution of the produce of the new mines of our own time.

In the month of December, 1870, to take official statistics published by Dr. Engel, Director of the Royal Prussian Statistical Office,* the price of beef, putting silbergroschen and pfennigen into English money, was 3*d.* a pound at Neidenburg, in the province of Prussia, at the east of the kingdom, while it was 8¼*d.* at Aix-la-Chapelle, in the Rhine province. In the same month butter was 9½*d.* at Neidenburg, 12½*d.* at Berlin, 14½*d.* at Magdeburg, in the province of Saxony, 15*d.* at Dortmund, in Westphalia, and 16*d.* at Aix-la-Chapelle. Straw was 10*s.* the schock at Braunsberg, in the province of Prussia, and £2 12*s.* at Saarbrücken, west of the Rhine. Take again the following statistics of a number of the most important articles at various towns. (See Table on next page.) The prices are given in silbergroschen and pfennigen in Dr. Engel's tables, but the proportions will be sufficiently indicated by the figures.

Dr. Engel's tables give prices at other towns in each of the different provinces, the naked statistics being presented in all cases without theory or comment. The war in France may probably have disturbed the markets in the towns nearest the military operations during the latest period for which the official statistics are published, and the military element is one which we shall have to notice again as one of the conditions besides the new gold affecting the movement of prices in Europe. But it by no means accounts for the inequalities, as is evident from the statistics of a number of years before the war. Going back, for instance, to 1865, we find butter 7*d.* a pound at Neidenburg, 10*d.* at Thorn, in the same eastern province, and 13¾*d.* at Aix-la-Chapelle, at the extreme west of the kingdom. The value of money, in short, is a local affair, even in Prussia, though one of the most advanced countries in

---

* *Zeitschrift des Königlich Preussischen Statistichen Bureaus.* Elfter Jahrgang, 1871. See also the statistics of prices in the volume published in 1867.

AVERAGE PRICES IN THE HARVEST YEAR AUGUST 1, 1870, TO JULY 31, 1871.

Town.	Province.	Wheat.	Rye.	Barley.	Oats.	Peas.	Potatoes.	Butter.	Beef.	Pork.	Straw.
Neidenburg, .	Prussia, . .	82·0	48·9	34·1	30·5	54·0	15·1	6·7	2·8	3·8	180·0
Thorn, . .	,, . .	91·0	58·6	49·1	39·8	62·9	22·10	10·3	4·4	5·0	308·8
Dantzig, . .	,, . .	92·8	59·11	46·11	32·6	62·6	23·11	10·3	7·1	6·1	222·9
Berlin, . .	Brandenburg, .	90·4	65·0	52·9	37·3	96·0	22·6	10·4	5·3	5·9	304·7
Magdeburg, .	Saxony, . .	91·7	67·3	54·6	39·6	97·1	25·5	11·10	6·8	6·8	342·3
Münster, . .	Westphalia, .	101·8	73·3	63·11	43·4	98·1	40·10	8·11	4·8	5·0	291·6
Dortmund, .	,, . .	105·5	74·9	58·7	41·11	108·6	37·3	10·9	5·7	6·3	406·7
Bochum, . .	,, . .	104·6	76·11	63·2	41·8	109·7	40·9	11·9	5·4	6·6	437·6
Düsseldorf, .	Rhine Province,	109·2	78·0	65·7	43·2	115·8	40·4	12·6	6·5	8·7	408·0
Aix-la-Chapelle,	,, ,, .	112·3	82·0	70·9	45·5	115·0	42·0	13·3	7·1	8·6	487·6

Europe, and one of the best provided with internal communications. Some of the differences are partially accounted for by differences in the fertility or in the harvests of different regions. Great fortifications, as at Cologne, Coblentz, Mayence, Königsberg, Dantzig, and Stettin, obstructing the growth and business of towns, and raising the rents of houses, occasion other diversities. Other local causes affecting supply or demand were recently assigned on the spot at other places in reply to my own inquiry. But if special local causes alone were at work, the rise in some localities would be attended by a fall in others, because the same sum of money cannot be in two places at once, and if part of the money previously current had been drawn off to new localities, there would be less left in the old ones; whereas we find a higher range of prices than formerly everywhere throughout Germany, though the differences are surprising. In Germany, as in England, combinations and strikes are now often referred to as the chief cause of rise in the present year in the prices of many things, and of the greater cost of living at particular towns. But this explanation fails to account for a continuous rise of prices for twenty years before strikes or combinations (which are of very recent appearance in Germany) were heard of; nor could a rise of the mass of commodities take place without either an increase in the money demand, or a diminution, which is not pretended, of the supply. A rise in money wages at the expense of employers may cause a change in relative prices, and a rise of things produced mainly by labour, but in that case things produced mainly by fixed capital, and whose price consists largely of profit, would sustain a corresponding fall. An altered distribution of money to the advantage of the working classes, again, would lead to an increased expenditure on their part; their comforts and luxuries might accordingly rise. But this in turn would be met by a corresponding diminution of expenditure on the part of other classes, and a corresponding fall in some articles. A fall in the house-rents of the middle classes, for example, would ensue, whereas what is particularly complained of is a rise. The payments of France, on account of the war, are in some places spoken of as one cause of advanced prices in the present year. The chief part of the money coming from that source seems, however, as yet either to have been withheld from circulation by the Government, or to have been expended west of the Rhine, in Alsace and Lorraine; and in any case those payments afford no explanation of the continuous advance of prices before July, 1871, the last month to which Dr. Engel's statistics come down. There are, I must allow, anomalies in German prices which remain inexplicable to me after much recent local inquiry; but some general results of importance seem to emerge beyond doubt from their examination in a number of different places.

The lesson, it is true, which investigation of facts impresses more and more on one's mind is distrust of economic generalizations; still they are of use if we are careful both, as far as possible, to cover under them only the proper particulars, and also to use them as guides to, instead of as concluding, inquiry. A generalization which may be advanced with reference to the present subject is that, in the first place, a much lower scale of the prices of land, labour, animal food, and other main elements of the cost of living to large classes, will usually be found to prevail in places without steam communication than in places similarly situated in other respects, but possessing railways or steam transport by water; in the next place, among places possessing steam communication, a considerably higher scale of prices of the staples referred to will for the most part be found in those which are centres of industrial or commercial activity or of foreign resort than in such as are of a stationary or colourless character; and, thirdly, as a general rule, there is a marked tendency to a higher elevation of prices in Germany as we travel from east to west. Hence Germany may be roughly divided into four monetary regions:—(1) places in arrear of the world's progress in respect of their means of locomotion as in other respects; (2) places communicating by steam with good markets, but not themselves the sites of much enterprise, or possessing any special attractions; (3) places which unite the best means of communication with local activity, or considerable resort from without; (4) among places falling within the last category, a higher scale of rents, wages, the price of animal food and other essentials will be found, *cœteris paribus*, in those which lie nearest the traffic and movement of Western Europe. Of the effect of the want of steam communication the reader may observe an example in the comparative prices given above, of Neidenburg on the one hand, without either railway or steam transport by water, and Thorn on the other hand, in the same province, seated both on the Vistula and on a railway. Again, for an example of the lower range of prices in comparatively stationary places, though well provided with means of locomotion, than in centres of industrial activity, compare prices, stated above, at Münster, in Westphalia, with those of Dortmund and Bochum, in the same province, but among the busiest spots in the Ruhr Basin. For an illustration, lastly, of the ascent of prices as we move westward in Germany, compare prices in the chief towns of the province of Prussia with those of Saxony and Westphalia, and these again with the prices of Aix-la-Chapelle, on the borders at once of Belgium, Holland, and Prussia, and on the high road to France and to the English Channel. This upward movement of prices as we move westward seems to be connected both with proximity to the best international markets, the increase of the manufacturing element and of industrial and commercial activity, and also with a third condition, itself not remotely allied to the two others—namely, the influence of education. In the two most eastern provinces of the kingdom, Prussia and Posen, it appears that above twelve per cent. of the recruits annually enlisted are unlettered; in Brandenburg, Saxony, and the Rhine Provinces, the percentage of unlettered recruits is considerably below one per cent. One discovers some correspondence between this scale of education, and the following scale of the average prices, in the decade 1861–70, of towns in the different provinces, from Dr. Engel's statistics :—

PROVINCE.	Wheat.	Rye.	Barley.	Oats.	Peas.	Potatoes.	Butter.	Beef.	Pork.	Hay.	Straw.
Prussia . . .	81.11	53.11	41.7	30.4	59.2	20.4	7.11	3.7	4.8	24.8	188.8
Posen . . .	79.7	55.8	44.10	31.8	58.5	15.3	8.7	3.10	4.10	25.7	194.2
Brandenburg .	83.7	59.11	47.4	34.1	73.2	18.10	9.8	4.7	5.2	27.7	249.0
Saxony . . .	83.3	64.7	51.3	33.8	79.3	21.4	9.7	4.9	5.4	36.2	234.2
Westphalia . .	91.8	69.1	57.7	38.7	88.4	29.3	8.9	4.8	5.5	31.11	282.2
Rhine Province	93.6	67.11	56.9	35.6	90.10	27.10	9.5	5.3	5.11	37.3	275.4

The higher range of prices in Western Germany, in short, springs from the greater abundance of money where business and traffic are best situated and most active, the manufacturing element furthest developed, and general intelligence highest. Knowledge, industrial energy, the value of land, labour, and time increase, and the commercial and money-making spirit becomes keener, for better for worse, as communication with the wealthiest and busiest countries of Western Europe becomes closer, and the German approaches the principal lines of western traffic, travel, civilization, and money expenditure.

Those who are conversant with the theory of the international distribution of the precious metals, expounded by Mr. Senior and Mr. Mill, may find evidence in the local prices of Germany that the principles which govern the partition of the world's currency among different countries, and the scale of international prices, apply also to the distribution of a national currency and the comparative prices of different places in the same country. The more efficient, productive, and valuable the industry of any country, or of any locality, and the cheaper and faster its produce can be carried to the best markets, the higher will be the scale of pecuniary earnings and incomes, and the higher consequently the prices for the most part of things in great demand, such as labour, land, and fresh animal food, of which the supply is limited, and which make a great figure in the cost of living. The producers for the foreign market get higher profits and wages; money flows in from abroad, and producers for home consumption, though no such nice equality of wages and profits as book theorems assume really exists, earn more than can be earned in less active and less advantageously situated places. If Yorkshire cloths and Lancashire cottons, carried by steam, could be made to suit the convenience and taste, and awaken a demand on the part of the whole population of European Russia and Asia, what would follow with respect to prices in England? Yorkshire and Lancashire would have a larger claim on the money of the world; there would be a rise in Yorkshire and Lancashire wages and profits in general, though by no means in the exactly equal ratio which economic fictions assume for wages and profits throughout the whole kingdom; both the working classes and their employers would have more to spend, and the comforts and luxuries of both, of which there was not a proportionately increased supply forthcoming, or not without additional cost, would advance in price. So in Germany, although one cause of prices being higher in places of great industrial activity or resort than in more purely agricultural or less frequented localities, may be that the supply needed, or part of it, must be brought from a greater distance, yet the principal cause is the difference of money demand and expenditure. The great rise in the cost of living at Berlin in the last year and a-half springs in the main from the fact that Berlin has become the capital not merely of Prussia, but of Germany, its political, intellectual, and financial centre. Hence a great influx of capital, people, and money, a great activity of business, an extraordinary demand for houses, building materials, and labour, an exorbitant rise in the prices of things into which they enter as principal elements, and a condition of the labour market which enables workmen in some trades to exact what are thought by employers exorbitant terms. The same monetary phenomenon presents itself likewise in small towns, which situation and local advantage have made places of much resort. At Heidelberg, for instance, I was lately told by a resident, who is a high authority with respect to German prices, that the cost of living to persons of moderate income, though rising many years before 1866, had advanced fifty per cent. since that date, and is still advancing, the main proximate cause in the last twelve months being the exactions by the working classes, in one trade after another, of a great advance in wages. But Heidelberg lies on the high road of travel, and almost at the intersection of the principal lines of European railway communication; it is one of a ring of towns of much resort, and itself possesses special attractions; the demands for higher wages have been grounded on the rise of commodities, and the increased pecuniary expenditure, of which the higher wages and prices afford proof, could not be forthcoming without a more plentiful circulating medium.

The comparison of local prices in Germany reconciles in principle two seemingly opposite theories respecting the international movement of prices consequent on the new gold mines, though neither theory is quite in accordance with facts. According to one theory, prices should have risen earliest and most in the countries whose industrial efficiency and whose means of communication were furthest advanced, and therefore more in England than in Germany or France. Another theory is that steam communication equalizes prices, raising them, therefore, most where they were formerly lowest, and therefore most in what formerly were backward and cheap countries and localities. Each theory contains a measure of truth, but the first overlooks the rapid diffusion of industrial inventions, activity, and improvements in transit, the consequent changes in the distribution of money and in the relative prices of different countries and different localities in the period of the new gold; while the second exaggerates the equalizing influences of steam locomotion. The real movement of comparative national and comparative local prices has not been a general equalization, nor as yet even a tendency towards it. What we find is, not a uniform elevation of the whole level, but the rise, as it were, of a great number of monetary peaks of different altitudes—a rise, that is to say, at a great number of points in continental countries to or near to the highest ranges in England, and again at a still greater number of other points, to altitudes considerably below the pitch reached at the points of highest development, but much above the level of places without improved communication. Railways and steamers are said to equalize prices; and so they do, creating equalities and tendencies to equality of two kinds. They tend to raise prices at many of the most advanced places on the Continent to, or nearly to, a par with those of the principal English markets, and again, to bring prices in previously remote and cheap places up towards the range generally prevailing along the lines of steam transport. But they also create new inequalities, and these, too, of two kinds. They raise prices at places obtaining the new means of communication above the range prevailing at places obtaining no similar advantage; and again, they concentrate capital, business, and money expenditure plethorically, as it were, at particular spots with peculiar natural resources or advantages of situation, and thus elevate prices enormously there at a time when an unwonted abundance of money is in the world. Improvements in locomotion develop the resources of the world, but the resources of different countries and of different localities are unequal, on the one hand, and the new means of locomotion develop their actual resources unequally, on the other hand, because not equally distributed. It is not, we must remember, the mere acquisition of means of rapid communication that raises money-earnings to the highest point, or that makes the greatest change in habits of expenditure and the pecuniary cost of living; what does so is the ingress of wealth, enterprise, and outlay, the generation not only of opportunities for pecuniary gain, but also of the habit of taking advantage of them, the influx not only of money, but also of the money-making spirit, the creation of a custom of looking, not for customary prices, but for the highest prices to be got for everything, every inch of ground, every trifling exertion, every minute of time; while, at the same time, the habits of consumers naturally become costlier as their incomes as producers become larger. So far are railways and steamers from diffusing these causes of extraordinary pecuniary gains and extraordinary prices equally throughout all the regions they traverse, or even all the places they actually touch, that they often draw capital, business, and money, not to but from places on the very lines of steam communication to others with greater advantages. Even at spots whose position and opportunities are such that the money-making spirit, the habit of seeking the utmost price, and the organization often necessary to obtain it, might be expected to develop themselves at once, they sometimes do not do so for years. In a district, for example, where the bulk of the inhabitants are owners of land, growing chiefly for their own consumption, they may not be tempted immediately by the offer which a new railway makes of high prices at a distance to send their produce to market. People are often reluctant to change their ways of life, even where they would be great pecuniary gainers. A few weeks ago, at a place in the Ruhr Basin, which must soon be absorbed in the whirl of industrial activity round it, but where life is still comparatively cheap, tranquil, and old-fashioned, an hotel-keeper answered the question, whether there were any great factories or industrial establishments yet,—'No, thank God!' It must be confessed that the new movement does not always add to the comfort or happiness of the district it invades. Take those little hamlets which one sees from time to time nestling in a ravine on the side of one of the low mountains of Siegerland, where every householder has his twenty acres of land, his share in a wood, his three or four cows, his pig, and perhaps a few sheep, whose own land produces his food, and the sale of whose wood supplies all his other wants. The mountain has ribs and bowels of iron; tall chimneys and high prices will soon rise at its base; the peasant may find that his wood buys less than before; he may descend from the rank of a landowner to that of a labourer, and perhaps be tempted to begin a new, anxious, and uncertain career in a town. But there is another side of the picture. The progress of industrial and commercial activity is inseparably bound up with that of science and art, as both cause and effect; and it is the chief of the agencies which, by a number of influences, direct and indirect, are elevating at last the condition of the toiling masses of Europe in one place after another.

The movement in place of prices in Germany, or of comparative local prices, is obviously connected with the movement in time, or the comparative prices of different periods, and therefore with the question concerning the changes in the value of money since the new mines were discovered, or the gold question. With a view to the solution of a different though closely related question, to which we shall have to recur, and which the title of his Essay explains,* an eminent German statistician has recently published an elaborate analysis of the

* Welche Waaren werden in Verlaufe der Zeiten immer theurer? [What commodities become constantly dearer in the lapse of periods of time?] *Statistische Studien zur Geschichte der Preise.* Von Dr. E. Laspeyres. Tübingen, 1872.

prices of 312 commodities from 1846 to 1865 in the market of Hamburg. Among the results is a classification of the 312 commodities in eleven groups, with the comparative prices of successive quinquennial periods indicated in the following Table, in which the prices of the first period, 1846–50, are represented by 100:—

Group.	Class of Commodities.	Number of Commodities.	Five years, 1846 to 1850.	Five years, 1851 to 1855.	Five years, 1856 to 1860.	Five years, 1861 to 1865.	Fifteen years, 1851 to 1865.
I.	Products of South European plants—wines, fruits, &c. .	23	100	121	143	136	133·7
II.	Agricultural products of Central Europe—corn, peas, beans, &c., ...	41	100	122	133	128	127·8
III.	Hunting and fishery products, . . .	19	100	116	135	131	127·8
IV.	Products of sylviculture, ...	17	100	109	113	160	127·2
V.	Produce of European cattle-rearing, . .	29	100	113	137	125	124·1
VI.	Edible Colonial products, ...	44	100	110	125	129	121·8
VII.	Non-edible Colonial products, . . .	44	100	105	115	123	114·0
VIII.	Fibrous manufactures—linen, woollens, spun silk, &c., . .	12	100	102	107	127	112·2
IX.	Chemical manufactures, ...	40	100	111	117	102	109·9
X.	Mineral and metal manufactures, . .	22	100	107	111	101	106·4
XI.	Products of mining and smelting—coal, iron, &c., . . .	24	100	107	108	97	104·1
		312 [?]	100	111·2	122·1	123·3	118·98

If, however, the reader examines the prices of the particular articles comprised in the eleven groups, he will find that the average prices of the groups do not show the real rise, the greater number of the more important commodities having risen much more in the period subsequent to 1846–50 than the averages indicate. Unfortunately, too, the table stops at the end of 1865, while a great rise in some commodities has taken place in subsequent years. Group XI. in the table shows, in fact, a fall in coal and iron in 1861-65 compared with 1846–50, whereas those great staples are now at extravagant prices in Germany as in England. The statistics presented by Dr. Laspeyres* do not enable us to make any close comparison between the movement of prices at Hamburg and at London, but so far as they go they indicate a considerably greater rise at Hamburg since the discovery of the new mines. On this point, it seems to me that the reason assigned by Dr. Laspeyres for a greater rise of cereals, &c. (group II.), at Hamburg than at London, namely, that England has derived greater benefit than Germany from improvements in transport and free trade in corn, hides the real distribution of benefits. Improvements in transport and trade tend to raise the pecuniary value of raw produce exported to the benefit of producers in the exporting countries, and to lower the price in the importing countries to the benefit of consumers. But Germany is an exporting, England a great importing country in the matter of corn, Germany being, in fact, one of the sources of the English supply. Dr. Carl Knies, the eminent professor of political economy at Heidelberg, pointed out in an essay on the 'Depreciation of Money' in 1859 that there were causes tending to a greater rise of prices in Germany than in England. 'First and foremost,' he observed, 'among the agencies creating important changes in prices come railways, diminishing the differences in the local values of money, by causing its influx into places where prices were low from places where they were high. Germany may be classed among the former, England among

* See p. 58 of his Essay.

Province.	Decade.	Wheat.	Rye.	Barley.	Oats.	Peas.	Potatoes.	Butter.	Tallow.	Beef.	Pork.	Hay.	Straw.
Prussia, ...	1841—50	67·4	42·1	31·11	22·0	46·7	15·9	5·5	4·6	2·4	3·0	19·1	143·11
	1861—70	81·11	53·11	41·7	30·4	59·2	20·4	7·11	5·2	3·7	4·8	24·8	188·8
Posen, ...	1841—50	66·0	44·0	34·5	24·4	47·8	14·0	5·10	3·9	2·9	3·4	22·8	166·4
	1861—70	79·7	55·8	44·10	31·8	58·5	15·3	8·7	5·3	3·10	4·10	25·7	194·2
Pomerania, . . .	1841—50	68·8	45·7	33·4	24·7	48·4	16·1	6·7	3·10	2·9	3·4	19·7	172·3
	1861—70	85·10	59·11	46·9	33·7	64·7	19·4	9·3	4·4	3·11	5·4	22·3	232·1
Silesia, ...	1841—50	65·2	46·2	35·11	24·4	52·4	17·1	5·7	4·4	2·9	3·5	22·5	141·3
	1861—70	79·9	58·1	45·4	30·8	65·9	18·3	8·5	4·9	3·11	4·11	30·3	188·3
Brandenburg, . .	1841—50	69·9	46·3	47·4	26·6	56·9	14·6	6·9	4·6	3·0	3·6	22·7	184·9
	1861—70	83·7	59·11	35·10	34·1	73·2	18·10	9·8	6·2	4·7	5·2	27·7	249·0
Westphalia, . . .	1841—50	76·4	56·6	42·10	28·9	68·5	20·9	5·5	4·0	2·11	3·9	20·6	160·3
	1861—70	91·8	69·1	57·7	38·7	88·4	29·3	8·9	5·8	4·8	5·5	31·1	275·4
Saxony, ...	1841—50	66·2	49·2	36·11	25·5	59·0	16·9	6·10	5·6	3·4	3·9	27·1	176·9
	1861—70	83·3	64·7	51·3	3·8	77·3	21·4	9·7	6·9	4·9	5·4	36·2	204·2
Rhine Provinces, .	1841—50	82·1	61·0	46·2	28·7	72·5	20·9	6·1	4·9	3·2	4·2	28·1	201·4
	1861—70	93·10	67·11	56·9	35·6	90·10	27·10	9·5	5·8	5·3	5·11	37·3	275·4

the latter. At a time when a general fall in the value of money is taking place in consequence of the abundance of gold, the change is diminished in England and augumented in Germany by the change in the movement of money.' But the same movement which has given Germany railways and steamers has given it steam for manufacture and mining as well as for locomotion, and all the mechanical and chemical inventions of England and France in addition to its own. If we add great legal and administrative reforms removing obstacles to production and trade, and the spread of education, we may see reason for greater relative progress and a greater relative increase of pecuniary incomes in many parts of Germany than in England, though the actual scale of incomes and prices may still be higher in England. The prices of Hamburg, it should be added, must not be taken as representing the movement of prices throughout Germany, where the real movement is made up of a number of different local movements. Hamburg, long one of the chief seats of German trade, has advanced much less in respect of industrial activity, means of communication, wealth, and the increase of money, than many other towns which have come to the front in the last twenty years. Dr. Engel's tables supply some additional information, showing, for example, the average prices of some important commodities in the chief towns of each province of Prussia in the two decades 1841–50 and 1861–70 respectively. (See Table on preceding page.)

If, however, we compare the average prices of 1861–70 with those of the immediately preceding decade 1851–60, we find that while the rise in butter, tallow, beef, pork, hay, and straw, has been a continuous one, wheat, barley, oats, peas, and potatoes were, on the contrary, on the average of years, higher in the decade 1851–60 than in 1861–70. The articles, however, which have risen continuously are much better measures of the purchasing power of money in Prussia than those which ranged higher in the first decade of the new gold period than in the second, above the prices of 1841–50. The prices of butter, tallow, beef, and pork, are taken on a more uniform system throughout the different markets of the kingdom than those of the other articles. The seasons produce much more violent fluctuations in grain and potatoes than in animal food; and animal food is both a much more important item than bread and potatoes in the economy of the middle and wealthier classes, and one better adapted to test an increased expenditure on the part of the working classes—butter especially, on which the working classes in the mining and manufacturing districts at least of Prussia spend much more than on meat. Not to encumber our pages with too many figures on one hand, and because, on the other hand, butter, of all the articles in Dr. Engel's statistics, affords the best criterion of the movement of prices and the cost of living, let us take the price of that article during a succession of years at various towns; the year 1841 affording, as Dr. Engel's tables show, a fair standard of pre-Californian prices for comparison:—

Price of the Pound of Butter in Pfennigen.

Year.	Königsberg.	Dantzig.	Posen.	Stettin.	Berlin.	Breslau.	Magdeburg.	Münster.	Cologne.	Aix-la-Chapelle.
1841	73	71	70	96	84	64	81	64	75	75
1851	71	72	70	88	84	78	89	60	68	67
1852	80	80	84	95	86	90	89	64	77	93
1854	90	91	101	100	91	93	97	75	85	96
1855	95	103	106	110	91	98	104	82	93	100
1856	101	110	104	113	112	97	108	85	102	112
1857	104	104	102	117	120	102	118	88	113	129
1859	103	101	98	107	119	90	109	80	109	130
1860	92	95	88	104	108	82	95	75	91	111
1862	106	106	107	125	111	94	111	89	110	124
1863	105	107	109	120	114	102	108	73	104	122
1864	104	105	110	120	117	110	114	87	118	128
1865	110	112	116	125	118	113	120	92	125	137
1870	111	118	128	132	124	115	140	105	134	161

These statistics exhibit, amid some curious irregularities, a continuous rise at all the towns in the list, but a much greater rise at Aix-la-Chapelle, where the price has more than doubled, than at Königsberg, where the rise is a little more than 50 per cent. We have, however, no statistics of places where the rise has been greater: places, that is to say, which before 1850 had neither railway communication nor industrial activity, and which now are in the front rank with respect to both. Aix-la-Chapelle was a considerable town, and had the advantage of a railway before the discovery of the new gold mines; but there are now mining and manufacturing centres which twenty years ago were not to be found on the map, and it is in such places that the scale of wealth, wages, rents, and the prices of animal food, has changed most.

Dr. Engel's statistics do not come down to the present year; but Mr. Scott's report on 'the condition of the industrial classes, and the purchase power of money' in Würtemberg, supplies figures showing a continuous rise in that part of Germany since 1850:—

COMMODITIES.	April, 1870.	April, 1872.
Beef, . .	6*d.*	6¼*d.*
Pork, . .	6*d.*	7*d.*
Veal, . .	5¼*d.*	6¼*d.*
Butter, . .	7¼*d.*	10½*d.*
Milk, . .	2½*d.*	3¼*d.*

The recent advance in these articles has, I am assured, been greater in some parts of Germany, though I am not enabled to authenticate the results of personal inquiry by official statistics. It is more important to note that no statistics exhibit the real increase in the cost of living in many German towns, since they do not exhibit the increase of town wages and house-rents, and of the retail prices of many things into which wages and house-rent enter as principal elements. The practical change in the value of money varies, of course, for different classes and different individuals, according to the course of their habitual expenditure, since some things have risen more than others, and some, both imported and manufactured in the country, not at all. The classes who seem to be least affected by it as consumers, are those who have no wages to pay, while their own wages have risen considerably, and who have often a cottage, a garden, and cow of their own. The classes with stationary incomes, in whose expenditure house-rent, animal food, and the wages of servants, form the chief items, are, of course, the chief sufferers.

On the whole, it is evident that there has been a great change in the value of money in Germany in the last twenty years, though it has been different in different localities, and we have no such array of statistics as would be necessary to determine the exact amount of the fall in any locality. Still less can we determine exactly the share of the new gold mines in the fall. There were causes tending to raise prices in Germany, though no new mines of extraordinary fertility had been discovered. One cause, altogether distinct from the mines in its nature, though indistinguishably associated with them in its operation, is the improvement in the industrial and commercial position of the Germans. In a country which has gold mines of its own, the production of gold depends partly on the powers and skill of the miners, and partly on the fertility of the mines. Let both the efficiency of the miners and the productiveness of the mines largely increase, and there will be a vast increase in the production of gold; but it will be impossible to say how much is due to the miners, and how much to the mines. Foreign trade, as economists put it, is the gold mine from which nations without actual mines of their own get their gold, and the fertility of the foreign mine and the efficiency of the Germans who work at it have increased together.

Both causes together, nevertheless, fall short of explaining the changes in German prices. Two other sets of causes have been at work at the same time: one augmenting the amount of the circulating medium and the rapidity of its circulation, the other affecting the supply of some of the chief articles on which the cost of living mainly depends. The improvements in locomotion and in commercial activity which have so largely augmented the money-making power of the Germans, have also quickened prodigiously the circulation of money; and the development of credit, likewise following industrial progress, has added to the volume of the circulating medium a mass of substitutes for money which move with greater velocity. You can send money by steamer and railway, but you can send credit by telegram, and a new million at New York may raise prices in a few hours at Frankfort and Berlin. A much smaller amount of money than formerly now suffices to do a given amount of business, or to raise prices to a given range; and to the increased amount of actual money now current in Germany we must add a brisk circulation of instruments of credit. It is true that some of the principal means of substituting credit for coin, and economizing the use of the latter, have little or no operation in Germany. Cheques, strange to say, are hardly in use, and there is no Clearing-house. But there is a mass of bank-notes; and bills of exchange, for very small as well as for large amounts, pass from hand to hand among people in business almost as freely as bank-notes; the same bill making often a great number of purchases before it reaches maturity. The transactions are, of course, liable to be reopened if the bills be not met in the end, but otherwise they answer as payment in cash. A small proportion of coin thus supports an immense volume of circulating credit. Were the circulating medium composed of coin alone, whatever the amount of the precious metals issuing from the mines or circulating in other countries, whatever the price of German commodities in the gold market abroad, no rise of prices of German commodities at home could take place without additional coin enough to sustain it. It might be the conviction of people in business in Germany, that, looking to international prices, and the relative cost of production of German exports and other German commodities, prices generally ought to be double their former amount; yet, in the absence of instruments of credit, only a doubled quantity of coin, or a doubled rapidity of its circulation, could actually double prices, and give German labour and productions their due value in relation to money. But, when credit comes in as a substitute for coin, it may, with a small proportion of money as a support, raise prices at home to the pitch which equal amounts of labour and abstinence fetch in the foreign market.

There has, then, been a plurality of causes, besides the increased quantity of gold in the world, augmenting what for shortness we may call the money demand for German commodities—the increased industrial and commercial powers of the Germans, the more rapid circulation of money, and the rapid augmentation of the circulating medium by a volume of credit. But the question of prices is a question concerning the supply of commodities no less than the money demand. An increased money demand does not of necessity raise the prices of commodities. That depends on the conditions affecting the supply of each class of thing, for which there is a greater money demand. A nation like the United States, possessing a vast territory of prodigious fertility, might, with peace and free trade, see the prices of almost all things falling in the markets of California itself. An important class of considerations, connected with the rise of prices in both Germany and England, is contained in the question Dr. Laspeyres has raised: 'What commodities become constantly dearer in the lapse of periods of time?' Adam Smith has given an answer which at least points in the right direction, if it involves an erroneous distinction between corn and other sorts of rude produce in the case of old countries which do not import the former: 'If you except corn and such other vegetables as are raised altogether by human industry, all other sorts of rude produce—cattle, poultry, game of all kinds, the useful fossils and minerals of the earth, &c.—naturally grow dearer as the society advances in wealth and improvement.' Among the sorts of rude produce particularly referred to by Adam Smith in his elaborate exposition of the subject as naturally growing dearer in the lapse of periods of time is wood, and German statistics afford an illustration. In Professor Rau's 'Grundsätze der Volkswirthschaftslehre,' the following prices of a given measure of the same wood at Würtemberg, in successive periods, are given :—

	Fl.	Kr.
1640—1680	0	37
1690—1730	0	57
1740—1780	2	14
1790—1830	8	22

Dr. Engel, again, gives statistics which show the continuous rise of carpenter's wood in another part of Germany since 1830 :—

	1830.	**1840.**	**1851.**	**1860.**	**1865.**
Carpenter's wood per klafter, in silbergroschen,	50	75	102	130	180

Of course, the rise in price of things which grow naturally dearer in the progress of society is enhanced by any sudden increase of money and fall in its general value, and it then becomes impossible to apportion the influence of the different agencies—increased consumption with growing scarcity or greater cost of production on the one hand, and greater abundance of money on the other. Every artificial obstruction to the supply of important commodities inflicts an aggravated loss on those whose money incomes remain stationary while money is falling in value. The rise in the price of animal food in Germany, where there is a wide distribution of landed property and a simple system of land transfer, may be ascribed mainly to natural causes; and a large part of the German population are either gainers by it as sellers, or unaffected by it as producers for their own consumption. It is otherwise in a country like England, in which laws in the supposed interest of an insignificant number limit the supply of land in the market, diminish its produce, and make food unnaturally dear. The gold question has added enormously to the importance of the land question in England, and the classes with fixed incomes are especially concerned in both.

Persons with stationary incomes in this country are, as it were, between several fires. They suffer from high prices, whether they spring from abundance of gold, from natural dearth of commodities, or from the increase of population and wealth. They suffer along with other classes, and the prosperity of other classes is a calamity to them. The main resources they had to look to on the discovery of the new gold mines were reforms in the laws relating to land in their own country on the one hand, augmenting and cheapening the produce of land, and industrial and economical progress in other countries on the other, assigning to these the principal share of the new treasure. Of all parts of Europe, England is that in which the fall in the value of money, measured in commodities—I do not say measured in labour—ought to have been least sensible, on account of the nature of its imports, the natural cheapening of manufactures, the improvements in husbandry which legislation might have indirectly effected, the example which all the rest of the civilized world had set with respect to land laws, and the immense demand for the treasure from the new mines which peace, liberty, industry, and trade might have opened up in other countries to circulate a vast increase of produce at much higher pecuniary value than remoteness and poverty have hitherto allowed them to bear. The new area in Europe, not to speak of Asia, which civilization would open for the employment of new money is enormous. The inequalities in the local prices of Germany, the rise in its most progressive localities, the comparatively low prices in its backward localities, point to one of the chief outlets to which people here, with fixed incomes, might have reasonably looked for the absorption of the new gold. Low as prices still are in many places in Germany, they are lower over great districts of Austria, and yet lower over the greater part of Russia, two countries, moreover, where inconvertible paper currencies resist the circulation of the precious metals.

As matters stand, the increase of money in England has far outstripped the increase of some of the most important commodities. And when one reflects that the money comes from a new world of peace and liberty, in which production never flags, while the demand for it in Europe is limited by the policy of an old military world, and the supply of commodities by the law of an old feudal world, the prospect before those with whom money does not increase with house rent and the price of food seems the reverse of encouraging.

XXII.

PRICES IN ENGLAND IN 1873.*

THE movement of prices in England is a less simple matter than the reasoning of some eminent economists indicates. The advance in the cost of living is considerably greater than appears from their calculations, and the new gold is but one of the causes acting on prices. An attempt has been made to measure the effect of the gold by comparing the average prices of a number of important commodities during the period since the new mines were discovered, with the average prices of a previous period. Mr. Jevons, who adds rare mathematical powers to high economic attainments, has adopted this method; but, in inquiries of this kind, the truth is seldom reached until several methods have been tried, and probable truth only, not mathematical precision, is attainable. The method of averages fails in several ways. It does not show the real movement of prices or the real depreciation of money; the tables omit some of the chief elements of the cost of living; the prices compared are wholesale prices, while the purchasing power of an income depends on retail prices; and, by ascribing the whole rise of prices to the new gold, this method conceals the material fact that the gold is only one of a plurality of causes lately tending to raise them.

A comparison of the average prices of successive periods of years may be useful to indicate the total profit and loss on transactions in the periods compared, but is delusive as a criterion of the change in the value of money. Suppose that in the first decade after the discovery of the new mines prices

---

* *Fortnightly Review*, June 1, 1873.

had risen twenty per cent., and in the second decade had fallen back to their old level, money at the end of the twenty years would be of the same value as at the beginning, yet the average prices of the whole twenty years would show a depreciation of twenty-five per cent. Suppose, on the other hand, that prices had risen steadily during both decades so as to range fifty per cent. higher at their close, the real fall in the purchasing power of money would be fifty per cent., yet an average would show a fall only of twenty-five: that is to say, only half the real fall. Take, as exemplifying the second supposition, the movement of prices in the sixteenth century, after the discovery of the American mines. Prices rose continuously in some parts of Europe until money had sunk to a third of its former value; here an average, including the lower prices of the earlier years of the movement, would far under-estimate the real depreciation. So in England now, if the cost of living to large classes be much greater than during most of the years since the new gold mines were opened, the average prices of the whole period afford no measure of the real diminution in the purchasing power of fixed incomes. If house rent, the wages of servants, indoor and outdoor, animal food of all kinds, coal, washing, many articles of clothing, horses and horse-keep, cost now in the aggregate, by a succession of rises, one-half more than they did a generation ago, a householder would be a good deal out in his reckoning were he to measure the present and future purchasing power, say of a thousand a-year, by the average prices of the past twenty-five years. The averages referred to, moreover, omit some of the chief items in the cost of living. No account, for example, is taken of the great rise in house rent and wages in recent years, nor of the additional charges which retailers make to consumers, partly to cover higher wages, shop-rents, and other items in the cost of their own business. The recent prices of many important articles, *e. g.* butchers' meat, have risen far more than prices in the wholesale market. The actual increase in the cost of living to large classes, therefore, far exceeds the advance shown in tables which Mr. Jevons and the 'Economist' have published. The living of the poorest class (of women especially), who pay no wages, rarely eat animal food, and whose chief expenditure is on bread, sugar, and tea, may, notwithstanding the rise of coal, cost no more than formerly; but, where the scale of expenditure ascends to servants, meat and butter every day, and a tolerable house, the change for the worse in the purchasing power of fixed incomes makes itself more heavily felt than any statistics show.

Free trade created in this country a demand for a larger currency; but the chief cause which has prevented a ruinous rise of prices in England is that other parts of the world have absorbed the bulk of the gold and silver sent into circulation. Take a single fact. In the twenty-two years, 1850–1871, inclusive, the imports of gold and silver into British India amounted to £235,000,000; the amount exported was only £27,000,000, and the mints of the three Presidencies coined upwards of £145,000,000. In that period, therefore, India alone absorbed £208,000,000's worth of gold and silver for currency and other purposes: that is to say, an equivalent to two-fifths of the addition made to the stock of the precious metals by the new gold mines in the twenty-two years. What probability is there that the development of Indian trade will be such in the next twenty-two years as to absorb £208,000,000 more?* The question forms part of a larger one. What chance is there that, for the future, the progress of the rest of the world in means of locomotion, production, and trade, will be such as to divert from England all but a small fraction of the new treasure the mines may yield?

The international and local distribution of the precious metals in the last twenty years has followed, in the main, the path of the industrial and commercial development abroad. Steamers, railways, the rise of manufactures, the growth of trade—internal and external—have caused a prodigious increase in the demand of foreign countries for money to carry on their

* Sir Richard Temple's able financial statement for 1873–4 shows that in 1872–3 the influx of treasure had almost ceased. The Mints of Calcutta and Bombay were in a state of inaction.

increased business, and represent the rise in both the quantity and the market value of their productions. The same change in the distribution of money has taken place over a great part of the world which took place earlier in England itself. Places formerly remote, undeveloped, and backward, ill-furnished with both means of locomotion and money, have gained access by steam to the best markets, have advanced in both industry and skill, have ceased to be poor and cheap, and have made vast additions to their currencies. But many of the foreign channels which railways and commerce have created for the streams of new money are now full—some full to overflowing. Many parts of the Continent, which not long ago were noted for cheapness, are now as notorious for dearness;* and although a great part of Europe has yet to be opened up by railways, it were rash to assume that the progress made in the next twenty years will be equal to that of the last twenty. The west of Europe is already reticulated with railways; the east will hardly in two decades overtake the west, and during their construction new railways raise the prices of English iron and coal, though when finished they find new outlets for money. An eminent authority points, indeed, to possible absorbents for much of the future gold in the resumption of payments in specie by France and the United States on the one hand, and the gold coinage of Germany on the other. The fact, however, which actually confronts us is, that France, the European country which had hitherto absorbed most of the new gold, is now driving it from its currency; and that Germany is exchanging silver for gold—the silver will be liberated for circulation elsewhere—but what we have to look to is, not the amount of gold only in the world, but the amount of gold, silver, and credit together, remembering that a great rise of prices in England can be brought about with a small importation of

* See, as regards Germany, the Essay, entitled 'Prices in Germany,' in the present volume (*supra*, pp. 332–355). It is greatly to be desired that the eminent French economists who have discussed the effects of the new gold mines, M. Chevalier, M. Levasseur, and more recently M. Victor Bonnet, would resume the investigation in connexion with later changes of prices in France.

specie. Suppose that English iron and coal, for example, sell fifty per cent. dearer in the foreign market by reason of the abundance of the precious metals abroad, they may sell as much dearer in the home market, mainly by an expansion of the credit circulation; and other English productions will then rise in price.

Other causes, besides the abundance of the precious metals, have raised the cost of living in England. The method of averages assumes the new gold to be the sole cause of the rise in prices arrived at, on the ground that 'the average must, in all reasonable probability, represent some single influence acting on all the commodities.' But why not a plurality of influences? Mr. Jevons' own work on coal proves the existence of one other cause besides the new gold. Mr. Tooke's 'History of Prices' supplies a still more decisive example. The high range of prices from 1793 to 1815 was ascribed by many persons exclusively to the over-issue of notes, and the consequent depreciation of the currency. Mr. Tooke demonstrated that the main causes of the rise lay in conditions affecting commodities, not money, and that the depreciation of the currency never exceeded 30 per cent., while corn, to take one commodity, stood at one time at 177*s.* the quarter. Mr. Newmarch has done good service accordingly, by insisting from the first on an investigation of the conditions of demand and supply affecting commodities, before coming to any conclusion respecting the influence on prices of the increase of gold. By means of such an investigation only can we ascertain whether the causes of the rise of prices are permanent or temporary, and what is more important, whether they are, as in the case of coal and animal food, to some extent within our control, or, like the fertility of the gold mines, altogether beyond it. It should, however, always be borne in mind, in speaking of demand and supply, that it is only in the shape of money-demand that the new gold can ever come into circulation, and that if there be independent conditions of supply and demand sufficient to cause a rise of prices, a great addition to the quantity of money in circulation must magnify the rise in proportion. But some reasoners go beyond this. They urge that since the demand which raises prices can be no other than a money-demand, to trace a rise of prices to an increase of demand is simply to trace it to the new gold. A rise of some commodities, it has been added, would, but for the new gold mines, have been compensated by a fall of others, since the total amount of money expended would otherwise not have increased. It is not so, however. The total expenditure of money will naturally advance with the increase of population, though no new sources of money be discovered, and prices may rise without any discovery of more fertile mines. Suppose the population of England to grow from twenty to thirty millions, English exports and money returns increasing nearly in the same ratio, and the average money-income of the population continuing at, say, £10 per head. Though individual incomes will not rise on this supposition, yet the total money-income of the nation will increase with the population from £200,000,000 to £300,000,000. Suppose, then, that half the income of each individual, on the average, is spent on house-rent, animal food, leather, coal, and some of its products, not an acre of land will have been added to the island, and house-rents may rise; meat, butter, milk, and some other products of land may grow considerably dearer; coal may have to be fetched from greater depths or poorer mines at high cost. There may thus be a considerable rise in the cost of living, and a corresponding fall in the purchasing-power of fixed incomes, as the consequence merely of the growth of population. Let new gold mines of extraordinary fertility come at the same time into play—let money-incomes rise on the average from £10 to £15 per head, and the rise of prices may beggar the classes whose incomes are stationary.

The actual situation of matters in England is, then, that a number of causes, of which the new gold is only one, have raised the cost of living, and that the cause which has hitherto diverted from England the chief effects of the new gold mines can hardly be counted on. One result with which we may be threatened may be exemplified by the fact that the race of scholars in Germany is said to be in danger of dying out before the rise of prices and the diminished power of fixed incomes. We cannot, however, control the production of gold, we cannot hasten the development of foreign countries, and thus provide for its absorption. The more need, therefore, to do what lies in our power at home to check the increasing cost of chief staples of expenditure, such as coal and the produce of land. Even Lord Derby tells us that the produce of land is only half what it should be; and the bearing of our land system on the matter is sufficiently illustrated by the statement in the last Agricultural Returns of Great Britain, that a decrease of 3,592,600 sheep, or 12 per cent. in the whole stock of sheep in Great Britain, took place between 1868 and 1871, chiefly, if not entirely, through the want of irrigation and grass.

It is not in political economy to tell how the cost of extracting coal can be diminished, or how the enormous waste of fuel may be lessened. But it might at least be expected of economists not to foster extravagant prices by fictions and fallacies. The equality of profits is a fiction under which producers and dealers are enabled to hide inordinate gains: at one time by keeping down wages, at another by charging exorbitant prices. The assumption that an omniscient competition equalizes profits has done infinite mischief, both theoretical and practical, by checking inquiry into the actual phenomena of trade, and the real distribution of wealth. The new gold itself is a novel condition from which an eminent economist anticipates a disturbance of relative prices and profits for thirty or forty years. What sort of equality is that which is liable to disturbance for more than a generation by even one of the numberless changes which industrial progress and discovery (to say nothing of political events) are perpetually importing into the conditions of trade? In London alone seventy-four new trades appear in this year's Directory, and it may be affirmed that before they were added not a capitalist in London knew so much as the names of the trades already existing. How, then, can it be maintained that capitalists are so well acquainted with the situation and prospects of every occupation that their competition equalizes profits? The truth is, we are almost in total darkness respecting the profits of many long-established businesses, and this darkness (which is often the cover of exorbitant prices) is due in great measure to an influential school of economists who have taken away the key of knowledge—the investigation of facts—which Adam Smith and Mr. Mill had put into our hands.

XXIII.

THE MOVEMENTS OF AGRICULTURAL WAGES IN EUROPE.*

THE question presenting itself in the Eastern Counties is really no mere local question or struggle, no mere trial of the right or power of English agricultural labourers to raise wages by combination, important and significant as is its assertion. It is a particular phase of a movement, or series of movements, general over Europe, arising everywhere mainly from similar causes, and exhibiting everywhere some similar phenomena, along with phenomena due to special causes in particular countries and localities. Farmers in the Eastern Counties no doubt imagine themselves in presence of an extraordinary difficulty. But there have been no combinations or strikes of agricultural labourers on the Continent, yet complaints of the rise of agricultural wages have been heard for years; it was one of the chief causes of the late French *Enquête Agricole;* a serious alarm on account of it is now felt in most parts of Germany (notwithstanding a recent general fall in the price of labour), and in some parts of Belgium. A survey of the principal facts in several representative countries may aid us to estimate the nature and strength of the forces with which the farmers in the Eastern Counties have to contend, and to judge how far general and permanent, how far local and temporary, causes are at work. The chief reason, however, for the present investigation is, that it is not an agricultural labour question only which is finding its issue at home and abroad, but one connected with all the most important economic phenomena

* *Fortnightly Review*, June 1, 1874.

and problems of the age, with the course of industrial and commercial development in Europe, the amount and distribution of money and its representatives, the changes in prices, the movements of population, the new ideas and powers of the working classes, and the operation of land laws and systems of rural economy ; though some of these great subjects can only be glanced at in the following pages.

Two not unrelated phenomena in all the chief countries of Europe, are a remarkable rise in the money wages of agricultural labour in recent years, and prodigious diversities in the rates paid in different parts of each country.

In Belgium, where farm wages had been rising for twenty years, they have lately sprung in some districts from 2 fr. 50 c. to 3 fr. 50 c. and upwards. In France, M. de Lavergne estimated the general rise in the decade 1855–1865 at 20 per cent., but it was much greater in many places, and continued down to the war. Dr. Baur and Baron Von der Goltz put it at 60 per cent. in the north of France in the last twenty-six years; and one cannot doubt that the rise throughout the country would have been greater, and would be still going on, but for the late war, the drain of money which has followed it, and the uncertain state of political affairs. In Germany there are four different classes of agricultural labourers (*Dienstleute*, *Gesinde*, *Einlieger*, and *Haüsler*), and a calculation of the rise in wages is much embarrassed by differences in the modes of payment, and payments in kind. For the present purpose we need concern ourselves only with the earnings measured in money of the two classes (called *Einlieger* and *Haüsler*, the latter having cottages of their own, and the former being lodgers) who share the designations of *Tagelöhner* and *freie Arbeiter*, day-labourers and free labourers. Baron Von der Goltz, Professor of Rural Economy in the University of Königsberg, a writer of great practical experience, in the new edition of his work on the German agricultural labourer's question, measures in money the rise of the wages of the classes of labourers referred to at 100 per cent. in the Rhine Province, and from 50 to 60 per cent. in the eastern province of Prussia, in the last ten to twenty years.* A table of agricultural wages in the last number of the Journal of the Agricultural Society for Rhenish Prussia puts the rise in one district at from 75 to 100 per cent. in the last four years, in another district at 200 per cent. in the last twenty years, and in a third at 200 per cent. in the last ten years.† At Tübingen in Würtemberg, Dr. Gustav Cohn tells me the rate was 1*s.* 2*d.* a-day in 1850–1855; 1*s.* 4*d.* in 1860–1865; 1*s.* 8½*d.* in 1866–1870; and is 2*s.* 0½*d.* in 1874. At Wissen, in the Rhine Province, on the border of Westphalia, Mr. Wynne, a resident English engineer, states: 'Ten years ago agricultural wages were 1*s.* 2½*d.* a-day, measured in money; about that time railway works commenced, and they rose very quickly. At present they are about 2*s.* a-day—a fall after the exaggerated rates of last year.' Mr. White, British Consul at Dantzig, one of the best informed and most intelligent Englishmen in Germany, although remarking (April 27) that 'the price of labour in Germany has quite lately entered into a retrogressive stage,' measures the general rise in the price of agricultural labour at from 50 to 100 per cent. in the last twenty years, and speaks of great alarm on the part of farmers with respect to the future. The foregoing estimates are in accordance both with facts ascertained by myself in several visits to Germany, and with recent information from authorities so high as Professor Nasse of Bonn, member of the Prussian Parliament, Mr. W. T. Mulvany of Düsseldorf,‡ and Herr Bueck, formerly secretary to an East Prussian Agricultural Society, and now to an important society in Rhenish Prussia. It may be concluded from these authentic data that the rise of farm wages in some parts of Germany much exceeds the rise, according to Mr. Caird's estimate, in England.

A second European phenomenon is prodigious inequality in the prices of agricultural labour in different parts of each

* *Die ländliche Arbeiterfrage.* Zweite Auflage, 1874, p. 125.

† *Zeitschrift des landwirthschaftlichen Vereins für Rheinpreussen.* Mai, 1874, p. 158.

‡ Formerly Poor Law Commissioner in Ireland, but for many years past the chief of great mining and other industrial enterprises in the Ruhr Basin and the Rhine Province.

country. In England they varied at the end of 1873, according to Mr. Caird, from an average of 12*s*. a-week in the southern to 18*s*. a-week in the northern counties: these averages, however, covering much greater local diversities. In 1870 they varied from 7*s*. a-week in Dorsetshire to 22*s*. in Yorkshire and Northumberland, and they still vary from 11*s*. to 25*s*. In Belgium the actual diversities are thus described in a letter from M. Emile de Laveleye: 'In the Campine the rate of agricultural wages is 1 fr. 25 c. a-day in summer, and 1 fr. in winter, without food or other addition. This rate extends to the environs of Hasselt and St. Trond, four leagues from Liége. In Flanders the rate is 1 fr. 50 c.; in the Ardenne it is 2 fr. 50 c. In the coal and metallurgic basins of Liége, Charleroi, Mons, it is from 3 fr. to 3 fr. 50 c.; and in a commune near Liége it is actually at this moment (May 1, 1874), 3 fr. a-day, and the labourer's food into the bargain.' With respect to Holland, I possess no more recent statistics than those given in the documents relating to foreign countries in the Report of the late French *Enquête Agricole*, where it is stated that the rate of wages varies from 1 fr. in some provinces to 2 fr. in others. With regard to France, statistics exist in abundance. Dividing the country into six regions, M. de Lavergne, in 1865, estimated the earnings of the French agricultural labourer at 600 fr. a-year in the north-west and south-east, at 360 fr. in the north-east, and only at 300 fr. in the west, south-west, and centre. These figures, being averages struck over many departments, included much wider variations. According to the *Enquête Décennale*, published in 1868, wages were 3 fr. 14 c. a-day, with 4 fr. 35 c. in harvest, in the Department of the Seine; 1 fr. 14 c., with 1 fr. 68 c. in harvest, in the Côtes du Nord. In 1869 Mr. J. S. Mill informed me that the rate about Avignon, where he resided, was 3 fr. a-day throughout the year. In the same year I found it as low as 1 fr. a-day in more than one place in Brittany; and Lord Brabazon's Report to the Foreign Office in 1872* gives an average rate of 2 fr. 50 c. in the Seine, 1 fr. 13 c.

* *Further Reports, &c., respecting the Condition of the Industrial Classes and the Purchase-power of Money in Foreign Countries.* 1872, pp. 43, 44.

in the Côtes du Nord, and 1 fr. 15 c. in the Morbihan. At present the tendency to a rise throughout France, which otherwise might show itself, is arrested by political uncertainty; but at four or five leagues from Paris, as the eminent economist, M. Victor Bonnet, informs me, the rate is 3 fr. 60 c. a-day; at from twenty to fifty leagues from Paris it varies from 2 fr. 50 c. to 2 fr.; and in some remote parts of the country without a railway it may perhaps be as low still as from 1 fr. 25 c. to 1 fr.

In Germany the lowest rates of agricultural wages are found in the eastern provinces of Silesia and Posen. In one district of Silesia they averaged, in 1873, only 8½*d.* a-day in summer, and 7*d.* a-day in winter; while in a district of the Rhine Province they were from 2*s.* 6*d.* to 4*s.* 6*d.* a-day in summer, and from 2*s.* 2½*d.* to 3*s.* in winter, and by task-work the labourer in this district earned from 2*s.* 6*d.* to 6*s.* a-day, according to the work and the season. In the Rhine Province itself prodigious diversities are found, for examples of which see the table of wages already referred to in the '*Zeitschrift des landwirthschaftlichen Vereins für Rheinpreussen*' for May, 1874. Even these instances fail to show the full extent of the inequality of the money earnings of an agricultural labourer's family in different parts of Germany. German women take an active part in farm work, and their wages vary from place to place, like the wages of their husbands and fathers. The number of working and earning days, again, is considerably greater in most parts of west Germany than in the north-east of the empire, although the length and severity of the winter in the latter region demands a larger expenditure in fuel and clothing. It is, too, much easier for the farm labourer in south-western than in north-eastern Germany to acquire a plot of land of his own, and the milder climate and better markets of the former enable him to make a larger addition to his wages by its produce than he could in the latter.

The inquiry follows, What are the causes of the two phenomena described—which might be easily shown to present themselves also in several other countries—the immense rise in the price of agricultural labour, and its prodigious local diversities?

The rise is supposed by many persons to be sufficiently accounted for by emigration and migration to towns—two agencies of great importance, but by no means adequate to account for the phenomenon. Emigration, in the first place, cannot have caused the rise in France or in Belgium, from neither of which has there been any emigration to speak of. From Germany the total emigration has been considerable, but the natural increase of population has more than replaced it; it has taken place chiefly in the parts of the empire where wages have risen least, and there has been but little emigration, if any, in recent years from the localities where wages are highest, and where they have risen most; in these localities immigration, in fact, not emigration, is the conspicuous movement. It is worthy of notice, moreover, that the chief emigration has been from provinces and districts where the population is thinnest, where large estates prevail, where little farms are fewest, and where the labourer despairs of getting a plot of land of his own.* In England, again, emigration has not hitherto much diminished the number of agricultural labourers, probably not at all in the districts where agricultural wages are highest; and though indirectly emigration from Ireland has had an appreciable effect on English wages by diminishing Irish immigration, the great recent rise in money wages in the southern counties certainly cannot be referred chiefly to that cause.

The migration of agricultural labourers to towns and mining and manufacturing districts is a more potent agent, the economic and social significance of which in several aspects can hardly be exaggerated. But it is demonstrable that it affords only a partial explanation of the rise in the price of agricultural labour. There has been no considerable migration from Flanders, yet agricultural wages have risen. In Germany, the migration of the rural population to Berlin and the chief industrial towns and districts in the west has been very great. But were that the sole cause of the rise in agricultural wages, how are we to account for the still greater rise of wages in

* Von der Goltz, *Die ländliche Arbeiterfrage*, pp. 114–121.

those very towns and manufacturing districts? In France, likewise, a great rise of town wages preceded, and, indeed, caused the migration of the rural population which continued down to the war. And in England, town, mining, and manufacturing wages have, although the movement is very unequal, on the whole risen greatly along with the price of agricultural labour, instead of sustaining a fall, as the migration theory, taken alone, would import. How is it, moreover, that farmers have been enabled to pay so much higher prices for labour in all the countries referred to? Whence has come the additional money to pay them, and to raise at the same time the prices of commodities all over Europe? The general rise in the money wages of agricultural labour must be connected with this general rise in the prices of commodities, and with the chief cause of the latter phenomenon, the immense augmentation and the more rapid circulation of money and its representatives since the new gold mines were discovered, and since railways and other inventions began to spread over Europe. To exemplify the rise in the prices of articles coming more or less within the consumption of the German labourer, Mr. W. Wynne has furnished me with the following table of prices, in Silbergroschen, at Wissen in the Rhine Province (5 Silbergroschen = 6*d.*) :—

Commodities.	1853.	1863.	1873–4.
Butter, per lb.,	3½ sgr.	4½ sgr.	13—14 sgr.
Eggs, per dozen,	2 ,,	3 ,,	9—10 ,,
Beef, per lb.,	3 ,,	4½ ,,	7 ,,
Veal, ,,	1⅚—2 ,,	Not stated.	4— 5 ,,
Potatoes, per cwt.	10 ,,	—	25 ,,
Linen, per ell,	2½ ,,	—	4½ ,,
Cloth, ,,	30—35 ,,	—	60—70 ,,
Coffee, per lb.,	5—6 ,,	—	10—12 ,,

As an instance of the rise of prices in north-east Germany, Herr Bueck states with respect to the district of Gumbinnen, in the province of Prussia,—'the Regierungsbezirk Gumbinnen obtained its first railway in 1860, and the price of one pound of butter was then 4 to 5 Silbergroschen, whereas at present it is 10 to 13 Silbergroschen ; the price of beef, which was then 2½ to 3 Silbergroschen, is now 6 Silbergroschen.' But although the rise in the prices of commodities, as well as in money wages, at home and abroad, and in both country and town, proves that one general agency is the increase and the greater activity of money and its representatives, the explanation thus afforded is by no means adequate to account for the movements of agricultural wages. The highest German authorities, scientific and practical, Professors Nasse and Von der Goltz, Mr. Mulvany, and Mr. Consul White, are agreed that the rise in money wages in Germany exceeds the rise in the price of the articles of the labourer's consumption.* The changes in wages, again, from year to year, and from decade to decade, do not correspond with the changes in prices. Not only has the price of rye, for example, which is the chief food of the German farm labourer, not risen in proportion to wages, but in the decade 1861–71 rye and all other cereals were cheaper than in 1851–61 ; yet money wages continually rose. Nor do the local variations of wages in Germany, or any other country, follow or correspond with the variations in the prices of commodities. Food and clothing are not dearer in the coal basin of the Meuse than in Flanders, yet agricultural labour is twice as well paid; and food is rather cheaper in the Ardenne than in Flanders, yet the farm labourer is paid about 75 per cent. more for inferior work. It is, in fact, impossible to get to the root of the rise in wages, without entering into the causes of the other striking phenomenon—their great local diversities.

---

* Professor Nasse says: 'That the economic condition of the agricultural labourer has improved here, and that the rise of wages has surpassed the rise of prices of the necessaries of life, admit of no doubt. The condition of the labourers who, as here is often the case, have a little property in land, has especially improved.' From another part of the Rhine Province Mr. W. Wynne writes: 'The rise is to a considerable extent a real one, as the labourer now lives better, and clothes himself better, takes more holidays, gets oftener drunk, &c.'

The causes of this second phenomenon are both general and local; some common to all countries in Europe, some peculiar to particular countries, some to particular regions or districts. The most general causes are, first, the unequal natural advantages of different regions and localities for manufacture or trade; secondly, their unequal development, especially by means of locomotion, and, above all, railways. Capital, money and its representatives, and the demand for labour, have increased most where the means of production and the means of communication with the best markets have improved most, where coal, iron, and mechanical power have multiplied the produce of the human hand, and where railways and other modes of communication have made most rapid progress. Broad exemplifications of the influence of these two sets of conditions (which are closely related, for superior natural advantages attract the means of development) are to be seen on every side at home and abroad. Many years ago, Mr. Caird pointed out that a line 'following the line of coal' divided England into two regions of high and low agricultural wages, and his recent statistics show that the same line of division still exists:—

'Average weekly wages in England:	1850.	1873.
Northern counties	11*s.* 6*d.*	18*s.* 0*d.*
Southern counties	8*s.* 5*d.*	12*s.* 0*d.*'*

In Belgium a similar line divides a region without mineral wealth, including Flanders and the Campine, from one rich in coal, iron, and manufactures, where wages range from 100 to 300 per cent. above the rates in the former region. In Germany, the country above all others in which the study of the subject abounds in interest and instruction, the line between high and low agricultural wages drawn by Von der Goltz is one between northern and southern Germany;† the former being the region

* Letter of Mr. Caird, *Times*, Jan. 3, 1874.

† In North Germany Von der Goltz includes the provinces of Prussia, Pomerania, Posen, Silesia, Brandenburg, Mecklenburg, Sleswig-Holstein, Brunswick, Oldenburg, Hanover, together with the northernmost parts of the Rhine Province and of Westphalia; the remainder of the present German empire forming South Germany, according to this division.

of low, and the latter of high agricultural wages. The rates of wages certainly justify this division, but they vary greatly from east to west in the north—from 1*s.* 8*d.* a-day in Mecklenburg to 8*d.* a-day in parts of Silesia and Posen—and a much more marked and characteristic division lies between north-eastern and south-western Germany. From Dresden westward wages range higher than eastward, but the main region of high farm-wages is from the neighbourhood of Frankfort-on-the-Maine to the Ruhr Basin, thence to Düsseldorf and Aachen, and southward through Rhineland to Baden.* In this region of high wages itself there are immense inequalities, but some of them form no exception to the principle of the division, others fall under another principle, likewise connected with natural advantages, which will be presently indicated. Speaking generally, the south-western region, whose boundary has just been roughly marked out, is the main region of German industrial and commercial enterprise, communication by steam, general activity, intelligence, and wealth. Vicinity to the chief countries and markets of western Europe, numerous lines of railway, a river crowded with steamers, coal, iron, and their products, cause a greater abundance and more rapid circulation of currency, a greater demand and competition for labour of all kinds, and a generally higher price for agricultural as well as town or mechanical labour, than is to be found in the north-east of the empire, which lies remote from the traffic, civilization, and progress of the western world, is much less completely provided with railways, and is in a more primitive condition as regards customs, ideas, and industrial life.† Take as an example of the

---

* Mr. Consul White, who has an extraordinary knowledge of the industrial economy of Germany, remarks on this view, as to which I lately consulted him: 'What you say of the south-west is, I think, on reflection the correct representation, and I quite agree in your delimitation. An English employer of labour, who has travelled over those parts quite lately, told me that at Nürnberg he found wages a trifle higher than at Dantzig, but from thence he found them highest at Frankfort-on-the-Maine, the Ruhr Basin, and Cologne. This tallies also with your views in the essay on "Prices in Germany" in the *Fortnightly Review*, November, 1872.'

† Low railway freights for raw material have been one cause of the industrial

influence of this diversity in the economic conditions of the two regions, the rates of agricultural wages in the districts of Düsseldorf on the Rhine, on the one hand, and Gumbinnen, in the province of Prussia, on the other hand, where the soil is good, but no manufactures or trade on a large scale exist:—

	DÜSSELDORF.	GUMBINNEN.
	s. d. s. d.	s. d. s. d.
Summer wages, per diem, Men, . .	2 6 to 4 0	1 0 to 1 9½
,, ,, ,, Women, .	1 6 ,, 2 0	0 6 ,, 0 9½
Winter ,, ,, Men, . .	1 6 ,, 2 0	0 7¼ ,, 1 0
,, ,, ,, Women, .	1 0 ,, 1 6	0 4¾ ,, 0 6

The same principle shows itself in local inequalities within each of the two great regions. The price of farm labour is much higher close to Berlin than throughout the greater part of Brandenburg, and considerably higher about Dantzig than in most rural districts of the province of Prussia. It is, in like manner, 75 per cent. higher in the Ruhr Basin, and near towns like Cologne, than in purely agricultural districts of Westphalia and the Rhine Province. One remarkable exception to the general principle (which, however, seems less real than apparent) is, that Silesia, the eastern province in which there is most manufacture and trade, and which possesses considerable mines, is also the province in which the price of farm labour is lowest. Mr. Consul White, remarking that 'it has always astonished him that Silesia, an industrial centre, has the lowest agricultural wages of all Germany,' adds, that he is told the cause lies in the cheap and thrifty modes of living of the peasantry, and suggests that the proximity of Poland and of Austria may also partly account for it in Upper Silesia. Von der Goltz also refers the low scale of Silesian wages partly to the low standard of expenditure of the inhabitants, partly to the relatively dense population. If, in addition to these conditions, we

progress, wealth, and high wages of western Germany. Should the attempt to raise them which is now being made be carried out, it is the opinion of high authorities that a serious decline in the rate of industrial progress will ensue.

reflect that this immense province is for the most part untraversed by railways, is contiguous to a vast region backward in that as in other respects, lies remote both from maritime ports and from western markets, we may fairly consider the exception only a partial one; though it proves that there are economic conditions which no single generalization will cover, and the roots of which may reach far down in past history. 'Every province,' says the illustrious rural economist, M. de Lavergne, of his own country, 'has its history, which has powerfully acted on its economic development;'* and the observation is yet truer of Germany than of France.

But another potent cause of inequalities in agricultural wages alike in Germany and in many other countries, lies in local diversities of climate and soil—a cause which the more merits attention that its operation is diametrically contrary to an old economic doctrine. It is where the work of cultivation has least variety and interest, where life has few charms, where winter is longest and coldest, where the wage-earning days are fewest, where the labourer finds it hardest to supplement his earnings by the produce of a little farm of his own, that the price of agricultural labour *per diem* is lowest in Germany, and Von der Goltz is certainly right in treating the climate as one cause of the low rate of wages in the north-east; though the chief cause seems, as certainly, the one previously pointed out, on which he does not dwell. In the south-western region itself we find this second class of natural causes in active operation, wages being usually much lower in barren mountainous districts than in those warm, fruitful valleys and plains which enable both the farmer and the labourer with a plot of ground of his own to rear close to excellent markets a variety of rich plants, tobacco, chicory, garden vegetables, hemp, which will not grow in less generous zones. After citing a number of local rates of agricultural wages in Würtemberg, Von der Goltz adds:—'From these data it follows that the rates in Würtemberg vary materially. In the least favourably situated districts they average from 47 to

---

* *Economie Rurale de la France*, 4me ed., p. 60.

49 kreuzers a-day; in those most favourably situated they rise to 78–80 kreuzers. This fact meets one in all parts of middle and south Germany, in which climate and cultivation exhibit such diversities.' It is a fact to which an analogy may be found in these islands, in which wages and profit, as well as rent, *cæteris paribus*, usually are higher on exceptionally good land, all three, and not rent only, falling on barren and mountainous soils, whatever economic theories may suppose.* The great inequalities of wages hence arising in Germany are, no doubt, partially compensated by the descent of the mountain labourer into the plains and valleys at harvest and other seasons, when there is an unusual supply of work; but throughout the rest of the year his earnings are smaller, while his wants are greater, on account of the cold, than those of the inhabitants of the lower districts. Baron Von der Goltz—almost the only economic defect of whose book is its tendency to sweep averages, the besetting sin of both statisticians and economists—seems much to overrate the compensatory influence of this periodical migration. The Irish labourer used, in like manner, to migrate to England for the harvest, but that did not raise his earnings to the English level; it only enabled him to exist for the rest of the year on Irish wages. Assuredly in Germany money wages have by no means followed the equitable principles of which economists, in their thirst after generalization rather than truth, and under the influence of eighteenth century notions of natural laws of equality and uniformity, have dreamt. It is where the skies are brightest, the air most genial, the work of husbandry pleasantest, life in every way most agreeable, that the price of farm labour is highest. It is here, too, that the labourer finds it easiest to get a property of his own, and that its produce is richest. 'The farther,' says Von der Goltz, 'we proceed from north and east to south and west, the more numerous is the class of landowning agricultural labourers, and the better is the condition of those who are so.' The fluctuations in the price of labour are no doubt greater in the industrial

* In the United Kingdom itself wages, profit, and rent are all three commonly highest, *cæteris paribus*, where the land is best.

districts of the south-west than in north-east Germany, partly for a reason not referred to by Von der Goltz, but mentioned to me by Professor Nasse, that where small farming predominates, there is a less regular supply of labour in the market; and partly, I am disposed to think, because both demand and supply are here affected by the fluctuations in manufacture and trade. But it is beyond all question that the permanent influence of the causes which produce these variations has been favourable to the agricultural labourer, and that, notwithstanding them, his condition has been a continuously improving one. The remark which Consul White makes with respect to the farm labourer throughout Germany, is especially applicable to him in Rhineland and the Ruhr Basin: 'Improved civilization has produced greater demands and requirements in this class; all authorities agree that they live, on the whole, better than they used to, and insist on getting better paid.'

In France, as in Germany, the chief causes of high agricultural wages are proximity to great industrial centres or easy communication with great markets, but we find also local causes of diversity, such as differences of climate or soil. The high wages about Avignon, for example, are attributable partly to the high prices produced by markets, such as Lyons and Marseilles, partly to the rich returns which the climate affords to cultivation, and partly to the skill of the cultivators. Writing in 1869 respecting the rise of wages there, above the rate ten years before, Mr. Mill said:—'All prices have risen at Avignon (which was already ten years ago a remarkably dear place), owing to the causes which made it then dear. There is a rapid sale for all agricultural produce in Paris, Lyons, and Marseilles; consequently all the prices in the market are high. . . . The cultivation round Avignon is carried to a high degree of perfection, and seems to have been so for centuries. The system of irrigation is elaborate, ploughing deep, the clearing of the land from weeds very perfect, fallows unknown except in the poor mountain soil, and the whole country is covered with trees of some sort, under which there is cultivation. I have been told that, owing to the peculiar advantages of irrigation, climate, and position between large towns, with easy railway and river communication, there is a constantly increasing tendency towards the cultivation of early fruit and vegetables. Already the exportation of these is very considerable, and it seems as though this cultivation must be favourable to small properties.'

In Normandy the rate of wages is as two to one compared with the rate throughout a great part of Brittany; and there are several reasons for the difference. Normandy is much nearer to the market of Paris; it has great manufacturing towns, and Brittany none; its soil is much more fertile, and the Norman population does not multiply like the Breton. Agricultural wages have greatly risen throughout France in the last twenty years, through the increase of French production and trade, the increased quantity and activity of money, railways, the demand for labour in the chief towns, the consequent migration of the rural population to the towns, their disinclination for large families, and the absorption of the peasantry (several millions of whom own small properties) in the cultivation of land of their own. But the local force of each of these causes varies, and the prices of agricultural labour are consequently very unequal.

In Belgium, again, although the principal cause (as in every progressive country in Europe) of diversity in the local rates of agricultural wages is the presence or absence of mines, manufactures, or commerce on a great scale, other causes are at work. Thus the low rate in Flanders and the Campine is due partly to the natural poverty of the soil; and the chief cause of the relatively high rate in the Ardenne, where the farm labourer earns twice as much as in Flanders (although his work is inferior, and the region has no manufactures or foreign commerce), is that there are 270 Flemings and only 100 Ardennois to the same number of hectares.

Thus there are various causes in each country for great local diversities of agricultural wages, but the most powerful and the most general cause is the unequal distribution of advantages for manufactures and commerce, and of good markets; and we can easily trace a close connexion between the great general rise in the price of agricultural labour in Europe in recent years, especially in part of west Germany and Belgium, and the great local inequalities in its price in each country. The currency of all Europe has been vastly augmented by new mines and instruments of credit; the rapidity also of the circulation of money has multiplied, and the prices of all things, labour included, which have not increased in proportion, have by consequence risen. Secondly, money has increased most, and the price of labour has risen most, in the districts whose money-getting powers have increased most through industrial development and rapid communication with the best markets. Thirdly, our continental neighbours have acquired in recent years those new arms of industry and commerce—iron, coal, the steam-engine, steam locomotion—which England possessed a generation earlier; prices consequently have risen in many parts of the Continent to the English scale from a much lower level; the demand and competition for labour, and the sums offered for its assistance, have increased abroad in proportion, and the French, German, and Belgian agricultural labourer has shared with the town workman in the new streams of money. An economist of merited parliamentary fame, lately spoke of machinery as one cause which has prevented a rise of wages in recent years in some trades in England;* and doubtless it sometimes has that effect, by superseding labour. Nevertheless the main cause of the comparatively high rate of wages throughout western Europe, and the main cause of high local rates of agricultural wages in each of its countries, is, in one word, machinery, or the steam-engine, creating new industries and immense accumulations of capital, finding swift sale for their produce in markets where gold and its representatives abound, and augmenting the price of all kinds of labour in the vicinity.

The real movements of agricultural wages throughout Europe will be seen to be in striking contradiction to generalizations, such as the tendency of wages to equality, which have passed with a certain school of English economists for economic laws:

* Mr. Fawcett, M.P., in an article in the *Fortnightly Review;* also in his *Manual of Political Economy* (5th ed.), pp. 137–9.

generalizations not without a measure of truth as indicating one of several forces, but mistaken by that school for the actual resultant of all the forces: generalizations, one may add, which were once useful and meritorious as first attempts to discover causes and sequence among economic phenomena, but which have long ceased to afford either light or fruit, and become part of the solemn humbug of 'economic orthodoxy.' During the last two generations, while some distinguished economists were asserting, not merely a tendency towards it, but an actual equalization of wages, the real tendency in all countries making progress was towards inequality—a tendency which, in fact, already showed itself in a marked manner a century ago, with the advance of commerce and manufactures, in both Great Britain and France, as statistics collected by Adam Smith and Arthur Young prove. The 'law' which economists ought to have laid down for the age from those two great writers' days to our own, was the law of great inequality in the local demand for labour, by reason of great inequalities in the advantages, development, and money-making powers of different localities. But the consequent inequalities in the prices of agricultural labour in England, it is important to notice, were formerly compensated for in a good measure by corresponding inequalities in the prices of commodities: food was cheap where wages were low, food dear where wages were high. Prices rose around the great centres of mining, manufacture, and trade to a scale greatly above that prevailing in purely agricultural districts, just as they have risen in the industrial districts of West Germany above the scale in Pomerania, Silesia, and Posen. A new inequality in agricultural wages in England took place with the equalization of the prices of food by railways and roads. In not a few parishes in the southern counties money wages remained almost stationary, at 7*s.* to 8*s.*, from 1770 to 1870, while meat rose in the interval from 2*d.*, and in some places actually only a 1¼*d.* a pound, to nearly the same price, say 10*d.*, as in Yorkshire and Northumberland, and milk and butter in proportion. When Mr. M'Culloch was laying down in successive editions of Adam Smith's treatise, that canals, roads, railways, &c., had 'brought the prices of all sorts of produce and the wages of labour in different districts much nearer to a common level than at the period of the publication of the "Wealth of Nations,"' he was right enough about the prices of produce, but so wrong about wages that they varied in England, at the time of his last edition, from 9*s*. to 22*s*., not unfrequently with a cottage and garden in the latter case, and without either in the former. Moreover, on the rise in the prices of food in the southern counties, brought about by their equalization through the kingdom, supervened a succession of further rises caused by the general increase of population, the increased wages and consumption in the manufacturing districts, and the increase of both the metallic and the credit circulation of the country. The recent rise of money wages in the southern counties had in fact been preceded by a fourfold fall in real wages measured in the price of animal food, and a great fall measured in cottage rents. The rise, therefore, during the last three or four years in the wages of the southern farm labourer—though in some cases from 7*s*. and 8*s*. to 12*s*. and 13*s*.—is, compared with his real wages a century ago, almost a nominal one only.

Another inequality which the application of steam to manufactures and locomotion brought about was a difference between the wages of mechanical and agricultural labour (unless in the manufacturing districts) out of all proportion to any differences in the severity of the employment and the skill and knowledge required. Adam Smith thought the ploughman in his time beyond comparison superior in skill, judgment, and discretion to the town workman or mechanic, and he certainly is not now inferior in the proportion of his pay. In so far as he is ignorant and inefficient, it is the effect, not the cause, of his low wages; and the groundlessness of a recent suggestion that the lower wages of the southern counties are attributable to an inferiority of race, is proved by the fact, which might have been learned from Mr. Caird, that a hundred years ago wages were higher in the southern than in the northern counties, in the proportion of 7*s*. 6*d*. to 6*s*. 9*d*. a-week. The truth is, that the sources of wages are unequally distributed by nature, but a more equal local development and a more equal distribution of labour might long ago have been brought about, had economists, in place of assuming equality, examined the facts, and ascertained the actual inequalities and their causes.

It remains briefly to indicate some of the conclusions to which the foregoing review of facts, and the present conditions of the situation, seem to point. A rise in the money wages of agricultural labour is a general European phenomenon, showing the operation of general causes. It is everywhere in part merely a nominal rise, but especially so in the southern counties of England, where a great fall in real wages, by reason of a continuous rise in prices, preceded it. In all countries in Europe there are great inequalities in money wages, but in most of them, Germany in particular, those inequalities are partially compensated by local differences in the prices of food, so that no such real inequalities in real wages exist there as in England; nor is it possible that such inequalities can continue here, now that the economic fictions which concealed them and their causes have been exposed. The future rate of money wages is indeed everywhere partly a question relating to the fertility of the gold mines and the abundance of money; but whatever may be the amount of money in circulation, it may be predicted that its distribution will be such as to secure a larger share than heretofore to the agricultural labourer in the southern counties of England. Temporary and local causes have lately checked the rise of agricultural wages in some countries, but all the permanent and general conditions tend to maintain it, especially in the lower levels. The recent decline in Germany is, in fact, a mark of the increasing influence of manufactures and trade on the price of agricultural labour, and of the disappearance of customary and stationary rates of agricultural wages, and of the excessive disproportion between them and the rates in other employments.* Everywhere in Europe farm labourers are

* Since this Essay was written, nearly five years ago, the diminished activity of manufactures and trade in Germany has been attended with a further decline in agricultural wages, which are not much higher in many places now than in 1867. Formerly the movements of trade did not affect German agricultural wages. [January, 1879.]

breaking the bonds of tradition and habit, everywhere acquiring new powers; in England they have, moreover, gained those potent forces of union which have long been the monopoly of town workmen, and farmers in the depth of the country are beginning to feel at once the effects of the competition of distant employers in towns and in the New World, and of the combination of their own labourers on the spot. When one considers the number and strength of the causes tending to the elevation of the agricultural labourer, and the breadth of the area over which they are operating, one can hardly err in affirming the ultimate futility of a local effort to put a stop to a movement which, on the one hand, has what may be called universal and permanent forces on its side, and, on the other hand, is fortified by special local conditions. The dark part of the prospect is, that England, in the outcome, may lose the chief part of its rural population, for it seems too plain that nothing will awaken its legislature or its landowners in time to the importance of making it the well-grounded hope of the industrious and thrifty farm labourer to acquire a little farm of his own.

XXIV.

THE INCIDENCE OF IMPERIAL AND LOCAL TAXATION ON THE WORKING CLASSES.*

THE working classes comprehend in this article all grades of working people, skilled and unskilled, in both town and country, domestic servants, and also that numerous body of small dealers whose earnings are derived more from their labour than from their little stock-in-trade. It is not very important whether foremen are included or not, but they are so here as receiving wages. To measure the burden imposed on this vast section of society by both imperial and local taxation is a problem of much complexity and difficulty, admitting of no exact solution, but the grounds for a rational judgment may be found. Two questions are involved: How much do the working classes contribute to the revenue of the State? and, How much do they actually lose by the system of taxation? The first may possibly be answered with some approximation to accuracy; but the second is really the principal inquiry, and it is one as impossible to answer in arithmetical terms, as it would have been to estimate in precise figures the pecuniary loss inflicted on the working classes by the corn duties. The theoretical canons commonly applied to determine the incidence of taxes afford but moderate assistance, and are often misleading. They furnish us amply with inferences from ideal 'average' or 'natural' rates of wages and profit, respecting the 'tendencies' of taxes in 'the long run' and 'in the absence of disturbing causes.' But taxes are paid immediately under the real conditions of life, and out of the actual wages and profits or other funds of individuals, not out of hypotheses or abstractions in the minds of economists. The

* *Fortnightly Review*, February 1st, 1874.

working classes have had especial reason to complain of the acceptance of such abstractions as realities, and of inferences from them as rules of practical finance. The doctrine of the equality of wages has done much to perpetuate the low wages of agricultural labour in the southern counties, that of the equality of profits has injured the labouring classes generally, alike as recipients of wages, as consumers, and as taxpayers; and the doctrine of a 'natural' rate of wages was the chief cause of the passing of the Corn Laws, the least mischief of which to the classes who live by labour was the rise in the price of bread. It was inferred that the labourer's pay must rise with the price of his food, and that taxes on wages are really taxes on profits,* and accordingly members of Parliament, on both sides of the House, discussed the duty on corn under the conviction that it could not fall on the labourer.† Mr. Ricardo himself opposed the duty in Parliament, simply on the ground that it would lower the profits of capitalists. In place of raising wages, it really lowered them, in a manner highly important to remember in an inquiry into the effects of existing taxation. 'Take the great change in the Corn Laws,' said Mr. Gladstone, in a celebrated Budget speech. 'You have created a trade in corn; by that trade you have created a corresponding demand for the commodities of which they (the working classes) are the producers, their labour being an essential element in their production, and it is the enhanced price their labour brings, even more than the cheaper price of commodities, that forms the main benefit they receive.' One of the chief causes of the impossibility of ascertaining with exactness the amount of the burden of existing taxation on the classes in question, is that the effect on wages must be taken into account. But, although I cannot pretend to furnish an accurate estimate, I think the following investigation, brief as it necessarily is, will be found to establish at least: (1.) That the real burden imposed on the working classes by the present system of taxation, imperial and local, is incal-

* Ricardo's *Principles of Political Economy and Taxation*, chap. xvi.

† See, on this point, the *Speeches* of Mr. Cobden (popular edition), p. 9.

culably greater than is generally supposed. (2.) That taxes which admittedly fall on them seriously affect them in various ways besides those ordinarily taken account of. (3.) That they are contributors to a number of taxes generally believed not to touch them at all.

Take, first, imperial taxation. Of the grievous inequality of the contribution levied from the working classes by the customs and excise duties, which produced nearly forty-seven millions of the sixty-five and a-half millions raised by imperial taxation in the last financial year (exclusive of the revenue from the post-office, telegraphs, crown lands, and miscellaneous receipts), there can be no question. The duty, for instance, on all qualities of tea is the same; the duty on a pound of the finest cigars is little heavier than on a pound of common unmanufactured tobacco; the duties on beer, spirits, and wine, make no distinction between rich and poor. It is, indeed, sometimes asserted that the wealthier classes pay, in addition to their own, their servants' taxes on tea, sugar,* and beer; but the very language in which one well-known writer defends this assumption, affords proof of its error: 'A gamekeeper,' says Mr. Dudley Baxter, 'is employed by a country gentleman at weekly wages, but lives in his own cottage, and pays his own taxes on beer and sugar. If the taxes are taken off, he reaps the benefit, and is therefore the true taxpayer. But a house-servant, if his provisions are paid for him, would not receive any benefit, so that his master is the taxpayer.'† Were the taxes referred to removed, the result would be that outdoor servants would have more money to spend, while indoor servants in the very same establishments would have no more than before, unless their wages were raised, as they could be, in proportion to the reduced cost of their board, without any loss to their masters. It is, indeed, a mere fiction that competition equalizes wages in all occupations and all over the kingdom; but such an inequality as the foregoing obviously could not continue. It is not, however, by the cost to them as

* The duty on sugar has been abolished since the first publication of this Essay.
† *The Taxation of the United Kingdom*, p. 48.

consumers, even adding the charges for the advance of the duties by the producers and dealers, that the sums of which customs and excise duties deprive the working classes can be measured. Not to mention that the forty to fifty millions advanced would otherwise be productively employed, yielding wages as well as profit on each turn of the capital, the system by which they are raised is a network of obstructions and restrictions to trade, production, and the employment of labour. For evidence in detail of the mass of impediments which customs and excise regulations oppose to the growth of commerce, manufactures, agriculture, capital, and wages, I must refer to a former Essay.* But I may instance one fact not particularized there. Conservatives and Liberals are now agreed that protective and discriminative duties impede the development of our resources, and diminish the demand for labour. Yet we still maintain four protective and discriminative duties—on sugar, spirits, wines, and tobacco. The sugar duties are framed for the protection of the British refiners, and the protection afforded appears to be disastrous, even to many of them.† The duty on foreign spirits protects the British against the German distiller, in ordinary years. The wine duties place all wine-producing countries other than France, and our trade with them, under a heavy disadvantage. The licensed British cigar-maker pays little more than the importer of raw tobacco, and the duty becomes virtually protective. These four duties, accordingly, by obstructing the natural course of commerce and industry, diminish the earnings of the working classes, besides taxing them on their expenditure. Just as the duty on foreign corn was a tax not only on the

---

* Financial Reform. *Cobden Club Essays*, 2nd Series, 1871–2.

† 'Since 1840 they had had no less than twenty-seven changes in the sugar duties, and since 1863 they had had four or five conventions with Foreign Powers for the purpose of protecting the refining trade, and also the revenue. The result had been this, that while there were twenty-three sugar refiners existing in London in 1862, only three or four were left in existence now. He had the curiosity to ascertain what proportion of foreign sugar and English sugar was sold in this town (Bradford). He went to one of the leading grocers and asked him the question, and was astonished to hear that he did not sell a single ounce of English made sugar, and that he found it more profitable to buy it from France.'—*Speech of Mr. Jacob Behrens at Bradford*, November 26.

bread, but also on the wages of working classes, so the sugar duties mulct them, not only as buyers of sugar, but also as sellers of labour; and the duties on wine, spirits, and tobacco are taxes on the wages of men and women who never drink a glass of strong liquor, or smoke a pipe in the year. It may, on account of the difficulty of levying the imperial revenue by direct taxation, be absolutely necessary; it may, for moral and sanitary reasons, be desirable to tax the consumption of stimulants; but in estimating the actual incidence and pressure of our system of taxation, we are bound to take account of the fact that the duties levied on commodities are not only taxes, and most unequal ones, on the working classes as consumers, but also taxes on their earnings as producers.

Another incidence of a number of taxes on the working classes as producers has been concealed by the doctrine that taxes on particular commodities and particular employments fall on consumers only, not on producers. The theory of taxation abounds in examples of the danger of the abstract and hypothetical method of reasoning in economics. The economist sets out with an assumption surrounded with conditions and qualifications, and perhaps itself open to question, such as that in the long run, and on the average, the profits of different occupations tend to equality, and presently forgetting all his qualifications and conditions, concludes that the profits of individuals must be equal; and therefore all special taxes advanced by producers must come back to them with equal or average profit. Individual profits really, in almost every business, vary from enormous gain to absolute loss. Profit depends, as Mr. Mill says, not only on the skill of the capitalist himself, and the conduct and honesty of those he deals with, but also 'on the accidents of personal connexion, and even on chance. That equal capitals give equal profits, as a general maxim of trade, would be as false as that equal age and size give equal bodily strength.'* Nevertheless, it is taken for granted that every special tax on a business is recovered 'with average profit,'

* *Principles of Political Economy*, Book ii., chap. xv.

though the net result of all a trader's advances is not unfrequently ruin, though all such taxes give an advantage to the larger capitalists, and though our customs and excise duties have been steadily driving small producers and dealers from one business after another. There is a numerous working class (as, from the small proportion of their capital to their work, they are properly considered) who are frequently losers by the taxes they advance. A petty retailer, to give real examples, takes out licences to sell spirits, beer, and tobacco; he advances the customs and excise duties on tea, sugar, and the rest of his stock; he pays perhaps sixpence in the pound on his shop; and after all these duties have been advanced, his shop is burned to the ground, or he falls sick and loses his business, or he is defrauded and becomes bankrupt; or a large dealer, to whom the taxes are 'a fleabite,' takes away his customers; or from one of twenty other causes the return to all his outgoings is ruin. Take another actual case. A cab driver saves a little money, and sets up a cab for himself; soon afterwards his cab is smashed in a street collision, and his horse is so seriously injured that it has to be shot. A large cab proprietor would feel the loss of one horse almost as little as the cost of his licence, but to the poor cabman I speak of his licence itself was a considerable outlay, and he will never recover it. There are thousands of poor men who every year embark their little savings or borrowed money in losing ventures of this sort on which they pay taxes; and not unfrequently one cause of their failure is the advantage which wealthier rivals find in those very taxes. Thus, excise and customs duties on commodities, trade licences, licences to keep horses and public carriages, &c. —though treated not only by theorists but even by chancellors of the exchequer as taxes on consumers alone—are often heavy direct taxes on a working class of producers, over and above the general diminution of wages which the whole system of so-called indirect taxation occasions.

Again, it is commonly assumed in estimates of the incidence of taxation, that the working classes are entirely unaffected by a number of imperial taxes which really fall on them. Thus probate and legacy duties, and stamp duties in general, the income-tax, the house-tax, the wine duties, the railway duty, and the duty on dogs, are usually supposed never to fall on working men or women, directly or indirectly. Now, in fact, the succession duty, in the first place, really falls upon many of them. Numbers of working men and women in towns and manufacturing districts have become owners of houses—originally in most cases through building societies—and succession duty is often paid on them. At Bradford, for instance, a high local authority answers as follows the questions given :—'Do any of the working classes own the houses they occupy?' 'A large number.' 'Do cases occur in which they pay probate and legacy, or succession duties?' 'Yes, frequently, as large numbers own house property.' Another good authority states with respect to the same town: 'Very many workmen own the cottages they live in. A smaller but still fair number own two, and some even four cottages. The cottages are worth from £100 to £150 each.' A London workman's house is sometimes worth from £400 to £500, and, if a leasehold, pays the higher succession duty on personalty. It does not so often happen that working men leave to their families other property of sufficient value to become liable to probate and legacy duty; yet it does sometimes happen, in the case alike of workmen, servants, and small dealers belonging to the working class. Servants, too, sometimes receive legacies, subject to duty from their masters, and working people of all classes sometimes succeed to personalty, or receive legacies from relatives who have made money as emigrants or otherwise. The house-tax, again, sometimes falls on the highest class of skilled workmen, and sometimes on workmen of a poorer class, either as lodgers or letters of lodgings. The income-tax, though directly incident on but a small number of the highest paid workmen or foremen, has an incidence on the working classes which one of the current canons of taxation conceals. It is laid down that taxes on the profits of all employments fall on capitalists only, and cannot be shifted on any other class. But there is in reality a perpetual migration along the borders between capital and labour, as there is also an intermediate class who individually may be regarded either as capitalists or workmen, according as capital or labour forms the main element in their earnings. To instance actual examples of the migration referred to: I have known the same man successively a butler, a grocer, and a court-crier; the same man an upper servant, a small trader, and a railway-platform inspector; the same man a groom, a cab proprietor, and the conductor of an omnibus; the same man a waiter, a tavern-keeper, and a waiter again; the same man a private servant, a servant in a hotel, and the proprietor of the hotel; the same woman a housekeeper, a shopkeeper, and the matron of a workhouse. It is quite a common thing for servants to set up shops with their savings; and the inducements to do so, as also their success in doing so, depend a good deal on the taxes on profits. Few, indeed, of the working classes are sufficiently versed in the real incidence of taxation to estimate the pressure of indirect imposts; but they are quite alive to the pressure of such a tax as the income-tax, and to the vexatious and often oppressive manner in which it has latterly, with grievous impolicy, been levied. So long as the exemptions of small incomes are not carried considerably further, Schedule D must fall indirectly on servants and other working classes, by diminishing the migration from their ranks to those of employers, and so lowering wages. Other commonly overlooked taxes on working people, as above said, are stamps on receipts, bills, &c.; the railway duty, the duty on dogs, and the wine duties. Small retailers and other dealers, carpenters, smiths, and other workmen, have often occasion to use stamps, besides which, stamp duties reach the labouring classes generally as consumers. The railway duty falls on them both as regular passengers and as excursionists; and the duty on dogs, though sometimes regarded by country gentlemen, in relation to the working classes, as a duty on poaching, is really often a duty on the sentinel who guards the poor man's or poor woman's cottage from tramps and peculating neighbours. Even the wine duties fall sometimes on working people in sickness, 'for the poor are sometimes sick,' as Mr. Gladstone once said on he subject; and the heaviest duties are imposed on the kinds of wine they use. The wine duties in such cases have, too, like several other taxes, another incidence on the poor, in the shape of privation. Law taxes have been said to fall heaviest on a class who, at first sight, seem not to be subject to them at all, namely, those who are too poor to go to law on account of its cost, and thereby forfeit their rights. Stamp duties on deeds are of this character; they constitute also part of the system which makes land—the common and favourite investment for the savings of working men on the Continent—an impossible investment for them in England.

Thus the pressure of imperial taxation in the mass on the working classes is enormous, though it cannot be accurately measured, and is not distributed equally over the entire body. In the financial year ending March 31, 1873, its different branches* yielded:—

Customs.	Excise, Licences, &c.	Stamps (including Probate, Legacy, and Succession Duties).	Land Tax and House Duty.	Property and Income Tax.
£	£	£	£	£
21,033,000	25,785,000	9,947,000	2,337,000	7,500,000

To the two first of these branches, which yielded more than two-thirds of the whole, the working classes contributed out of all proportion to their incomes; and the other branches, in place of compensating for that inequality, added heavily to the burden sustained by many working people. But this statement affords no adequate measure of the relative pressure of taxation, since it omits the incalculable losses in wages which the system of raising it occasions.

Bearing these considerations in mind, let us glance at an arithmetical estimate by one of our most distinguished econo-

* Exclusive of the Post Office, Telegraph Service, Crown Lands, and Miscellaneous Receipts. See Statistical Abstract, 1873.

mists, of the relative contributions of different classes to both imperial and local taxation: one which seems to estimate as accurately as is possible the chief taxes on expenditure, save that it adds to the burden on the wealthier class the duties on the consumption of their servants, the objection to which has been stated already. Summing up the results of an investigation into the taxes falling on three typical families—the first, a common labourer's, with an income of £40 a-year; the second, an artisan's, with £85 a-year; and the third, a middle class family, with £500 a-year—Mr. Jevons arrives at the following Table:*—

Description of Tax.	Percentage of Income paid in Taxes, by Families expending in the Year, repectively:—		
	£40	£85	£500
On Necessaries, ...	2·1	1·7	·8
On Stimulants, ...	5·5	4·1	1·8
Direct Taxes, ...	—	—	2·7
Legacy and Probate Duties, . .	—	—	·8
Rates and Tolls, ...	2·5	2·4	1·9
Total Taxation, . .	10·1	8·2	8·0

It will be seen that, according to this estimate, the weight of taxation decreases as the income increases, being 10·1 per cent. on the common labourer's income, and only 8·0 per cent. on an income of £500 a-year; and it seems clear that if the estimate had been carried up to the higher incomes, the burden would be seen to bear an inverse proportion to the ability to bear it. Yet the estimate omits a number of items which, as we have seen, must be included in the real pressure, direct and indirect, of taxation on the working classes. To Mr. Jevons'

* *The Match Tax.* By W. Stanley Jevons, p. 64. As the estimate occurs only incidentally in the able essay referred to, it could not well be exhaustive, but it furnishes a good basis for calculation.

estimate ought to be added the incidence, direct or indirect, or both, of the income-tax, the house-tax, the probate, legacy, succession, and other stamp duties, trade licences, taxes on shops, and on public carriages, railways, horses, and dogs, and sundry taxes paid by a number of small dealers. Above all, I submit, with unfeigned respect to Mr. Jevons, that a large addition ought to be made for the losses in wages arising from the system of indirect taxation.

Another estimate, by Mr. Leone Levi, reckons the taxes paid by the working classes out of their total taxable income, at twelve-and-a-half per cent., and the taxation of the upper and middle classes at twelve per cent. This estimate includes some of the taxes on labour omitted by Mr. Jevons, but omits a number of others which it has been shown ought to be included. And so far is Mr. Levi's estimate from taking any account of the loss of wages, or even allowing for the additional cost of taxation occasioned by the advance of duties by dealers (which Mr. Jevons puts at twenty per cent.) that he strangely assumes that the advance causes an addition to wages.* Nevertheless he concludes that the whole burden of taxation on the upper and middle classes is 'rather less than that which falls on the income of the working classes.'

Both the estimates just referred to include the important element of local taxation. The question now follows, whether local taxation redresses or aggravates the very unequal burden which, it has been shown, imperial taxation casts on the working classes?

Some recent writers on local taxation set out with the assumption that local rates in England are always levied on the occupier, but the proposition does not hold good in the case of the occupiers of premises of small rateable value; † the greatest diversity of practice exists in different towns and parishes with respect to the levy of rates on owners and small occupiers.

---

* *Estimate, &c.* By Leone Levi, p. 10.

† See with respect to the levy of poor-rates, in the case of small occupiers, the *Poor Rate Assessment and Collection Act*, 1869. The levy of other rates is affected by a number of Acts, and the powers given to authorities.

But the real incidence of rates does not depend on their levy from owner or occupier, and the subject is one of great complexity, though some economists find a simple key to its solution in the doctrine of an equality of the profits of different occupations and investments. Neither farmers, house builders, nor people in trade, they argue, will take less or can get more than 'average,' 'ordinary,' or 'natural' profits; none of them, therefore, will bear special taxation, and the rates in the case of farmers will fall on land-rent; in the case of houses (unless in special situations, where the ground owner is affected), on the occupiers; in the case of the premises of traders, on consumers. Respecting the profits of farmers, I will only say, so far are they from being determined by a knowledge of the profits of other occupations, that a farmer seldom knows the profits of any other business in the nearest market town, and never knows the profits of farming itself in the different parts of the kingdom. Farming is a speculative business, depending very much on the seasons and other local conditions, and its profit varies in different localities, under different landlords, with different farmers, at different periods. We can only make sure that farmers in general will shift the burden of rates from their own to other shoulders if they can. And the question follows, Are there no shoulders but the landlord's to which they may shift it? Are there not two other possible sources besides rent, from which they may recoup themselves for special local taxation, namely, wages and prices? As regards prices, foreign competition has hitherto presented no insurmountable obstacle to a rise in the price of a great part of farming produce, such as fresh meat, milk, butter, eggs, and sundry vegetables; the price of corn itself depends a good deal on the domestic supply. Then as to wages, the truth is, that while economists have been assuming, contrary to Adam Smith, a free competition and an equal rate of wages throughout the kingdom, farmers have had all along the price of labour very much under their own control in a number of places. 'The wages of labour on Salisbury Plain,' Mr. Caird wrote, in his famous 'Letters on English Agriculture in 1851,' in which he showed that agricultural wages varied from six to sixteen shillings a-week, 'are lower than in Dorsetshire. An explanation of this may partly be found in the fact that the command of wages is altogether under the control of the large farmers, some of whom employ the whole labour of a parish. Six shillings a-week was the amount given for ordinary labourers by the most extensive farmer in South Wilts, who holds nearly five thousand acres of land, great part of which is his own property. Seven shillings, however, is the more common rate; out of that the labourer has to pay one shilling a-week for the rent of his cottage.' Twenty years later, wages in Dorsetshire were generally from seven to eight shillings a-week;* and if we look to the low wages of labour in many parts of the country on the one hand, and the high price of farm produce on the other, it is impossible not to see that farmers in many places have been able to put the burden of rates on labourers as well as consumers, and have exercised the power; so that, in fact, labourers have been mulcted in both wages and prices. We find here the explanation of a difficulty which seems to have puzzled both members of the committee of the House of Commons on Local Taxation (1870) and witnesses. It was argued, on the one hand, that the great increase of rates must have come out of the pocket of the farmer, since rents had not fallen; and, on the other hand, that it must have come out of the landlord's pocket, since agricultural profits had not fallen. It seems not to have occurred to either landlord or farmer that a rise in the price of farm produce, without a corresponding rise in farm wages, reconciles the two statements respecting profits and rent, and proves at the same time the incidence of the rates on consumers and labourers:—

'2373. Are you an owner of land in Somersetshire?—I am.

'2374. Do you farm your own land?—I do.

'2375. Have you given attention to the subject of rating? —I have.

* * * * *

---

* On the different rates of wages of agricultural labour in England and their causes, see the present writer's *Land Systems of Ireland, England, and the Continent*, pp. 353–4, 357–79.

'2432. Is this a fair way to state your opinion, that the owner does not reduce the rent in consequence of the rise in the rates?—Certainly he does not; I believe that during the last thirty years, when the rate has nearly doubled, nearly the whole of the increase has been paid by the occupier.

'2433. Because there has been no readjustment of the rent?—Exactly; rents are not readjusted very often. Farming is one of those fluctuating businesses that an owner does not readjust his rent very often, perhaps not even for one or more lives.

'2435. Then you have this curious result, that though a farmer's profits must be enormously affected by a rise in the rates, which you have described as 100 per cent., nevertheless it has had no influence on the rent?—Very little indeed.

'2445. Have the farmers' profits diminished generally in your neighbourhood?—No; I think not.'

But more general incidences of the rates, both in country and town, have to be considered. In the first place, on whom do the rates on the houses occupied by working people, both in country and town, fall? Secondly, what is the effect of the poor-rate on wages? It would save a world of trouble to follow, in respect to the first question, the formula that the builders of houses and investors in house property must get the average rate of profit, and therefore the rates must fall on the occupiers, whether working people or not. It gives, too, an air of complete command over the subject, and of rigorous logic, to argue strictly from assumptions such as the equality of profits. But there are really no such short cuts to the end of economic inquiries. In one of the excellent articles on finance which M. Leroy-Beaulieu, an economist of very high reputation, and editor of the *Economiste Français* has recently contributed to that useful journal, it is shown that there are no external characteristics by which the State can measure, for the purpose of an income-tax, the profits of business. 'The system is in its very nature defective. One of its principal faults is, that it can throw no light on the individual profits of each trader: it has, in fact, for its base the supposed average profit which each class of traders may reasonably obtain. In this system, therefore, individual injustices must alway sbe numerous.'—(*Economiste Français*, December 20, 1873.) Nevertheless, the State has a thousand times better means of ascertaining the actual profits of every business than any private person in business can have, inasmuch as it can make it the business of a large staff to collect information on the subject in every locality, while each man in business must mind his own business, instead of the business of other people all over the country. What would be thought of a project to assess the taxpayers under Schedule D to the income-tax, on an assumption that every man actually makes the same percentage of profit on his capital? Such, verily, is the assumption on which the common theory of the incidence, alike of local rates, of customs, and excise duties, is based: a theory which suits large and successful capitalists, no doubt; it justifies both low wages and high prices; and it serves as a screen for enormous profits from the competition of 'low men'—to borrow the language of a high authority in such matters—who would 'cut in' if they knew the real state of affairs. A flagrant *ignoratio elenchi* in economics has arisen from this readiness to 'cut in'; it is put forward as proving that profits are, by consequence, equalized. The fact that capital deserts losing businesses for others in which extraordinary profits are made, proves only that profits are actually very unequal. The new capital, moreover, often comes in only for a loss at the turn of the tide, after the earlier men in the trade have doubled their capitals, and a fresh inequality is the real consequence. Take the common case of building-ground to be let for ninety-nine years, and consider for one moment the nature of the assumption that the profit on houses is determined by the knowledge which capitalists have of the profits of all investments, and the consequent equalization of building with other profits. The profits of each occupation vary, as we have seen, with different individuals, from immense gain to utter ruin, and vary at different times in the case of the same individual. We are told by Mr. Brassey's biographer that there were times when he would have died a poor man; and he might have died a poor man had the economic assumption been well founded, and had other people known the real state of his business. The same capitalist, in several cases known to myself, is making profits on different investments under his own management, varying from upwards of 100 per cent. to a balance on the wrong side. Adam Smith, writing at a time when the number of employments for capital was comparatively insignificant, when the modes of carrying on business were almost stationary, when speculation was a much less active element than now, and when all the conditions of an estimate of the profits of different businesses were comparatively simple, said :—'It is not easy to ascertain what are the average wages of labour even in a particular place, and at a particular time. We can, even in this case, seldom determine more than what are the most usual wages; but even this can seldom be done with regard to the profits of stock. Profit is so fluctuating that the person who carries on a particular trade cannot always tell you himself what is the average of his annual profit. It is affected not only by every variation of price in the commodities he deals in, but by the good or bad fortune both of his rivals and of his customers, and by a thousand other accidents to which goods, when carried either by sea or land, or even when stored in a warehouse, are liable. It varies, therefore, not only from year to year, but from day to day, and even from hour to hour. To ascertain what is the average profit of all the different trades carried on in a great kingdom must be much more difficult; and to judge of what it may have been formerly, or in remote periods of time, must be altogether impossible.'

The doctrine by which eminent economists of our own day affect to determine the incidence of rates assumes much more than the knowledge of which Adam Smith demonstrated the impossibility. It assumes that capitalists not only know the past and present profits of all occupations and investments, but foreknow them at remote periods—to the end of a long building-lease, for example. Yet it is clearly impossible for persons contemplating the building or buying of new houses to foretell, even for twenty years, the profits that single investment will yield. The movements of business and population, the demand for houses and other buildings, the increase of wealth and money, and the general range of incomes and prices, the supply of new houses on the spot, the means of locomotion bringing other districts within reach, all defy calculation. The underground railway defeated the expectations of many house-owners in London. There are indeed house-agents who will affect to tell you the rate of profit on houses, just as there are actuaries who profess to be able to capitalize and assess to the income-tax the profits of every man in every business, though of two men assessed at the same rate, one will be bankrupt within the year, and the other will make money for half a century, and die richer than Mr. Brassey. The truth is that the profits of house property, the rents that can be exacted from occupiers, and the incidence of rates, depend on no such fiction as 'the average rate of profit,' but on the demand for and the supply of houses, and these conditions vary from time to time, and from place to place. The house-builder, having cast in his lot with house and ground, and covenanted to pay a ground-rent, determined, not by any knowledge of the profits of all occupations, but simply by the local demand for and supply of building-ground, afterwards makes such terms as he can with his tenants. And the constant increase of population, the narrow limits of distance from their business within which it is convenient to most people to live, and the cost and trouble to existing occupiers of removal, give the owner, in most cases, the stronger position, and enable him to throw any increase in the rates on the occupier. But, on the other hand, if rates were abolished, house-owners in most places might exact some addition to their rent, and to that extent they may be said to pay a part of the present rates in reduced rents; their power of raising the rent on the abolition of rates being limited, not by any 'average rate of profit,' but by the supply and demand for houses, and the encouragement to building which the prospect of higher rents might occasion. No universal or strict rule, therefore, can be laid down on the subject; but, generally speaking, the occupier is the weaker party, and the chief burden of the rates can be laid upon him.

In the case of occupiers of the working class, the inquiries I have been able to make lead to the conclusion that, generally speaking, the bulk of the rates falls either directly, or indirectly in rent, upon them; but as rent usually could and would be somewhat raised, were rates to be done away with, a part may be said to fall on the houseowner. It would be unfair, at the same time, to take no account of the fact that on some large estates, owing to the liberality of the landlords, the payment of the rates on the cottages of labourers falls altogether on the former. So differently, indeed, are labourers circumstanced in respect of both house-rents and rates, as well as of wages, in different places, that in one parish I know of, belonging to a large proprietor, the labourer pays only £2 12*s.* for a decent cottage and garden, and nothing for rates; while in neighbouring parishes, in which the rate of wages is the same, he pays £6 for a worse house without garden, and the rates in addition. The estate of the great landlord is, to speak fairly, in most cases, the best estate for the labourer to live on. Where great landlords and great estates injure the working classes, are as buttresses of a system which keeps land out of the market, obstructs agriculture, manufactures, and trade, and causes the very notion of little farms to appear a chimera to the untravelled Englishman.

The only conclusion we can come to with respect to the incidence of rates, as between owner and occupier, is that generally the working man, as occupier of a house in country or town, pays (sometimes to a man as poor as himself) all the rent that can be screwed out of him. A little more could be screwed out of him were there no rates, and to that extent the rates may be said to fall on the owner, the remainder being borne by the workman. Even where the local authorities exempt the occupier from the payment of rates on the score of poverty, the rent is often raised in proportion. But it must not be forgotten that, whatever may be the incidence of the rates, as between owner and occupier, working men are now, in a considerable number of cases, the owners of the houses they occupy, and bear the whole burden of the rates, even where their houses are mortgaged. In not a few cases, moreover, the owners of the cottages occupied by workmen are themselves working men; and here, too, whatever the incidence of the rates, as between owner and occupier, working men pay the entire amount. It is estimated that there are 2000 building societies in England, and although the English building societies do not build, they advance money to working people both to build and to buy houses, and the number of houses consequently owned by men and women of those classes in some places is truly prodigious.* 'We have,' says a witness connected with some of the chief building societies in Birmingham, in evidence before the Friendly and Building Societies' Commission, '13,000 houses in Birmingham belonging to our working men. We have streets more than a mile long, in which absolutely every house belongs to the working classes.' The value of a working-man's house, and the amount of the rates on it, are sometimes considerable. 'To-morrow,' says another witness before the Commission, 'I have to settle an advance to a workman on the Metropolitan Railway; we are to lend him £360; he has bought a house for £420.' The amount of local taxation on a town workman's house is, in short, sometimes actually not far below the amount paid by a millionaire, who keeps only an office in town, and lives in a parish where rates are low. But it is not town workmen only who pay rates as owners of houses. The famous Mr. Joseph Arch, for example, has long been a village ratepayer, as owner of a house left to him by his mother.

Two other classes of working people ought not to be left unnoticed, who are neither owners nor occupiers of whole houses, but letters of lodgings and lodgers. The vestry clerk of St. Leonard's, Shoreditch, gave the following evidence before the Poor-rates Assessment Committee of 1868, with respect to inhabitants of houses of £10 a-year rateable value in that parish:—

'2543. Do you know in what way those people are employed

* A useful Essay on English Building Societies has been published by Mr. Ernst von Plener (lately First Secretary to the Austrian Embassy in London, now a Member of the Austrian Parliament), the author of a *History of English Factory Legislation*, of which an English translation was procured by Mr. Mundella.

who live in those houses?—A great many of them have stalls in the street, and they go out with hearthstones, and there are a great many birdcatchers and brickmakers.

'2544. Are there many bricklayers and masons' labourers in your parish?—Yes, there are a good many bricklayers, and a good many cabinet-makers.

'2546. Do those people chiefly take in lodgers in their houses?—A great many of them take a house—for instance, widows, and those sort of people—and let it out to lodgers.'

The vestry clerk of Bethnal Green also gave evidence:—

'2707. Are the people who occupy a £10 house, even though they pay a weekly rent, unable to pay their rates?—In many instances they take in lodgers, and with that they are scarcely able to get along.'

It may be assumed, for the reasons given above respecting occupiers, that in such cases the letter of the lodging in the first instance generally pays at least the greater part of the rates in rent, but the question follows—Is it finally paid by the lodging-letter or by the lodgers? The stoutest advocate of 'the average rate of profit,' as the key to the incidence of taxation, will hardly contend that costermongers, sellers of hearthstones, birdcatchers, bricklayers, and poor widows in Shoreditch are accurately informed respecting the rates of profit to be made in every trade and investment. The case, indeed, falls within one of the exceptions which Adam Smith emphatically made to the doctrine of a tendency of the gains of different occupations in the same neighbourhood to equality—exceptions which deprive the doctrine of all application to the profits of English trade at the present day. There is no general principle to determine the incidence of rates in the case of the lodgings of poor workpeople. We can only assume that the letters of such lodgings get as much rent as they can, but its payment is precarious; and even if they succeed in shifting both their own rent and the rates on their lodgers, they pay themselves for the exemption in discomfort and injury to health. And whether they or the lodgers are the real ratepayers, the rate falls on a working class. Nor does the incidence of local taxation on the working classes end there. Both as consumers and as producers, they are likewise contributors to local rates levied on shops and other trade premises, and to tolls and dues for roads, bridges, canals, ferries, fairs, markets, and harbours. They contribute as consumers, like other classes, when the price of the commodities they use is enhanced by such local taxation. And they pay much more heavily as small producers and dealers, when their business is unremunerative, and they fail to recover their outgoings. It has been demonstrated already that so-called indirect imperial taxes are often crushing direct taxes on poor working men and women with a small stock in trade; and local taxation, too, is sometimes the last straw that breaks the back of the petty trader. It is, therefore, certain that, on the whole, the working classes bear out of their scanty incomes an amount of local taxation in rates which forms a heavy addition to their imperial taxation. What, then, if nearly one-half of the whole amount levied in rates is applied in a manner which makes it, in fact, to a great extent a deduction from wages? What if, in addition, a great part of the remainder of the local revenue is applied to purposes from which the owners of property derive the chief, and, in some cases, the whole advantage, as in the case of various permanent local improvements, and other objects of local expenditure which raise the value of land and buildings?

Out of nearly twenty-two millions of local taxation in England and Wales, between seventeen and eighteen millions are raised directly by rates, and of this amount about eight millions are applied, directly or indirectly, to the relief of the poor. But that the relief of the poor cheapens labour, and is to a considerable extent taken out of wages, as Mr. Purdy and Mr. Thorold Rogers have argued, appears incontrovertible. I by no means go the length of saying that its operation in that respect can be nicely calculated, or that the whole of the fund raised for the relief of the poor—who must not in that sense be confounded with the working classes, many of whom never get any relief, and who are not the only classes relieved—is practically a deduction from wages. But it is certain that, were it not for the poor-rate, there would be a smaller supply of labour, and a higher rate of wages Both the preventive and the positive checks to population would act in increased force. There would be fewer improvident marriages and more emigration, on the one hand; and more deaths from sickness and want, more vagrancy and mendicancy, on the other hand. If the poor-rate were abolished, the difference would not all go into the pockets either of landlords or farmers in the country, or of owners or occupiers in towns; for wages would certainly rise in both country and town. And it follows that many members of the working classes contribute in poor-rates to a fund from which they not only derive no advantage, but which is so applied that it diminishes their own earnings. They are taxed, therefore, twice to the poor-rate; and they are taxed further for local improvements, from which a wealthier class derives the chief benefit. It is not, indeed, possible to measure exactly the amount of benefit derived by different classes from the objects of either imperial or local taxation. And few falser maxims of finance have ever been propounded than that of the great French economist, M. Say, which Sir William Harcourt appears to follow, that 'the best system of finance is to spend little, and the best taxation is that which is least in amount.' On the contrary, as Mr. Wells observes in a Report on the local taxation of New York, 'probably there is no act which can be performed by a community, which brings in so large a return to the credit of civilization and general happiness, as the judicious expenditure, for public purposes, of a percentage of the general wealth raised by an equitable system of taxation. It will be found to be a general rule that no high degree of civilization can be maintained in a community, and indeed no highly civilized community can exist, without comparatively large taxation.' Mr. Wells cites, in the same Report, the wise remark of Mr. Jevons:—'There is sure to be a continuous increase of local taxation. We may hope for a reduction of the general expenditure, and we shall expect rather to reduce than raise the weight of duties; but all the more immediate needs of society—boards of health, medical officers, public schools, reformatories, free libraries, highway boards, main-drainage schemes, water supplies, purgation of rivers, improved police, better poor-laws—these and a score of other costly reforms must be supported mainly out of local rates.' The working classes undoubtedly share the benefits of such institutions, but a much larger share often accrues to a wealthier class, whose contribution, in proportion to their ability, is immeasurably smaller. Local improvements in towns, for example, whether made by municipal authority or by great companies, often raise prodigiously the value of the property of the rich, while causing only loss and distress to working people, whom they disturb from their dwellings, whose rents they raise, and who do not remain long enough to participate in the ultimate advantages.

As in the case of imperial, so in the case of local taxation, I make no pretence to offer an exact estimate of the relative burdens imposed on the working and other classes. But the candid reader who has followed the investigation which my limits have narrowly circumscribed must, I think, be convinced that, on the one hand, imperial taxation falls with enormously disproportionate weight on the working classes; and, on the other hand, local taxation, in place of redressing, greatly aggravates the inequality. I will venture only to add that, under these circumstances, to abolish the income-tax on Schedule D (which includes many of the wealthiest and least taxed men in the world), instead of repealing the duties on sugar and tea, would be a monstrous injustice. In a debate in the House of Commons on local taxation, in 1872, Mr. Rathbone, M.P. for Liverpool, said: 'Local taxation, as at present levied, pressed heavily on labour as compared with capital, and the wealthiest classes were allowed to escape from paying anything like their fair share of the rates. In the case of London, or any other seaport where merchants were the wealthy class, and their visible personal estate consisted mainly of ships and stock-in-trade of great value, the anomaly became apparent. It was this class who directly or indirectly derived benefit from the labouring classes, so long as they were earning wages, and escaped almost entirely when they became chargeable. From inquiry into a number of cases he had ascertained that many large merchants and brokers were only paying one-half to two per cent. (in rates), while the labouring men in their employ were paying twice to seven times as much in proportion to their income. In a word, a merchant, or shipowner, deriving an income of £15,000 a-year from a capital of £150,000, paid £62 in rates on his counting-house and warehouses, and £65 on his suburban residence assessed at £450 a-year. The young doctor or solicitor paid £14 out of his income of £600 a-year on his £60 house; and the labourer £2 8*s.* 9*d.* out of his £1 4*s.* a-week on his 4*s.* cottage. Thus an income of £15,000 a-year paid less than 1 per cent.; an income of £600 a-year paid 2⅓ per cent.; and an income of £1 4*s.* a-week paid 4 per cent.'

Take also the evidence of a witness before the Select Committee on Local Taxation:—

'2792. You are a Justice of the Peace at Liverpool?—I am.

'2793. Have you been a member of the Town Council at Liverpool?—Yes, for many years.

'2938. . . . A gentleman comes and hires an office in Liverpool, and he makes his £50,000 a-year in it; but he goes and lives in Cheshire, and pays nothing to the rates of Liverpool beyond the rates that are levied on his office.'

The Chairman of the Middlesex Quarter Sessions, again, stated with respect to the metropolitan county in which so many millionaires live:—

'Unfortunately the rates do not keep pace with a man's wealth; there is many an individual that has £10,000 a-year, whose rates are perhaps no more than upon a house of £500 a-year, and there is the injustice, I think, of the poor-rate.'

The levy of a large portion of the revenue by indirect taxation gives, however, the smaller incomes included in Schedule D a claim to exemption, and the argument for it is fortified by the fact that otherwise the income-tax must, for reasons given above, fall indirectly on the working classes. Those classes are, moreover, virtually subjected to a heavy income-tax (though one which brings nothing into the treasury of the State) in the diminution of wages resulting from customs and excise duties and regulations. A remodelled succession duty, equalizing the duties on real and personal property, and raising both in the case of remote successions, but reducing both in case of successions to property of small value, seems the best remedy for the inequalities of the income-tax as regards permanent and temporary incomes—inequalities which are not peculiar to the income-tax, being incident also to all duties on articles of common consumption. To substitute a naked property-tax for the income-tax is to tax the houses and savings of poor working people in order to exempt the income of the Rothschilds from taxation.

XXV.

BRITISH COLUMBIA IN 1862.*

OUR most distant North American colonies, British Columbia and Vancouver Island, move in a course the very reverse of what Adam Smith has called the natural progress of opulence. He argues that as subsistence is necessarily prior to comfort and luxury, the cultivation and improvement of the country must, in the nature of things, precede the growth of towns, and the greater part of the capital of a rising community must be first directed to agriculture, next to manufacture, and last of all to foreign commerce. This necessary order of things is also, he observes, in conformity with the natural inclinations of mankind; agriculture being the pleasantest of all occupations, and being unattended with the risks of trade. From these premises the philosopher concludes that if human institutions had not thwarted nature, the towns would nowhere have increased beyond what the improvement and cultivation of the territory in which they were situated could support, until the whole of that territory was completely cultivated. But he points out that this natural order of progress was inverted in the growth of all the States of Europe after the dissolution of the Roman Empire. The foreign commerce of these cities introduced all their fine manufactures, and manufactures and commerce together gave birth to the principal improvements of agriculture. The causes which forced the different countries of Europe into 'the unnatural and retrograde order' are investigated in the Third Book of the Wealth of Nations; and the explanation amounts in brief to this, that the mediæval laws and customs affecting the ownership and tenure of land discouraged agriculture, while the

* *Saturday Review*, October 25, 1862.

inhabitants of towns arrived at independence and liberty much earlier than the occupiers of the soil.

But how are we to account for the phenomenon that the youngest colonies of Great Britain in North America are following the same paths of progress as the feudal States of the Middle Ages? The very first consequence of the rush to the mines of British Columbia in 1858 was to create the flourishing town of Victoria in Vancouver Island, which before was merely a factory of the Hudson Bay Company. On the mainland, the less populous and less prosperous town of New Westminster, the capital of British Columbia, grew up, between which and the mining districts are now several smaller towns. All these towns are purely commercial. In Vancouver Island agriculture is still in its infancy. In British Columbia it can hardly be said to exist as yet. In the latter the colonial population, as distinct from the native Indian tribes, consists almost exclusively of miners, shopkeepers, carriers, or packers, town and road labourers, and military and civil officials—the mining element largely preponderating during the mining season. Some time ago the Victoria 'Daily British Colonist,' a sensibly written, but villainously printed paper, observed:—'The town and country begin to swarm with men, most of them inured to labour. The majority are, perhaps, better acquainted with agriculture than with any other art. Yet all profess to be bound for Cariboo. Agriculture seems never to be taken into account.' This is a state of things not only irreconcilable, in appearance at least, with Adam Smith's doctrine, but diametrically opposed to the precepts of a yet more famous philosopher respecting a colonial community. 'The people wherewith you plant,' according to Lord Bacon, 'ought to be gardeners, labourers, smiths, carpenters, joiners, fishermen, fowlers, with some few apothecaries, engineers, cooks, and bakers. But,' he adds, 'moil not too much underground, for the hope of mines is uncertain, and useth to make the planters lazy in other things.'

Were there no land fit for either pasture or tillage in British Columbia, it would be needless to say anything more about the cause of the backwardness of agriculture. No one now disputes that Vancouver Island possesses, in addition to a climate closely resembling that of England, several rich tracts of arable and pasture land, which are however only beginning to be settled. But as to the agricultural capabilities of British Columbia, there has been some controversy, which appears to have arisen from a confusion between the coast and inland districts. In the former, mountains and forests predominate, but the minès are all in the interior, and beyond the range of the Cascade Mountains. There is abundant room for a large farming population. In the country of the Thompson, the Bonaparte, and the Pavilion Rivers, for example, as well as in that of the Similkameen and of the O'Kanagan Lake, there are great tracts of excellent land. The soil and climate are not the obstacles to the growth of agriculture in British Columbia. The traveller there may indeed be reminded of the gloomy horrors of 'those matted woods where birds forget to sing,' to which the exiles from the Desérted Village were driven; but we have unquestionable evidence that between the Thompson and the Quesnelle Rivers there are vast undulating table-lands where there is not more than sufficient wood for the settlers' requirements. The traveller, for instance, from Kamloops may canter his horse for days without a check from the nature of the ground, turning him out to grass at night. Such being the capabilities of this country, the 'British Colonist' impresses upon its readers that there is a way in which a fortune can be made in British Columbia without breasting the snow on the hills or packing beans and bacon on their backs from creek to creek in Cariboo:—'That way is simply by taking farms on the road to Cariboo. That way is by raising hay, oats, wheat, potatoes, beans, pork, beef, and mutton. These are the commodities that can be most easily exchanged for gold. There is not a country under the face of heaven that now offers such brilliant inducements to the farmer as British Columbia.'

How is it then that such brilliant inducements have been held out in vain if they exist? Is it simply an instance of the truth of Bacon's observation, that the hope of mines useth to make the planters lazy in other things? Or is there anything peculiar to the economic condition of a gold country tending to the discouragement of agriculture, and to the removal of the order of industrial development that Adam Smith describes as the natural one? Upon Adam Smith's own principles it follows that the industries which supply the prime necessaries of the miner's life and occupation must be the first to settle themselves near the gold diggings, and this alone would account for commerce taking precedence of agriculture, since the miner cannot wait for food until it is grown in his new country, and he wants many things besides the food that the most fertile soil can supply him with. He wants, for instance, first of all things, whisky. 'If you ask,' says a Cariboo correspondent of the 'British Colonist,' 'why provisions are so high, look at the nature of the first invoices which invariably follow civilization, and the predominant article will invariably be whisky.' The miner wants also tools, boots, and other articles, which will not grow out of the ground, and which he must get from the merchant, and not from the farmer. For this reason alone we might look for the appearance of ships before farms in a mining colony, and the growth of towns before the cultivation of the country. But this is not the whole of the matter. Another principle, known to the student of modern political economy, is on the side of commerce against agriculture. That is, when a country has a pre-eminent advantage over other countries in the production of one or two commodities, it may be more profitable to import than to produce at home commodities for the production of which it has not so decided a superiority. It may be that British Columbia has pastures richer than any in the British Isles; yet it may be cheaper to bring English cheeses and Irish cattle round Cape Horn than to find them in the colony. The 'British Colonist' speaks of Cariboo prices as offering a bounty on farming near Cariboo, but forgets that those prices also impose an enormous tax on the farmer, who has to pay for labour and every other requisite at an extravagant rate. Gold is cheap at Cariboo, and dear abroad; it flies from the cheap to the dear market, and the first people to surround the miner are those who act as his agents and carriers to and from foreign countries. Packers, storekeepers, merchants, are the people he deals with, because they fetch what he wants from places where gold is comparatively scarce, and labour comparatively cheap. The metallic riches of British Columbia make agriculture proportionately costly in the colony, since every labourer looks for a miner's earnings, and farm labourers are not to be had unless for enormous wages. It is not, then, absence of fertile land, nor the presence of Red Indians and mosquitoes that forms the main impediment to farming in British Columbia; it is the presence of mines of still greater fertility for the time than its richest soils. The distance of the mines from the coast, the distance, again, of the colonial harbours from Oregon and San Francisco, may afford protection to the colonial producer of fresh meat and vegetables for the gold diggings; but the growth of cereals to any extent, or anything in the nature of elaborate agriculture, is not likely to be seen in British Columbia for years. Its exports of gold for some time will probably be great, and its imports of provisions in exchange will as probably not be small.

XXVI.

AUVERGNE.*

In the magnificent picture of the physical geography of France, with which the genius of Michelet has illustrated its history, only a few harsh touches are given to the province of Auvergne, depicted briefly as a land of inconsistencies and contradictions, cold beneath a southern sky, and inhabited by a southern race shivering on the ashes of volcanoes; a land of vineyards, whose wine does not please, of orchards, of which distant strangers eat even the commonest fruits, and one to whose mountains thousands of emigrants yearly return without a new idea. It is, in fact, a land of contrasts, physical and moral; containing regions whose features, social and economic, as well as geological, are widely dissimilar. Yet the contrasts involve no real contradictions. The chief physical contrast is between mountain and plain, and remarkable economic and social diversities spring from it. But mountain and plain are correlatives and complements, not contradictions, to one another; and differences of life, occupation, usage, thought, and feeling in their inhabitants are but consequences of the same laws of human nature, operating under diverse conditions, and afford excellent illustrations of the mode in which differences of structure and character in human societies, often superficially attributed to diversity of ancestral origin or race, are really produced.

* *Fortnightly Review*, December, 1874.—Some controversy exists on the point whether, in translating the name l'Auvergne, the English article should be used, as in the case of the Bourbonnais, the Lyonnais, the Vivarais, the Ardennes, the Seine, the Creuse, &c., or whether we should say simply Auvergne, as in the case of Normandy, Brittany, Picardy, Flanders, &c. A German philologer whom I consulted on the point, and in whose opinion a French philologer also consulted, concurs, draws the following distinction between the cases in which the article should be used in English, and those in which it is more idiomatic to discard it:—

It is not the scenery of Auvergne that this essay seeks to describe, but some of its chief economic and social phenomena; they are, however, so related to some of its physical features, that the latter cannot be left altogether unnoticed. Of the two departments into which the ancient province once called Arvernes, from the Arverni, is now divided, that of the Cantal, formerly La Haute Auvergne, is wholly a mountainous region; while the richer, more populous, and far more important department of the Puy-de-Dôme—so named from the huge mountain overhanging Clermont-Ferrand, its capital—contains both mountainous districts, and also the famous plain or valley named the Limagne, traversed by the railway from Gannat to Issoire; of which, thirteen hundred years ago, King Childebert said, 'there was but one thing he desired before he died, that was to see the beautiful Limagne of the Auvergne, which was said to be the masterpiece of nature, and a land of enchantment.' A century earlier Sidonius Apollinaris wrote from a country-seat in this rich valley, 'The Auvergne is so beautiful that strangers who have once entered it cannot make up their minds to leave it, and forget in it their native land.' The strangers who enter Auvergne at the present day are for the most part either geologists about to inspect its extinct volcanoes and other similar phenomena, or invalids on their way to the mineral waters of Royat, La Bourboule, or Mont Dore, or ordinary tourists coming to see both its exhausted craters and its baths. The geologists and the tourists usually make up their minds to leave the province after a few days; and a few weeks at the baths generally suffice to give the invalids strength and resolution to return home. Least of all, perhaps, is the visitor who comes (as has happened more than once to the present writer)

'The Bourbonnais, the Lyonnais, the Vivarais, are adjectival formations, and therefore naturally take the article in English. The French departments, again, being the names of rivers and mountain chains, take the article in English, just as we say the Seine, the Loire, the Alps, the Pyrenees, of the rivers and mountains themselves. But the only French province which could properly take the article in English would be such as La Marche, where English idiom, too, would require us to say the March, or the Border. There is nothing to distinguish the case of Auvergne from that of Normandy and Brittany, where the article is omitted in English, though used in French.'

fresh from Switzerland to the Limagne, likely to be moved to the enthusiasm of Sidonius Apollinaris by its scenery; especially just after the harvest, when its corn-fields, like shorn sheep, are bare and unpicturesque. But the ancient could as little have sympathized with the modern traveller's admiration for Switzerland. What he loved was a land of corn and wine and fruit, and that the Limagne is. His associations with gigantic mountains, frowning rocks, tremendous precipices, deserts of ice and snow, were horror, hunger, danger, and death. Auvergne itself has mountains and rocks, which, picturesque as they are, have few charms for those to whom they are associated only with privation and hardship. A woman, of whom I asked my way a few weeks ago in the highlands of Mont Dore, said, 'This is not a nice country, with all these mountains and rocks,' adding, with a horizontal movement of her hand, 'I like a flat country.' Her associations with mountain scenery were black bread with a few chestnuts and potatoes, water unreddened with the wine at which Michelet sneers, hard times in winter, and hot and weary work in summer, with only one preservative from thirst—not to have a habit of drinking. 'Je n'ai pas l'habitude de boire, ainsi je n'ai pas soif,' she replied to a question suggested by my own feelings under a burning sun. In the plain of the Limagne she knew that the labourer often owned the ground on which he worked, might, if he pleased, drink the juice of his own grapes, and might, if he sold, as Michelet says, the common apples from his orchard in a distant market, instead of eating them himself, get 450 francs to the hectare for them, with as much more for the grass amidst which they grew. Having heard an old woman in a cottage in the Limagne say to a visitor, to whom she offered a slice off a huge melon, that she was very fond of melons, which are cheap in that region, I asked my friend on the Mont Dore mountain if she liked them. 'Je les aimerais mieux,' she replied, 's'ils venaient dans les montagnes.'

A contrast full of instruction and interest, when viewed in relation to its causes, between the mountain and the plain in Auvergne, is the different distribution of landed property. In the mountainous districts of the Puy-de-Dôme, the term large property—*la grande propriété*—is applied, as a general rule, only to properties of a hundred and fifty acres and upwards; properties under forty acres being there classed as *la petite propriété*, and those between forty and a hundred and fifty acres as *la moyenne propriété*. In the Limagne, on the other hand, from twenty to five-and-twenty acres make a large property in popular thought and speech, and a multitude of the small properties do not exceed a quarter of an acre. The soil in this fertile plain has in the last two generations, especially the last twenty years, passed almost wholly out of the possession of wealthier and larger owners into that of *petits propriétaires*, who cultivate it with their own hands. The Report on the Puy-de-Dôme, contained in one of the twenty quarto volumes of the 'Enquête Agricole,' after referring to the want of capital in the mountainous parts of that department, says, 'In the plain, the want of capital does not make itself felt, in consequence of the sale of land in small lots, which has permitted of the liquidation of property by paying off mortgages; but the species of proprietors has changed, and the man of means, the former proprietor, has become a capitalist, who has invested the proceeds of his land in securities.' This diversity in the distribution of landed property results partly from economic causes, partly from profound differences in the feelings and ideas generated by opposite conditions of life in mountain and plain. The economic causes are by no means the most interesting, but they must not be overlooked. In the mountains, on the one hand, both the comparative infertility of the land and the nature of pastoral husbandry tend to maintain comparatively large farms, and to prevent their being broken up by sale in small parcels. In the Limagne, on the other hand, the aptitude of the soil and climate for the production of rich plants—the vine, for example—requiring minute cultivation, and peculiarly suited to spade-husbandry; the rise in the price of such productions in recent years; the rise, moreover, of wages—adding nothing to the expenses of the cultivator who employs no hired labour, but heavily to those of the large farmer;—the increased gains and savings of both small cultivators and labourers, and their consequently increased purchases of land, make a combination of causes tending to minute subdivision. Adam Smith, remarking that it was a matter of dispute among the ancient Italian husbandmen whether it was advantageous to plant new vineyards, adds, that the anxiety of the owners of old vineyards in France in his own time to prevent the planting of new ones indicated an opinion that the high profits of vine-growing could last no longer than the restrictive laws which they had procured for that purpose. The increased growth of the vine around Clermont-Ferrand in the last five-and-twenty years shows what the small proprietors in the Limagne now think on the subject. In the arrondissement of Clermont alone, between thirty and forty thousand acres of both hill-side and plain are now covered by vineyards, which formerly were to be seen only on certain slopes with the best aspects.

Yet, after allowing all due weight to the causes referred to, it remains certain that causes of a totally different order have powerfully contributed to the maintenance of larger properties in the mountainous districts than in the plain, namely, the greater strength in the former of ancient usage, old family feeling, and religious sentiment in both sexes. In the plain both the sale of land in small plots and the partition of inheritances by the law of succession tend to break up family properties; in the mountain neither has hitherto operated considerably. The Report of the 'Enquête Agricole' on the Puy-de-Dôme makes no attempt to trace to their sources the curious diversities of usage and sentiment which it describes; but the description itself is worth citing. 'The transmission of property takes place in a manner essentially different in the plain and the mountain. In the plain an inheritance is almost always partitioned or sold when a succession (of more than one child) takes place; if partitioned, each of the heirs takes a part of each parcel; if it is sold, it is so in detail, and by the smallest fractions, in order the more readily to find buyers. Everything thus contributes to indefinite subdivision in the plain. In the mountains they cling to the conservation of the inheritance unbroken, and do all that is possible in order not to destroy the work of the family, and not to divide the paternal dwelling. The daughters willingly consent to take religious vows, and renounce the patrimony of their parents ; those who contract marriage agree to leave to the head of the family their share of the inheritance. It is the same with the sons, of whom some become priests, others emigrate, consenting not to claim their share of the property ; and it is one of the sons who remains at home, working with the father and mother, who becomes in turn proprietor of the paternal dwelling. Thus the principle of the law of equal partition is eluded, and it comparatively seldom happens that the other children assert their claims, so accepted is the usage in the manners of the mountain.'

In Auvergne, as in the department of the Creuse, one reason for the great annual migration of the peasants to the towns, which, in France, where there is no exodus to foreign countries, goes by the name of emigration, is doubtless the comparative unproductiveness of mountain land. It cannot give bread to all the young men born on it. But a more potent reason, in Auvergne, though one less in accordance with old economic hypotheses, is that the younger sons, as the 'Enquête Agricole' states, seek a subsistence elsewhere, in order to leave the property undivided to the elder brother ; or occasionally it is the elder brother who emigrates, relinquishing his share to a younger one remaining at home. Thousands of Auvergnats are consequently to be found labouring in remote cities, as masons, sawyers, porters, water-carriers, blacksmiths, chimney-sweeps ; and it is a saying in the surrounding provinces, when some hard work has to be done, 'Il faut attendre le passage des Auvergnats.'

They have a character in French towns, and French novels, for clownishness and stupidity, derived doubtless from the nature of their occupations, as hewers of wood and drawers of water. But they show no lack of native shrewdness, according to my observation, when questioned on any subject. And M. de Lavergne remarked to me lately, that the Auvergnat displays more sagacity in timing his migration than the peasant of his own department, the Creuse—M. de Lavergne is deputy for the Creuse—does. The Auvergnat leaves his home at the beginning of winter, when the country is buried in snow, returning in summer, when work of different kinds is going on. The Creuse peasant, on the other hand, goes to Paris, Lyons, or some other town, when summer is coming on, and comes back in winter, when there is nothing to do. Michelet taunts the Auvergne emigrants with bringing back some money, but no new ideas. The sum they bring to the poor department of the Cantal is put at five million francs (£200,000) a-year, in the Report of the 'Enquête Agricole' on that department—a sum hardly to be despised. But the renunciation by the emigrants of their share in the family property certainly shows, if not an extraordinary imperviousness to new ideas, an extraordinary tenacity of old ones, and in particular of two ideas which are among the oldest in human society—subordination to the male head of the family, and conservation of the family property, unalienated and unpartitioned. The number of younger sons from these mountains who become priests is a still more remarkable phenomenon, though traceable in the main to the same causes. M. Bonnet, of Clermont-Ferrand, being asked in the course of his evidence before the 'Enquête Agricole,' what was the proportion of young men in the plain and the mountains, respectively, of the Puy-de Dôme, who devoted themselves to the clerical profession, replied, 'In the Limagne very few young men devote themselves to the religious profession. It is from the mountains they come. Half the clergy of the diocese come from the arrondissement of Ambert.'

A few weeks ago, I happened myself to sit beside a party of priests at dinner, and learned that four out of the six were born in the Auvergne mountains, which likewise contribute largely to recruit the convents with nuns. M. Bonnet, being asked whether the mountain families do not induce the daughters to take religious vows, in order to prevent the partition of the family estate, replied, 'To that I answer in the affirmative. The parents, in consequence of the piety which reigns in the mountains, are not sorry to see their daughters embrace the religious profession, and at the same time to see the family property thereby less divided. In general, the eldest son remains at home, and the father frequently leaves to him the part disposable by will. And when a daughter enters a convent, if the portion she brings to it does not absorb her share in the inheritance, she on her side usually makes her will in favour of the already favoured brother.'

Thus in the Auvergne mountains at this day, 'the younger brother sinks into the priest,' just as Sir Henry Maine describes him as doing under the influence of primogeniture in feudal society. The daughter, too, enters the convent just as she did in the middle ages, and from the same causes which actuated her then—family sentiment and male primogeniture on the one hand, and 'the piety which reigns in the mountains' on the other hand, which is, in fact, a survival of mediæval piety, preserved by certain conditions of life and environment. A reason, it is true, sometimes assigned for the number of young women who become nuns in the department of the Puy-de-Dôme is that there are no girls' schools in the mountains; the daughters of parents who can afford it are, therefore, sent to convents to be educated, and the education they receive both unfits them and gives them a distaste for the rude life of a mountain farmhouse. They learn to make lace and embroidery, but not to mend stockings or to make butter or cheese. It is, neverthless, undisputed that religious feeling and family ideas fill the chief place among the motives which lead both the daughters to take vows, and the younger sons to become priests.

I have nowhere met with any attempt to trace to their ultimate causes the curious social phenomena just described; but one may, I think, point with certainty to the difference of environment and conditions of life in the mountain and in the plain, as the source of the superior force of religion, family feeling, and ancient usage in the former. On its moral and social side, the contrast between mountain and plain is the contrast between the old world and the new; between the customs, thoughts, and feelings of ancient and modern times.

The principal sources of change and innovation in the plain—towns, manufactures, trade, easy communication with distant places, variety of occupation and manner of life—are inoperative in the mountains. Even in summer, the mountain lies aloof from the town and its life, communication between them is tedious for people on foot; the country carts are of the most primitive make, and drawn by slow oxen or cows. Where a heavy load has to be brought up hill on the best roads in the department, for instance, from Clermont towards Mont Dore, I have seen six horses yoked in a curious order to draw it—first one wheeler, then two abreast, with three leaders in tandem. In winter the whole mountain region is under snow, the roads are often impassable, and the members of the mountain family are shut up together with their dumb companions, the cattle. Then the life of the mountain pastoral farmer is the same from father to son, and from age to age; the whole neighbourhood, too, follows the same occupation, and leads the same life, so that there is a surrounding mass of uniform and primitive usage and thought. But the family is the earliest of social bonds, and it is by studying it as it survives in places such as the Auvergne mountains, that we can best realize something of the force of that ancient bond, and something of the nature of the sentiments which led to the patriarchal authority of the elder brother on the one hand, and the conservation of the family property under his guardianship and control on the other. Sir Henry Maine calls the origin of primogeniture, as affecting the devolution of land in the middle ages, one of the most difficult problems of historical jurisprudence; and it has a peculiar difficulty in England to which he has not referred. How was it that during a period when society was decidedly becoming more orderly, and patriarchal rule was giving place to regular government, the division of socage lands among all the sons was superseded by primogeniture, the principle already established in the case of land held in military tenure? A tendency to uniformity in the law, produced by the institution of itinerant royal courts, and the bias of the judges, contributed probably to the change; but something more is required to explain it. The courts proceeded to make custom, instead of the old law of gavelkind, determine the succession to socage lands; but the question follows, how did a custom come into existence contrary to the old law, and to the apparent interest of the majority of the family? And the existence at this day, in the Auvergne mountains, of a custom directly opposed to the positive law of the land helps us to understand how the English courts were supported by family feeling in assuming a custom of primogeniture contrary to the old law of division.

The force of religious feeling, 'the piety which reigns in the mountains,' as M. Bonnet calls it in a passage cited above, has its root, doubtless, partly in the same conservation of ancient sentiment, thought, and belief, which gives the family property to one son, partly in other ideas and feelings generated by the conditions of mountain life. As the difference between the mountain and plain is a phase of the difference between the old world and the new, so is it a phase of the difference between country and town. The mountain is, as it were, the country in its rudest primitive form, while the plain is, as it were, a great suburb of the towns it contains and has continual intercourse with. The *petit propriétaire* in the Limagne has the money-making spirit as strongly developed as the town tradesman; sometimes he himself lives in the town, and in any case he has frequent transactions of buying, selling, and other relations with it. But the money-making and commercial spirit evidently tends to individualism, and to the disintegration of the family; and it has ever been found also to foster a secular spirit and repugnance to sacerdotal dominion. In towns, moreover, and also (though in a smaller degree) in the surrounding plain, men see chiefly the power of man, and unconsciously gather confidence from their own numbers against both the powers of nature, which are supreme in the mountain, and those supernatural powers which the powers of nature suggest to rude minds. The difference between the force of religious sentiment and reverence for the clergy in town and country in Catholic countries is striking. One has but to look at the way in which a Flanders priest is saluted in the streets of Ghent, for instance, and at some miles' distance in the country, for evidence of the opposite influence in this respect of town and country life. At Clermont-Ferrand, the respectable working-man commonly holds aloof from the clergy, declines their aid, even when in need, and is averse from joining societies for the mutual benefit of the members, because the clergy take a part in their management. Indications of the prevailing disposition in that town towards ecclesiastical authority have repeatedly come under my notice. One day, last September, I was reading a newspaper in a café, when an old woman going by observed in the most sarcastic manner and tone in reference to a person beside me, 'Ce monsieur appartient à Monseigneur l'Evêque, puisqu'il a acheté la Gazette d'Auvergne.' Pointing to another person, she continued, 'Ce monsieur-là appartient à Monsieur le Préfet, puisqu'il a acheté le Journal du Puy-de-Dôme.' Then seeing both journals in my hand, 'Voilà un monsieur qui a acheté tous les deux. Il ne sait pas encore à qui appartenir. C'est une question difficile.' No old woman in the mountains of a diocese which draws half its clergy from their youth could have spoken with such levity of an episcopal dignitary. The persistence in the Auvergne mountains of ancient ideas and feelings on such subjects as both the clergy and family property, notwithstanding that thousands of their peasants spend half the year in large towns, affords an instructive example, on the one hand, of the profound influence of physical geography on the mental constitution of man, and the history of the different branches of the race, and, on the other hand, of the operation of laws of human nature and motives to human conduct, powerfully affecting the economic structure of society, the division of occupations, the amount and the distribution of wealth, which are absolutely ignored in what still passes with some professed economists for a science of wealth.

Among the most active agencies in the town which rarely reach the mountains in Auvergne is the newspaper, the influence of which at Clermont-Ferrand I have heard ecclesiastics deplore, although they themselves employ it to the utmost of their power. Arthur Young tells that he could not find a single newspaper in a café in that town in the autumn of 1789, though the air was alive with revolutionary rumours. In the autumn of 1874 he might have found half-a-dozen in any one of several cafés, besides having them pressed upon him by newsvendors incessantly passing by. The local journals are not sparing of rhetoric, or lacking in party spirit. The number of the journal which the old woman called the organ of Monseigneur l'Evêque, contained a furious article against radicalism, of which the following passage is a specimen :—'The radical lives on hatred. Irritated against authority, irritated against society, irritated against God, he hates everything, he hates even himself. Hatred devours him, and hatred supports him. To glut his hatred he would give his life, and he wishes to live only to glut it. He breeds, imbibes, and feeds on hatred; and, like the garment of Nessus, it burns him, being in that respect an anticipation of eternity.' If the Auvergne radical is a good hater, it seems that the Auvergne ecclesiastic is so too. M. de Lavergne, speaking of the immense subdivision of landed property in the Limagne since 1789, and the vast increase in the number of spade-cultivators, remarks in his 'Rural Economy of France' that the prevalence of such severe manual labour has a tendency to produce rough and violent manners. Such manners certainly are sometimes exhibited in the Limagne, but not by spade-cultivators only.

The minute subdivision of land during the last twenty-five years in the Limagne, whatever may be its tendencies for good or for evil in manners and other respects, assuredly cannot be ascribed to over-population, once regarded in England as the inevitable consequence of the French law of succession. It is true that between 1789 and the middle of this century the population of the Puy-de-Dôme increased, as M. de Lavergne says, from 400,000 to 600,000.* But later statistics supplied to me by M. Adolphe F. de Fontpertuis, an economist well known

* *Economie Rurale de la France*, 4me ed., p. 364.

to English readers of the 'Economiste Français' and the 'Journal des Economistes,' exhibit an opposite movement—

	1851.	1866.	1872.
Population of the Puy-de-Dôme, .	601,594	571,690	566,463

And the Report of the 'Enquête Agricole' on the department states, 'All the witnesses have declared that one of the principal causes of the diminution of the population is the diminution of children in families. Each family usually wishes for only one child; and when there are two, it is the result of a mistake (une erreur), or that, having had a daughter first, they desire to have a son.' A poor woman near Royat, to whom I put some questions respecting wages and prices, asked whether my wife and children were there, or at one of the other watering-places, and seemed greatly surprised that I had neither. She thought an English tourist must be rich enough to have several children; but when asked how many she had herself, she answered with a significant smile, 'One lad; that's quite enough.'

Our conversation on the point was as follows:—

'Votre dame et vos enfants, sont ils à Royat?'

'Non.'

'Où donc? à Mont Dore?'

'Moi, je n'ai ni enfants ni femme.'

'Quoi! Pas encore!!'

'Et vous, combien d'enfants avez-vous?'

'Un gars; c'est bien assez. Nous sommes pauvres, mais vous êtes riche. Cela fait une petite différence.'

If over-population gives rise to tremendous problems in India, the decline in the number of children in France seems almost equally serious. If two children only are born to each married couple, a population must decline, because a considerable number will not reach maturity. If only one child be born to each pair, a nation must rapidly become extinct. The French law of succession is producing exactly the opposite effect to what was predicted in this country. Had parents in France complete testamentary power, there would not be the same reason for limiting the number of children. M. Léon Iscot, accordingly, in his evidence on this subject before the 'Enquête Agricole' on the Puy-de-Dôme, said, 'The number of births in families has diminished one-half. We must come to liberty of testation. In countries like England, where testamentary liberty exists, families have more children.'

Whatever may be thought of the change which is taking place in France in respect of the numbers of the population, there is one change of which no other country has equal reason to be proud. Its agricultural population before the Revolution was in the last extremity of poverty and misery, their normal condition was half-starvation; they could scarcely be said to be clothed, their appearance in many places was hardly human. No other country in Europe, taken as a whole, can now show upon the whole so comfortable, happy, prosperous, and respectable a peasantry. The persons examined before the 'Enquête Agricole' on the Puy-de-Dôme, a department with many disadvantages of situation and climate, grumbled about many things, as landowners and farmers universally do; but they were unanimous on the point that the peasantry and labouring class were 'better fed, better clothed, and better lodged' than a generation ago; and in all these respects a visible improvement has taken place, even within the last ten years. You still, it is true, often see boys and girls in the Puy-de-Dôme without shoes and stockings, but rarely ever otherwise than comfortably clad in all other respects. The absence of shoes and stockings is a sign, not of poverty, but of the retention of ancient custom. In the north of Ireland it is still not uncommon to see girls on the road in a smart dress and bonnet, and holding a parasol over their heads, with their shoes not on their feet, but in their hands. And in a good many parts of the south of France a century has made no great change since Adam Smith wrote, 'Custom has rendered leather shoes a necessary of life in England. The poorest person of either sex would be ashamed to appear in public without them. In Scotland, custom has rendered them a necessary of life to the lowest order of men, but not to the same order of women, who may, without any discredit, walk about barefooted. In France, they are necessaries neither to men nor to women; the lowest ranks of both sexes appearing there publicly, without any discredit, sometimes in wooden shoes, and sometimes barefooted.' That it is no discredit either to boys and girls in the Puy-de-Dôme to go barefooted, and, on the other hand, that modern fashion is beginning to creep even into the mountain villages, I saw evidence the other day in the village of La Tour d'Auvergne, where children smartly *chaussés* in the latest style were playing with others without shoes or stockings. The Auvergne children, one may observe, do play; they are not, like the children in Swiss villages, serious little old men and women, too busy and grave for laughter or play. Children and adults alike in Auvergne seem for the most part in rude health, though in the mountains they may sometimes owe more to the air than to the food, and in some villages crétins are still to be seen—a consequence, doubtless, of the filthy condition of the cottages within and without. The horrid malady of crétinisme has lately been driven from some Swiss valleys by an improvement of the houses. In the Puy-de-Dôme this autumn I saw many instances of a change which is the sure precursor of an elevation of the standard of habitation, namely, the substitution of tiled for thatched roofs. One hears people say there, indeed, that this change is no improvement; that the thatch is not only cheaper, but warmer in winter, and cooler in summer. It is, however, a source of constant danger from fire to the whole village; and in every country in western Europe the change from the straw roof to tiles or slates is found to be accompanied by material progress. M. L. Nadaud puts into the mouth of an interlocutor in his 'Voyage en Auvergne,' 'You will never make of an Auvergne village a Flemish village. Climates form the habits and tastes.' Climate certainly plays a great part in determining the economic condition of mankind; and its agency, along with other physical influences, has been too generally overlooked by economists in their eagerness to explain the whole economy of society by reference to the single assumption of a desire of every one to obtain additional wealth. But climate did not make the Flemish village. It grew up by degrees in the middle ages out of liberty, manufactures, and markets for village productions. And the fact that the Auvergne villager is beginning to roof his dwelling with tiles from another province shows that liberty and facilities for trade may yet make a Flemish village of the Auvergne one. Even of the remote and mountainous Cantal, M. de Lavergne said several years ago, 'The discoveries of modern civilization have been long unknown in Upper Auvergne; its towns are but rude villages, and its rustic dwellings have but too often the repulsive aspect of extreme poverty, yet competence and comfort are making their way into them by degrees.'

A general rise of wages has taken place in Auvergne in the last fifteen years, but the rise has been very unequal. The demand for labour has increased much more in some communes than in others, and, on the other hand, the supply is much scantier in some than elsewhere. 'In one commune,' says the Report of the 'Enquête Agricole,' 'there are but four labourers; everyone therefore fights for them, and when they work for one employer, it is impossible for the others to get their work done.' At Saint-Maude, near Issoire, M. de Saint-Maude stated to the commission that it was out of the power of large proprietors there to farm their own land, on account of the scarcity of labour and its extravagant price. 'The price of a day's labour is from 4 to 5 francs, and a meal besides, with wine. Wages have more than doubled since 1852. Women, above all, have seen their wages trebled.'* In another place, however, the rate was shown to be only 1 fr. 25 cents. in winter, and 2 fr., with food, in summer; and in a third, 1 fr. 50 cents., without food, during the greatest part of the year, with 1 fr. 25 cents., and food, in harvest. In the autumn of the present year, after the harvest, I found 3 francs a-day the rate in several parts of the Limagne, and a person from Normandy, who was present when I made some inquiries on the subject, remarked that this was more than is paid in that wealthy province—a statement quite in conformity

---

* *Enquête Agricole, Puy-de-Dôme,* p. 296.

with M. Victor Bonnet's statistics.* The assertion of M. de Saint-Maude respecting the rise of women's wages is likewise in accordance with a statement of a high authority on French economics, M. Paul Leroy-Beaulieu, that the pay of women for agricultural labour has risen more than that of men in recent years—a fact, he adds, only to be rejoiced at, women having formerly been much underpaid in comparison with men. With respect to the relative movement in recent years of agricultural and town wages in Auvergne, the following figures are taken from some unpublished statistics, which Mr. Somerset Beaumont, late M. P. for Wakefield, collected at the close of last year, showing the comparative rates in agriculture and several other employments in 1868 and 1873, at Clermont-Ferrand and in its neighbourhood:—

		1868.		1873.	
		fr.	*c.*	*fr.*	*c.*
Agricultural Wages, per diem, without food,	During the harvest, .	3	17	4	0
	In ordinary seasons, .	2	24	2	50
Masons, ...		3	0	3	50
Carpenters, ...		3	0	4	50
Joiners, ...		3	0	3	50
Locksmiths, ...		3	25	3	50
Servants, per annum—Men, ...		300	0	400	0
,, ,, Women, ...		150	0	200	0

The reader will observe that these variations are by no means in harmony with the old assumption of abstract political economy, that the diversity of wages in different employments corresponds to diversities in the nature of the work; as though all the poor workmen throughout every country could know exactly all the differences of wages and work in all occupations, and choose their own trade accordingly. The wages of carpenters at Clermont were lower in 1868 than those of locksmiths;

* See Essay, 'Agricultural Wages in Europe,' *supra*, p. 368.

in 1873 they were much higher, and were so, not because the nature of either employment had changed, but simply for the same reason that agricultural wages had risen in some communes much more than in others, namely, that the local conditions of demand and supply had changed.

Among causes both of a rise and of local inequalities in wages, prices, and the cost of living in Auvergne are its watering-places, Royat, Mont Dore, and La Bourboule, which may be classed together as constituting a third social and economic region. Auvergne, as already said, is a land of contrasts, and the contrast which this third region presents to the two others already described is worth notice, not only as contributing to a description of the province, but also as illustrating the influence of local physical conditions on social phenomena, and exemplifying the causes which produce distinct types of human life, character, and pursuit.

One difference which strikes the eye at once between the watering-place and the two other regions is, that while the latter display dissimilar social and economic features, yet those features are in both cases indigenous; it is the Auvergnat you see, unlike as he appears in mountain and plain. But the watering-place, though in Auvergne, is not of it, socially speaking. You find yourself, on entering it, among Frenchmen from every part of France, except the province in which it is situated; its chief social phenomena are exotic, not native. The only pervading type of character here is also altogether unlike the types which the two other regions develop. The representative man of the Limagne is the spade-husbandman, wringing the uttermost farthing from his little property; the patriarchal head of the pastoral household, the priest, the nun, the emigrant labourer, are the representatives of the mountain. But in the watering-place, the only representative character is the invalid; the people round you differ in every respect but one, that they are almost all seeking the cure of some malady. In the mountain, family sentiment, religion, ancient usage, are the dominant principles; in the rich agricultural plain, the paramount object is to make money wherewith to buy land; at Royat, Mont Dore, and Bourboule the dominant motive which determines the occupations of producers and the demand of consumers is the desire, not of wealth, but of health. But this desire brings wealth to the watering-place, which thereby becomes a monetary region in which the cost of living is higher than in other parts of the province, and is so in conformity with the main principle governing the diffusion of money and the movements of prices. The general principle traceable throughout the immense monetary changes of our time—one which the assumption that wages and profits are equalized by competition has led not a few economists to miss—is that the distribution of the increased currency of the world has followed the path of local progress, and of the development of local resources or advantages, of whatever kind. Superior local advantages for manufactures and trade in one place, for scenery or amusement in another, for the cure of disease in a third, cause a relatively large influx of money, and send up the prices of labour and important commodities above the rates prevailing in places making inferior progress, or offering no special attraction to money. Only one classification, as already said, fits the majority of the visitors to the watering-places of Auvergne, namely, that they are for the most part invalids; but whatever they are, and however they spend their lives, they spend here in the mass a great sum of money at hotels, and on baths, carriages, saddle-horses, sedan-chairs, shops, the casino, &c.; and as their numbers yearly increase, local prices rise. Not many years ago, Royat, Mont Dore, and Bourboule were three villages of no reputation, with village prices. Bourboule, in particular, was then a mere hamlet of the meanest order; now the visitor forgets the old hamlet in a cluster of new hotels, and villas, with rows of smart little shops, which disappear at the close of the season. Bourboule was mentioned in guide-books not long ago as having from seventy to eighty visitors in the season; this autumn it had several thousands, most of whom remained for several weeks. There were members of the National Assembly, authors, country gentlemen, Parisians, provincial townspeople, military men, ecclesiastics, besides a multitude of nondescript young gentlemen and ladies. Eminent above all was a writer of European fame, M. Léonce de Lavergne, especially entitled to mention here, not only as having described the rural economy of both the Limagne and the mountains of Auvergne, but also as having foretold the growth of its watering-places in one of the celebrated works by which he is best known to most English readers, 'L'Economie Rurale de la France.' In his own country he has long held a high place, both in the world of letters and in the political world, having formerly occupied a considerable post in M. Guizot's government, and being now one of the most influential and respected members of the National Assembly, although the infirmity of his health has prevented his taking a conspicuous part in its public proceedings. His presence at Bourboule this autumn may be instanced as an example of the operation of the physical causes which are giving both wealth and celebrity to places formerly as poor as unknown, and changing the scale of prices in proportion. The charge for pension this autumn at Bourboule was from twelve to fifteen francs a-day, according to the length of the stay—a rate, perhaps, not immoderate, considering that it included wine, but one which would have seemed incredible a few years ago. At Clermont-Ferrand, the passing and uncovenanted stranger still pays only four francs for an excellent dinner in the principal hotels, with wine and fruit unlimited. Clermont, indeed, with the other chief towns of the Puy-de-Dôme, might fairly be classed together as constituting a fourth region with distinct social and economic phenomena: one indication of this being that, close as are the commercial and other relations between the towns of the Limagne and the surrounding plain, the villagers in the latter generally regard the townspeople with a feeling approaching to hostility. It was, however, the aim of this essay to sketch only some of the most striking and distinctive social and economic features of a province as yet little known in those respects in England; and its towns, though not without peculiar characteristics, seem hardly to call for a special description. The sketch which has been given of the phenomena of the rest of the province may suffice to illustrate the importance of taking account, in economic investigations, of physical geography and environment, and the necessary fallaciousness of a theory which professes to account for the division of labour in every country, the amount and distribution of its wealth, and the movements of money and prices, by deductions from the principle of pecuniary interest.

What do we learn respecting the real division of employments in Auvergne, the motives which determine it, the distribution of landed property and other wealth, the scale of wages and prices, from the assumption that every individual pursues his pecuniary interest to the uttermost? Is it simply the desire of pecuniary gain which makes one Auvergnat a porter at Lyons, another a priest at Clermont, and the sisters of both perhaps nuns, while an elder brother of each has the whole family property? In one only of the three regions described is pecuniary interest the dominant principle; and even in that region there are inequalities of wages and profits, with other economic phenomena utterly at variance with doctrines which, by a curious combination of blunders, have been called by some writers 'economic laws.' The faith of a school of English economists removes mountains. In France, where labour moves from place to place, and from agriculture to other employments, much more freely than in England, mountains certainly do not prevent the migration of labour. Yet even in France the migration by no means takes place on such a scale, or with such facility, as nearly to equalize wages; and in the places from which it is greatest, the department of the Creuse and the province of Auvergne, the main cause is not pecuniary interest. The younger brother in Auvergne goes from his home to a distant city in obedience to traditional family sentiments; and the peasant goes from the Creuse to Paris as a mason, not because he has calculated the difference of earnings in the two places, and in different employments (for he could make more in many cases by remaining at home), but because his father went to Paris before him, and his comrades do so around him. The relation of the economic phenomena of society to its moral, intellectual, and political condition is undreamt of by the old school of economists. Even in the case of men, it is manifestly vain to look for an explanation of the causes which determine the economic condition either of individuals or of classes, without reference to laws, customs, moral and religious sentiment; how much more is it so in the case of women? Let me adduce one instance, showing how, even in the smallest details, the economic structure of society, as regards the occupations and earnings of women, is influenced by moral and other causes, quite apart from individual pecuniary interest. At a hotel in Clermont-Ferrand, in which, as is commonly the case in large French hotels, a man does the work of housemaid, a Swiss visitor remarked to me lately, that you will rarely find perfect cleanliness and neatness where such is the case; yet in France, he added, 'it is a necessary evil. A young or good-looking housemaid has no chance of keeping her character in a French hotel; in Switzerland she is as safe as in a church.' I answered that possibly she might be as safe in the mountains of Auvergne as of Switzerland; for climate is certainly one of the causes which produce a difference in this respect between French and Swiss morals. Other causes, too, might be assigned, but I refer here to the moral difference in question only as exhibiting the influence of moral causes on the economic structure of society down to the minutest details.

There is another subject on which the social and economic phenomena of Auvergne may be seen to throw considerable light, namely, the mode in which diversities of human character and life are produced, and the real origin of differences of national character, customs, and condition, which are vulgarly attributed to difference of race—that is to say, to ancestral and inherited differences of physical and mental constitution. Greater differences of human life, motive, and pursuit are to be found in parts of the province of Auvergne, a few miles from each other—in adjacent districts of mountain and plain, for example—than some which are often pointed to between Frenchman and Englishman as the consequences of an original difference of race. The people of every country like to be told that they possess an inherent superiority to every other, and the doctrine of race flatters every race and every nation. The Englishman, the Frenchman, the German, the Spaniard, the Jew, above all the Chinaman, each thinks himself of a superior race. When we descend from nations to smaller divisions of mankind, to provinces for example, the same claim is commonly set up by each to superiority over the other divisions. An Auvergnat lately asked me if I did not observe that the Auvergnats were a finer and more vigorous race than the rest of Frenchmen, and the question reminded me that a Comtois once asked me the very same question in favour of the men of his own province, la Franche Comté. Divide provinces into departments or counties, and one finds that county pride can soar quite as high as provincial or national pride. Descend further from counties to yet smaller divisions, to villages for instance, and you will find neighbouring villages in Germany with a profound contempt for each other, and an exalted consciousness of their own hereditary superiority. Take still minuter groups, and you may discover in every country many thousands of families, in all ranks of life, the members of each of which believe that they come of a better stock, and possess finer natural qualities than their neighbours. From the family come down to the individual, and the real root of the popular doctrine of race in all its forms is reached, being no other than individual conceit. The doctrine of race not only does not solve the problems which really arise respecting national diversities of character, career, and condition, but prevents those problems from being even raised. And it is impossible to acquit a dogmatic school of economists of all blame in respect of the ignorance of ascertainable causes of social diversities which the vulgar theory of race exhibits. The method of abstract reasoning from crude assumption, in place of careful investigation of economic phenomena and their causes, has prevented the discovery of a mass of evidence respecting the real origin of differences in the aims, qualities, and circumstances of mankind in different countries and situations, such as the mountain and the plain of Auvergne, for example, upon which a true theory of the causes of the diversities commonly attributed to race, might have been built.

THE END.